PATHS TO POWER

Paths to Power includes state-of-the-art essays on U.S. foreign relations from the founding of the nation through the outbreak of World War II. Essays by William Earl Weeks, Kinley Brauer, Edward P. Crapol, Richard H. Collin, David Steigerwald, Brian McKercher, Justus D. Doenecke, and Michael A. Barnhart review the literature on American diplomacy in the early Republic and in the age of Manifest Destiny, on American imperialism in the late nineteenth century and in the age of Roosevelt and Taft, on war and peace in the Wilsonian era, on foreign policy in the Republican ascendancy of the 1920s, and on the origins of World War II in Europe and the Pacific. The result is a comprehensive assessment of the current literature, helpful suggestions for further research, and a useful primer for students and scholars of American foreign relations.

MICHAEL J. HOGAN is a professor of history at the Ohio State University and editor of *Diplomatic History*, the journal of record for specialists in American diplomatic history and national security studies. He is the editor of five volumes on aspects of American diplomatic history, including *The End of the Cold War: Its Meaning and Implications* (1992), *America in the World: The Historiography of American Foreign Relations Since 1941* (1995), *Hiroshima in History and Memory* (1996), and *Ambiguous Legacy: U.S. Foreign Relations in the "American Century"* (1999). He is also the author of *Informal Entente: The Private Structure of Cooperation in Anglo-American Economic Diplomacy, 1918–1928* (1977); of *The Marshall Plan: America, Britain, and the Reconstruction of Western Europe, 1947–1952* (1987); and of *A Cross of Iron: Harry S. Truman and the Origins of the National Security State, 1945–1954* (1998). He is recipient of numerous fellowships and prizes, including the Quincy Wright Prize of the International Studies Association, the George Louis Beer Prize of the American Historical Association, and the Stuart L. Bernath Prize of the Society for Historians of American Foreign Relations.

D1118229

Paths to Power

The Historiography of
American Foreign Relations to 1941

Edited by
MICHAEL J. HOGAN
The Ohio State University

CAMBRIDGE
UNIVERSITY PRESS

PUBLISHED BY THE PRESS SYNDICATE OF THE UNIVERSITY OF CAMBRIDGE
The Pitt Building, Trumpington Street, Cambridge, United Kingdom

CAMBRIDGE UNIVERSITY PRESS
The Edinburgh Building, Cambridge CB2 2RU, UK   www.cup.cam.ac.uk
40 West 20th Street, New York, NY 10011-4211, USA   www.cup.org
10 Stamford Road, Oakleigh, Melbourne 3166, Australia
Ruiz de Alarcón 13, 28014 Madrid, Spain

First published 2000

Printed in the United States of America

Typeface Sabon 11/13 pt.   System Adobe PageMaker® 6.5

*A catalog record for this book is available from
the British Library.*

Library of Congress Cataloging-in-Publication Data

Paths to power : the historiography of American foreign
relations to 1941 / edited by Michael J. Hogan.
p. cm.
Includes bibliographical references and index.
ISBN 0 521 66287 7. – ISBN 0 521 66413 6 (pbk.)
1. United States – Foreign relations – Historiography.
I. Hogan, Michael J., 1943– .
E183.7.P29 2000
327.73 0072 – dc21   99–28048
                                   CIP

ISBN 0 521 66287 7   hardback
ISBN 0 521 66413 6   paperback

With appreciation to Matthew Davis, Jennifer Walton, Nate Citino, Bruce Khula, Susan Landrum, Bruce Karhoff, Amy Staples, Paul Pierpaoli, Josef Ostyn, Darryl Fox, Paul Wittekind, Toby Rosenthal, Kurt Schultz, and especially Ann Heiss. I couldn't have done it without you.

Contents

The Authors

MICHAEL A. BARNHART is professor of history at SUNY-Stony Brook. He has written *Japan Prepares for Total War: The Search for Economic Security, 1919–1941* (1987) and *Japan and the World Since 1868* (1995) and has edited *Congress and U.S. Foreign Policy: Constraining the Use of Force in the Nuclear Age* (1987). From 1991 to 1996 he served as editor of *The Journal of American-East Asian Relations*.

KINLEY BRAUER is professor of history at the University of Minnesota. He has edited a volume on *Austria in the Age of the French Revolution, 1789–1815* (1990) and is the author of *Cotton vs. Conscience: Massachusetts Whig Politics and Southwestern Expansion, 1843–1848* (1967), for which he received the McKnight Foundation Humanities Award. He has also published extensively on American foreign relations before the Civil War and is currently working on a study of Russian-American relations in the nineteenth century and a biography of William Henry Seward.

RICHARD H. COLLIN is professor emeritus of history at the University of New Orleans. He is the author of *Theodore Roosevelt, Culture, Diplomacy, and Expansion: A New View of American Imperialism* (1985) and *Theodore Roosevelt's Caribbean: The Panama Canal, the Monroe Doctrine, and the Latin American Context* (1990). He is currently writing a book about "Collectors, Tariffs, and the New Museums: The Creation of an American Art Patrimony, 1890–1940."

EDWARD P. CRAPOL is professor of history at the College of William and Mary. He is the author of *James G. Blaine: Architect of Empire* (1999) and the editor of *Women and American Foreign Policy: Lobbyists, Critics, and Insiders* (2d ed., 1992).

JUSTUS D. DOENECKE is professor of history at New College of the University of South Florida. He received his Ph.D. in 1966 from Princeton University, where he studied with Arthur S. Link. He has published many books and articles on Cold War isolationism, the Garfield-Arthur presidency, and the Manchurian crisis of 1931–1933. His *In Danger Undaunted: The Anti-Interventionist Movement of 1940–1941 as Revealed in the Papers of the America First Committee* (1991) received SHAFR's Arthur S. Link Prize for documentary editing.

MICHAEL J. HOGAN is professor of history at The Ohio State University and editor of *Diplomatic History*. In addition to editing several volumes on American foreign relations, he is the author of *Informal Entente: The Private Structure of Cooperation in Anglo-American Economic Diplomacy, 1918–1928* (1977), *The Marshall Plan: America, Britain, and the Reconstruction of Western Europe, 1947–1952* (1987), and *A Cross of Iron: Harry S. Truman and the Origins of the National Security State, 1945–1954* (1998). He is the recipient of numerous prizes, including the Quincy Wright Book Prize of the American Studies Association, the George Louis Beer Prize of the American Historical Association, and the Stuart L. Bernath Prize of the Society for Historians of American Foreign Relations.

BRIAN MCKERCHER is professor of history and chair of War Studies at the Royal Military College of Canada. A specialist on inter-war Anglo-American relations and the editor or co-editor of nine books on diplomatic and military history, he has written *The Second Baldwin Government and the United States, 1924–1929: Attitudes and Diplomacy* (1984), *Esme Howard: A Diplomatic Biography* (1989), and *Transition of Power: Britain's Loss of Global Preeminence to the United States, 1930–1945* (1998). Elected a Fellow of the Royal Historical Society in 1996, he is the general editor of *The Praeger Studies in Diplomacy and Strategic Thought*.

DAVID STEIGERWALD is associate professor of history at The Ohio State University, Marion. A Fulbright scholar in 1995–96, he is the author of *Wilsonian Idealism in America* (1994), *The Sixties and the End of Modern America* (1995), and numerous essays on twentieth-century America. He is now at work on a book regarding technological change and recent conceptions of culture in a global setting.

WILLIAM EARL WEEKS teaches history at San Diego State University. He is the author of *Building Continental Empire: American Expansion from the Revolution to the Civil War* (1996) and *John Quincy Adams and American Global Empire* (1992).

Preface & Acknowledgments

The essays in this volume were originally published in *Diplomatic History*, the journal of the Society for Historians of American Foreign Relations (SHAFR). I am indebted to the Society for permission to republish the essays here, and to the authors for revising their essays and waiving their claim to any republication fees. Those fees, together with royalties from the sale of this volume, will be contributed to the Lawence E. Gelfand-Armin Rappaport Fund. Tom Patterson and I established that fund several years ago to honor our former graduate advisors, both founding members of SHAFR, and to support the editorial office of *Diplomatic History*.

I am also indebted to Frank Smith, my editor at Cambridge University Press. Thanks to his efforts much of my work as the editor of *Diplomatic History* has been pulled together in this and other volumes that I hope will be of service to graduate students and scholars in the field. Thanks are due as well to The Ohio State University for its support of the journal, to the Mershon Center at Ohio State for its help with the Graduate Workshop in Diplomatic History, to Nate Citino and Bruce Khula for aid in preparing the manuscript, and to Kurt Schultz for expert copyediting. But my deepest gratitude is to the graduate students who have helped me with *Diplomatic History* over more than a dozen years, starting with the newest set, Matthew Davis and Jennifer Walton, and working back to Nate Citino, Bruce Khula, Susan Landrum, Bruce Karhoff, Amy Staples, Paul Pierpaoli, Josef

Ostyn, Darryl Fox, Paul Wittekind, Toby Rosenthal, Kurt Schultz, and especially Ann Heiss, who served first as editorial assistant, then as assistant editor, and now (since 1992) as associate editor of the journal. All of us in SHAFR are indebted to these colleagues, and none more so than I.

Columbus, Ohio   MJH
May 1999

1

Introduction

MICHAEL J. HOGAN

This volume of essays concludes a project that began a dozen years ago, when I became the editor of *Diplomatic History*, the journal of record for specialists in the history of American foreign relations. That project grew out of the conviction that such a journal should inform its readers of the recent literature and newest trends in the field. With this conviction as a guide, I began to solicit and publish a variety of methodological and historiographical articles. The methodological articles, which elaborated the new conceptual approaches used by diplomatic historians, were later reprinted in *Explaining the History of American Foreign Relations*, a collection that I co-edited with Thomas G. Paterson in 1991. Four years later I edited a second collection of articles drawn largely from the same journal and published as *America in the World: The Historiography of American Foreign Relations since 1941*. As the title indicates, the essays in this volume reviewed the recent literature on American diplomacy in the period from World War II through the Cold War. This period had so captured the attention of diplomatic historians that the volume included nineteen essays running more than six hundred pages. But even while preparing *America in the World* I was already recruiting and publishing historiographical reviews of the literature on American foreign relations from the early Republic to the Second World War – more than a hundred and fifty years of diplomacy that had been slighted but not completely ignored by historians. The result was eight essays first published in *Diplomatic History* and now revised and republished in this volume.

As I noted at the start of *America in the World*, historiographical essays are extremely difficult to write, but immensely rewarding. Even when they do little more than summarize the literature, they still perform an invaluable service to scholars and students who find it difficult to stay abreast of their field. This is perhaps even more the case with the essays in this volume, if only because the diplomacy of the early Republic, of the nineteenth century in general, and even of the period between 1900 and 1941 has long been a subject that most historians teach rather than research. Indeed, the historiography of American foreign relations before the First World War has become something of a "wasteland," to borrow a phrase that Jonathan Dull used to describe the study of American foreign relations before the Constitution. Nor is it just the paucity of new work that merits this judgment. Drew McCloy, Steven Watts, and other scholars of the nineteenth century have produced brilliant works on which diplomatic historians can draw. But to the extent that diplomatic history itself has spawned fresh ideas and ways of thinking, it has done so largely in work that deals with the twentieth century and especially the Cold War. With that conflict behind us, it can only be hoped that diplomatic historians will refocus their energies on other topics and earlier periods. The essays in this volume are born of that hope.

These essays can be divided into two categories – those dealing with the early Republic, the middle period, the late nineteenth century, and the Progressive Era, and those dealing with Wilsonianism, the interwar period, and the origins of World War II in Europe and the Pacific. The four essays in the first part, though written by different authors at different times, nonetheless make some of the same points. Though respectful of older works and established approaches, they are tired of the familiar categories of analysis and of the old debates between realism and idealism, traditionalism and revisionism. All four authors urge the next generation of historians to focus on new topics and ideas, and all four see the concept of empire as the central story of American diplomacy through the nineteenth century.

William Earl Weeks, Kinley Brauer, and Edward Crapol see more continuity than discontinuity in American diplomacy over the nineteenth century. In particular, they see the quest for over-seas commercial empire as a powerful theme running through the whole period, and they reject the notion that a more traditional colonialism took hold only at the end of the nineteenth century. On the contrary, the continental empire of the pre–Civil War period, particularly the capture of Mexican and Indian territory and the subjugation of non-white populations, laid the groundwork for extra-continental expansion in the late nineteenth century and especially for the occupation and control of the Philippines. Weeks, Brauer, and Crapol urge diplomatic historians to explore the con-tinuities evident in these landed acquisitions and in the whole history of American commercial expansion, to analyze the ideol-ogy and rhetoric of American empire, and to explicate the role of key policymakers.

Writing about the diplomacy of the early Republic, Weeks also notes the linkages between foreign policy and domestic politics, particularly the connection between efforts to free the seas and expand commerce and the larger project of civil, political, and religious liberty that defined the Republican experiment. He calls attention to recent work that examines the place of foreign policy in the debates over federalism, elaborates the American convic-tion that overseas commercial expansion was essential to the sur-vival of Republican political institutions, and explores the ten-sion between the American commitment to republicanism and the sectional divisions and military institutions that grew out of American expansion.

Like Brauer and Crapol, and like Richard Collin, Weeks also stresses the need to see American expansion in the nineteenth cen-tury as part of the larger project of Western imperialism. These historians want their colleagues to put American imperialism into an international context and to fashion a history that is more comparative and therefore free of the ethnocentric and exceptionalist biases that supposedly marked an older generation of scholarship. To Collin, such an approach would have the ad-ditional advantage of demolishing the hegemonic paradigm that he claims has dominated so much of the literature on American foreign relations – a paradigm that stresses the economic, military, and strategic aspects of American foreign policy and that sees American expansion as more unified, coherent, and deliberate than was actually the case. In Collin's vision, the hegemonic paradigm should give way to an alternative analytical model that he calls symbiosis. He does not define symbiosis very clearly, but it seems to combine a new emphasis on cultural affairs and on the interaction between states with a conservative postrevisionism that refuses to moralize about American imperialism in the same fashion as revisionists and other advocates of the hegemonic approach.

At times Collin's essay seems to read like a defense of American imperialism as the white man's burden, a tendency we do not find in the essays by Weeks, Brauer, and Crapol, all of whom are also inclined to see U.S. imperialism as far more purposeful than Collin will concede. Nevertheless, all four authors urge a history that treats the process by which American imperialism worked, puts that process in international context, compares it with that of other countries, and escapes the old moralisms, the old attempts to see U.S. policy as exceptional, and the old dichotomies between idealism and realism, traditionalism and revisionism.

The authors also share other themes, including a new emphasis on culture and on the role of nongovernmental groups. Intrigued by the corporatist or associational model that some historians have used to explain American foreign policy in the twentieth century, these historians urge their colleagues to look carefully at the role played by private actors, and not just the economic functional groups that are usually at the center of a corporatist approach. Weeks, Brauer, and Crapol also call for a history of American foreign relations that includes women, African Americans, Native Americans, and ethnic groups. Influenced by cultural and social history, including ethnic studies and women's history, they are particularly struck with the need to explain more clearly the influence of race and racism on the rhetoric and ideology of American imperialism, the relationship between the U.S. government and American Indians, and the role that women played as missionaries or in overseas benevolent associations, the peace movement, and the anti-imperialist movement.

The next set of essays, four altogether, also critique old approaches and call for new directions. David Steigerwald, surveying the recent literature on Wilsonian diplomacy, concludes that contemporary developments, notably the end of the Cold War and the dissolution of the Soviet Union, have eroded the utility of both the realist critique of Woodrow Wilson and its revisionist counterpart. Borrowing from E. J. Hobsbawm, he suggests an approach that focuses less on Wilson than on the changes in the global system over which he presided. Like those scholars who deploy a corporatist model, he stresses how the development of modern capitalism produced economies dominated by large concentrations of private power and increasingly regulated by an administrative state. But he also notes, like Hobsbawm, how the modern nation state emerged just as ethnic and racial consciousness was intensifying and as national economies were becoming more dependent on world markets.

To Steigerwald, in other words, the paradox of modern diplomacy is to be found in the tensions that necessarily exist between the unifying forces associated with nationalism and with the rise of the modern nation state and the disunifying forces associated with ethnic, racial, and religious consciousness and with the integration of national markets into a global economy. Wilson was one of the first modern leaders to wrestle with these tensions. But the same tensions influenced other leaders as well, and Steigerwald sees new opportunities for scholars who seek to connect Wilson's experience to the global history of nationalism after World War I, and especially to the efforts by leaders everywhere to balance the forces of nationalism against the growing internationalism of the market and the centrifugal pull of racial, religious, ethnic, and linguistic identities.

The second essay in this group is by Brian McKercher, a Canadian scholar who surveys the literature on the interwar period. McKercher, too, seems convinced that nothing is to be gained by following the well-worn paths trod by traditional historians who labeled the 1920s an isolationist decade, and by revisionist historians whom he dismisses as Marxists and economic determinists. Such oversimplifications are not likely to inspire confidence in

McKercher's readers; nor is his effort to credit all new insights to
non-American scholars who have worked on the interwar period,
and especially to a tiny group that he calls the London school and
that includes, not surprisingly, McKercher himself. McKercher's
chauvinism might be hard to swallow, but he understands the
need to internationalize the study of American foreign policy and
his essay also includes a good summary of the recent literature on
such key figures as Wilson and Roosevelt, on the economic diplomacy of the 1920s, on the isolationist debates of the 1930s, and
on U.S. relations with Latin America, Asia, and Europe.

The last two essays, by Justus D. Doenecke and Michael A.
Barnhart, survey the literature on U.S. intervention in the Second
World War. Barnhart traces the literature on the origins of the
Pacific War from its initial focus on Japanese-American relations
and the disaster at Pearl Harbor to the multinational studies of
recent years, which are increasingly concerned with coalition
building in Asia and the Pacific, with the influence of internal
politics on the foreign policies of particular states, and with the
role of Britain, China, and other powers, as well as the United
States and Japan. Doenecke, focusing on the European side, provides a broad and detailed survey of the literature in several categories. These include works on Roosevelt and other key figures,
on bilateral relations between the United States and various countries, on the role of the State Department, the armed forces, and
the intelligence establishment, and on the debates in Congress
and in the public at large over the benefits of neutrality or intervention. Doenecke's survey touches on a rich body of work, but
the results leave him wanting more than the literature delivers.
Like Barnhart, he laments the lack of new methodologies, of new
ways of thinking, and of a single work that pulls the pieces of the
story together in a synthetic history of the period.

Such a lament is common in the following essays, which also
offer a set of recommendations that do not differ markedly from
those suggested in the introduction to *America in the World*. As
noted above, the authors see a desperate need for synthesis. They
survey topics and periods for which archival documents have long
been available and for which we have a mountain of scholarly

books and articles. But very few historians have tried to step back from the documents and write a general survey that draws heavily on the insights available in the monographic literature. Still worse, we have even fewer works that leap from a general survey to a synthesis that is creative in its own right. One thinks of Robert Beisner's *From the Old Diplomacy to the New, 1865–1900* (2d ed., Arlington Heights, IL, 1986), or of Michael Hunt's ⟵ *Ideology and U.S. Foreign Policy* (New Haven, 1987), to name two of the few such works available. Many of the authors in this volume are intrigued by the possibility of bringing the corporatist or associational model to bear on such a synthesis, but no one has stepped forward to accept this challenge.

Nor have diplomatic historians done enough to explore the insights to be derived from scholars in other fields. To be sure, Weeks has been influenced by the literature on Republicanism, Crapol has been a pioneer in the study of women and foreign policy, and Barnhart has written international history. But much more needs to be done in these areas, as all of the authors admit. Although historians can take great pride in writing diplomatic history as American history, the authors in this volume see international history and comparative national history as new frontiers waiting to be explored more fully. There seems to be a consensus on this point, and some of the authors, especially Weeks, Brauer, and Crapol, also urge diplomatic historians to draw more heavily on the lessons to be learned from social history, discourse studies, and literary theory. Although they do not want to lose sight of the state and state power, they nonetheless hope to decenter the field to some extent. They urge diplomatic historians to become more interested in traditional nonstate actors, such as corporations, labor unions, banks, and agricultural interests; in less traditional private actors, such as women, African Americans, Native Americans, and ethnic groups; in the influence of race, racism, and gender on foreign policy; and in the ideology, rhetoric, and political culture of American diplomacy. The time is ripe for synthetic work, but that work cannot be creative in today's intellectual market, nor reach much beyond the field, unless it borrows heavily from the insights of scholars in other disciplines.

2

New Directions in the Study of Early American Foreign Relations

WILLIAM EARL WEEKS

The study of early American foreign relations has been in the doldrums for a generation. Diplomatic historians have largely overlooked the foreign policy of the early republic while they have debated the major issues of the twentieth century, especially the Cold War. The preeminence of the United States in this century, the apocalyptic stakes involved in the Cold War, and the promise of new archival material are some of the factors that have combined to create a sense that the concerns of the twentieth century are more important than early American foreign relations. Recent historiographers have noted the sparseness of new work in the early period. Jonathan Dull characterizes American foreign relations before the Constitution as "a historiographical wasteland"; Kinley Brauer describes the period 1815–61 as "the Great American Desert."[1] Indeed, if one judges by the amount of work done recently, the field of antebellum American foreign relations is a desert, while Cold War studies are a triple-canopy rain forest.

The apparent end of the Cold War may signal a shift in emphases. The magnitude and speed of the Soviet collapse and the sud-

1 Jonathan Dull, "American Foreign Relations Before the Constitution: A Historiographical Wasteland," in *American Foreign Relations: A Historiographical Review*, ed. Gerald K. Haines and J. Samuel Walker, (Westport, CT, 1981); Kinley J. Brauer, "The Great American Desert Revisited: Recent Literature and Prospects for the Study of American Foreign Relations, 1815–1861," *Diplomatic History* 13 (Summer 1989): 395–418. See also "Foreign Policy in the Early Republic Reconsidered: Essays from a SHEAR Symposium," *Journal of the Early Republic* 14 (Winter 1994): 453–96.

den irrelevance of Marxist-Leninist ideology suggest that communism was not as formidable an enemy as was sometimes believed. Moreover, the censorship and destruction of the documentary record of the 1950s has cast doubt on how much historians will be allowed to know about recent events. Blanche Wiesen Cook has gone so far as to ask if "there is a future at all" to the history of recent American foreign relations.[2]

What does seem evident is the extent to which this truly has been the American century, the century in which American power and influence has dwarfed that of any other nation. The surrender of the Soviet Union in 1989 spelled victory for the United States in a seventy-five-year war with autocracy, fascism, and communism. The proclamation of a "new world order" represents the culmination of a national mission to transform the world. The roots of this national mission can be traced at least to 1776. American notions of internal political development, international trade, and international law that were visionary in the eighteenth century have emerged victorious in a form remarkably faithful to their original conception. Successive monarchical and Communist challenges to this *novus ordo seclorum* have been defeated. While one cannot attribute all the changes in international law, politics, and economics throughout the last two centuries to American influence, the preeminence of the American model is indisputable, especially considering that the recent bicentennial of the French Revolution revolved less around its global significance than around whether or not it was even a good idea. The Communist revolution stands revealed as a historic failure. Even if the outlines of the passing of U.S. hegemony are now becoming apparent, the idea of the American way of life, symbolized by some form of liberal capitalism, remains ascendant. The reality of this dominance and the speed with which it was achieved suggest that virtually no period in the history of American foreign affairs can be viewed as unimportant.

The Columbus Quincentenary is another factor that may encourage more attention to the study of early American foreign

2   Blanche Wiesen Cook, "U.S. Foreign Relations History – Is There a Future at All?" *Perspectives* 29 (November 1991): 11–14.

relations. Whatever one's views regarding the virtues or vices of European expansionism, it is clear that the mixing of peoples, technologies, and values that characterized European colonialism has been one of the major developments in human history. Five hundred years later, the world is about to become a "global village." What Walter LaFeber has termed the "American Age" is in fact a part of the Age of Europe. The traditional (and still widespread) view that casts foreign relations solely as a contest between the United States and Europe must begin to take into account that international relations during the last five centuries have also been a struggle between Euro-American peoples and non-Euro-American peoples and, on a more basic level, have been made up of innumerable individual social, political, military, and economic encounters between people of diverse backgrounds. Within this altered framework, American foreign policy is perceived not only in opposition to the European tradition but as a fundamental part of it as well. This revised perception of American foreign relations suggests many hitherto unasked questions and puts old questions in a new light.

Hence the time may be right for a reexamination of the entire history of American foreign relations as part of an enlarged understanding of both American and world history. This essay examines recent work on the period between 1787 and 1828 (although the phrase "early American foreign relations" might rightfully be said to refer to the entire antebellum era). The quality and quantity of this work proves that even a desert is capable of sustaining a substantial amount of life. On the whole, however, the field has remained a scholarly backwater, in part because historians of previous generations often appeared to have answered all the major questions, leaving little new ground to break. Succeeding generations have to examine old issues in a new light; they cannot have the exhilarating experience of being the first to chronicle a major event or era. The immense shadow cast by the work of the giants who first explored the field means that any scholar who plans to do work in early American foreign policy must still confront the extensive legacy of these earlier generations.

The most imposing of all these early historians is Henry Adams, one of the first and still possibly the greatest historian the United States has ever produced. Adams's nine-volume *History of the United States of America during the Administrations of Thomas Jefferson and James Madison* remains unsurpassed in its weaving of politics, culture, economics, and diplomacy into a coherent portrait of the Jeffersonian revolution.[3] It reminds contemporary specialists that the nation's foreign policy can only be understood in the larger context of the time. Adams's interpretations continue to inspire some of the most significant work of recent years.[4] The grace with which his *History* is written is alone reason enough for it to be read today.

Only slightly less influential than Adams in defining early American foreign policy has been Samuel Flagg Bemis. Of his many works, his two-volume biography of John Quincy Adams is the most enduring.[5] While *John Quincy Adams and the Foundations of American Foreign Policy* is better known, it is *John Quincy Adams and the Union* that probes Adams the man. Although Bemis was an unabashed nationalist, the thoroughness of his research alerts scholars that their efforts can only complement rather than replace his work. Like that of Henry Adams, the work of Samuel Flagg Bemis is a major point of departure for any student of the foreign policy of the early republic.

Just below Adams and Bemis in historiographical significance are a number of scholars whose output was both distinguished and prolific. They include Julius Pratt, Dexter Perkins, Charles C. Griffin, Arthur P. Whitaker, George Dangerfield, Alexander DeConde, Richard Warner Van Alstyne, William Appleman Williams, Bradford Perkins, and Richard B. Morris.[6] Collectively,

---

3 Henry Adams, *History of the United States of America during the Administrations of Thomas Jefferson and James Madison*, 2 vols. (1889; reprint ed., New York, 1986).

4 See Robert Tucker and David Hendrickson, *Empire of Liberty: The Statecraft of Thomas Jefferson* (New York, 1990).

5 Samuel Flagg Bemis, *John Quincy Adams and the Foundations of American Foreign Policy* (New York, 1949); idem, *John Quincy Adams and the Union* (New York, 1956).

6 See, for example, Julius Pratt, *Expansionists of 1812* (Baltimore, MD, 1925); Dexter Perkins, *The Monroe Doctrine, 1823–1826* (Cambridge, MA, 1927); Charles C. Griffin, *The United States and the Disruption of the Spanish Empire, 1810–1822: A Study of the Relations of the United States with Spain and the Rebel Spanish Colonies* (New York, 1937); Arthur P.

their work has articulated early American foreign relations so extensively that it is small wonder that (with some notable exceptions) scholars for a generation have looked to later eras for less well trod ground.

Yet it is clear that changing times will yield changing interpretations, no matter how imposing the edifice of previous scholarship. In recent years historians have produced a number of significant books on American foreign relations. One of the most important is Jerald Combs's *American Diplomatic History: Two Centuries of Changing Interpretations*. Combs demonstrates that from the publication in 1826 of Theodore Lyman's first diplomatic history of the United States, interpretations of American foreign relations have been influenced by the historical moment in which they were written: even those "who thought present concerns and personal opinions should play no part in historical analysis" were influenced by the times they lived in, and "even the most 'scientific' historians failed to keep their assumptions and attitudes from affecting their historical interpretations of past American diplomacy."[7] While some of Combs's interpretations are debatable, his volume is an invaluable overview of the evolution of American diplomatic historiography. Although the breadth of his work limits the depth of his analysis and suggests the need for book-length treatments of each era that probe more fully the histories and historians of the time, it is a fine introduction to what could be an entirely independent area of study.

Peter Novick's *That Noble Dream: The "Objectivity Question" and the American Historical Profession* confirms Combs's point about the influence of present concerns on the writing of history for the American historical profession as a whole. Novick's re-

---

Whitaker, *The United States and the Independence of Latin America, 1800–1830* (Baltimore, MD, 1941); George Dangerfield, *The Era of Good Feelings* (New York, 1952); Alexander DeConde, *Entangling Alliances: Politics and Diplomacy under George Washington* (Durham, NC, 1958); Richard Warner Van Alstyne, *The Rising American Empire* (New York, 1960); William Appleman Williams, *The Contours of American History* (Cleveland, 1961); Bradford Perkins, *Castlereagh and Adams: England and the United States, 1812–1823* (Berkeley, 1964); and Richard B. Morris, *The Peacemakers: The Great Powers and American Independence* (New York, 1965).

7   Jerald A. Combs, *American Diplomatic History: Two Centuries of Changing Interpretations* (Berkeley, 1983), 75.

intro- duction historiography

search into the private papers of dozens of eminent historians conclusively demonstrates that objectivity was an ideal honored but not practiced, especially during the early years of the Cold War when historians were attracted to the idea of the disinterested scholar attempting to be objective yet determined to teach lessons validating the American way of life. It is important to note that Novick is not substituting an open-ended relativism as the alternative to objectivity. He believes that history is ultimately an appeal to the facts, however problematic the construction of those facts may sometimes be. It is to be hoped that his work will dissuade historians from rejecting alternative explanations as "not objective" and encourage a more precise delineation of the epistemological, philosophical, and moral assumptions that animate the various schools of historical thought.[8]

Along the same lines, Alexander DeConde, in his 1985 presidential address to the Pacific Historical Association, frankly asserted that "historians have rarely been impartial." He noted the pervasive ethnocentrism of "civilized" historians, particularly where war was concerned: "They have consistently glorified the warfare, the distinctiveness, the presumed superiority, and the chauvinism of their own people, often while serving as conscious agents of imperialism." He also candidly suggested that because so many historians are employees of state or government institutions, their claims to impartiality are compromised.[9]

Collectively, Combs, Novick, and DeConde provide strong support for the claim that historians, like the people they write about, do not work outside the bounds of history. Their work shows that advocacy history did not begin with the New Left of the 1960s, or even with the work of Charles Beard and Carl Becker earlier in the century. Historians of American foreign relations have consistently allowed their work to serve the values in which they believe. In 1961 Samuel Bemis himself revealed how he disdained the role of the disinterested historian when in his presi-

---

8 Peter Novick, *That Noble Dream: The "Objectivity Question" and the American Historical Profession* (Cambridge, England, 1988), chap. 10.
9 Alexander DeConde, "Clio, Clientage, Ethnocentrism, and War: Some Reflections," *Pacific Historical Review* 55 (February 1986): 3, 16.

dential address to the American Historical Association he attacked what he perceived to be a tendency among Americans to over-analyze themselves. "Too much self-study, too much self-criticism is as weakening to a people as it is to an individual," he said. Americans were "debauched by mass media of sight and sound, pandering for selfish profit . . . fed full of toys and gew-gaws, our military preparedness held back by insidious strikes for less work and more pay, our manpower softened in will and body in a climate of amusement. Massive self-indulgence and massive responsibility do not go together."[10] Correct or not, Bemis's remarks are not those of a neutral observer.

The idea of objective truth is pernicious insofar as it justifies suppressing alternative truths that are by definition not objective. In this sense objectivity is hardly the noble dream that it was alleged to be. Objectivity presupposes that historians occupy a position outside history, that they can check their spiritual, moral, and political commitments at the door when they enter the archives. The record shows that this has not been the case. Nor is it necessarily desirable for it to be so. Paradoxically, acknowledging one's subjectivity might be the key to effective communication between scholars of diverse points of view.[11] The search for a collective understanding of history is not the same as an objective understanding that pretends to be abstracted from the community and historical era within which it is produced. Perhaps all one can ask is that historians deal honestly with the historical record, be faithful to their individual consciences, and not be the puppets of any institutional or ideological agendas.

The now-evident biases and shortcomings of older works on early American foreign relations do not negate their value as a solid foundation for new work. The challenge for modern scholars is to reinterpret early American foreign relations and its histo-

10 Samuel Flagg Bemis, "American Foreign Policy and the Blessings of Liberty," in his *American Foreign Policy and the Blessings of Liberty and other Essays* (New Haven, CT, 1962), 14.

11 See Christopher Thorne, *Border Crossings: Studies in International History* (Oxford, 1988), chap. 2. See also David M. Fitzsimons, "Thomas Paine's New World Order: Idealistic Internationalism in the Ideology of Early American Foreign Relations," *Diplomatic History* 19 (Fall 1995): 569–82.

riography using contemporary approaches to history. Insofar as traditional diplomatic histories have isolated foreign relations from the larger trends of American and world history, the task is one of reintegration.

An example of more recent work that illustrates the connection between American foreign relations and the major themes of national development is Frederick W. Marks's *Independence on Trial.* Marks's bold thesis is that "foreign policy . . . was of overwhelming significance" in spurring constitutional reform and that "taken as a whole, problems relating to the conduct of foreign affairs far outweighed any other combination of issues facing the confederation." Condemning the failure of previous historians to consider the role of foreign policy in the making of the Constitution, Marks argues that the inability to retaliate effectively against foreign trade restrictions united the new nation, as did looming threats to national security.[12]

Marks extended and modified his views in a 1987 article, "Power, Pride, and the Purse: Diplomatic Origins of the Constitution." Restating his idea that "the strongest driving force behind the Constitution by far was a crying weakness in foreign affairs," Marks nonetheless concedes that prior to 1786 few people believed that the problems of national defense and commercial policy could not be solved within the framework of the Articles of Confederation. Yet Marks sees events moving quickly in 1786 to create a mood of national paralysis and spur widespread talk of secession. The crisis of 1786 culminated with Shays's Rebellion, which Marks characterizes as "secession coupled with subversion."[13]

Subsequent scholarship has cast a different light on some of Marks's ideas. Norman Graebner's "Isolationism and Antifederalism: The Ratification Debates" documents that Antifederalists believed that the threat to national security was exaggerated. Graebner cites Patrick Henry's plea that "the Con-

---

12 Frederick W. Marks III, *Independence on Trial: Foreign Affairs and the Making of the Constitution*, 2d ed. (Wilmington, DE, 1986), x.
13 Frederick W. Marks III, "Power, Pride, and Purse: Diplomatic Origins of the Constitution," *Diplomatic History* 11 (Fall 1987): 318, 312.

stitution be debated on its merits and not forced on the American people with descriptions of danger that did not exist." He notes that Antifederalists did not believe government under the Articles of Confederation would lead to disaster and that they favored reform that would allow a uniform commercial policy. He also stresses that the Antifederalists accused the Federalists of "over-promising in their vision of national growth and progress under the new plan of government." In sum, the Antifederalists per-ceived that the threat of danger from abroad was being used to stampede the nation into ratifying a document "that dictated . . . pervading infringements on the states and, potentially, on the lib-erties of the people."[14]

In a similar vein, Lawrence S. Kaplan's "Jefferson and the Con-stitution: The View from Paris, 1786–1789" demonstrates that Jefferson was at first hesitant about the Constitution because he thought it was a stronger central government and not a danger from abroad that posed the greatest threat to individual liberty. He feared Shays's Rebellion not because it posed a threat to pub-lic order but because it could serve as an excuse to establish a repressive central authority. Although he supported strengthen-ing congressional power to regulate commerce, Jefferson none-theless was concerned that the Constitution opened the door to "the possibility of America losing in the name of law and order the vital distinctions between the Old and New Worlds."[15]

The work done to date suggests that while a connection be-tween foreign policy and the origins of the Constitution exists, the questions of national defense and commercial policy were primarily (as Marks's own work implies) only arguments put forth

14   Norman Graebner, "Isolationism and Antifederalism: The Ratification Debates," *Dip-lomatic History* 11 (Fall 1987): 340, 342, 352. See also Jonathan Marshall, "Empire or Liberty: The Antifederalists and Foreign Policy, 1787–1788," *Journal of Libertarian Studies* 4 (Summer 1980): 233–54; and Eugene R. Sheridan, "The Recall of Edmond Charles Genet: A Study in Transatlantic Politics and Diplomacy," *Diplomatic History* 18 (Fall 1994): 463–88.
15   Lawrence S. Kaplan, "Jefferson and the Constitution: The View from Paris, 1786–1789," *Diplomatic History* 11 (Fall 1987): 323. See also Elise Marienstras, *L'Amerique and La France: Deux Revolutions* (Paris, 1990); and Marie Jean Rossignol, *Le Ferment Nationaliste: Aux Origines de la Politique Exterieure des Etats-Unis, 1789–1812* (Paris, 1994).

to win the campaign for ratification.[16] It seems more precise to say that it was the related impulses toward nation and empire, symbolized by the appeals to national unity and national greatness at the core of the Federalist argument, that were the motive forces behind the Constitution. The yearning for nation and empire long predated the crisis of 1786 and was by no means universally felt even after the ratification of the Constitution. Indeed, ratification was made possible only by downplaying the Constitution's centralizing and imperial potential. Yet Hamilton made it clear what the stakes were in the opening paragraph of *The Federalist*: "The subject speaks of its own importance; comprehending in its consequences nothing less than the existence of the UNION, the safety and welfare of the parts of which it is composed, the fate of an empire in many respects the most interesting in the world."[17]

For advocates of nation and empire, ratification of the Constitution was but one of a long series of victories over the particularistic and isolationist tendencies of much of the country. It is also important to recall that the Federalists, like the revolutionary faction, were probably a minority of the total population. The truth is that the Constitution was drafted in secret by a body that exceeded its authority and ratified by a process that Graebner notes was "controlled" by the Federalists.[18] The worthiness of the endeavor cannot alter these basic facts about the Constitution's origins. Indeed, they provide key insight into the nature of the nationalist and imperialist tendencies in the early republic.

The tension between domestic politics and international affairs is explored in Stephen Peter Rosen's "Alexander Hamilton and the Domestic Uses of International Law." Rosen suggests that Hamilton had a double-edged view of international law: the anarchy of the international state system meant that international

16 See Frederick W. Marks III, "Foreign Affairs: A Winning Issue in the Campaign for Ratification of the Constitution," *Political Science Quarterly* 86 (September 1971): 444–69.
17 Alexander Hamilton, James Madison, John Jay, *The Federalist*, introduction by Clinton Rossiter (1788; reprint ed., New York, 1961), 33. See also Leonard W. Levy, *Original Intent and the Framers' Constitution* (New York, 1988), chap. 2; and Roger H. Brown, *Redeeming the Republic: Federal Taxation and the Origins of the Constitution* (Baltimore, MD, 1993).
18 Graebner, "Isolationism and Antifederalism," 353.

law necessarily reflected the balance of power. Therefore Hamilton believed it "folly" for a weak nation like the United States to attempt to alter international law.[19]

Domestically, Hamilton invoked international law as a means to restrain what were perceived to be the irresponsible impulses of the masses. In Rosen's words, "the initial concern was how to make the American people deferential to international realities. By demanding that American citizens obey international law, Hamilton was demanding that they obey international realities." International law was not enforceable internationally, but it could be enforced domestically: "By transforming power politics into the obligations of law, ratified and enforced by the national government, citizens are brought under legal control. . . Law was a constant theme in Hamilton's essays because he needed to restrain his fellow citizens." Similarly, Rosen asserts that the Farewell Address was chiefly concerned "not with the idea of permanent neutrality but with the principle of popular deference to the elected officials who conduct the nation's foreign affairs and to the law of nations."[20]

Rosen's understanding of Hamilton is paralleled in Forrest McDonald's *Alexander Hamilton*. Casting Hamilton as a champion of a hierarchical and deferential social order, McDonald suggests that the Farewell Address "was an eloquent plea, by two men who loved their country, for their fellow citizens to return to their senses." McDonald argues that because the Treasury was responsible for collecting tariff revenues and overseeing foreign debts, Hamilton had to be more active than Jefferson in foreign affairs. When one links Hamilton's substantial role in foreign affairs to his successful efforts on the domestic front to establish "the procedures by which people interacted, rather than attempting to ordain what they should do," it becomes clear that "the bastard son of a Scotch pedlar" (as John Adams termed the secre-

---

19   Stephen Peter Rosen, "Alexander Hamilton and the Domestic Uses of International Law," *Diplomatic History* 5 (Summer 1981): 195.
20   Ibid., 196, 201. See also Daniel G. Lang, *Foreign Policy in the Early Republic: The Law of Nations and the Balance of Power* (Baton Rouge, LA, 1985).

tary of the treasury) was perhaps the most influential American of the 1790s.[21]

The widespread habit of casting the foreign policy debate of the 1790s as a straightforward clash between Hamilton's cool realism and Jefferson's wooly-headed idealism has been persuasively countered in Lawrence S. Kaplan's *Entangling Alliances with None*, a collection of essays on the Federalist and Republican eras. Kaplan argues that it was a fear of British domination that drove Jefferson's alleged pro-French policies, not a misguided Francophilia. Kaplan makes it clear that Jefferson was both less Francophile and less Anglophobe than he is often portrayed. Most important, Kaplan demonstrates that the realist/idealist dichotomy is problematic by reminding us that both Jefferson and Hamilton were part of a "consensus of 1789" characterized by "the support of a strong central government capable of maintaining freedom from European entanglements and profits from European commerce."[22]

Yet Kaplan makes a crucial distinction between Hamilton and Jefferson that suggests why the latter might appropriately be labeled an idealist. He notes that Jefferson consistently believed that his politics were just and "moral by virtue of their American character." Unlike Hamilton, Jefferson tended to cast issues of national interest in terms of transcendent moral categories, a practice Kaplan describes as "a characteristic American approach to international relations."[23] Jefferson's vision of a world remade by American ideas contrasts starkly with Hamilton's conception of national greatness achieved within the limits of the established international order.

---

21 Forrest McDonald, *Alexander Hamilton: A Biography* (New York, 1979), 322, 122. See also Edward Pessen, "George Washington's Farewell Address, The Cold War, and the Timeless National Interest," *Journal of the Early Republic* 7 (Spring 1987): 1–25; and Peter Onuf and Nicholas Onuf, *Federal Union, Modern World: The Law of Nations in an Age of Revolutions, 1776–1814* (Madison, WI, 1993).

22 Lawrence S. Kaplan, *Entangling Alliances with None: American Foreign Policy in the Age of Jefferson* (Kent, OH, 1987), 78.

23 Ibid., 23. See also Ralph Ketcham, *Presidents above Party: The First American Presidency, 1789–1829* (Chapel Hill, NC, 1984); Thomas C. Ray, "'Not One Cent for Tribute': The Public Addresses and American Popular Reaction to the XYZ Affair, 1798–1799," *Journal of the Early Republic* 3 (Winter 1983): 389–412; and Michael Kitzen, "Money Bags or Cannon Balls: The Origins of the Tripolitan War, 1785–1801," ibid. 16 (Winter 1996): 601–24.

That historians have conceptualized the foreign policies of the Federalist era as a struggle between realism and idealism again evidences how the present has shaped the study of American foreign relations. The realist school arose in the 1940s as a response to the new international situation. The United States found itself in a position of unparalleled power and global leadership, and its traditional moral categories seemed incompatible with the ambiguities of its new role. To writers such as Hans Morgenthau, George Kennan, and Walter Lippmann, realism meant a foreign policy through which the United States would make its international aspirations conform to its capabilities and interests. Kennan argued that this realist approach characterized the conduct of American foreign relations until 1898, when President McKinley mistakenly led the United States into the ranks of the colonial powers. This blunder was compounded by the great crusade of World War I, in which Woodrow Wilson promised the American people more than he knew he (or they) could deliver, that is, a world "safe for democracy."[24] For the realists idealism and morality became associated with a tender-minded naivete that was damaging to the national interest and, insofar as these virtues were disassociated from power, ineffective in advancing the values in whose name they were invoked. Realism, with its aura of results-oriented tough-mindedness, became so influential that in 1964 Norman Graebner described early American foreign policy as "fundamentally amoral."[25]

Yet the term "realism" connotes a second meaning, one which casts doubt upon the validity of the concept as a tool of analysis. In this second meaning, realism is characterized by a sober willingness to see the world as it is, not as we would like it to be. As a worldview it is related to the classic conservative notion that it would be dangerous to assume that humans are driven by anything other than their baser impulses. It assumes that warfare

24   George F. Kennan, *American Diplomacy, 1900–1950* (Chicago, 1951); Hans Morgenthau, *Politics Among Nations: The Struggle for Power and Peace* (New York, 1948); Morgenthau, *In Defense of the National Interest: A Critical Examination of American Foreign Policy* (New York, 1951); Walter Lippmann, *The Cold War* (New York, 1947).
25   Quoted in Jerald A. Combs, "Norman Graebner and the Realist View of American Diplomatic History," *Diplomatic History* 11 (Summer 1987): 256.

is inevitable and pacifism is folly. The pessimistic understanding of human nature implicit in the realist outlook may be correct, but the realist school fails, in general, to judge American politics and policymakers in the same tough-minded way it does the rest of the world. Even the most realistic American statesmen are portrayed idealistically, with motives that are not seen as selfish or depraved. Hence, Forrest McDonald presents Hamilton's actions as the essence of realism, yet Hamilton himself is seen as motivated by a keen sense of justice and the common good. It may be that the only truly realistic interpretations of American foreign policy are revisionist accounts that attribute every act, no matter how apparently altruistic, to a selfish nationalism.[26] In order to remain viable, the realist school must confront this contradiction between its framework for understanding the actions of other nations and its framework for understanding the actions of the United States.

Some might suggest that the concept of realism can be salvaged by substituting the word "pragmatic" for "realist." A pragmatist historian might say that American foreign policymakers tempered their idealism with considerations of the power at the nation's disposal. On closer examination, however, even this position is untenable. Much of the nation's history can be understood as the triumph of the visionary over the practical, beginning with the American Revolution. Realist calculations about power would have prevented the War of Independence. The realist school does not adequately take into account the power of the human spirit to triumph over material disadvantage. Indeed, one of the most remarkable things about the American nation (until now at least) has been the extent to which its economic and military power has caught up to and kept pace with its messianic, world-redeeming pretensions.

The unsentimental assumptions about the nature of humanity that underlie the realist position raise the question of the role of commercial expansionism in American foreign policy. Changing

---

26 Because of his basic skepticism as to the motives of the makers of American foreign policy, Gabriel Kolko, the reigning bete noir of diplomatic history, might best be considered a realist.

times have again affected the historiographical debate. Economic motives, largely invisible in the 1940s and 1950s, came to center stage in the 1960s via the work of William Appleman Williams and other members of the so-called Open Door school. This interpretation continues to generate controversy.[27] Nonetheless, while it is clear that Open Door enthusiasts may at times have exaggerated or oversimplified presumed economic motives, it is equally clear that there is an emerging consensus that places commercial expansionism at the center of early American foreign policy.

One of the books that has made a substantial contribution to this consensus is *Economics and World Power: An Assessment of American Diplomacy since 1789*, edited by William H. Becker and Samuel F. Wells. An illuminating collection of lengthy articles by a distinguished group of historians, this volume is explicitly intended to assess the accuracy of the Beard-Williams thesis regarding the centrality of economic motives in American foreign policy and more generally to consider the influence of economic factors in America's rise to world power. The essays by James A. Field, Jr., and Kinley J. Brauer show that antebellum American foreign policy, if not bound by the alleged economic determinism of the revisionist school, was dominated by economic concerns. Field details how from 1789 to 1820 "the central importance of economics was axiomatic" to American statesmen, and shows that "the central aim of foreign policy . . . was to extend commercial relations while avoiding political entanglement," although this proved more difficult than anticipated. He articulates an "ideology of commerce" that the Republicans hoped would serve as a "powerful weapon" in a struggle to "free the seas and better the condition of mankind." This struggle to free the seas and liberate commerce was linked to a larger program of civil, political, and religious liberty that defined the American revolutionary experiment and distinguished it from the corrupt institutions and practices of Europe. Ultimately, Field agrees with

27   See Arthur M. Schlesinger Jr.'s critique of the Open Door school in *The Cycles of American History* (Boston, 1986), chap. 7.

Theodore Lyman's 1826 judgment that American diplomacy to that time was "altogether of a commercial character."[28]

Similarly, Kinley J. Brauer views the period 1821 to 1860 as a time when "American leaders were well aware of the vital relationship between American prosperity and American diplomacy." Brauer sees "the central concerns" of policymakers being "widening old markets and opening new ones, expanding production, and promoting industry." Again, this commercial vision was part of a larger American ideology oriented around "economic and political self-determination, representative and limited government, freedom of the seas, and personal liberty." Brauer reasons that "since a crucial part of American prosperity and growth stemmed from international trade, since nature and history had dictated that America's primary relations with other nations would be economic, economic considerations provided the fundamental framework for American foreign relations during this period."[29]

Brauer is careful not to imply that there was unanimity within the United States regarding the direction and pace of commercial expansionism. He traces an ongoing sectional division: "As the American economy divided along regional lines, sectional leaders developed and promoted distinctive foreign policies calculated to serve the economic interests of their constituents." Brauer's work also shows that scholars examining the role of economics in American foreign policy must remember that there is no single business community, only business communities. The traditionally clubby nature of the American foreign policy establishment has made it susceptible to the influence of well-connected individuals advocating policies that serve a narrow segment of the economy and may or may not be in the national interest. Perhaps

28 James A. Field, Jr., "1789–1820: All Economists, All Diplomats," in *Economics and World Power: An Assessment of American Diplomacy since 1789*, ed. William H. Becker and Samuel F. Wells, Jr. (New York, 1984), 31, 53. See also James A. Field, Jr., *America and the Mediterranean World, 1776–1882* (Princeton, NJ, 1969).
29 Kinley J. Brauer, "1821–1860: Economics and the Diplomacy of American Expansionism," in *Economics and World Power*, 59, 65, 113. See also Alfred E. Eckes, Jr., *Opening America's Market: U.S. Foreign Trade Policy Since 1776* (Chapel Hill, NC, 1995), chap. 1; John E. Crowley, *The Privileges of Independence: Neomercantilism and the American Revolution* (Baltimore, MD, 1993); and William E. Unrau, *The White Man's Wicked Water: The Alcohol Trade and Prohibition in Indian Country, 1802–1830* (Lawrence, KS, 1996).

the most prominent such individual in the early republic was John Jacob Astor, whose financial and social connections to the political elite allowed him to secure ongoing federal support for his North American fur trading empire.[30]

My work on the Monroe era has found a vigorous program of global commercial expansionism based on the principles of reciprocity when possible, retaliation when necessary, and naval preparedness. Mary W. M. Hargreaves's detailed study of *The Presidency of John Quincy Adams* also emphasizes the central role of commerce in the foreign policy of that ill-fated administration. Commercial expansionism during the Jackson presidency has been documented in John Belohlavek's *Let the Eagle Soar*, revising the traditional notion of Jackson's quiescence in foreign affairs. Finally, the 1983 reissue of Norman A. Graebner's classic *Empire on the Pacific* carries the study of commercial expansionism to mid-century.[31]

Economic motives have become key to understanding early American foreign policy. One might ask how it could be otherwise. Interpretations of American foreign policy that deny or minimize the role of commercial interests seem implausible when one considers the degree to which economic abundance has defined the American way of life. Americans are, as David M. Potter's still-respected book observes, "people of plenty." Potter's notion that the primary aim of the American government has been "to keep our population in contact with the sources of wealth" resonates with a conception of American foreign policy whose major goal is to facilitate the expansion of private commerce.[32] Indeed, so well established is the relationship between the nation

30   The central role of John Jacob Astor in shaping early American foreign policy is beginning to come into focus. See James A. Ronda, *Astoria and Empire* (Lincoln, NE, 1990); Field, "All Economists"; William Earl Weeks, *John Quincy Adams and American Global Empire* (Lexington, KY, 1992), chap. 2; and James R. Gibson, *Otter Skins, Boston Ships, China Goods: The Maritime Fur Trade of the Northwest Coast, 1784–1841* (Seattle, 1992).

31   Weeks, *John Quincy Adams*; Mary W. M. Hargreaves, *The Presidency of John Quincy Adams* (Lawrence, KS, 1985); John Belohlavek, *"Let the Eagle Soar:" The Foreign Policy of Andrew Jackson* (Lincoln, NE, 1985); Norman Graebner, *Empire on the Pacific: A Study of American Continental Expansion* (1955; reprint ed., Santa Barbara, 1983).

32   David M. Potter, *People of Plenty: Economic Abundance and the American Character* (Chicago, 1954), 123.

and economic abundance that the burden of proof is on those historians who would deny or minimize the role of commerce in shaping American foreign policy. They would need to describe the mechanism by which the pervasive American concern with material prosperity was prevented from dominating foreign policy in the way it dominates so many other areas of our lives.

To emphasize the central role of commerce in the making of foreign policy is not necessarily to lapse into a simplistic economic determinism. Recent work outside the bounds of diplomatic history has shed light on how commerce, foreign policy, and ultimately, national survival were linked in the opinion of the elite. Joyce Appleby's *Capitalism and a New Social Order: The Republican Vision of the 1790s* suggests that the commerce attendant upon the capitalist mode of producing and distributing goods was perceived as indispensable to sustaining and spreading the republican revolution. Appleby emphasizes that the Jeffersonian mind linked capitalism to the promise of prosperity essential to the success of the republic. In this context, France and England in the 1790s "became symbols of two alternate futures or fates for the United States: England as the model of sober, ordered constitutional government . . . and France, presenting a vision of what a society of free men might be." Appleby's work highlights how a view of the international scene can be a projection of a domestic ideological, political, and psychic struggle.[33]

Equally illuminating is Drew McCoy's *The Elusive Republic: Political Economy in Jeffersonian America*. McCoy argues that the problems created by an agricultural surplus, a concern over the maintenance of public virtue, and fears of inevitable decline spurred the Jeffersonians into a program of territorial and commercial expansion. In McCoy's terms "expansion across space" was meant to forestall "development through time," or the corruption associated with an urban, industrial society. He writes, "America needed open markets as well as open space to make republicanism work." The Jeffersonian faith that "expansion of American trade would have a missionary impact on the rest of

33   Joyce Appleby, *Capitalism and a New Social Order: The Republican Vision of the 1790s* (New York, 1984), 57.

the world" reveals the extent to which the vision of material prosperity implicit in the notion of the Open Door is the preeminent
American value. McCoy's description of that faith is a reminder
that America's most enduring export has been a revolutionary
ideology that promises nothing less than a new world order based
on the principles of liberal capitalism. McCoy's work also lends
support to the idea first advanced by Beard and subsequently developed by Williams that expansionism was a means of dealing
with domestic crises, both current and anticipated.[34]

One of the most thought-provoking works in recent years on
early American foreign relations is Robert Tucker and David
Hendrickson's *Empire of Liberty: The Statecraft of Thomas
Jefferson*. Tucker and Hendrickson's severe indictment of Jefferson
builds on the insights of Henry Adams and is perhaps influenced
in larger measure by the authors' own conceptions of statecraft in
the modern world. Jefferson is portrayed as the preeminent revolutionary of his time, "perhaps the greatest expansionist" with a
"virtually limitless vision of expansion of the Empire of Liberty."
Yet Jefferson's imperial ambitions had less to do with the expansion of the boundaries of the United States than with the defense
of liberty and the republican institutions that sustained it. The
authors are correct to remind us that Jefferson did not envision
the world becoming *part* of the United States but rather *like* the
United States, that is to say, republican. Jefferson believed strongly
that republican institutions could not truly be safe in the United
States until they existed everywhere. Significantly, Tucker and
Hendrickson give implicit support to the Open Door school's contention that territorial expansion was motivated in part by a desire to defuse domestic tensions when they argue that Jefferson
believed that "it was through expansion . . . that the republican
character of the Union would be preserved."[35]

Tucker and Hendrickson find crucial contradictions in Jefferson's
ideology and leadership. They believe that his commitment to a

34 Drew McCoy, *The Elusive Republic: Political Economy in Jeffersonian America* (Chapel
Hill, NC, 1980), 132, 86. See also David K. Adams and Cornelis A. van Minnen, *Reflections
on American Exceptionalism* (Staffordshire, England, 1994).
35 Tucker and Hendrickson, *Empire of Liberty*, 159, 161, 162. See also Doron S. Ben-Atar,
Origins of Jeffersonian Commercial Policy and Diplomacy (New York, 1993).

world eschewing European balance-of-power politics was made absurd by his own grandiose expansionist plans, which the authors believe could not succeed without the force, fraud, and hypocrisy characteristic of continental diplomacy. They see Jefferson's successful Louisiana diplomacy as the result of fortune rather than foresight and his vigorous assertion of neutral rights as "a fiction belied by the plain facts of the case." Jefferson's ideological zeal blinded him to the necessity of conciliating Great Britain, tilted his policy toward France, inspired the massive usurpation of liberty during the embargo, and ultimately led to the war his statecraft shrank from. The authors' summary critique of Jefferson's leadership restates the realist position. They fault Jefferson for investing "the narrowest of American interests with a status so exalted that they could not be compromised" and for according neutral rights "a status far higher than that accorded the principle of the balance of power," and they conclude that his adherence to those principles affords "a profound illustration of how the insistence on 'reason and morality' without reference to 'power and expediency' can subtly derange a statecraft, subvert the modest tasks of diplomacy, and end by betraying both physical security and economic interest."[36]

In refusing to take republican ideology seriously, Tucker and Hendrickson forget that American foreign policy has been built on a series of grandiose and unrealistic aspirations, from attempting to overthrow the European mercantile system to trying to create a world "safe for democracy." The unifying thread has been a visionary desire to bend the world to the American model. To fault Jefferson's diplomacy for only partially realizing his messianic aspirations is to measure his effectiveness as a statesman by an unrealistic yardstick. Nor is it appropriate to define expansionism as Jefferson's "raison d'état." Using the terms and cat-

---

36 Tucker and Hendrickson, *Empire of Liberty*, 193, 221. See also Burton J. Spivak, *Jefferson's English Crisis: Commerce, Embargo and the Republican Revolution* (Charlottesville, NC, 1979); Clifford L. Egan, *Neither Peace nor War: Franco-American Relations, 1803–1812* (Baton Rouge, LA, 1983); Ronald L. Hatzenbuehler and Robert L. Ivie, *Congress Declares War: Rhetoric, Leadership, and Partisanship in the Early Republic* (Kent, OH, 1983); and Richard J. Ellings, *Embargoes and World Power: Lessons from American Foreign Policy* (Boulder, CO, 1985).

egories of traditional European diplomacy to analyze Jeffersonian statecraft obscures the revolutionary quality of republican foreign policy. Although necessity may have prompted American statesmen to make certain concessions to the European system, it was their ambition to transform the international economic, legal, and political status quo. The indisputable long-term success of this ambition renders moot criticisms that Jeffersonian foreign policy failed by not adhering to the principles of European realpolitik.

In the past decade several significant works have explored ideas concerning war, the military, and republican government. Lawrence D. Cress reevaluates the role of the military in republican thought in *Citizens in Arms*. By examining evolving ideas about the military "within the larger context of eighteenth-century republican ideology," Cress shows how the Jeffersonians moved out of necessity from their traditional suspiciousness of standing armies to a point where "the American army had become as much an institution of the country as the Constitution itself." Cress outlines how the development of a commercial, sophisticated society led to a public largely unwilling and unable to defend itself. The question then became "how could the republic guarantee its security if the citizenry could not be depended upon to serve the public good?" Given a citizenry that was largely unwilling to serve in the army and the related fact that its ranks were made up primarily of the poor and disenfranchised, Cress might better have titled his book *Citizens Not in Arms*.[37]

In a similar way, Theodore Crackel's *Mr. Jefferson's Army* reinterprets the traditional view that Jefferson held "whiglike, antiarmy, sentiments." Crackel argues that the Jeffersonians feared a standing army controlled by Federalists and that Jefferson, along with Henry Dearborn, "undertook a social and political transformation" of the army "in an effort to insure its loyalty to the new regime." Central to this "chaste reformation" was the creation of a military academy to train officers loyal to the republican

37   Lawrence D. Cress, *Citizens in Arms: The Army and Militia in American Society to the War of 1812* (Chapel Hill, NC, 1982), xii, 177, 76.

government. Much of this work was undone by the Madison administration, but that did not entirely negate Jefferson's "truly republican solution" of a regular army led by (if not made up of) citizens.[38]

One of the most enlightening recent works on American attitudes toward war is Reginald Stuart's *War and American Thought from the Revolution to the Monroe Doctrine*. Stuart traces the evolution of the limited war theories of the eighteenth century into what he calls "the American war myth" of the post-1815 period. Stuart sees the War of 1812 as decisive in linking the idea of limited war to the national interest, thereby creating a belief in the inevitability of war and a willingness to use force to defend U.S. interests. He notes how after 1815 "definitions of national interest mushroomed" to the point where "American foreign policy became more offensive than defensive, more aggressive than passive, more self-righteous than studiously impartial." Andrew Jackson, described by Stuart as "the American war myth incarnate," symbolized this emerging ethos. Speaking out against war became difficult, because antiwar sentiments were frequently equated with anti-Americanism.[39]

Another book with profound implications for foreign policy scholars is Steven Watts's *The Republic Reborn: War and the Making of Liberal America*. Watts examines the cultural and intellectual transition from republicanism to liberal capitalism, and concludes that the War of 1812 played "a crucial role" in this process by "energizing and validating larger liberalizing impulses in early nineteenth-century America." He argues that "what was projected on to the looming conflict of 1812 – fantasies and nightmares, visceral emotions and lofty ideals – often influenced people's views and actions more than a detached analysis of policy and instrumentality." For many, the war with Britain was "an immense blank slate on which they wrote their hopes and fears."

38   Theodore J. Crackel, *Mr. Jefferson's Army: Political and Social Reform of the Military Establishment, 1801–1809* (New York, 1987), 2, 14, 183. See also Joan R. Challinor and Robert L. Beisner, eds., *Arms at Rest: Peacemaking and Peacekeeping in American History* (New York, 1987).
39   Reginald C. Stuart, *War and American Thought: From the Revolution to the Monroe Doctrine* (Kent, OH, 1982), 160, 174.

Ultimately, it functioned as "a clarion call for American 'civil religion.'" In effect, Watts's work (in a manner reminiscent of Roger Brown's *The Republic in Peril: 1812*) suggests that the War of 1812 stemmed not from the struggle for neutral rights, territorial expansionism, national honor, or the Indian threat, but rather from an insecure national psychology. It is perhaps as reasonable an explanation as any.[40]

Reginald Horsman's "The War of 1812 Revisited" updates the ongoing discussion of what Donald Hickey has termed "the forgotten conflict." Horsman highlights the evolving nature of our understanding of the war by modifying the positions he himself took on the war thirty years ago. While still emphasizing that the conflict was "an offshoot of the European war," Horsman now argues "that there were many politicians in the United States who saw the invasion and retention of Canada as a useful side benefit of a war that had become necessary largely because of British maritime policies." As one of the first to challenge Julius Pratt's work pointing to expansionism as the cause of the war, Horsman now believes that the pendulum has swung back to a point where expansionist motives are being understated. J. C. A. Stagg's *Mr. Madison's War* also reemphasizes the American ambition for Canada, but sees the planned conquest of Canadian territory as part of Madison's plan to coerce Great Britain economically.[41]

More remains to be done on this enigmatic conflict. Horsman suggests that scholars look at the regional and state economic and social effects of the war and examine the Canadian view as well. The role of the Floridas needs to be reconsidered, perhaps as part of some general reevaluation of Pratt's thesis in *Expansionists of 1812*. The work of cultural and intellectual historians should also be integrated into our understanding of the war. After all, this relatively brief and bloodless conflict gave rise to a

---

40 Steven Watts, *The Republic Reborn: War and the Making of Liberal America, 1790–1820* (Baltimore, MD, 1987), xvii, xix, 271.
41 Reginald Horsman, "The War of 1812 Revisited," *Diplomatic History* 15 (Winter 1991): 118–19. See also J. C. A. Stagg, *Mr. Madison's War: Politics, Diplomacy, and Warfare in the Early American Republic, 1783–1830* (Princeton, NJ, 1983); Dwight L. Smith, *The War of 1812: An Annotated Bibliography* (New York, 1985); and Donald Hickey, *The War of 1812* (Urbana, IL, 1989).

people's general, a star-spangled banner, and a vigorous nationalism. It should not be forgotten.

A key figure in early American foreign relations and indeed, all
of American history, is John Quincy Adams. Long reputed to be
America's "greatest secretary of state," Adams has not exactly
been ignored by historians. Yet it is the manner in which his
personal destiny and the destiny of the nation intersected that
makes Adams a figure of enduring significance. This is the focus
of my own work.

Groomed almost from birth for leadership by his famous par-
ents, Adams believed himself preordained to play a crucial role in
a nation he believed destined by God to remake the world in its
image. A leading spokesman for nationalism and national unity,
he styled himself as the "man of the whole nation," a leader devoted to principle and above party or sectional differences. His
well-known support for continental expansionism should not obscure his global vision of a world order based on freedom of the
seas, freedom of commerce and navigation, and republican government.

Adams's most significant diplomatic achievement was the Transcontinental Treaty of 1819 with Spain. Taking over the long-
stalled negotiations in 1817 in a position of diplomatic weakness,
Adams (assisted by Jackson's Seminole War campaign) crafted an
agreement that finalized the Louisiana Purchase, secured the
Floridas, and, in conjunction with the Convention of 1818 with
Great Britain, established the nation's first transcontinental claim.
The treaty (and the matrix of policies that made it possible) established the conditions that allowed Monroe and Adams to make
their famous 1823 proclamation of hemispheric superiority.[42] The
Transcontinental Treaty is also significant in that by excluding
Texas it established a dynamic that would influence the Ameri-
can political debate until the Civil War.

The gap between relative power and relative accomplishment
is the true measure of statesmanship. Surely no other statesman
in American history accomplished as much as Adams did with so

---

42 See Weeks, *John Quincy Adams.*

little economic and military power. Questions of personal responsibility for this achievement are meaningless. Adams's pre-
dominant influence does not diminish Monroe's role as an artful
conciliator of a high-powered cabinet that included John C.
Calhoun and William Crawford. Monroe possessed the most
important trait a president can have – the ability to recognize
sound advice. His leadership resulted in the ultimate success of
Jeffersonian foreign policy and a presidential record in foreign
affairs that can rightfully be said to surpass that of either Jefferson
or Madison.

Adams also made a lasting contribution to American nationalism by formulating a distinct rhetoric of empire. An immensely
learned man who viewed history through the lens of an undoubt-
ing nationalism and the psyche of a latter-day Puritan elder, Adams
more than anyone of his time gave official voice to the emerging
ideology of nationalist expansionism, most notably in his defense
of Jackson's Seminole War campaign of 1817–18. Bemis writes,
"Adams all but coined the myth-making phrase 'manifest destiny.'"[43]

Three assumptions underlay the rhetoric of empire: the unique
virtue of the United States, its mission to regenerate the world in
its own image, and the nation's God-given destiny. Within the
assumptions of this rhetoric, any foreign policy issue could be
cast as a providential struggle between American righteousness
and foreign depravity. Adams's rhetoric of empire built on traditions that existed prior to its conception; it established a rhetorical framework for nationalist expansionism that was subsequently
elaborated and modified by future statesmen.

The recurring theme of virtue, mission, and destiny that ani-
mates so much of the official record suggests that the makers of
American foreign policy have been part of a rhetorical tradition
that has tended to define the range of responses available to American leaders. This rhetorical tradition explains many of the continuities of American foreign policy. The mystical nationalism im-

---

43 Bemis, *John Quincy Adams and the Union*, 481. For the best short collection of Adams's
writings see Walter LaFeber, *John Quincy Adams and American Continental Empire* (Chicago, 1965).

plicit in the rhetoric of empire has made it resistant to factual contradiction; its appeal to a spine-tingling patriotism and the nation's sentimentalized image of itself has made it effective both in gaining public support for official policies and in quelling dissent.[44]

It is not surprising that Adams in his later years became a prophet of civil war. He never wore the garb of national unity comfortably. His nationalist phase obscured the differences regarding the nature of the republic that separated him from putative allies such as John C. Calhoun. As early as 1820, Adams's diary records frank premonitions of a civil war to purge the institution of slavery from the land of liberty. His incendiary career in the House was marked by a seeming desire to precipitate the conflict. His decades-long anticipation of war between the states (and similar anticipations by other prominent national leaders such as Calhoun) suggest that, as Bernard Bailyn observed in reference to the American Revolution, the Civil War occurred in the minds of men long before it became a reality.[45]

The year 1815 marks the turning point in antebellum American foreign relations and perhaps in antebellum American history as a whole. The end of the War of 1812 saw old controversies fade in importance and new concerns arise. The transition from republicanism to liberalism is but one major shift with implications for the study of foreign relations. Rising American nationalism, widening sectional differences, an incipient democratic movement, and a redoubled commitment to territorial, commercial, and ideological expansion are just some of the trends that gathered speed in subsequent years. In geopolitical terms an emerging harmony of interests began to control Anglo-American

44   See William Earl Weeks, "John Quincy Adams's 'Great Gun' and the Rhetoric of American Empire," *Diplomatic History* 14 (Winter 1990): 25–42. See also Kenneth M. Coleman, "The Political Mythology of the Monroe Doctrine: Reflections on the Social Psychology of Hegemony," in *Latin America, The United States, and the Inter-American System*, eds. John D. Martz and Lars Schoultz (Boulder, CO, 1980), 95–114; Lawrence Kaplan, "The Monroe Doctrine and the Truman Doctrine: The Case of Greece," *Journal of the Early Republic* 13 (Spring 1993): 1–22; and David S. Heidler, "The Politics of National Aggression: Congress and the First Seminole War," ibid., (Winter 1993): 501–30.

45   See Leonard L. Richards, *The Life and Times of Congressman John Quincy Adams* (New York, 1986); and Weeks, *John Quincy Adams*, chap. 8.

relations leading eventually to the "special relationship" between Great Britain and the United States that has been so important in this century. It might also be said that the age of Manifest Destiny began in 1815 in the wake of the Battle of New Orleans and with the creation of a popular hero in Andrew Jackson, the individual who embodied this emergent new nationalism.[46]

The robust, "spread-eagle" expansionism of the period 1815–61 makes ironic the frequent characterization of this period as a quiescent time in American foreign relations. Assertions that the United States turned to internal concerns during this time implicitly accept the notion that continental expansionism was in fact manifest destiny and not the result of an aggressive foreign policy. The vigorous extension of commercial relations and the numerous military and scientific expeditions undertaken during this time belie the notion that the nation was isolated from global affairs. Indeed, the vigor with which the United States expanded both continentally and globally before 1861 contradicts the view that the imperialism of the 1890s was an aberration or a new departure in American foreign policy. That the relatively quiet 1870s and 1880s are often cited as evidence of a hiatus in territorial expansionism is eloquent testimony to the breakneck pace of American development. The seeds of 1890s expansionism were planted early in the century.

Albert Weinberg's *Manifest Destiny: A Study of Nationalist Expansionism in American History* remains the most sophisticated work on a complex ideology. Weinberg's extensive research into a range of public and private sources reveals the intricate and contradictory connections between ideas of nation and empire and right and wrong. As Weinberg observes, an expansionist nation "never admits it is doing violence to its moral instincts." The pursuit of national self-interest in the guise of national altruism is the thread that connects the Revolutionary era's notion of "natural right" to the 1930s creed of "world leadership."

---

46 On Anglo-American relations see Kinley J. Brauer, "The United States and British Imperial Expansion, 1815–1860," *Diplomatic History* 12 (Winter 1988): 19–37; Reginald Stuart, *United States Expansionism and British North America, 1775–1871* (Chapel Hill, NC, 1988); and J. Leitch Wright, *Britain and the American Frontier, 1783–1815* (Athens, GA, 1975).

Weinberg also points to the use throughout American history of an open-ended definition of security as a means to justify acts of aggrandizement. His work illustrates how manifest destiny, rather than being confined to the 1840s, is in some sense the controlling idea of American nationalism.[47]

Reginald Horsman's recent article "The Dimension of an Empire for Liberty: Expansionism and Republicanism, 1775–1828," emphasizes how the activities of frontiersmen, the overseas commercial endeavors of private individuals, and fears (both real and imagined) about security combined to render moot the question of whether or not a republic could be extensive. Principle consistently yielded to expediency when expansionism beckoned. Horsman points out that while the Jeffersonians envisioned North America ruled by predominantly white and republican regimes, they did not assume that the entire continent would necessarily become part of the United States. He notes, too, that "after 1815, security was less important as a motive for territorial acquisitions than a desire to give support to agricultural and commercial expansionism."[48]

Horsman also rediscovers the sectional divisiveness inherent in the expansionist consensus of the era. He sees "sectional fears" as "an essential ingredient" in the expansionist debates of the 1780s and beyond. While during the first half-century of American foreign policy the Northeast feared being outvoted by southern and western interests, by 1825 "this situation was to be reversed, and the South came to consider itself as being sacrificed . . . to a commercial and antislavery region."[49]

Horsman's emphasis that opposition to expansionism "was not just a temporary tactic used against the Federalists in 1787 and

---

47 Albert K. Weinberg, *Manifest Destiny: A Study of Nationalist Expansionism in American History* (Baltimore, MD, 1935), 73. See also Richard Slotkin, *The Fatal Environment: The Myth of the Frontier in the Age of Industrialization, 1800–1890* (New York, 1985).

48 Reginald Horsman, "The Dimensions of an 'Empire for Liberty': Expansion and Republicanism, 1775–1825," *Journal of the Early Republic* 9 (Spring 1989): 15. See also idem, *The Diplomacy of the New Republic, 1776–1815* (Arlington Heights, IL, 1985).

49 Horsman, "The Dimensions of an 'Empire for Liberty,'" 19. See also Howard Jones, *Mutiny on the Amistad: The Saga of a Slave Revolt and Its Impact on American Abolition, Law, and Diplomacy* (New York, 1987); and Walter LaFeber, *The American Age: United States Foreign Policy at Home and Abroad since 1750* (New York, 1989), chap. 5, which emphasizes sectional divisions over expansionism as a major cause of the Civil War.

1788, and then forgotten" is critical. Horsman notes that those "who feared that constant expansion would create a government they did not want, and that the republic in pursuing its ambitions for agrarian and commercial growth was changing its nature and abandoning the republican idealism that had inspired the . . . Founding Fathers," were "constantly thwarted" in their attempts to restrict expansionism. Yet the point to remember is that these naysayers were correct: expansionism (and more particularly, how to use the newly acquired territories) led directly to the collapse of the republic. The exuberant expansionism of the era existed alongside an increasingly bitter debate over the future of the republican revolution. There was not one manifest destiny but several, and by the 1850s the euphoria of territorial acquisition could no longer contain the divisiveness of these alternative visions. In the end the nation paid a steep price in blood, treasure, and ideals for regions acquired at what first seemed to be relatively little cost.[50]

The celebratory narrative of American history overlooks the fact that prophecies of the collapse of the republic because of reckless expansion came true. Studies of antebellum foreign policy must calculate the full costs of expansion. Successive U.S. administrations consciously disregarded the republican idea of government based on consent of the governed, beginning with the forced incorporation of fifty-thousand French creoles into the United States as a result of the Louisiana Purchase and culminating in the Union army's invasion and occupation of the South, which rendered that idea absurd. Both the northern and southern visions of a voluntary association of states became "lost causes," sacrificed to the emerging imperatives of nation and empire. As Lewis P. Simpson writes, "the failure of antebellum southern society was also the failure of antebellum New England society. . . The irreconcilable tension between these opposing salvational efforts doomed the first American Republic."[51]

---

50   Horsman, "The Dimensions of an 'Empire for Liberty,'" 1, 19.
51   Lewis P. Simpson, *Mind and the American Civil War: A Meditation on Lost Causes* (Baton Rouge, LA, 1989), 32.

A major and still only partially understood aspect of American foreign policy is its relation to race and racism. Historians have shown that in the first decades of the nineteenth century there was a heightened sense of Anglo-Saxon racial pride and superiority and a simultaneous decline in the belief in the natural equality of all races. The expectation that assimilation would eliminate the perceived inferiority of the nonwhite races was replaced by a conviction that certain groups could not be assimilated. A pathbreaking work in this controversial and complex area of study is Reginald Horsman's *Race and Manifest Destiny.* Horsman defines the specific roots of the American ideology of racial destiny, but is careful to locate that ideology in its European context. He argues that "between 1815 and the mid-1850s an American Anglo-Saxon ideology was used internally to bolster the power and protect the status of the existing population and externally to justify American territorial and economic expansion." In the case of American Indians, this shift toward a harsher view of the nonwhite races helped to create a consensus in favor of removal. The harshness of the project was mitigated in the minds of the white majority by "the widespread intellectual and popular view that the replacement of an inferior by a superior race was a fulfillment of the laws of science and nature." In a manner reminiscent of Weinberg, Horsman shows how white Americans adapted this racial ideology to Mexicans in order to justify expansion along the southwestern frontier. While he acknowledges the persistence of the enlightenment view on race, he concludes that by the 1850s American thinking was characterized by a belief in the inferiority of much of the nonwhite world and by a conviction that global progress could be achieved by American commercial expansion into "backward" areas.[52]

---

52 Reginald Horsman, *Race and Manifest Destiny: The Origins of American Racial Anglo-Saxonism* (Cambridge, MA, 1981), 189, 191, 298. See also Richard Drinnon, *Facing West: The Metaphysics of Indian-Hating and Empire Building* (Minneapolis, 1980); Michael H. Hunt, *Ideology and U.S. Foreign Policy* (New Haven, CT, 1987); Alexander Saxton, *The Rise and Fall of the White Republic: Class Politics and Mass Culture in Nineteenth-Century America* (London, 1990); and Anders Stephanson, *Manifest Destiny: American Expansionism and the Empire of Right* (New York, 1995).

Much work remains to be done in the field of U.S. relations with American Indians. For reasons that are not clear, historians of American foreign relations usually have not considered Indian relations to be part of the field, although the long history of treaty making and the government's own policy (at least until 1830) suggest that Indian policy is not an internal affair. But new studies of early U.S.-Indian relations must not focus upon the federal government; to do so would obscure the fact that policy was driven more by the actions of frontiersmen, fur traders, speculators, slaveholders, and pioneers than by diplomats. The myriad encounters between whites and Indians along the frontier and their complex relation to federal policy suggest the need for a body of regional and bilateral studies of the interaction of Europeans, Americans, and American Indians. This new scholarship must resist the tendency to see indigenous peoples as a problem to be overcome. Rather, such studies must draw upon the knowledge and insights of native American studies and anthropology, as well as direct research into the history of the various American Indian tribes.[53]

Emily S. Rosenberg has sketched the outlines of such scholarship. She calls on historians to "walk the borders of global power" by "analyzing power systems from various perspectives situated on the periphery." Insofar as it pertains to relations with American Indians, such a work would refrain from the uncritical use of terms such as "savage," "hostile," and "civilization" as categories of explanation. Indeed, significant work could be done to analyze how such terms have subtly defined Indian-white rela-

---

53　On Euro-Indian relations see Francis Jennings, *Empire of Fortune: Crowns, Colonies and Tribes in the Seven Years War in America* (New York, 1988); Dorothy V. Jones, *License for Empire: Colonialism by Treaty in Early America* (Chicago, 1982); William G. McLoughlin, *Cherokees and Missionaries, 1789–1839* (New Haven, CT, 1984); Brian W. Dippie, *The Vanishing American: White Attitudes and U.S. Indian Policy* (Middletown, CT, 1982); J. Leitch Wright, Jr., *Creeks and Seminoles: The Destruction and Regeneration of the Muscogulge People* (Lincoln, NE, 1986); Gregory E. Dowd, *A Spirited Resistance: The North American Indian Struggle for Unity, 1745–1815* (Baltimore, 1992); and Colin G. Calloway, *The American Revolution in Indian Country: Crisis and Diversity in Native American Communities* (Cambridge, England, 1995). Francis Paul Prucha, *The Great Father: The United States Government and the American Indians*, 2 vols. (Lincoln, NE 1984), is of limited usefulness owing to its focus on federal policy even as Prucha acknowledges the inability (or unwillingness) of the federal government to enforce its will over the frontiersmen.

tions in scholarship done to date. As Rosenberg observes, "a peripheral vantage is not a geographic location but a habit of mind. . . . A peripheral view comes less from where we stand than from the critical questions we frame." Rosenberg is insightful in pointing out that a call for a new international history by itself does not guarantee that such a history would transcend parochialism. Questions of perspective and scope must be addressed in order for the term international history to have clear meaning. Indeed, despite all the good intentions behind such calls for a new international history, the term itself parochially presumes that the nation shall remain the primary unit of analysis.[54]

Insofar as international history addresses the issue of cultural, economic, and political interaction along the frontier, it intersects with the New Western History, proving yet again how limiting disciplinary categories can be. One of the most promising areas for a truly multiperspectival approach is the eastern Pacific rim from Alaska to Alta California during the late eighteenth and early nineteenth centuries. There, amid a Euro-American struggle for empire, individuals from diverse nations and races interacted. The underlying issue of shifting sovereignty definitely makes this a foreign relations problem. James Ronda's *Astoria and Empire* details how John Jacob Astor's plans for a vast fur trading network extending from Western Europe to the northwest coast and then to China guided American foreign policy in the region during the first two decades of the nineteenth century, a time when the northwest coast was, relatively speaking, more remote from Washington than were the Philippines in 1898. Ronda recounts the efforts of Astor and his associates to play off against one another the various nations and tribes contending for influence in the region in order to gain control of the lucrative fur trade. *Astoria and Empire* illustrates how a special interest became the national interest to such an extent that in 1813 John Quincy Adams declared that "the finger of nature" pointed the United States in the direction of the Columbia River region.[55]

54 Emily S. Rosenberg, "Walking the Borders," *Diplomatic History* 14 (Fall 1990): 568.
55 Ronda, *Astoria*, 334. On the New Western History see William G. Robbins, "Laying

In a similar vein, John H. Johnson has elaborated the cultural and economic foundations of U.S.-Latin American relations in *A Hemisphere Apart*. By examining relations with Hispanic America as a product of domestic influences, as a reaction to Latin American actions, and as a function of British attitudes and policies, Johnson is able to construct a conceptual framework that identifies the sources of official policy.[56] N. N. Bolkhovitinov has performed this task for Russian-American relations in his extensive documentation of early economic, scientific, social, and political contacts between citizens of the two nations.[57]

What the work of Ronda, Johnson, Bolkhovitinov, and others makes clear is that international relations are not defined entirely or even primarily by official actions. International relations between the United States and the polities in the region extending along a great arc from the west coast of South America to China were the result of complex and as yet dimly understood interactions between many nations, tribes, and individuals. Scholars of early American foreign policy must pay more attention to this western and southern arc in order to place the national experience in broader historical perspective.

Historians must shift from a multiarchival to a multicultural approach not in order to make their work politically correct but rather to make it historically significant. The Quincentenary has stimulated an awareness that Columbus's explorations spurred the growth of a web of complex interactions that have led to today's emerging global civilization. Previous studies of this process which focused on Europe or the United States are now anachronistic; scholars must consider new approaches if their work is

Siege to Western History: The Emergence of New Paradigms," *Reviews in American History* 19 (September 1991): 313–31.
56   John J. Johnson, *A Hemisphere Apart: The Foundations of United States Policy toward Latin America* (Baltimore, MD, 1990). See also Walter LaFeber, *Inevitable Revolutions: The United States in Central America* (New York, 1983); Peggy K. Liss, *Atlantic Empires: The Network of Trade and Revolution, 1713–1826* (Baltimore, MD, 1983); and Lester D. Langley, *The Americas in the Age of Revolution, 1750–1850* (New Haven, CT, 1996).
57   Nikolai N. Bolkhovitinov, *The Beginnings of Russian-American Relations, 1775–1815*, trans. Elena Levin (Cambridge, MA, 1975); Bolkhovitinov, *Russia and the United States: An Analytical Survey of Archival Documents and Historical Studies*, trans. J. Dane Hartgrove (Armonk, NY, 1986). Still valuable is Howard I. Kushner, *Conflict on the Northwest Coast: American-Russian Rivalry in the Pacific Northwest, 1790–1867* (Westport, CT, 1975).

to build upon rather than recapitulate that of prior generations. They must evaluate new archival sources (or reassess work previously done) using a broader framework than they have used in the past. The story of "America and . . ." remains important, but interpreters of that story will be obliged to frame their interpretations within an emerging global perspective if their work is to resonate beyond the narrow ranks of diplomatic historians.

Part of this new perspective concerns the integration of women into the study of foreign relations. At first glance, women seem nearly invisible in early American foreign relations; *Women and American Foreign Policy*, a collection of essays edited by Edward Crapol, has nothing on women prior to 1830. Yet the power of women cannot be ignored. The influence of Abigail and Louisa Adams over the psyche and career of John Quincy Adams is still but partially understood. The subtle influence of women upon American statesmen and foreign diplomats needs further examination.[58]

More promising still would be a gendered approach to American foreign relations. The study of American foreign relations is dominated by men and therefore is especially ripe for the fresh perspectives that gender as a category of historical analysis can provide. The traditional exclusion of women from positions of power (and from the writing of foreign relations) makes a gendered approach potentially enlightening. Joan Wallach Scott has outlined such an approach by observing how gender has long been "a primary way of signifying relationships of power" and as such can now be used by scholars as "a way to decode meaning and to understand the complex connections among various interactions."[59] Such a method might prove valuable in understanding

---

58   Edward P. Crapol, ed., *Women and American Foreign Policy: Lobbyists, Critics, and Insiders* (New York, 1987). See also Paul C. Nagel, *The Adams Women: Abigail and Louisa Adams, Their Sisters and Daughters* (New York, 1987). Suggestive is Judith M. Hughes, *Emotions and High Politics: Personal Relations at the Summit in Late Nineteenth Century Britain and Germany* (Berkeley, 1983).

59   Gender is used to describe the set of socially constructed categories that comprise the notion of "woman." See Joan Wallach Scott, *Gender and the Politics of History* (New York, 1988), 42, 45–46.

what Joan Hoff-Wilson has termed the "macho factor" in American foreign relations.[60]

In spite of the widespread calls for new perspectives in American foreign relations, it remains to be seen whether novel approaches will be accepted within the profession or by the society at large. Views of American foreign relations from outside the republican revolution are likely to look radically different from views from within. The uproar over the Smithsonian's "The West As America" exhibit (described by Daniel Boorstin as "a perverse, historically inaccurate, destructive exhibition") suggests that traditional interpretations will not yield quietly to new ways of looking at the past.[61]

Nonetheless, the end of the Cold War may allow for a new candor in the study of American foreign relations. The emergence of new perspectives on the record and meanings of American foreign relations does not necessarily negate the importance of the American national experience.[62] One need not be a chauvinist to assert that the history of the United States is exceptional – one need only look at the record. The nation's unparalleled rise to global preeminence and its role as the first (and to date only) superpower means that scholars must continue to examine American nationalism and American imperialism. Whatever judgments one might make about it, the experience of the wealthiest and most powerful nation in history is of vast significance to humanity. Historians need to probe the reasons for the extraordinary rise of the United States and analyze its ascent within the context

---

60 Joan Hoff-Wilson, "Conclusion: Of Mice and Men," in *Women and American Foreign Policy*, 184. See also Susan Jeffords, *The Remasculinization of America: Gender and the Vietnam War* (Bloomington, IN, 1989). For a perceptive commentary on "gendered" approaches to the study of foreign relations see Emily S. Rosenberg, "Signifying the Vietnam Experience," *Reviews in American History* 19 (September 1991): 438–44. See also "Culture, Gender, and Foreign Policy: A Symposium," *Diplomatic History* 18 (Winter 1994): 47–70.
61 "The West As America: Reinterpreting Images of the Frontier," National Museum of American Art, Washington, DC, March 15–July 7, 1991; *Los Angeles Times*, 13 June 1991. Plans for the exhibition to be shown in Denver and Saint Louis were canceled. See also Vivien Green Fryd, *Art and Empire: The Politics of Ethnicity in the U.S. Capitol, 1815–1860* (New Haven, CT, 1992).
62 See Ian Tyrrell, "American Exceptionalism in an Age of International History," Michael McGerr, "The Price of the 'New Transnational History,'" and Ian Tyrrell's response, *American Historical Review* 96 (October 1991), 1031–57, 1058–67, 1068–72.

of world history, while resisting the tendency of previous American exceptionalists to attribute, either implicitly or explicitly, the success of the American nation to the progressive unfolding of God's will. American history has occurred in the realm of human affairs, and Americans carry the burdens of guilt and responsibility inextricably associated with great power.[63] Our histories must reflect this basic truth.

63   On this point see Reinhold Niebuhr, *The Irony of American History* (New York, 1952), ◁—
chap. 2.

3

The Great American Desert Revisited: Recent Literature and Prospects for the Study of American Foreign Relations, 1815–1861

KINLEY BRAUER

Like the "Great American Desert" of old, the period between 1815 and 1861 might as well be regarded as a desert in the recent historiography of American foreign relations.[1] Once a period of vital concern to diplomatic historians in which a generation established their scholarly reputations, contemporary historians of American foreign relations have all but abandoned the Middle Period as an area of investigation, with the consequence that the diplomacy and foreign policy of the era is heading toward oblivion.[2] Many colleges and universities have dropped courses

---

1 As a result of Major Stephen Long's exploring expedition in 1819, maps published in the 1820s often carried the legend "Great American Desert" over the territory between the tree line and the Rocky Mountains. Major Long regarded these treeless plains as an area unsuitable for "civilized," settled existence and fit only for nomadic tribes. See *An Atlas of Early Maps of the American Midwest*, comp. W. Raymond Wood (Springfield, IL, 1983); *The Northern Expeditions of Stephen H. Long: The Journals of 1817 and 1823 and Related Documents*, ed. Lucile M. Kane, June D. Holmquist, and Carolyn Gilman (St. Paul, MN, 1978); and Roger Nichols and Patrick L. Halley, *Stephen Long and American Frontier Exploration* (Newark, DE, 1980). Writes Helen Hornback Tanner, "Stephen Long's 1823 characterization of the plains as the Great American Desert imprinted American minds for decades." Tanner review of *Mapping the North American Plains: Essays in the History of Cartography*, ed. Frederick C. Luebke, Francis W. Kaye, and Gary E. Moulton (Norman, OK, 1987), in *Journal of American History* 75 (June 1988): 222.

2 Samuel Flagg Bemis, Dexter Perkins, Frederick Merk, Arthur P. Whitaker, Norman Graebner, and Richard W. Van Alstyne all published studies that quickly became standards for methodology and analysis. The more important works covering topics in this period are

dealing with American foreign relations, and courses on the mid-nineteenth century are the first to go. Non-diplomatic historians of nineteenth-century America rarely mention the international relations of the United States in their studies.[3] This trend can be reversed. Just as the seemingly desolate Great American desert masked a rich land that beckoned explorers, so too does the foreign relations of the Middle Period contain a number of unan-

Samuel Flagg Bemis, *John Quincy Adams and the Foundations of American Foreign Policy* (New York, 1949); Dexter Perkins, *The Monroe Doctrine, 1823–1826* (Cambridge, MA, 1927) and *The Monroe Doctrine, 1826–1867* (Baltimore, MD, 1933); Frederick Merk, *Albert Gallatin and the Oregon Problem: A Study in Anglo-American Diplomacy* (Cambridge, MA, 1950), *The Oregon Question: Essays in Anglo-American Diplomacy and Politics* (Cambridge, MA, 1967); idem, with Lois Bannister Merk, *Manifest Destiny and Mission in American History: A Reinterpretation* (New York, 1963); Merk, *The Monroe Doctrine and American Expansionism, 1843–1849* (New York, 1966); Arthur P. Whitaker, *The United States and the Independence of Latin America, 1800–1830* (Baltimore, MD, 1941); Norman A. Graebner, *Empire on the Pacific: A Study in American Continental Expansion* (New York, 1955); and Richard W. Van Alstyne, *The Rising American Empire* (New York, 1960). For a complete listing of their publications see *Guide to American Foreign Relations since 1700*, ed. Richard Dean Burns (Santa Barbara, 1983).

3   For information on the exclusion of nineteenth-century diplomatic courses from college curricula see Ralph Levering, "The Importance of the History of American Foreign Relations," *OAH Newsletter* 12 (May 1984): 20–22. Despite the considerable efforts of editors of *Diplomatic History*, the premier journal of the history of American foreign relations, to solicit submissions of manuscripts dealing with the period before the Civil War, the overwhelming number of essays continue to explore problems in the twentieth century and particularly the Cold War. Of the nearly three hundred research articles published in *Diplomatic History* since its first issue in 1977, only thirty deal with nineteenth-century topics, and of those only ten (four written by the same person!) deal with the period between 1815 and 1861. By comparison, over one hundred articles have dealt with topics in the early Cold War years between 1945 and 1953. The ten Middle Period articles in *Diplomatic History* are Kenneth E. Shewmaker, "'Untaught Diplomacy': Daniel Webster and the Lobos Islands Controversy" 1 (Fall 1977): 321–40; Harry Ammon, "The Monroe Doctrine: Domestic Politics or National Decision?" 5 (Winter 1981): 53–70, with a response by Ernest May; Kenneth E. Shewmaker, "The 'War of Words': The Cass-Webster Debate of 1842-43" 5 (Spring 1981): 151–64; Kenneth E. Shewmaker, "'Hook and line, and bob and sinker': Daniel Webster and the Fisheries Dispute of 1852" 9 (Spring 1985): 113–29; Robert L. Paquette, "The Everett-Del Monte Connection: A Study in the International Politics of Slavery" 11 (Winter 1987): 1–21; Kinley J. Brauer, "The United States and British Imperial Expansion, 1815–60" 12 (Winter 1988): 19–37; Kenneth E. Shewmaker, "'Congress only can declare war' and 'the President is Commander in Chief': Daniel Webster and the War Power" 12 (Fall 1988): 383–409; William Earl Weeks, "John Quincy Adams's 'Great Gun' and the Rhetoric of American Empire" 14 (Winter 1990): 25–42; Luis Martínez-Fernández, "Caudillos, Annexationism, and the Rivalry Between Empires in the Dominican Republic, 1844–1874" 17 (Fall 1993): 571-97; and Jay Gitlin, "Private Diplomacy to Private Property: States, Tribes, and Nations in the Early National Period" 22 (Winter 1998): 85–99. See the comment by a former editor of *Diplomatic History* in Warren I. Cohen, "The History of American-East Asian Relations: Cutting Edge of the Historical Profession" 9 (Spring 1985): 105.

swered questions and unexploited areas that deserve renewed consideration.

The current lack of interest and dearth of scholarship in the diplomacy of the Middle Period has not gone without notice.[4] Lester D. Langley, in discussing the historiography of the period from 1812 to 1840, included only six diplomatic studies published between 1960 and 1973; the bulk of his examination rested upon works written considerably earlier. Anna Kasten Nelson, in dealing with the years between 1840 and 1865, suggested that an all-consuming interest in the twentieth century, the decline of interest in the political history of the nineteenth, and the willingness of revisionists to rely on the interpretations of Richard Van Alstyne lay at the root of the problem.[5]

Nelson's judgment is not entirely correct. Nineteenth-century political history remains a flourishing field.[6] In addition, a few revisionists, most notably William Appleman Williams and Walter LaFeber, have written on the period, although Williams's interpretation was clearly aimed at the post–Civil War period, and LaFeber's work has been restricted to an introductory essay and interpretative textbook summaries.[7] The chief problem seems to be that political history has moved in new directions, so that the

4   See Charles S. Maier, "Marking Time: The Historiography of International Relations," in *The Past Before Us: Contemporary Historical Writing in the United States*, ed. Michael Kammen (Ithaca, NY, 1980), 355–87; and the essays by Michael H. Hunt and Walter LaFeber in "Responses to Charles S. Maier, 'Marking Time: The Historiography of International Relations,'" *Diplomatic History* 5 (Fall 1981): 353–82. See also Hunt, "New Insights But No New Vistas: Recent Work on Nineteenth-Century American-East Asian Relations," in *New Frontiers in American-East Asian Relations: Essays Presented to Dorothy Borg*, ed. Warren I. Cohen (New York, 1983), 18.

5   See Lester D. Langley, "American Foreign Policy in an Age of Nationalism, 1812–1840," and Anna Kasten Nelson, "Destiny and Diplomacy, 1840–1865," in *American Foreign Relations: A Historiographical Review*, ed. Gerald K. Haines and J. Samuel Walker (Westport, CT, 1981), 32–47 and 49–63, respectively.

6   See, for example, Joel H. Silbey, *The Partisan Imperative: The Dynamics of American Politics before the Civil War* (New York, 1985), who begins his study, "Scholars have devoted a great deal of attention to the pre–Civil War era in the United States, never more so than at present" (xi).

7   See William Appleman Williams, *The Roots of the Modern American Empire: A Study of the Growth and Shaping of Social Consciousness in a Marketplace Society* (New York, 1969); Walter LaFeber, ed., *John Quincy Adams and American Continental Empire: Letters, Speeches, and Papers* (Chicago, 1965); Lloyd C. Gardner, Walter F. LaFeber, and Thomas J. McCormick, *Creation of the American Empire*, 2 vols. (Chicago, 1973); Walter F. LaFeber, *Inevitable*

"new political history" appears to bear little relevance to concurrent foreign relations. Also, as Nelson suggests, the revisionists remain firmly rooted in the late nineteenth and twentieth centuries, at least as far as original research goes.

Studies of foreign relations of the Middle Period published more than thirty years ago have not served as models for fresh investigations. Nearly all of them are narrowly conceived diplomatic histories that rely on traditional methodology. They deal with intergovernmental relations concerning strategic and legal questions and issues related to territorial expansion, and they emphasize the role of elites in establishing and implementing policy. Furthermore, as exhaustive works often based upon multiarchival research in several languages, they are clearly intimidating to scholars who lack foreign language fluency, especially in areas of current interest outside Western Europe, and who have difficulty securing grants for overseas research.[8] And the major issues, U.S. involvement in the Latin American wars of independence, the Monroe Doctrine, the acquisitions of Florida, Texas, California, and the Oregon territory, and the Mexican War, have all been well covered, leaving scholars interested in exploring new aspects of these topics from similar perspectives and by similar methods to conclude that little is left to be done.

Scholars thus contributed only a few comparable studies during the mid-1950s and 1960s. Bradford Perkins moved into the well-trod pathway of Anglo-American relations in the 1820s and added a cultural dimension to his diplomatic study. Henry Blumenthal provided an excellent examination of Franco-American relations between 1830 and 1871. And David Pletcher added a much-needed and long-overdue reexamination of American territorial expansion in the 1840s and the Mexican War.[9] These

Revolutions: the United States in Central America (New York, 1984); idem, *The American Age: United States Foreign Policy at Home and Abroad Since 1750*, 2 vols. (New York.1994); and idem, *The Clash: A History of U.S.-Japan Relations* (New York, 1997).

8 Concerning the lack of facility with foreign languages among diplomatic historians see Alexander DeConde, "What's Wrong with American Diplomatic History," *SHAFR Newsletter* 1 (May 1970): 1–16.

9 See Bradford Perkins, *Castlereagh and Adams: England and the United States, 1812–1823* (Berkeley, 1964); Henry A. Blumenthal, *France and the United States: Their Diplomatic*

excellent works have enriched and in some cases corrected our understanding of the period, but they have not substantially or significantly altered the approaches of their predecessors. Neither have they sparked a renewed interest in the period.

The reasons for the continued avoidance of foreign relations in the Middle Period are many and varied. As Ernest May, Charles Maier especially, and many others have pointed out, traditional diplomatic history began its decline as scholars developed new methodologies, often drawn from other disciplines, that allowed them to ask new and exciting questions that previously had not been open to historical investigation.[10] Social historians became able to examine history "from the bottom up," and political historians developed new techniques for examining both small-group and mass behavior. Furthermore, contemporary social changes revived interest in ethnic groups, blacks, and American Indians and created virtually an entirely new field in women's history. Students thus shifted their primary interest to nonelites and to groups that have never been of particular interest to traditional diplomatic historians.

While historians of contemporary American foreign relations, Maier notwithstanding, have with great imagination and success

---

Relations, 1789–1914 (Chapel Hill, NC, 1970); idem, *A Reappraisal of Franco-American Relations, 1830–1871* (Chapel Hill, NC, 1959); idem, *American and French Culture, 1800–1900: Interchanges in Art, Science, Literature, and Society* (Baton Rouge, LA, 1975); and David M. Pletcher, *The Diplomacy of Annexation: Texas, Oregon, and the Mexican War* (Columbia, MO, 1973). Approximately two-thirds of Perkins's most recent study, *The Creation of a Republican Empire, 1776–1865*, vol. 1 of *The Cambridge History of American Foreign Relations,* deals with the period before 1815 and relies heavily on Perkins's earlier research. The material on the period between 1815 and 1861 is a useful narrative summary.
10   Among the many essays that comment on the declining fortunes of diplomatic history, one of the best is Ernest R. May, "The Decline of Diplomatic History," in *American History: Retrospect and Prospect,* ed. George Athan Billias and Gerald N. Grob (New York, 1971), 399–430. See also Thomas J. McCormick, "The State of American Diplomatic History," and Lawrence Evans, "The Dangers of Diplomatic History," in *The State of American History,* ed. Herbert J. Bass (Chicago, 1970), 119–41 and 142–56, respectively; Richard W. Leopold, "The History of United States Foreign Policy: Past, Present, and Future," in *The Future as History: Essays in the Vanderbilt University Centennial,* ed. Charles F. Delzell (Nashville, TN, 1977), 231–46; Peter Paret, "Assignments New and Old," *American Historical Review* 76 (February 1971): 119–26; Gordon A. Craig, "Political and Diplomatic History," in *Historical Studies Today,* ed. Felix Gilbert and Stephen R. Graubard (New York, 1971), 356–71; and William Langer, "The Next Assignment," *American Historical Review* 63 (February 1958): 283–504. Compare David Patterson, "What's Wrong (and Right) with American Diplomatic History," *SHAFR Newsletter* 9 (September 1978): 1–14.

applied these new methods and techniques to their work, few diplomatic historians of the Middle Period have made the attempt.[11]
Consequently the study of mid-nineteenth century foreign relations has suffered from both the broad decline of interest in diplomatic history and the failure of specialists in the period to apply
fresh methods and concepts to their work.

One of the major reasons modern diplomatic historians have
not moved back into the pre–Civil War period stems from their
particular urge to find useful lessons for the guidance of contemporary foreign policy. When diplomatic historians lost interest in
elaborating upon the basic guiding principles of American foreign policy and became more concerned with strategic and economic questions, they turned their attention to more "relevant"
modern periods.[12] Realist critics of the decline of American power
began their studies with the 1880s, when the United States supposedly shifted from limited and practical to unlimited and idealistic goals, and from continental and hemispheric to global concerns.[13] Revisionist critics of American economic expansionism/
imperialism, who in the 1950s and 1960s shifted attention away
from international relations to the study of foreign policy, concentrated on the time when the United States became an industrial power.[14]

These studies dramatically altered the very nature of historiographical debate and firmly focused attention on the post–Civil
War period. Those concerned about the use, misuse, and arrogance of power were clearly most interested in American foreign

11 See Maier, "Marking Time," 355–87; and especially the essay by Melvyn P. Leffler in
"Responses to Maier," 365–71. See also Cohen, "American-East Asian Relations," 101–12.
12 Bemis and Perkins in the 1930s found justification in the Middle Period for isolationism
in the interwar period. Their similar justification for American Cold War policies can be
found in Samuel Flagg Bemis, "American Foreign Policy and the Blessings of Liberty," *American Historical Review* 62 (January 1962): 291–305; and Dexter Perkins, "The Monroe Doctrine—Its History and Values" (Paper delivered at the Harry S. Truman Library, Independence, MO, 30 March 1963), *Bobbs-Merrill Reprint Series in History*, H–310 (Indianapolis,
1967). See also Gaddis Smith, "The Two Worlds of Samuel Flagg Bemis," *Diplomatic History*
9 (Fall 1985): 297, 299.
13 See George F. Kennan, *Realities of American Foreign Policy* (Princeton, NJ, 1954).
14 Curiously, revisionists generally did not incorporate the methodological advances of
other disciplines into their studies. In emphasizing the importance of economics in foreign
policy, they have concentrated on ideology and have used undifferentiated aggregate economic data.

relations in the twentieth century. And those interested in both the broad and narrow issues of the Cold War found little reason to move further back than 1917 for the sources of American foreign policy. Study of Revolutionary and Early National Period diplomacy became in the minds of many an exercise in antiquarianism; the Middle Period became an irrelevancy.

A significant contributing element in this light is the assumption of a profound discontinuity between pre– and post–Civil War America. The tendency of the major works on this period to emphasize contiguous continental expansion, which ended in 1853, the deaths of the most important actors (Adams, Jackson, Webster, Clay, and Calhoun) in the 1840s and 1850s, and the cataclysm of the Civil War itself, combined with the massive increase in the pace of industrialization, have given the impression that an entirely new stage of diplomacy began after the Civil War. The common notion is that during the 1850s certain far-seeing individuals planted the seeds of modern American foreign relations, and that after a period of gestation, a new, aggressive, imperialistic foreign policy emerged. The birth dates are variously given as 1865, 1880, or 1898 – or even 1917.[15]

In addition, the perception that the foreign policies of the Middle Period were narrowly conceived, limited, reactive, and ad hoc has caused many scholars and students to search for more challenging and cohesive periods to study. In his important essay on the relation of culture and power in international relations, Akira Iriye argues that the combination of isolationism, exceptionalism, and individualism divorced considerations of power from those of culture in American diplomacy. "Foreign policy," writes Iriye

---

15 See, for example, Walter LaFeber, *The New Empire: An Interpretation of American Expansion, 1860–1898* (Ithaca, NY, 1963). In this major interpretation of the postwar period, LaFeber begins with the comment, "Modern American diplomatic history began in the 1850's and 1860's . . . by the time William Seward became Lincoln's Secretary of State in 1861, a new empire had started to take form" (p. 1). Similarly, Ernest N. Paolino, *The Foundations of the American Empire: William Henry Seward and U.S. Foreign Policy* (Ithaca, NY, 1973), argues that Seward was considerably less a territorial expansionist than he was a commercial expansionist. Paolino devotes the bulk of his examination to the "foundations" laid while Seward was secretary of state in the 1860s. Charles Vevier, "American Continentalism: An Idea of Expansion, 1845–1910," *American Historical Review* 65 (January 1960): 237–53, found the roots of the modern American empire in the mid-1840s.

of the period, "was mostly informal, extemporaneous, and unsystematic because there was little thought that domestic developments called for anything else."[16]

Unlike Iriye, who seems to have written off the pre–Civil War period, others have proposed a number of fruitful directions for further study. Maier and Nelson have suggested that more work needs to be done on the role of ideology in American expansionism; Langley and Michael H. Hunt have called for fresh studies of international economic and cultural relations; and Emily Rosenberg has urged historians of American foreign relations to move "beyond a focus on formal transatlantic diplomacy into an examination of the cultural and economic discourses that shaped an American nationalism and helped construct a wide variety of contests over issues of boundaries and representation."[17]

In various ways these scholars have challenged their colleagues to reevaluate the Middle Period and to focus their attention on new questions and areas of inquiry. In addition, Langley and Alexander DeConde have called into question the assumption of broad and growing Anglo-American harmony in the period; DeConde, complaining about the heavy emphasis on Anglo-American relations, has urged scholars to devote more study to American relations with other nations; Nelson has proposed studying the effects of structural and functional interests in American foreign relations; Walter LaFeber has asked for a fresh consideration of the relation between partisan divisions and foreign policy; and Hunt has recommended that scholars apply to the period a "comparative imperial approach" that will "reinvigorate the study of eighteenth- and nineteenth-century foreign relations experience

16   Akira Iriye, "Culture and Power: International Relations as Intercultural Relations," *Diplomatic History* 3 (Spring 1979): 120.
17   Hunt, "Responses to Maier," 357, and generally 355–56; Nelson, "Destiny and Diplomacy," 50–52, 57, 60–61; Maier, "Marking Time," 375–77; Langley, "Age of Nationalism," 34-37; Emily S. Rosenberg, "A Call to Revolution: A Roundtable on Early U.S. Foreign Relations," *Diplomatic History* 22 (Winter 1998): 69. Referring to recent examinations of the Revolution and Early National Period that "routinely consider the new nation within an international and multicultural context," Rosenberg also criticizes historians of early American foreign relations who "define the history of America's international involvement so narrowly to exclude this scholarship." She concludes, "If there seems to be a paucity of work in early American diplomatic history, it arises from the overly narrow definition of the subdiscipline itself" (Rosenberg, "Call to Revolution," 70).

and ... relate it to the twentieth century in terms of the imperial paradigm."[18]   Finally, in an observation as valid for the entire Middle Period as it is for the part about which he was writing, Langley has concluded that "the most noticeable flaw in the voluminous and often brilliant historiography of this era is the absence of an integrated synthesis spanning the entirety of American diplomacy from Ghent to the expansionist 1840s."[19]

These suggestions present problems of their own.   Although they do point to many existing gaps in the literature, there is little discussion of how the study of foreign relations might be brought into closer harmony with the present direction of historical scholarship, or how the methodologies, techniques, and scholarship of social, political, and women's-studies historians can be integrated into the study of American foreign relations in the mid-nineteenth century.   Nor do they suggest fundamentally new questions for the period.[20]

Historians of American foreign relations have approached their tasks from two different directions. The first, and one most closely related to the old diplomatic studies, centers on the external relations of the United States with foreign nations and regions. The second, commonly associated with revisionist historians, focuses on the internal construction of American foreign policy. Differences between the two are often only differences in degree, and the best of both demonstrate the close interrelationship between both external and internal forces in the construction and implementation of American foreign relations.[21]

18   Langley, "Age of Nationalism," 34–37; DeConde, "What's Wrong with Diplomatic History," 7–8; and LaFeber, "Responses to Maier," 364. DeConde, cited above, has attributed the emphasis on Anglo-American harmony partly to Anglophilia among establishment historians.

19   Langley, "Age of Nationalism," 43. See also essays by Lawrence S. Kaplan, Bradford Perkins, Kinley Brauer, John M. Belohlavek, and William Earl Weeks in "Foreign Policy in the Early Republic Reconsidered: Essays from a SHEAR Symposium," *Journal of the Early Republic* (Winter 1994) 14: 453–95.

20   See, however, Michael J. Hogan and Thomas G. Paterson, eds., *Explaining the History of American Foreign Relations* (New York, 1991). This volume contains uniformly superb essays on definition, theory, and methodology. Typically, the contributors are all specialists in twentieth century American foreign relations, and with rare exception, their references and "explanations" are most useful to scholars of more recent periods.

21   An excellent textbook that emphasizes this relationship explicitly is Wayne S. Cole, *An Interpretive History of American Foreign Relations*, rev. ed. (Homewood, IL, 1974).

Scholars interested primarily in the external relations of the
United States have three excellent models for further study. In his
study of American relations with the nations of the Mediterranean, James A. Field, Jr., has not only considered the activities of
diplomats, consuls, and commercial agents but also examined
both religious and secular missionaries who sought to bring God
and the American political and cultural system to North Africa
and the Levant.[22] Similarly, Michael H. Hunt has examined the
activities of diplomats, merchants, and missionaries in China,
exploring at the same time Chinese perceptions of and experiences in the United States, while Norman E. Saul has explored
the official, private, and cultural aspects of Russian-American
relations in the period, adding a comparative context as well.[23]
These accounts are broad, imaginative, and innovative and move
far beyond the boundaries set in earlier diplomatic histories.

The emphasis in each of these works on the commercial activities of Americans is characteristic of examinations of American
relations with nations and regions outside the North Atlantic community. Regarding other areas, George E. Brooks, Jr., has fully
described the nature and importance of legitimate (that is,
nonslave) trade on both coasts of Africa in the mid-nineteenth
century, and an extensive article literature exists on mercantile
activities in South and Southeast Asia.[24] Most of these studies,

---

22   James A. Field, Jr., *America and the Mediterranean World, 1776–1882* (Princeton, NJ,
1969). For a similar evaluation of Field's contribution see John H. Schroeder's introduction
to "American Diplomatic and Commercial Relations with Europe, 1815–1861," in *Guide to
American Foreign Relations*, 217–18.
23   Michael H. Hunt, *The Making of a Special Relationship: The United States and China to
1914* (New York, 1983); Norman E. Saul, *Distant Friends: The United States and Russia,
1763–1867* (Lawrence, KS, 1991). Saul, a specialist in Russian history and fluent in the
Russian language, has provided the first examination of Russian-American relations in the
nineteenth century based on Russian as well as American materials. For a full discussion of
Russian-American trade in the period see Walther Kirchner, *Studies in Russian-American
Commerce, 1820–1860* (Leiden, 1975).
24   George E. Brooks, Jr., *Yankee Traders, Old Coasters, and African Middlemen: A History of American Legitimate Trade with West Africa in the Nineteenth Century* (Boston,
1970). See also James W. Gould, "American Imperialism in Southeast Asia before 1898,"
Journal of Southeast Asian Studies 3:2 (1972): 306–14; Seward W. Livermore, "Early Commercial and Consular Relations with the East Indies," *Pacific Historical Review* 15 (March
1946): 31–58; Sharom Ahmat, "American Trade with Singapore, 1819–65," *Journal of the
Malaysian Branch of the Royal Asiatic Society* 38 (December 1965): 241–57; and idem, "Some
Problems of Rhode Island Traders in Java, 1799–1836," *Journal of Southeast Asian History*

however, minimize the involvement of the American government by focusing on the activities of private agencies. Scholars have thus adhered to the notion that overseas commercial activity was predominately private in nature and that the federal government, committed to a laissez-faire policy, became involved only sporadically and only for the limited purpose of protecting general American interests.[25]

Field and Hunt, however, have challenged this notion by suggesting that the government was more deeply involved in the commercial expansion of the United States than previously has been believed. A number of recent scholars carry this thrust forward. John H. Schroeder, in particular, has demonstrated that between 1820 and 1850 the navy played an increasingly important part in American commercial expansion. By the latter date, "the navy not only protected and defended American lives, property, and trade overseas, it now also helped identify new markets, collected valuable commercial and nautical information, concluded diplomatic agreements, and opened new areas to American enterprises."[26]

Schroeder has carefully analyzed the vicissitudes of federal naval policy and has described in detail both the appeals from special interests abroad for naval support and the activities of naval captains. Perhaps most important is his success in adding an official dimension to American commercial expansion and relating those policies to the ideology of expansion. Moreover, Schroeder has considered official naval and commercial policies in Latin America, an area surprisingly ignored by historians who have usually concentrated on American activities in favor of more distant and exotic areas.

6 (March 1965): 94–107. An intensive examination of Indian-American trade can be found in Goberdhan Bhaghat, *Americans in India: Commercial and Consular Relations, 1784–1860* (New York, 1951).

25   On this point see Kinley J. Brauer, "Economics and the Diplomacy of American Expansionism, 1820–1860," in *Economics and World Power: An Assessment of American Diplomacy since 1789*, ed. William H. Becker and Samuel F. Wells, Jr. (New York, 1984), 55–118.

26   John H. Schroeder, *Shaping a Maritime Empire: The Commercial and Diplomatic Role of the American Navy, 1829–1861* (Westport, CT, 1985), 4.

Historians of American foreign relations have traditionally left the detailed consideration of commercial relations between the United States and Europe to economic historians, and Schroeder is correct in noting that "the theme of diplomatic and commercial relations with Europe is not central to the history of American foreign policy in the period from 1815 to 1861."[27] Normally, diplomatic historians have considered only the negotiation of specific commercial treaties and have described with broad strokes the exchange of goods between the United States and individual nations of Europe. They have left it to economic historians to describe such related issues as commercial organization and precise commercial connections and to relate the results of their investigations to the broad domestic and international development of the American economy.[28] Rarely have traditional diplomatic historians integrated this work into their studies.

Commercial expansion has been at the center of attention in recent studies of most administrations between 1815 and 1860. Mary W. M. Hargreaves has argued that President John Quincy Adams "set as his priority in foreign relations the advancement of

27 Schroeder, "Diplomatic and Commercial Relations with Europe," in *Guide to American Foreign Relations*, 217. See Paul A. Varg, *United States Foreign Relations, 1820–1860* (East Lansing, MI, 1979). In this narrative synthesis of the period, Varg has argued that among the many sources of American foreign policy "the promotion of trade was the most basic" (xv). The bulk of his study, however, deals with non commercial matters and the diplomacy of territorial expansion. See also Kirchner, *Russian-American Commerce*; and John W. Rooney, Jr., *Belgian-American Diplomatic and Consular Relationships, 1830–1850: A Study in the Foreign Policy of the Mid-Nineteenth Century* (Louvain, 1969).
28 Among nondiplomatic historians, the best of the older studies are Norman S. Buck, *The Development of the Organization of Anglo-American Trade, 1800–1850* (New Haven, CT, 1925); Eldon Griffin, *Clippers and Consuls: American Consular and Commercial Relations with East Asia, 1845–1860* (Ann Arbor, MI, 1938); and Ralph W. Hidy, *The House of Baring in American Trade and Finance: English Merchant Bankers at Work* (Cambridge, MA, 1949). More recent examinations include Stephen Chapman Lockwood, *Augustine Heard and Company, 1858–1862: American Merchants in China* (Cambridge, MA, 1971); Jacques A. Barbier and Allan J. Kuethe, *The North American Role in the Spanish Imperial Economy, 1760–1819* (Manchester, 1984); D. J. Jeremy, *Transatlantic Industrial Revolution: The Diffusion of Textile Technologies between Britain and America, 1790–1830s* (Cambridge, MA, 1981); and Peggy K. Liss, *Atlantic Empires: The Network of Trade and Revolution, 1713–1826* (Baltimore, MD, 1982). For more general treatments see also Mira Wilkins, *The Emergence of Multinational Enterprise: American Business Abroad from the Colonial Era to 1914* (Cambridge, MA, 1970), the first part of which deals with the period under consideration; Douglass C. North, *The Economic Growth of the United States, 1790–1860* (New York, 1966); and George Rogers Taylor, *The Transportation Revolution, 1815–1860* (New York, 1951).

the nation's commercial interests"; John Belohlavek has written that commercial expansion was "the major thrust of Jacksonian foreign policy"; and Edward P. Crapol and Thomas Hietala have emphasized the commercial expansionism of the Tyler and Polk administrations. Crapol has argued that by the 1840s Tyler's "vision of national destiny was aimed at moving the United States from the status of a dependent peripheral nation to that of a core nation that rivaled Great Britain in the strength of its commerce, shipping, and overall economy," and Hietala has suggested that, "with the possible exception of Jefferson and Monroe, no other presidents can match the records of Tyler and Polk for bold initiatives in promoting the expansion of American trade before the Civil War."[29]

Hargreaves, best known as an editor of the papers of Henry Clay, has written a highly detailed study of the administration of John Quincy Adams in which fully one-third is devoted to Adams's foreign policy. Hargreaves demonstrates convincingly that Adams developed a broad national strategy aimed at securing open doors and competitive equality in all overseas ports. Toward those ends he advocated broad reciprocity with the established nations of Europe, complete access to colonial markets, and a program that would eliminate and preclude all special commercial arrangements between the great powers and weaker independent nations.[30]

If Hargreaves has focused on the ideology and diplomacy of Adams's commercial relations with the Atlantic nations of Europe and Latin America, Belohlavek has adopted a more global view. In his careful examination of America's commercial diplomacy and purposes in relations with Western Europe and Russia, the Mediterranean, Asia, and Latin America, Belohlavek argues that "Jacksonian diplomacy was a vital part of the American diplomatic continuum rather than a departure from it," and that

---

29   Mary W. M. Hargreaves, *The Presidency of John Quincy Adams* (Lawrence, KS, 1985), 89; John M. Belohlavek, *"Let the Eagle Soar!" The Foreign Policy of Andrew Jackson* (Lincoln, NE, 1985) 10; Edward P. Crapol, "John Tyler and the Pursuit of National Destiny," *Journal of the Early Republic* 17 (Fall 1997): 480–81; Thomas R. Hietala, *Manifest Design: Anxious Aggrandizement in Late Jacksonian America* (Ithaca, NY, 1985), 56.
30   Hargreaves, *Adams*, 67–91 passim.

Jackson was far more restrained and able than previously understood.[31] Belohlavek concludes that "Andrew Jackson formulated and exercised the most expansive and aggressive foreign policy between the presidencies of Thomas Jefferson and James K. Polk ... and helped to lay the foundations for the more dynamic diplomatic actions of the modern presidency."[32]

In two highly provocative articles, Crapol has examined the interrelationship between nationalism and sectional imperatives as well as the influence on foreign policy of abolitionism, ideology, economics, sectionalism, and partisan politics in the 1830s and 1840s, and has concluded that Tyler, too, had an expansive and aggressive foreign policy. Crapol challenges the notion that Tyler was primarily committed to the sectional interests of the South, southwestern expansion, and narrow agrarian and slave interests. He highlights Tyler's nationalism and contends rather that "Tyler envisaged a comprehensive foreign policy that would provide mutual, if not equal, benefits to all sections ... [and believed] that territorial and commercial expansion would allay sectional differences, preserve the Union, and create a nation of power and glory unparalleled in history."[33] Crapol further emphasizes the centrality of commercial considerations in his examination of the foreign policy programs of the antislavery movement and Liberty Party, neither of which have received adequate attention from scholars. He argues that antislavery leaders constructed a distinctive foreign policy initially based upon a broad program of commercial expansion aimed at taking control of the federal government away from southern slaveholder interests. One element of that program called for an appeal to the British to repeal their Corn Laws in the expectation that repeal would end American dependence on cotton exports to Britain, bring prosperity to the northwest, and firmly unite the north and west against the slave south. Crapol maintains that Tyler also promoted free trade and responded to the antislavery initiative by sending Duff Green to Britain to lobby for repeal of the Corn Laws. Tyler expected that

---

31   Belohlavek, *Jackson*, 253.
32   Ibid., 257.
33   Crapol, "Tyler and National Destiny," 468.

repeal would serve southern as well as northern and western interests, but this was only one part of an aggressive commercial
expansionism that included a liberal Anglo-American commercial agreement, a commercial agreement with China, and possible annexation of the Hawaiian Islands.[34]

Hietala, writing from an American studies perspective, is more
explicit than Hargreaves or Belohlavek in tying commercial and
territorial expansion together.[35] "During the 1840s," writes
Hietala, "American ambitions were global, not just continental,
and commercial as well as territorial . . . A determined quest for
export markets was a principal impetus behind the domestic and
foreign policies of the 1840s."[36] In this consideration of American commercial expansionism, Hietala emphasizes Americans'
bitter hostility and fear of British imperialism and the impetus
given to westward expansion by increasing interest in Asian trade.[37]

Hietala's analysis of American commercial policy during the
late 1840s carries forward a number of important themes raised
by Hargreaves and Belohlavek. All three studies, and Schroeder's,
present the United States as a commercial nation with global
interests as well as a nation determined to create a continental
empire. Hietala's intertwining of territorial and commercial expansionism (he dismisses the importance of Americans' sense of
mission and thus essentially ignores the involvement of noneco-
nomic interests overseas), his emphasis on the continuity between
the 1840s and the 1890s and after, and particularly his discussion
of the effects of domestic economic and social change on foreign
policy are especially valuable. In contradistinction to Hargreaves
and likely due to his interest in the relation between expansion-

---

34 Edward P. Crapol, "The Foreign Policy of Antislavery, 1833–1846," in *Redefining the
Past: Essays in Diplomatic History in Honor of William Appleman Williams*, ed. Lloyd Gardner
(Corvallis, OR, 1986), 85–103. See also Betty Fladeland, *Men and Brothers: Anglo-Ameri-
can Antislavery Cooperation* (Urbana, IL, 1972).
35 In his consideration of the American response to industrialization and longing for the
Jeffersonian ideal, and American racism, Hietala is heavily indebted to Leo Marx, *The Ma-
chine in the Garden: Technology and the Pastoral Ideal in America* (New York, 1964); Marvin
Meyers, *The Jacksonian Persuasion: Politics and Belief* (Stanford, 1957); and Richard Drinnon,
Facing West: The Metaphysics of Indian-Hating and Empire Building (Minneapolis, 1980).
36 Hietala, *Manifest Design*, 55.
37 See ibid., 55–94. These themes are also well examined in Graebner, *Empire on Pacific*.

ism and fear of blacks at home and Indians and Mexicans on the American frontier, Hietala emphasizes the role of racism in American expansion.[38]

All of these authors agree that the administrations they have studied established a well thought out program. The American government provided diplomats, consuls, and commercial agents with clear and consistent instructions; their success in securing agreements varied over time and place. These authors directly challenge the notion that Americans were relatively uninterested in overseas commerce, that they merely reacted to opportunities without clear policy objectives, and that individuals conducted commercial affairs on their own and without the active support and occasional goading of American officials.

They also suggest that the ideological content of American foreign policy consisted of considerably more than simply an ideology of territorial expansion. Commercial agents no less than religious missionaries actively and consciously promoted the export of American political, economic, and social ideas overseas and sometimes joined with diplomats in attempts to subvert foreign governments and cultures. In their discussion of various aspects of this "American Mission," these authors have done a great deal to break down the notion promoted by intellectual historians who argue that until the end of the century Americans were isolationists who turned their backs to the outer world and established no ideological basis for American foreign policy. In 1975, Rush Welter criticized his fellow intellectual historians by arguing that "we have yet to grapple successfully with the intellectual dynamics of American foreign policy." In his analysis Welter concluded that Americans resolved the conflict between their missionary impulse and their commitment to isolationism by resolving to serve other nations passively through benign example and the grant of asylum only.[39]

---

38 Hietala, *Manifest Design*, 10–54, 132–72. Writes Hietala, "There are . . . two sides to the missionary impulse that has so often marked United States foreign policy: actions purported to be benevolent and generous often became chauvinistic and condescending, and the ostensible beneficiaries frequently became victims instead" (p. 133).

39 Rush Welter, *The Mind of America, 1820–1860* (New York, 1975), 46. For similar views concerning American isolationism, see Richard W. B. Lewis, *The American Adam:*

Hunt, Reginald Horsman, and Anders Stephanson have also challenged the view that American foreign policy lacked an ideological basis in the mid-nineteenth century, and their interpretations differ to some extent from Welter's. Hunt, whose primary interest is in the twentieth century, finds broad ideological continuity throughout the American experience and suggests that during the eighteenth and nineteenth centuries Americans developed a coherent and popular foreign-policy ideology that emerged in the twentieth into a "powerful mutually reinforcing body of thought."[40] Similar to Iriye, however, Hunt contends that "ideology exercised a limited influence over the decisions made during the nation's first century, since the government was rendered cautious by its relatively limited resources and the sometimes sharp political disagreements dividing the informed public."[41]

Anders Stephanson suggests that Americans had a fully developed ideology that changed as American society, culture, and its economy evolved. In a brief but highly sophisticated study of the ideology of Manifest Destiny throughout American history, Stephanson argues that Manifest Destiny provided Americans with a powerful secular ideology infused with "religious overtones" that expressed their self-perception and provided a justification and explanation, but not an inducement, for both continental and global expansion. Like Welter, Stephanson also argues that Manifest Destiny provided Americans with a concept of mission that led to both passive and active ways of relating to other nations, first passively as "an exemplary state *separate* from the corrupt fallen world," and then actively as an aggressive state committed to "regenerative *intervention*." Stephanson contends that separation was the more dominant of the two impulses in the period.[42]

Innocence, Tragedy and Tradition in the Nineteenth Century (Chicago, 1955); and David W. Noble, *Historians Against History: The Frontier Thesis and the National Covenant in American Historical Writing since 1830* (Minneapolis, 1965). See also Brauer, "Economics and the Diplomacy of Expansionism," 61–65.
40   Michael H. Hunt, *Ideology and U.S. Foreign Policy* (New Haven, CT, 1987), xii. Hunt's focus is on the twentieth century, and he devotes less than a third of his study to the period before the late nineteenth century.
41   Ibid., 17.
42   Anders Stephanson, *Manifest Destiny: American Expansionism and the Empire of Right* (New York), xii. "Manifest Destiny did not 'cause' President Polk to go to war against

Horsman, on the other hand, centering on the evolution of American racial thought between 1815 and 1850 and its effect on white relations with blacks, Indians, and Mexicans, has emphasized racist ideology as the driving force in both territorial and commercial expansionism.[43] Horsman also contends that during the 1850s, well after they had turned from a commitment to regenerating "inferior" peoples to their enslavement and replacement, the American people looked across the seas. They expected that Anglo-Saxons, in pursuing aggressive commercial expansion in Latin America, the Pacific islands, and Asia, would similarly dominate and replace native populations.[44] Horsman suggests that such notions resolved the implicit conflict between aggressive overseas expansionism and anticolonialism.

These examinations of commercial and ideological expansionism led directly to a reconsideration of early American imperialism along the lines urged by Hunt. William Earl Weeks has argued persuasively that John Quincy Adams was "one of the great theologians of American nationalism and American imperialism,"[45] and contends that imperialism (that is, building an empire) "was, along with enhanced security, the chief motive for the creation of a union of states. An expansionist consensus unified

---

Mexico," Stephanson writes, "No particular policy followed from this discourse as such; though certainly conducive to expansionism, it was not a strategic doctrine . . . What I do argue, however, is that manifest destiny is of signal importance in the way the United States came to understand itself in the world and still does; and that this understanding has determinate effects" (p. xiv). For Stephanson's discussion of the religious roots of Manifest Destiny and its evolution between 1820 and 1860 see ibid., 3–27 and 31.

43   Reginald Horsman, *Race and Manifest Destiny: The Origins of American Racial Anglo-Saxonism* (Cambridge, MA, 1981). Parallel to Hietala's discussion of the malevolent aspects of the American mission, Horsman suggests that by the mid-1840s "American theorists on race were providing a mass of material defending innate differences between races . . . [that] were being used in Europe by those who were challenging the long-established views on the unity of the human race." He adds that, "although the United States shared in a general Western movement toward racialist thinking, American writers in the years from 1830 to 1850 led Europeans in expounding views of innate racial differences" (pp. 116, 157). From this, it is easy to infer that Americans, as experts, provided much of the "scientific" basis for the virulent racism of late nineteenth and especially twentieth century Europe.

44   Horsman, *Race and Manifest Destiny*, 286–92.

45   William Earl Weeks, "American Nationalism, American Imperialism: An Interpretation of United States Political Economy, 1789–1861," *Journal of the Early Republic* 14 (Winter 1994): 493. Weeks here was referring to his argument in his *John Quincy Adams and American Global Empire* (Lexington, KY, 1992).

the nation and provided the ultimate rationale for its existence.
. . . The breakdown of the expansionist consensus in the 1850s
was nearly synonymous with the breakdown of the nationalist
consensus, and the result was civil war."[46] Hietala maintains that
"the United States . . . was no exception to the development of
Western imperialism but rather an integral part of it. Racism,
commercial ambitions, nationalism, and, to a lesser extent, missionary fervor characterized the United States as much as any
other nation of the mid-nineteenth century."[47] Hietala is explicit
in demonstrating the direct link between the expansionism of the
1840s and the imperialism of the 1890s.[48] From a different perspective, this author has recently argued that the basic structure
and ideology of overseas informal imperialism as it developed in
the early twentieth century also had its roots firmly planted in the
Middle Period.[49]

The precise ways in which Americans, with or without active
government participation, sought to capture new markets, dominate entire economies, acquire the services of local collaborators,
and remodel foreign cultures merits considerable further work.
Toward this end, more work also needs to be done on the activities of diplomats, missionaries, and philanthropists active in the
period. Hunt has already provided a valuable indication of the
rich possibilities for such an analysis in his discussion of the interplay of these groups in his study of nineteenth-century Chinese-
American relations.[50] Unfortunately, neither Schroeder nor
Hietala, who are most interested in the global expansion of the
American empire, nor Hargreaves, Belohlavek, and Weeks, who

46   William Earl Weeks, *Building the Continental Empire: American Expansion from the
Revolution to the Civil War* (Chicago, 1996), ix.
47   Hietala, *Manifest Design*, 172. See also Hietala's full discussion of "an elaborate ideology of republican empire" in his chapter "American Exceptionalism, American Empire" (pp.
173–214). Earlier, Horsman also suggested that virtually all the Social Darwinian ideas,
racism, and nationalistic expressions in the imperialist debate at the end of the century found
expression in the Middle Period (*Race and Manifest Destiny*, 286–92).
48   Writes Hietala, "Policy makers such as McKinley, Hay, and Theodore Roosevelt moved
beyond continentalism and sought a global empire for the United States, but the transition is
not as dramatic as is usually assumed. In retrospect, the objectives of the expansionists of the
1890s closely resembled those of their predecessors in the 1840s" (*Manifest Design*, 212).
49   Brauer, "Imperial Expansion," 19–37.
50   Hunt, *Special Relationship*, esp. 1–79.

are not, have approached their studies from an international history perspective. All are far more concerned with foreign policy formation and rely almost solely on American materials.[51]

No discussion of American imperialism in the midnineteenth century can presume to be undertaken without primary consideration given to formal diplomatic and private relations with American Indian nations in North America. The study of diplomatic relations with American Indians remains a virtually untouched field. As Walter L. Williams has noted, Americans in the period and American scholars ever since have had a difficult time defining the Indians as either an internal or an external group, with the result that "Indians have been largely ignored as a factor in American diplomatic history."[52]

Williams has pointed out that, before 1831, American Indian nations were regarded as independent and sovereign. As such, the American government engaged in formal diplomacy and concluded several treaties with them. In 1831, however, the American government adopted the position that American Indians consisted of dependent, nonsovereign nations and relegated individual Indians to the status of colonial subjects. Theoretically, formal diplomatic relations should have ended, but in fact treaty-making continued until 1871.[53] Jay Gitlin has pointed out, furthermore, that "the roughly one hundred treaties concluded between the United States and various Indian peoples from 1826 to 1840 reveal an ongoing debate within Indian communities, between Indians and non-Indians, and between state and federal officials" on the relationship of Indians and non-Indians.[54] No matter how

51   Of the four monographs, Belohlavek used microfilms of British diplomatic materials and Hargreaves used published British documents, but neither relied on these materials heavily. Schroeder and Hietala cite no foreign archival material in their bibliographies. All, however, did rely on some published foreign documents found in collections and American source materials.

52   Walter L. Williams, "United States Indian Policy and the Debate over Philippine Annexation: Implications for the Origins of American Imperialism," *Journal of American History* 66 (March 1980): 810.

53   A year earlier, the Supreme Court ruled that existing treaties could be unilaterally abrogated by congressional statute (ibid., 811–12).

54   Jay Gitlin, "Private Diplomacy to Private Property: States, Tribes, and Nations in the Early National Period," *Diplomatic History* 22 (Winter 1998): 87.

one defines "imperialism," American relations with North American Indians satisfies that definition.[55]

One of the reasons historians of foreign relations have ignored American Indians is that rarely have Indian nations been taken seriously and never have they been considered on a par with Middle Eastern, Latin American, or Asian nations, much less than with European. American-Indian relations, involving not only the federal government and merchants but also farmer-planters, were not fundamentally different from the relations with the nations of Latin America, Africa, and areas of Asia.[56] Recent studies by Richard White demonstrate clearly that the Sioux nations, at least, presented the United States with a formidable competitor in the conquest of the American west.[57] Wilbur R. Jacobs's examination of the Anglo-French struggle for Indian support before 1763 and especially Dorothy V. Jones's excellent study of the relations between England and the United States with American Indians in

---

55 Not all historians agree. Although David F. Healy argues that imperialism "means the forcible extension of governmental control over foreign areas not designated for incorporation as integral parts of the nation" and "the essential element is that one society must in some way impose itself upon another in a continuing unequal relationship," the United States practiced expansionism, which evolved into "true imperialism . . . only in the later nineteenth century." Healy avoids using imperialism to describe the conquest of Indian lands and the northern Mexican provinces by suggesting that with regard to the Indians the United States practiced genocide rather than imperialism and with regard to the Mexicans, "less than 2 percent of the Mexican population was involved" (David Healy, "Imperialism," in *Encyclopedia of American Foreign Policy*, ed. Alexander DeConde, 3 vols. [New York, 1978], 1: 409). Ten years earlier, however, Robert W. Tucker sardonically commented, "To the extent that this expansion was undertaken at the expense of the indigenous population, it was still not imperialism because there were so few Indians (imperialism, in this view, begins with the millions not with the thousands, and with overseas territories not with contiguous territories.)" See Robert W. Tucker, *Nation or Empire? The Debate over American Foreign Policy* (Baltimore, MD, 1968), 41.

56 See Arthur N. Gilbert, "The American Indian and United States Diplomatic History," *The History Teacher* 8 (February 1975): 229–41. On Indian-white economic relations see Robert J. Trennert, Jr., *Indian Traders on the Middle Border: The House of Ewing, 1827–1854* (Lincoln, NE, 1981); Gitlin, "Private Diplomacy to Private Property'" 85–99; and Daniel H. Usner, Jr., "American Indians on the Cotton Frontier: Changing Economic Relations with Citizens and Slaves in the Mississippi Territory," *Journal of American History* 72 (September 1985): 297–317.

57 See Richard White, "The Winning of the West: The Expansion of the Western Sioux in the Eighteenth and Nineteenth Centuries," *Journal of American History* 65 (September 1978): 319–43; and idem, *Roots of Dependency: Subsistence, Environment, and Social Change Among the Choctaws, Pawnees, and Navahos* (Lincoln, NE, 1983).

the colonial period suggest a highly complex and sophisticated interrelationship that might well be applied to the later period.[58]

Despite Iriye's skepticism regarding American foreign relations in the pre–Civil War era, American diplomatic, commercial, and cultural relations with North American Indians provide an obvious field for the study of the relationship between power and culture. The relationship between Protestant Anglo-Americans and the Indians of Canada, the American west, and Mexico clearly presents a complex story of accommodation, conquest and victimization, survival, and withal, a clash of cultures. Although a number of specialists in American Indian studies and social historians have examined this conflict, it remains open to specialists in American foreign relations, and Gitlin is quite correct in urging diplomatic historians to move beyond interpretations that "cling to the static poles of conquest and victimization."[59]

Broadening diplomatic history into international history, examining the nature of commercial expansionism in the Middle Period, and analyzing the roots of post-Civil War imperialism are one means of reinvigorating the study of America's pre–Civil War foreign relations. Another approach is to reexamine the domestic sources of pre–Civil War foreign policy. Close examination of the effect of domestic political divisions on American foreign relations, as LaFeber has suggested, is only a first step toward a reconsideration of American foreign policy in the period.[60] In addition to partisan considerations, which Hargreaves thoroughly examines in relation to Adams's foreign policy, more attention is needed on the social, economic, and ideological bases of various

---

58 See Wilbur R. Jacobs, *Diplomacy and Indian Gifts: Anglo-French Rivalry along the Ohio and Northwest Frontiers, 1748–1763* (Stanford, 1950); and Dorothy V. Jones, *License for Empire: Colonialism by Treaty in Early America* (Chicago, 1982).

59 Gitlin, "Private Diplomacy to Private Property," 87. For one such study see J. Wendel Cox, "A World Together, a World Apart: The United States and the Arikaras, 1803–1851" (Ph.D. diss., University of Minnesota, Minneapolis, 1998).

60 Ernest R. May has ably analyzed the enunciation of the Monroe Doctrine from this perspective in *The Making of the Monroe Doctrine* (Cambridge, MA, 1975). See also Frederick Merk, "Presidential Fevers," *Mississippi Valley Historical Review* 47 (June 1960): 3–33, which deals with partisan battles over the Oregon question in the 1840s. See also David Eugene Woodard, "Sectionalism, Politics and Foreign Policy: Duff Green and Southern Economic and Political Expansion, 1825–1865" (Ph.D. diss., University of Minnesota, 1996).

political and regional groups as they relate to foreign policy matters.

Although historians of foreign relations have traditionally focused on the federal government and national policies, many who specialize in domestic history have examined foreign policy from a narrower perspective. Samuel Eliot Morrison paved the way with his classic 1921 study of Massachusetts commerce before the Civil War. Robert G. Albion, in two fine older studies, investigated the activities of New York merchants in the Atlantic trade; Jonathan Goldstein analyzed the activities of Philadelphia merchants in the China trade; Ernest M. Lander, Jr., examined the response of South Carolina to the Mexican War; and C. Stanley Urban, Robert E. May, and Richard Tansey covered special Southern concerns in the 1840s and 1850s. Samuel J. Watson has presented a superb study of the measured and cautious response of army officers on American borders and frontiers to American expansionism. Watson's study is a fine counterpoint to the growing literature on American filibustering in the period, the most recent of which include excellent studies by Frank Lawrence Owsley and Gene A. Smith and by Tom Chaffin.[61] Among spe-

---

61   Samuel Eliot Morrison, *The Maritime History of Massachusetts, 1783–1860* (Boston, 1921); Robert G. Albion, *Square-Riggers on Schedule: The New York Sailing Packets to England, France, and the Cotton Ports* (Princeton, NJ, 1938); idem, *The Rise of New York Port, 1815–1860* (New York, 1939); Jonathan Goldstein, *Philadelphia and the China Trade, 1682–1846: Commercial, Cultural, and Attitudinal Effects* (University Park, PA, 1978); Ernest M. Lander, Jr., *Reluctant Imperialists: Calhoun, the South Carolinians, and the Mexican War* (Baton Rouge, LA, 1980); C. Stanley Urban, "New Orleans and the Cuban Question During the López Expeditions of 1849–1851: A Local Study of 'Manifest Destiny,'" *Louisiana Historical Quarterly* 22 (January 1939): 149–83; idem, "New Orleans and the Caribbean, 1845–1860," ibid. 39 (January 1956): 48–73; Robert E. May, *The Southern Dream of a Caribbean Empire, 1854–1861* (Baton Rouge, LA, 1973); idem "Manifest Destiny's Filibusters," in Robert J. Johannsen et al., *Manifest Destiny and Empire: American Antebellum Expansionism* (College Station, TX, 1997), 146–79; Richard Tansey, "Southern Expansionism: Urban Interests in the Cuban Filibusters," *Plantation Society* 1 (June 1979): 227–51; Samuel J. Watson, "The Uncertain Road to Manifest Destiny: Army Officers and the Course of American Territorial Expansionism, 1815–1946," in Johannsen et al., *Manifest Destiny and Empire*, 68–114. On filibustering see, in addition to the works of Urban and May above, Frank Lawrence Owsley and Gene A. Smith, *Filibusters and Expansionists: Jeffersonian Manifest Destiny, 1800–1821* (Tuscaloosa, AL, 1997); and Tom Chaffin, *Fatal Glory: Narciso López and the First Clandestine U.S. War Against Cuba* (Charlottesville, VA, 1996). For an earlier examination comparable in scope to the Lander study and dealing with only a slightly longer timespan

cialists in American foreign relations, Paul A. Varg has examined the involvement of New England in American foreign relations between 1789 and 1850.[62] In all of these studies, and others, the authors have pointed out that there was both considerable breadth and division in the purposes and conduct among various special interests in American foreign affairs.

Much of this work, however, has been restricted to considerations of elite groups examined by traditional methodologies, and there has been minimal consideration of the activities of women, blacks, immigrant groups, and others less prominent in the foreign policy-making structure. This neglect can be justified only by assuming that the power elite worked in a vacuum, that the others had no involvement or effect worth examining, or that in any case, it is impossible to examine or to measure the roles of the masses. Enough work exists to dismiss the notion that elites functioned in isolation either from other elites or from nonelite groups. Few in the present climate of historical opinion would wish to argue that women and blacks, at least, are not worth further study, and recent advances in the historical discipline have opened up entirely new areas of study that now permit historians to ask and to answer new questions.

Here is where much of the new political history and recent advances in social history become especially pertinent to the study of foreign policy. Specialists in the new political history have applied the methodologies of political science, sociology, psychology, and statistics, the last aided by advanced computerized quantification techniques, to the organization of political parties in the period and to the nature of their cohesion and later disintegration. They may disagree about the relative importance of sectional, ethnocultural, economic, and partisan considerations in the political history of the Middle Period, but they have made it clear that American politics was shaped by a wide variety of in-

see Kinley J. Brauer, *Cotton vs. Conscience: Massachusetts Whig Politics and Southwestern Expansion 1843–1848* (Lexington, KY, 1967). See also John M. Belohlavek, "Economic Interest Groups and the Formation of Foreign Policy in the Early Republic," *Journal of the Early Republic* 14 (Winter 1994): 476–84.
62   Paul A. Varg, *New England and Foreign Relations, 1789–1850* (Hanover, NH, 1983).

terests and groups, each of which maintained its distinctiveness
while functioning within a broad political association.[63]

Contemporary social historians have used the same methodologies and techniques as political historians and anthropologists
to study groups, defined by gender, race, ethnicity, wealth, or status, that were either kept out of positions of power and authority
or that for a variety of reasons never made it into the established
power structure. Social historians have generally divided into
those who study the contribution of discrete social units to the
growth and development of the nation and those most concerned
with the development of the units themselves. Both types of studies are valuable to the historian of foreign relations.

The great danger in concentrating intensively on discrete units,
however, is that the relation of each unit to the others can become
unclear, so that the resultant foreign policy that emerges from the
interplay of the totality becomes invisible. There is, therefore, an
essential need for a new working synthesis that would relate new
work to a broader picture.[64]

The developing movement toward a corporatist synthesis of
late nineteenth- and twentieth-century American foreign policy
addresses the problems implicit in such fragmented study and provides a possible fruitful direction for future work in mid-nineteenth century studies.[65] Clearly, the corporatist synthesis cannot

63 See Allen G. Bogue, "The New Political History in the 1970s," in *Past Before Us*, 231–
51. For an indication of the nature of the debate among political historians see, for example,
Joel Silbey, *The Shrine of Party: Congressional Voting Behavior, 1841–1852* (Pittsburgh, 1967),
which stresses partisan politics as the key to voting patterns; and Eric Foner, *Politics and
Ideology in the Age of the Civil War* (New York, 1980), which emphasizes sectional and
economic considerations.
64 For an excellent discussion of this point see Thomas Bender, "Wholes and Parts: The
Need for Synthesis in American History," *Journal of American History* 73 (June 1986): 120–
36.
65 For a discussion of the "corporatist synthesis" see Thomas J. McCormick, "Drift or
Mastery? A Corporatist Synthesis for American Diplomatic History," *Reviews in American
History* 10 (December 1982): 318–30; and Michael J. Hogan, "Corporatism: A Positive Appraisal," *Diplomatic History* 10 (Fall 1986): 363–72. See also John Lewis Gaddis, "The
Corporatist Synthesis: A Skeptical View," ibid., 357–62. For a broader, more theoretical
view see Alan Cawson, *Corporatism and Political Theory* (New York, 1986); Alan Cawson,
ed., *Organized Interests and the State: Studies in Meso-Corporatism* (Beverly Hills, 1985);
and Reginald J. Harrison, *Pluralism and Corporatism: The Political Evolution of Modern
Democracies* (Boston, 1980).

simply be transposed to the earlier period. As it has been formulated to date, the corporatist synthesis relies heavily on the political, economic, and social organization of the more modern period and is not applicable to a period when political parties were in flux and suffered a high degree of instability, when powerful labor organizations did not exist, and when corporations were relatively small and regionally based. One might argue, in fact, that the greatest weakness of the corporatist synthesis in its present stage is that, unlike the old Open Door thesis or the generally unsatisfactory idealist-realist dichotomy, it is too restrictive and fails to serve as a unifying and consistent interpretative framework for the entire span of American foreign relations.

Such need not be the case, however. Drawing upon the broad implications of the corporatist synthesis and recent studies in political and social history in the period before the Civil War, it has become clear that a host of small special-interest associations joined together into large, collaborating political, economic, and social units.[66] Each of the special interests advanced specific domestic and foreign policies in varying degrees and competed within broader associations for increased authority. At the same time, the broader associations competed for political dominance in the nation.

One might hypothesize that the result of this struggle was the creation of a dynamic but fragile structure that was held together by a powerful, charismatic leader (Jackson) who had the support of the majority of spokesmen for various interests and associations and who balanced or controlled their demands, by a dominant national political party (the Democrats), and by a consensus ideology (expansionism). The structure that was built in the nationalistic decade following the War of 1812 survived to the 1850s. However, as sectionalism increased after 1825 and as the United

---

66   The propensity of Americans to form associations has long been recognized. For a brilliant contemporary statement see Alexis de Tocqueville, *Democracy in America*, 2 vols. (Paris, 1835 and 1840; Vintage edition, New York, 1955), 1, chap. 12. Writes Tocqueville, "In no country in the world has the principle of association been more successfully used or applied to a greater multitude of objects than in America . . . the partisans of an opinion may unite in electoral bodies and choose delegates to represent them in a central assembly. This is, properly speaking, the application of the representative system to a party" (1:198–99).

States underwent enormous economic, political, and demographic changes, the number of associations comprising the system multiplied and increasingly took on a regional character. Compromises and accommodations were made, but often only after increasingly bitter controversy at all levels. During the 1850s, the absence of effective executive leadership, the breakdown of national political parties, and the development of an irreconcilable sectional dispute over the character and direction of American expansionism paralyzed the federal government so far as the construction and conduct of foreign affairs were concerned, ended the broad system of compromise and accommodation, and culminated in secession and civil war.[67]

Opening up the period to this kind of an organizing principle would allow, if not require, historians of mid-nineteenth century American foreign relations to modernize their approach to the period and to bring diplomatic studies back into the mainstream of historical writing. By breaking down American political organization into more precise social and economic components, diplomatic historians would necessarily have to consider the involvement of new groups in the foreign policymaking process. Three of the most important groups within this framework are women, blacks, and ethnic Americans. Until the 1950s or so, the first two were essentially ignored by historians and the latter were treated only filiopietistically.

The lack of interest in the role of women in American foreign relations of the Middle Period is easily explained. Women in the period were prevented from serving as diplomats or commercial agents, held no elective offices, could not vote, and never presented themselves as a self-defined group that had a special or distinct foreign policy agenda. Furthermore, because scholars most often only considered women as a group, they missed the

---

67   See Brauer, "Economics and the Diplomacy of American Expansionism, 1820–1860," 82–112; and William W. Freehling, *The Road to Disunion: Secessionists at Bay, 1776–1854* (New York, 1990), pts. 6 and 7. See also William Earl Weeks, *Building the Continental Empire: American Expansionism from the Revolution to the Civil War* (Chicago, 1996); and Michael A. Morrison, *Slavery and the American West: The Eclipse of Manifest Destiny and the Coming of the Civil War* (Chapel Hill, NC, 1997), both of whom build upon this theme.

significant role women played as individuals.[68] Responding to this problem, Edward P. Crapol has compiled a collection of essays that deal with specific women who functioned as "lobbyists, critics, and insiders." The three essays that deal with women who were prominent in the Middle Period, Lydia Maria Child, Jane M. Cazneau, and Anna Ella Carroll, confirm the impression that women adopted positions and promoted policies that covered a wide spectrum and were indistinguishable from their male contemporaries.[69]

Studying women as individuals and with the same level of seriousness and attention applied to the study of individual men is essential; however, as long as historians believe that individual women merely participated in activities dominated by men and followed established male pathways they are likely to continue to submerge the role of women as women in American foreign relations. Drawing upon feminist scholarship, Emily Rosenberg has criticized scholars who apply "universalized formulations based solely on male experience" and ignore the fact that "in nearly every society, social systems and cultural discourse divide sharply along lines of gender." She suggests that feminist scholarship has exposed "blind spots in male-dominated histories" and "has challenged some of the language and categories of male-dominated analyses of global issues."[70] Clearly, what is needed are new questions and further investigation of areas in which women made a distinctive and commanding impact.

Two spheres in which women were especially active and in which they played leading roles were the antislavery and mis-

---

68 See Hilda L. Smith, "Women's History and Social History: An Untimely Alliance," *OAH Newsletter* 12 (November 1984): 4–6.

69 See Edward M. Crapol, "Lydia Maria Child: Abolitionist Critic of American Foreign Policy," Robert E. May, "'Plenipotentiary in Petticoats': Jane M. Cazneau and American Foreign Policy in the Mid-Nineteenth Century," and Janet L. Coryell, "Duty with Delicacy: Anna Ella Carroll of Maryland," all in *Women and American Foreign Policy: Lobbyists, Critics, and Insiders*, ed. Edward P. Crapol (New York, 1987), 1–18, 19–44, and 45–66, respectively.

70 Emily S. Rosenberg, "Walking the Borders," in *Explaining the History of American Foreign Relations*, 31. Referring to the growing literature of gendered discourse, Rosenberg also adds that "examination of gendered overtones of so much foreign policy language and symbolism can provide fresh, provocative insights into the wellsprings of policy formulation and legitimation" (p. 32).

sionary movements. In both cases, women were in the vanguard
of those who promoted liberal, humane, religious causes, and there
was a clear line into the women's rights movement.[71] Both the
antislavery movement and the missionary cause had obvious international implications. Abolitionists struggled to break
slaveholder domination of the federal government so as to secure
recognition of Haiti, end the trans-Atlantic slave trade, destroy
slavery throughout the Western Hemisphere, frustrate the annexation of Texas, and facilitate the movement of fugitive slaves into
Canada. Crapol credits Lydia Maria Child with "the initial intellectual formulation of what became the slave power thesis" and
gives her a pivotal role in creating an antislavery foreign policy
program.[72]

Missionaries were active in promoting and serving overseas
missions. With regard to the missionary movement, Sandra Taylor has explored the role of women in Japan in the 1860s and
Jane Hunter has done the same for China at the end of the century, suggesting implicitly that considerably more ought to be done
for the period between 1830 and 1861.[73] No one seriously interested in intercultural relations can ignore the missionary
movement. Neither can anyone interested in the missionary movement ignore the role of women in spreading the gospel and
promoting American values overseas.

If investigation into the role of women in American foreign
policy is underway, analysis of the role of blacks as a distinctive

71 See Page Smith, *Daughters of the Promised Land* (New York, 1970).
72 See Crapol, "Foreign Policy of Antislavery," 86 and passim.
73 See Fiona Bowie, Deborah Kirkwood, and Shirley Ardener, *Women and Missions: Past and Present: Anthropological and Historical Perceptions* (Providence, RI, 1993); Patricia Grimshaw, *Paths of Duty: American Missionary Wives in Nineteenth-Century Hawaii* (Honolulu, 1989); Patricia Ruth Hill, *The World Their Household: The American Woman's Foreign Mission Movement and Cultural Transformation, 1870–1920* (Ann Arbor, MI, 1985); Frederick J. Heuser, "Culture, Feminism, and the Gospel: American Presbyterian Women and Foreign Missions, 1870–1923" (Ph.D. diss., Temple University, 1991); Sandra Taylor, "The Sisterhood of Salvation and the Sunrise Kingdom: Congregational Women Missionaries in Meiji Japan," *Pacific Historical Review* 48 (February 1979): 27–45; Gael Graham, *Gender, Culture, and Christianity: American Protestant Mission Schools in China, 1880–1930* (New York, 1995); and Jane Hunter, *Gospel of Gentility: American Women Missionaries in Turn-of-the-Century China* (New Haven, CT, 1984). See also Clifton J. Phillips, *Protestant America and the Pagan World: The First Half Century of the American Board of Commissioners for Foreign Missions, 1810–1860* (Cambridge, MA, 1969).

and self-conscious group in pre–Civil War American foreign relations remains to be inaugurated.[74] Like women, blacks were universally prevented from assuming official positions in either domestic or foreign affairs. Unlike women, however, blacks had clear, definite, and distinct interests in a number of foreign policy issues relating not only to the slave trade, abolition, and escape to a more congenial environment but also to American relations with Liberia and Haiti and to the establishment of colonies of free blacks and freedmen in Central America and the Caribbean.[75] And, as Hietala has recently reminded us, much of the Texas movement revolved around issues dealing with the reduction or expansion of slave territory, issues in which blacks clearly had a primary and compelling interest.[76]

For the most part, diplomatic historians have simply ignored blacks as agents involved in American foreign relations in the Middle Period. The most well known studies deal with official policies and the programs of white humanitarian-philanthropists and racists (the two were not always distinguishable).[77] In his

74   The literature on blacks as a distinct group is extensive, although the appeal by John Hope Franklin for a new analysis that emphasizes the integration of blacks in American historical development has not been fully met and the new thrust by social historians and black scholars has been to emphasize distinct and separate aspects of the black experience. See Franklin, "New Perspectives in American Negro History," *Social Education* 14 (May 1950): 196–200; and a recent assessment of the new direction in August Meier, "Whither the Black Perspective in Afro-American Historiography," *Journal of American History* 70 (June 1983): 101–5.
75   On blacks' interest in emigration to Africa and Latin America see John Edward Baur, "Mulatto Machiavelli, Jean Pierre Boyer, and the Haiti of his Day," *Journal of Negro History* 32 (July 1947): 307–53; Howard Holman Bell, "The Negro Emigration Movement, 1849–54: A Phase of Negro Nationalism," *Phylon* 20 (November 1959): 132–42; Sheldon H. Harris, *Paul Cuffe: Black America and the African Return* (New York, 1972); Hollis R. Lynch, "Pan-Negro Nationalism in the New World before 1862," *Boston University Papers on Africa* 2 (1966): 147–79; Louis B. Mehlinger, "The Attitude of the Free Negro Toward Colonization," *Journal of Negro History* 1 (July 1916): 276–301; August Meier, "The Emergence of Negro Nationalism," *Midwest Journal* 4 (Winter 1951–52 and Summer 1952): 96–104 and 95–111, respectively; Dorothy Sterling, *The Making of an Afro-American: Martin Robinson Delany, 1812–1885* (Garden City, NY, 1971); Adelaine Cromwell and Martin Wilson, *Apropos of Africa: Sentiments of Negro-American Leaders on Africa from the 1800's to the 1950's* (London, 1969); Henry N. Sherwood, "Paul Cuffe and His Contributions to the American Colonization Society," *Proceedings of the Mississippi Valley Historical Society* 6 (1912–1913): 370–402; Robert G. Weisbrod, "The Back-to-Africa Idea," *History Today* 18 (1968): 30–37; and Moses J. Wilson, *The Golden Age of Black Nationalism, 1850–1925* (Hamden, CT, 1978).
76   See Hietala, *Manifest Design*, 124.
77   See Clarence C. Clendenen and Peter Duignan, *Americans in Black Africa up to 1865*

excellent study of the *Amistad* mutiny, Howard Jones does consider the testimony of black mutineers, but his investigation deals primarily with the effect of the controversy on the white antislavery movement. Jones's study stands out as one of the few, other than those concerned directly with territorial expansion, that directly relates the racial conflict to American foreign relations. Jones points out that the Amistad controversy strained relations with Spain and threatened to revive fears about British interest in Cuba.[78]

Notwithstanding the considerable literature by specialists in Afro-American history on black interest in emigration and other foreign questions, that material has rarely been integrated into considerations of American foreign relations in the period. And Afro-Americanists, even when they deal with international questions, seldom relate black efforts to the broader picture of American foreign relations. Floyd J. Miller, for example, has carefully analyzed the efforts of northern free blacks to found colonies in both Africa and Latin America from 1816 to 1863 and to promote mass emigration to Haiti in the 1820s and 1860s and to Canada in the 1850s. In the process, he has ably described the ideas, purposes, and activities of such black leaders as Paul Cuffe, Lewis Woodson, and Martin Delany and their relations with white advocates of colonization and has demonstrated that American blacks in the North had considerable organizational support and engaged in massive propaganda and lobbying activities. Although

(Stanford, 1964); Early L. Fox, *The American Colonization Society* (Baltimore, MD, 1919); and P. J. Staudenraus, *The African Colonization Movement, 1816–1865* (New York, 1961). See also Ronald T. Takaki, *Iron Cages: Race and Culture in Nineteenth-Century America* (New York, 1979).

78   Howard Jones, *Mutiny on the "Amistad": The Saga of a Slave Revolt and Its Impact on American Abolition, Law, and Diplomacy* (New York, 1987). For other works that relate to the racial conflict and issues unrelated to territorial expansion see Barton J. Bernstein, "Southern Politics and Attempts to Reopen the African Slave Trade," *Journal of Negro History* 51 (January 1966): 16–35; Peter Duignan and Clarence C. Clendenen, *The United States and the African Slave Trade, 1619–1862* (Stanford, 1962); Warren S. Howard, *American Slavers and the Federal Law, 1837–1862* (Berkeley, 1963); Hugh G. Soulsby, *The Right of Search and the Slave Trade in Anglo-American Relations, 1814–1862* (Baltimore, 1933); Alan R. Booth, "The United States African Squadron, 1843–1861," *Boston University Papers in African History* 1 (1964): 77–117; and Ronald T. Takaki, *A Pro-Slavery Crusade: The Agitation to Reopen the African Slave Trade* (New York, 1971).

Miller does refer at times to blacks' negotiations with British, Canadian, and Haitian officials, he does not deal with the foreign policy implications of the black program, nor does he make any attempt to relate black movements to national programs.[79] Much work thus remains to be done on the involvement of blacks in both America's international relations and the development of foreign policy in the pre–Civil War period.

The involvement of ethnic groups in American foreign relations has been well treated in relation to twentieth-century issues, and particularly in the eras of World War I and the early Cold War. The importance of these works makes it all the more surprising that so little has been done on the pre–Civil War period, and especially during the years of the first great wave of Irish and German immigration in the late 1840s and 1850s and the substantial Chinese immigration to the Pacific Coast states. Only the last were without effective spokesmen or political power.

Because women and blacks lacked the franchise, they had to find white male champions to lobby established leaders or appeal directly to the masses through propaganda, or in the case of blacks, to develop a nationalist consensus within the community at large. Such was not the case with ethnic groups, whose power of the ballot gained them their own spokesmen and won broad external support for their causes.

Political, social, and labor historians have published many studies on the role of immigrant groups in American politics, labor, and culture. Using advanced methodologies and techniques, these scholars have virtually destroyed the myth of the melting pot and have argued instead that ethnic consciousness persisted and that these groups maintained distinct special interests, many of which concerned relations between the United States and their native countries.[80] A number of individuals were deeply involved in the

---

79 Floyd J. Miller, *The Search for a Black Nationality: Black Emigration and Colonization, 1787–1863* (Urbana, IL, 1975).
80 See Rudolph J. Vecoli, "Ethnicity: A Neglected Dimension of American History," in *State of American History*, 70–84; Oscar Handlin, "Historical Perspectives on the American Ethnic Group," *Daedalus* 90 (Spring 1961): 220–32; and Milton M. Gordon, "Assimilation in America: Theory and Reality," ibid., 263–85, esp. 270–74. Dale T. Knobel has used content analysis to demonstrate that popular attitudes toward the Irish played a prominent part

promotion of commerce and the transference of national cultures in both directions across the Atlantic. As self-appointed, tacit, or chosen spokesmen for their groups, these people played an important role in American foreign relations in the Middle Period.

Among the European immigrant groups, the Irish were perhaps the most prominent. Important as a self-conscious group during the 1820s and 1830s, the Irish became a vital political force in the United States in the late 1840s and 1850s when millions fled the Great Hunger in Ireland. Diplomatic historians have invariably described the tactic of "twisting the lion's tail" by politicians to secure Irish votes. Similarly, British observers of American politics and diplomacy often noted the baleful effect of the chase for Irish votes on Anglo-American affairs.

Rarely have these scholars treated the Irish as more than a passive element in the political process. Those who insist on the existence of a steady growth of Anglo-American friendship before the Civil War and who base a good part of their understanding on common heritage, language, and culture often pretend that the Catholic, Anglophobic Irish Americans simply did not exist.[81] It is here that the elitism in traditional diplomatic history most clearly has distorted understanding.

Diplomatic historians have similarly neglected other ethnic groups. Unlike Irish Americans, who were generally "troublemakers" in that they promoted the independence of Ireland and created strains in Anglo-American relations, German Americans appear mostly concerned with promoting stronger relations between the United States and their native land. By actively de-

---

in preserving Irish distinctiveness. See Knobel, *Paddy and the Republic: Ethnicity and Nationality in Antebellum America* (Middletown, CT, 1986).

81   Many of the studies promoting the concept of Anglo-American affinity use the phrase "English-speaking peoples" to advance their case for cultural affinity and growing harmony. Rarely do the authors of these studies mention that a large, active, and rapidly growing segment of this linguistic group was bitterly hostile to Britain. H. C. Allen downplays the importance of Irish-American hostility toward Britain, partly by mentioning the "strain, albeit a highly recessive one, of orange in the green of Irishmen in America." H. C. Allen, *Conflict and Concord: The Anglo-American Relationship Since 1783* (New York, 1959), 100–101. Charles S. Campbell, in *From Revolution to Rapprochement: The United States and Great Britain, 1783–1900* (New York, 1974), emphasizes the common Anglo-American heritage and gives only passing mention to the considerable importance of Irish Americans in American politics (pp. 112–13).

manding support for German liberal movements and calling for increasing German-American commerce, German émigrés in the United States echoed two of the most important elements in American foreign relations before the Civil War – the fulfillment of the American mission and the expansion of American trade. Chinese immigrants to the United States, clearly important in American domestic development, also were important in American-East Asian relations during the Middle Period. Michael H. Hunt has provided a valuable introduction to the study of the role of Chinese immigrants in American relations with China in the mid-nineteenth century and indicates ways historians of foreign relations might treat all immigrant and ethnic groups in this period.[82]

As the preceding discussion suggests, the study of American foreign relations in the period 1815–61 has hardly been exhausted, and its neglect has been scandalous. Those scholars most interested in international history might well reconsider Anglo-American relations and examine America's cultural relations with the nations of continental Europe.[83] Recent studies of early American commercial globalism suggest a need for the examination of America's cultural conflicts with nations and societies in Asia, Africa, and Latin America, and an examination of the relations of the American government and people with American Indians is long overdue. Those wishing to focus on the development of American foreign policy not only have a promising new approach before them but, thanks to the publication of many studies in political and social history in the period, also have clear indications of new topics in need of investigation.

The study of American foreign relations in the midnineteenth century remains a rich field for future investigation. Its redevelopment will do much to provide a firmer basis and better understanding of more recent periods and help to restore the integra-

---

82 See Hunt, *Special Relationship*, 41–79.
83 For an excellent new examination of the prominence of Anglo-American relations and hostility toward Britain in this period see Howard Jones and Donald A. Rakestraw, *Prologue to Manifest Destiny: Anglo-American Relations in the 1840s* (Wilmington, DE, 1997); and Sam W. Haynes, "Anglophobia and the Annexation of Texas: The Quest for National Security ," in Johannsen et al., Manifest Destiny and Empire, 115–45.

tion of foreign relations generally into the exciting new directions well underway in the study of other areas of American history.

4

Coming to Terms with Empire: The Historiography of Late Nineteenth-Century American Foreign Relations

EDWARD P. CRAPOL

Over the past twenty years or more there has been a good deal of hand-wringing and soul-searching among historians of American foreign relations about the dismal state of the craft. This self-criticism, increasingly seconded by specialists in international relations and international history, has centered on the field's traditionalism, narrowness, parochialism, and ethnocentrism. All too frequently nonspecialists, and occasionally even specialists, have dismissed the study of American diplomatic history as a hopeless backwater of scholarly activity and inquiry.[1]

For many diplomatic historians the most unsettling critique of their field was Charles S. Maier's 1980 essay, "Marking Time: The Historiography of International Relations." A historian of modern Europe, Maier charged that American diplomatic history

The author wishes to thank Joseph A. Fry, Robert L. Beisner, Melvyn P. Leffler, and Anthony Esler for their helpful comments on earlier drafts of this essay.

1   Thomas J. McCormick, "State of American Diplomatic History," in *The State of American History*, ed. Herbert Bass (New York, 1970), 119–41; Alexander De Conde, "What's Wrong with American Diplomatic History?" *SHAFR Newsletter* 1 (May 1970): 1-16; Ernest R. May, "The Decline of Diplomatic History," in *American History: Retrospect and Prospect*, ed. George A. Billias and Gerald N. Grob (New York, 1971), 399–430; David S. Paterson, "What's Wrong (and Right) with American Diplomatic History? A Diagnosis and a Prescription," *SHAFR Newsletter* 9 (September 1978): 1–14; Alan Brinkley, "Writing the History of Contemporary America: Dilemmas and Challenges," *Daedalus* 113 (Summer 1984): 121–42; Christopher Thorne, "After the Europeans: American Designs for the Remaking of Southeast Asia," *Diplomatic History* 12 (Spring 1988): 206–8; Michael J. Hogan and Thomas G. Paterson, eds., *Explaining the History of American Foreign Relations* (New York, 1991), ix.

was a "languishing" field without an innovative methodology, "hobbled" by "overstated dichotomies" and an "intrinsic resistance to new techniques."[2] In the spring of 1981, at its annual meeting in Detroit, the Organization of American Historians devoted a panel to "The State of Diplomatic History," and some panel members confronted Maier's charges directly. Spirited responses to Maier's blanket indictment of the craft also appeared in the Fall 1981 issue of *Diplomatic History*.[3]

Perhaps the most convincing of the immediate replies to Maier's pessimistic assessment of the field were Walter LaFeber's and Joan Hoff-Wilson's. In their rebuttals both Lafeber and Hoff-Wilson charged that he had overlooked exciting new paths of inquiry and methodologies, such as corporatist theory, that had appeared in the 1970s. LaFeber acknowledged Maier's point that American diplomatic history remained a subfield of U.S. history, but maintained that this was "how it should be" because in the twentieth century the United States was the only nation "that continually exercises power globally while maintaining a liberal system at home" and "the parts cannot be separated." However, many other scholars, including Warren I. Cohen, editor of *Diplomatic History* at the time, conceded that Maier's critique was, "in most of its particulars, an accurate indictment."[4]

The debate has continued over the past two decades, as American diplomatic historians have searched for ways to revitalize their field. Proponents of a corporatist synthesis, under the leadership of Thomas J. McCormick, Joan Hoff-Wilson, and Michael J. Hogan, temporarily seized the high ground. In an influential 1982 essay entitled "Drift or Mastery? A Corporatist Synthesis for American Diplomatic History," McCormick confirmed Maier's charges that the field lacked verve, vitality, and excitement. He

2   Charles S. Maier, "Marking Time: The Historiography of International Relations," in *The Past Before Us: Contemporary Historical Writing in the United States*, ed. Michael Kammen (Ithaca, NY, 1980), 355–87.
3   "The State of Diplomatic History," session at the Seventy-Fourth Annual Meeting of the Organization of American Historians, Detroit, Michigan, April 1–4, 1981; "Symposium - Responses to Charles S. Maier, 'Marking Time: The Historiography of International Relations,'" *Diplomatic History* 5 (Fall 1981): 353–82.
4   Walter LaFeber and Joan Hoff-Wilson, Responses to Maier, 362–64, 377–82; Cohen, ibid., 353.

identified two primary weaknesses in the practice of modern American diplomatic history: the absence of systematic analysis and the failure to create a synthesis. Offering a sophisticated analysis of corporatism that could be applied to the study of twentieth-century foreign relations, McCormick premised his prescriptions for further research and investigation on the equation that "Wilsonianism = global corporatism."[5]

In her response to Charles Maier, Joan Hoff-Wilson had made similar claims for the redemptive powers of corporatist theory. At that juncture in the debate she expressed the hope that corporatist analysis might enable foreign policy specialists to establish "the long-sought-after post Cold War historiographical consensus."[6] Hoff-Wilson's fascination with the search for scholarly consensus was short-lived, however. By 1985 she came to the conclusion that the pursuit of historiographical consensus was a futile quest. She pointed out that since its emergence in the 1920s, the subfield of diplomatic history had never achieved consensus in its interpretations of the record of American foreign relations, and she doubted that it would anytime in the near future. Although she still believed the corporatist approach was important, she now argued "that we need an ethical imperative behind our writings rather than historiographical consensus."[7]

To guide diplomatic historians in this quest for an ethical imperative, Hoff-Wilson approvingly cited suggestions made by Arthur Schlesinger, Jr., in the early 1970s. Schlesinger named five subjects of moral concern that he thought scholars of American foreign relations should deal with: war crimes/atrocities, the nuclear arms race, colonialism, racism, and world poverty. To this list, which, with the possible exceptions of colonialism and racism, applied exclusively to the post-1945 era, Hoff-Wilson added a sixth imperative: "the environmental impact of technology." In conclusion, she declared unequivocally that she had

5　Thomas J. McCormick, "Drift or Mastery? A Corporatist Synthesis for American Diplomatic History," *Reviews in American History* 10 (December 1982): 318–30.
6　Hoff-Wilson, "Responses to Maier," 381–82.
7　Joan Hoff-Wilson, "The Future of American Diplomatic History," *SHAFR Newsletter* 16 (June 1985): 12.

abandoned the goal of historiographical consensus, which she now dismissed as "a false issue" and "not our major problem."[8]

These thoughtful, groping, often defensive responses to the issues raised by Maier, along with the subsequent calls for new methodological and topical approaches to the field that his critique prompted, did not put an end to the attacks on the craft of diplomatic history. In the late 1980s Sally Marks and Christopher Thorne, two specialists in European diplomatic history, joined the fray by repeating the now familiar charges that the study of American foreign relations was narrowly ethnocentric and deadeningly parochial. The alleged failure of American diplomatic historians to master foreign languages and to use foreign archives explained, at least for these critics, why their Americanist brethren persistently and myopically focused on the world as perceived by leaders and policymakers on the western side of the Atlantic.[9] More recently, nonspecialist Dina M. Copelman has reiterated previously leveled charges that the subfield is male-dominated, elitist, and sexist. In commenting on papers presented at a symposium in memory of William Appleman Williams, she noted that the "new diplomatic history" created at Wisconsin in the late 1950s and 1960s was quite traditional in its explanation of how power is dispersed and used in the system. She concluded that the Wisconsin School perpetuated "a style of diplomatic history (focusing on the deeds and thoughts of male leaders) that still seems somewhat closed to issues of how power is gendered."[10]

The ongoing criticisms of the field and the frequently expressed misgivings about its vitality and usefulness as an area of scholarly inquiry have not been confined to twentieth-century practitioners of the craft or to Europeanists and other nonspecialists. Certainly, a number of us who concentrate on late nineteenth-century American foreign relations are as unhappy with the stalemated nature of diplomatic history as are our twentieth-century

---

8 Ibid, 19.
9 Sally Marks, "The World According to Washington," *Diplomatic History* 11 (Summer 1987): 265–82; Thorne, "After the Europeans," 201–8. See also Robert J. McMahon, "The Study of American Foreign Relations," *Diplomatic History* 14 (Fall 1990): 554–64.
10 Dina M. Copelman, "Reflections on a Tradition That I Am Not a Part of But Which Is a Part of Me," *Radical History Review* 50 (Spring 1991): 105.

colleagues. The pessimism of the 1970s and 1980s has been apparent in our discussions of the field; we too have rehashed the same old issues and confronted the intellectual cul-de-sac presented by "obsessional over-stated dichotomies."

This sense of frustration and dissatisfaction was perhaps most provocatively expressed by James A. Field, Jr., who declared that the "worst chapter in almost any book" was usually the one on post-Civil War diplomacy and late nineteenth-century American imperialism.[11] Another surveyor of the study of American foreign relations in the years 1865–1900, Hugh DeSantis, called Field's characterization exaggerated and unfair, although he conceded that in most books the chapter on American imperialism, though not necessarily the worst, "might well be the most tedious."[12] Dissatisfied at different levels with the state of the art, both Field and DeSantis confined their analyses to issues specific to the late nineteenth century. Neither was much concerned about broader critiques of the discipline, nor did they address the perceived maladies of the craft of American diplomatic history as a whole.

Of the two overviews of the historiography of late nineteenth-century diplomatic history Field's was, as his title suggested, the more disparaging. He charged that, allowing for occasional individual modifications, the prevailing explanation of American imperialism that appeared in most textbooks was a "curious narrative" that had been constructed over the past fifty years or so on foundations erected originally by Julius W. Pratt and subsequently altered in eclectic fashion by Richard Hofstadter, William Appleman Williams, Walter LaFeber, and Thomas J. McCormick. This composite handiwork was "an inverted Whig interpretation of history" and was marred by the same presentism and "the same perceptions of false continuities and imputations of sin" that characterized the Whig view of the past. In Field's

11   James A. Field, Jr., "American Imperialism: The Worst Chapter in Almost Any Book," *American Historical Review* 83 (June 1978): 644–68.
12   Hugh DeSantis, "The Imperialist Impulse and American Innocence, 1865–1900," in *American Foreign Relations, A Historiographical Review*, ed. Gerald K. Haines and J. Samuel Walker (Westport, CT, 1981), 65.

opinion it was also "too rational" and "too unitary" as well as "excessively ethnocentric." To substantiate his charges, he provided a bill of particulars detailing what he believed to be the common failings of this interpretation of American imperialism.[13]

For all of its amusing qualities and occasionally telling insights, the "worst chapter" critique was seriously flawed. Field grossly distorted the scholarship on late nineteenth-century American foreign relations published during the previous fifteen years. In order to establish his arbitrary argument about the too unitary and too rational nature of the standard textbook interpretation, he presented evidence selectively, ignoring scholarship that did not support his harsh appraisal of the prevailing interpretation of the period. Occasionally, he made assertions about late nineteenth-century issues that revealed a limited familiarity with some of the period's most basic primary sources. Responding to Field's article, Robert L. Beisner observed that Field might have devastated those scholars who attributed "great influence to Social Darwinists and other intellectuals," but beyond that he offered little that was new – with the exception of some "new descriptive material."[14]

The material that Beisner praised in Field's essay comprised three observations about the period: that American naval policy in the 1890s was defensive and hemispheric and not offensive and imperialist, that in foreign relations and economic activity the citizens and government of the United States looked eastward to the Atlantic and Europe and not westward to the Pacific and Asia, and that a global network of telegraphic cables, which did not include a link between the United States and East Asia, was quite significant to an understanding of the events of the period. This last point about the importance of the international telegraphic network was Field's most original and useful observation. The other two points had been discussed previously and were seriously questioned in works he overlooked or chose to exclude.[15]

13 Field, "Worst Chapter," 645–46.
14 Robert L. Beisner, "Comments on Field's 'Worst Chapter,'" *American Historical Review* 83 (June 1978): 674–75.
15 For scholarship that undercuts Field's contention that historians ignored the continuing Atlantic orientation of the American economy and the nation's diplomacy see Howard B.

Despite his intellectual tendency to go for the jugular, one suspects that Field consciously set up strawmen that he could easily
knock down. The degree of calculated overstatement and exaggeration in his critique also leads one to suspect that it was designed deliberately to provoke his guild colleagues. Intentionally
or not, he succeeded in doing just that.[16]

DeSantis also may have believed that Field blatantly overstated
his argument, but he did concur with him that scholarship on the
period has been overly ethnocentric and, he added, characterized
by a wrongheaded insistence on the uniqueness of the American
experience. In his analysis of the historiography of the years 1865–
1900, DeSantis identified three prevailing interpretations of the
period. Historians in all three categories were preoccupied, according to DeSantis, with "seeking to discover how and why
America went wrong in 1898." Traditionalists such as Samuel
Flagg Bemis explained the imperial adventure as "a momentary
fall from grace." Progressive historians and their allies, the New
Left revisionists, viewed end-of-the-century overseas expansionism in the same messianic light, only they believed that it was an
unfortunate episode in the American national experience, when
the forces of evil triumphed over the forces of good. Realist scholars, according to DeSantis, saw the events of 1898 in another
light; they believed that America's leadership ignored national
interest in a burst of imperial missionary zeal. All three interpretations, although different in their particulars, adhered to a belief
in American exceptionalism. DeSantis concluded that late nine-

---

Schonberger, *Transportation to the Seaboard: The Communications Revolution and Ameri-*
can Foreign Policy, 1860–1900 (Westport, CT, 1971); Tom E. Terrill, *The Tariff, Politics, and*
American Foreign Policy, 1874–1901 (Westport, CT, 1973); Edward P. Crapol, *America for*
Americans: Economic Nationalism and Anglophobia in the Late Nineteenth Century (Westport,
CT, 1973); and Edward P. Crapol and Howard B. Schonberger, "The Shift to Global Expan-
sion," in *From Colony to Empire: Essays in the History of American Foreign Relations,* ed.
William A. Williams (New York, 1972). Field also overlooked Peter Karsten's *The Naval*
Aristocracy: The Golden Age of Annapolis and the Emergence of Modern American Navalism
(New York, 1972). Karsten saw the Navy in the years 1845–1925 as the "cutting edge" of a
diplomacy of economic expansion and asserted that "the naval officer was a vigorous ally of
the U.S. businessman abroad – in Asia and the Pacific, in Latin America and the Caribbean,
and in Europe, Africa, and the Mediterranean" (ibid., 141–45).
16   Field, however, was initially mildly surprised at what little reaction he elicited from Walter
LaFeber and Robert Beisner. See his "Reply," *American Historical Review* 83 (June 1978):
679–83.

teenth-century American foreign policy appeared to be "uniquely good in the case of the traditionalists, uniquely bad to the progressives, and uniquely naive according to the realists."[17]

This simplistic categorization, which alleges that historians in all three camps have been unable to break free of a commitment to American exceptionalism, exaggerated and distorted the historiography of the period almost as much as Field's "worst chapter" critique. It also did violence to the interpretative subtleties developed by the supposed adherents of the three schools. For example, Norman Graebner, one of the realists De Santis discussed, is too perceptive and sophisticated a scholar to subscribe to the notion that turn-of-the-century American leaders were uniquely naive and bumbling when it came to the national interest. Speaking of that generation's impressive imperial achievements, Graebner acknowledged that "these triumphs were not accidental"; American leaders realistically pursued the nation's interests and clearly understood the "continuing relationship between ends and means."[18]

DeSantis's overview was thus flawed, although certainly less so than Field's contentious appraisal. Both had ideological and other axes to grind; neither did complete justice to the prevailing scholarship on American foreign relations during the years 1865–1900. To his credit, however, DeSantis did note that some diplomatic historians of the post-Civil War era were finally breaking free of the exceptionalist framework. One new avenue of discourse was suggested by Robert Beisner's *From the Old Diplomacy to the New, 1865–1900*, which opened the way for study of the process of modernization of late nineteenth-century American foreign relations through "a more systematic application of social science theory to historical analysis." Other scholars have been probing sociocultural connections and differences among nations and tying these factors to the emergence of conflict in international relations. DeSantis also suggested that specialists might provide further empirical investigations of overseas economic expansion,

17 DeSantis, "Imperialist Impulse," 65.
18 Norman A. Graebner, *Foundations of American Foreign Policy: A Realist Appraisal from Franklin to McKinley* (Wilmington, DE, 1985), 351.

which, coupled with theoretical analyses of the nature of imperialism, "might provide more direction to the present desultory debate over whether imperialism, expansionism, and annexationism are the same or different phenomena." Despite his frustration with the apparent stalemate among historians of late nineteenth-century diplomacy, DeSantis remained hopeful. He concluded that "historiographical prospects for the future may not be as bleak" as a number of his colleagues feared.[19]

To what extent has this optimism about the field proved warranted over the past decade? Arguably, the tone within the foreign relations scholarly community has been noticeably more upbeat of late. Since the early 1990s historians have coordinated efforts to respond to critiques of the field and to explain and clarify recent trends in the writing and practice of American foreign relations for specialists and nonspecialists alike. In June 1990 the *Journal of American History* published a round table on American foreign relations. Thomas Paterson, who introduced the discussion, acknowledged that the craft had blind spots but asserted that the contributors to the round table had succeeded in underscoring diplomatic history's "transformation, diversity, vitality, and connections with other subfields in American history." In the fall of 1990 *Diplomatic History* published a symposium that was conceived as a direct response to the criticisms Christopher Thorne leveled at diplomatic history in 1988. Several Americanists, three of whom had also participated in the *JAH* round table, reacted to Thorne's suggestions that *Diplomatic History* and its parent organization, the Society for Historians of American Foreign Relations (SHAFR), be renamed to reflect a commitment to international history and to inaugurate a more internationalist, less ethnocentric and parochial, scholarly enterprise.[20]

19 DeSantis, "Imperialist Impulse," 77, 82, 80.
20 "A Round Table: Explaining the History of American Relations," *Journal of American History* 77 (June 1990): 93–180; "Writing the History of U.S. Foreign Relations: A Symposium," *Diplomatic History* 14 (Fall 1990): 553–605; Thomas G. Paterson, "Introduction," *Journal of American History* 77 (June 1990): 93; Thorne, "After the Europeans," 207. See also Christopher Thorne, "Diplomatic History, Some Further Reflections," *Diplomatic History* 14 (Fall 1990): 602–5.

Scholarly vitality and diversity clearly abounded in both of these forums. Topics covered included culture, ideology, gender, world systems, dependency, national security, corporatism, bureaucracy, and psychology. There was a discussion of the merits of national history as opposed to international history and a proposal to walk the borders "of a variety of global power systems to see how things might look from different peripheries." A number of the round table and symposium essays, along with several other previously published think pieces dealing with international relations models, balance of power, public opinion, and mental maps, have been compiled by Michael J. Hogan and Thomas G. Paterson in a handbook that conveniently explains the state of the art of American foreign relations.[21]

Whether all this intellectual ferment means that the field has been transformed, is no longer marginalized, and has gained the respect of other Americanists is open to question. Paterson candidly and somewhat apologetically acknowledged as much when admitting that if the hodgepodge of suggested new directions looked "too much like fragmentation and hopeless disarray, let us remember that the field is in flux. We are still finding out if one approach makes more sense than another and when; we are still determining what is central and fundamental and what is peripheral or superficial."[22]

The major shortcoming of this more than two-decade-old debate about the future of the craft of American foreign relations has been the limited applicability of its solutions for those of us who work on eighteenth- and nineteenth-century diplomacy. The prevailing emphasis within the field is presentist, and the debate about its future has been keyed to contemporary issues, because well over half of the members of the craft specialize in the post-1941 period.[23] Not surprisingly, most of the prescriptions for revitalizing the field are focused on the twentieth century and are

21 Hogan and Paterson, eds., *Explaining the History*.
22 Paterson, "Introduction," 96.
23 McMahon, "The Study of American Foreign Relations," 563; John Lewis Gaddis, "The Emerging Post-Revisionist Synthesis on the Origins of the Cold War," *Diplomatic History* 7 (Summer 1983): 171.

primarily if not exclusively aimed at the World War II and Cold War eras. For a nineteenth-century specialist many of these pre-scriptions would be difficult to put into practice. For example, both corporatism and dependency are essentially twentieth cen-tury phenomena, as are three of Schlesinger's ethical imperatives – war crimes/atrocities, the nuclear arms race, and world pov-erty. Other avenues of inquiry, such as international relations models, mental maps, and national security, appear to have only minimal usefulness for exploring nineteenth-century issues.[24]

It would be difficult to argue that late nineteenth-century histo-riography has undergone a transformation comparable to that of the World War II and Cold War eras or that scholarship on the 1865–1900 period is marked by the same vitality and diversity that appears to be the norm for the post-1941 period. One major reason for this scholarly lag is that late nineteenth-century spe-cialists are not blessed, as are their World War II and Cold War colleagues, with the enormous scholarly windfalls that occur when millions of government documents and private papers are made available to the public. Another reason may be that great inter-national upheavals, such as the events surrounding the end of the Cold War, do not influence studies of late nineteenth-century di-plomacy to quite the extent they do scholarship on the latter half of the twentieth century. One exception to this general rule may be the early 1990s public discussion of and media hype surround-ing the issue of "imperial overstretch" and late twentieth-century America's alleged decline in power and status. Stimulated in part by the publication in 1987 of Paul Kennedy's *The Rise and Fall of the Great Powers*, this intellectual debate should eventually alter scholarly inquiry into turn-of-the-century American imperialism.[25]

Clearly, however, a number of the new directions suggested by the present campaign to revitalize the craft do apply to the 1865–

---

24 James Chace and Caleb Carr argued that the United States throughout its history "con-sistently has sought absolute security through unilateral means." See *America Invulnerable: The Quest for Absolute Security from 1812 to Star Wars* (New York, 1988). Arthur M. Schlesinger, Jr., recently hypothesized that "the pursuit of national security" might be the explanation for American empire (*The Cycles of American History* [Boston, 1986], 141).

25 Paul Kennedy, *The Rise and Fall of the Great Powers: Economic Change and Military Conflict from 1500 to 2000* (New York, 1987).

1900 era of American foreign relations and have already influenced scholarship and enriched our understanding of the period. One area that scholars have recently begun to explore has been the role of gender in foreign relations. Prompted in good measure by the sustained impact of the new social history and recently energized by the vitality of women's history, a number of studies have attempted to integrate women and issues of gender into the pattern of the nation's foreign relations. The activities of female missionaries and other global emissaries of privately funded benevolent associations, such as the Young Women's Christian Association (YWCA), represented an obvious point of convergence for gender and diplomacy. So too did women's participation in the late nineteenth-century peace movement, the campaign for international arbitration of national disputes, and, closer to home, the anti-imperialist crusade opposing the McKinley administration's policy of overseas territorial expansion in the Caribbean and the Pacific.[26]

American women missionaries have been the subject of two pioneering studies by Patricia R. Hill and Jane Hunter. In *The World Their Household*, Hill explored, among other things, the process of cultural transformation. Her careful and perceptive analysis of the women's foreign mission movement showed how it promoted cultural imperialism in the non-Western world and revealed "its symbiotic relationship with changing cultural paradigms of ideal womanhood in America."[27] Jane Hunter, in her excellent study of women missionaries in turn-of-the-century China, discovered that females comprised 60 percent of the American missionary effort there. This "feminization of the mission force" in China went hand-in-hand with American empire-building. Hunter maintained that "supporters of American empire

---

26 Emily Rosenberg, "Gender," *Journal of American History* 77 (June 1990): 116–24; Charles DeBenedetti, *The Peace Reform in American History* (Bloomington, 1980); Edward P. Crapol, ed., *Women and American Foreign Policy: Lobbyists, Critics, and Insiders*, 2d ed. (Wilmington, DE, 1992).

27 Patricia R. Hill, *The World Their Household: The American Woman's Foreign Mission Movement and Cultural Transformation, 1870–1920* (Ann Arbor, MI, 1985), 3. See also Joan Jacobs Brumberg, *Mission for Life* (New York, 1980), chap. 4; and Patricia Grimshaw, *Paths of Duty: American Missionary Women in Nineteenth-Century Hawaii* (Honolulu, 1989).

considered Christian religion a necessary accompaniment to American expansionism, and in some cases the very justification for it." In a fascinating insight into the link between empire, gender roles, and women's search for productive careers in late nineteenth-century America, Hunter pointed out that "much as proponents of economic empire saw Asia as a potential solution for the domestic problem of surplus goods, so certain women saw in missions a potential solution for a more personal problem – a tentative energy for which there was no acceptable home market." This observation put a new spin on the longstanding but still pertinent debate about whether overseas expansion was partly an exercise in exporting social problems. It also suggested possibilities for further research into women's roles on the cutting edge of empire and, as Emily Rosenberg has proposed, into the ambiguities associated with being a member of both the "inferior sex" and the "superior race" in imperial settings such as China in the late 1890s.[28]

Nancy Boyd offered a different interpretation of the role of women as agents of cultural imperialism abroad in her study of the overseas activities of the American Young Women's Christian Association. She questioned whether the work of the YWCA actually fit the category of cultural imperialism. In her view the YWCA women were emissaries of Christ, of "American womanhood," and "of a global woman's movement." In that capacity YWCA representatives improved the lives of indigenous women in India and China, for example, by trying to eliminate such practices as suttee, child marriage, and footbinding. If these women were cultural imperialists because they exported "the uniquely Western idea that women should be leaders, free to develop in their own way," Boyd believed "they gladly claimed the title."[29]

---

28   Jane Hunter, *The Gospel of Gentility: American Women Missionaries in Turn-of-the-Century China* (New Haven, CT, 1984), xiii, xvi, 7; Rosenberg, "Gender," 118n.4.
29   Nancy Boyd, *Emissaries: The Overseas Work of the American YWCA, 1895–1970* (New York, 1986), 57–58. See also Ian Tyrrell, *Woman's World/Woman's Empire: The Woman's Christian Temperance Union in International Perspective* (Chapel Hill, NC, 1991). For a perceptive discussion of the issue of "cultural imperialism" see Paul W. Harris, "Cultural Imperialism and American Protestant Missionaries: Collaboration and Dependency in Mid-Nineteenth Century China," *Pacific Historical Review* 60 (August 1991): 309–38.

Boyd understood that the status and role of American women abroad was not defined that simply, however. She uncovered some of the ambiguities females encountered in their service within the imperial-colonial contexts of the non-Western world. These emissaries of Christ and enlightened womanhood understood that, while they "preached against war and imperialism," their "very presence depended on both." YWCA women also accepted, albeit with some reservations, the privileges that the "superior race" enjoyed. Their dilemma, according to Boyd, was that "they could not have done their work without servants, a luxury that few could have afforded at home, to maintain their lodgings, purchase and prepare their food. They deplored the class system that provided them with servants, but they did not rebel against it, partly because they could think of no alternative means of providing the working poor with a livelihood."[30]

In addition to these studies of women who walked the borders of empire as missionaries and emissaries abroad, scholars have recently given us studies of American women who opposed the nation's imperialistic policies and attempted to raise public awareness of the consequences of imperialism and to offer alternative courses of action for American diplomacy. In the immediate aftermath of the Civil War, Lydia Maria Child, a tireless abolitionist opponent of antebellum U.S. territorial expansionism by "fraud and force," fought the Grant administration's "greed for annexation" in the Caribbean. Later in the century, as John M. Craig has demonstrated in his admirable study of Lucia Ames Mead, women were leaders of the peace reform movement and were in the forefront of the anti-imperialism campaign.[31] Another scholar, Judith Papachristou, found that in the 1890s a small cadre of women sought to form a distinct "female foreign policy constituency out of an existing network of more than a million women

30　Boyd, *Emissaries*, 58, 252–54.
31　Crapol, "Lydia Maria Child: Abolitionist Critic of American Foreign Policy," in *Women and American Foreign Policy*, 13–17; John M. Craig, *Lucia Ames Mead and the American Peace Movement* (Lewiston, 1990). For another perspective see James A. Field, Jr., "Winning the Peace: The New Diplomacy in a World of Change," in *Arms at Rest: Peacemaking and Peacekeeping in American History*, ed. Joan R. Challinor and Robert L. Beisner (Westport, CT, 1987), 75–97.

who belonged to the popular women's clubs and organizations of the time." One of these women's social purity groups, the Women's Christian Temperance Union (WCTU), established in 1887 a Department of Peace and International Arbitration to promote discussion of the issues of war and peace. In her analysis of the foreign policy activism of the WCTU and other women's organizations Papachristou claimed that women developed a unique and "distinct female perspective on foreign policy." Whether women succeeded in creating a more moral and humane outlook than men on the nation's foreign relations is arguable, and the work of other scholars, including this writer, would call into question Papachristou's emphasis on the importance of a unique female perspective.[32]

Although these pathbreaking studies of female missionaries and peace reform activists have opened up new interpretive opportunities for the study of late nineteenth-century foreign relations, the majority of specialists have either ignored or resisted the implications of this new scholarship. Women's history and social history are too often dismissed as peripheral and unimportant diversions that distract from the true concerns of the diplomatic historian – power and the exercise of power, which in turn are anchored in the belief that the state should remain the center of scholarly attention. Two members of the craft, Charles R. Lilley and Michael H. Hunt, have recently presented a conceptual response to those who argue that diplomatic history must of necessity focus on the state and state power. Recognizing that the main problem was how to bond social structures to issues of power and political events, Lilley and Hunt acknowledged that "the most formidable challenge handed down by the social history approach is to find a place for non-state actors in our hardy, state-dominated conception of foreign relations." They directly questioned one of the basic assumptions shared by many diplomatic historians, "that the state *should* stand at the center of our attention and that non-state actors, such as corporations or private-interest

---

32 Judith Papachristou, "American Women and Foreign Policy, 1898–1905: Exploring Gender in Diplomatic History," *Diplomatic History* 14 (Fall 1990): 493–96, 506–7; Joan Hoff-Wilson, "Conclusion; Of Mice and Men," in *Women and American Foreign Policy*, 173–88.

groups, assume importance by virtue of their connections to the foreign policy and international activities of the state."[33]

To overcome the fairly pervasive skepticism about and resistance to a new way of looking at things among practitioners of the craft and to find ways to move beyond a narrowly state-centered mode of inquiry, Lilley and Hunt proposed an imaginative and innovative three-sphere conceptual framework that would accommodate traditional state power and at the same time make room for the nonstate actor. In their scheme each sphere would be autonomous but loosely tied to the other two through areas of mutual overlap and emphasis. State power would be the focus of the first sphere. The focus of the second, which presumably would include women's history and gender issues, would be an international social history that explored nongovernmental agencies and their influence on the flow of ideas and culture across national boundaries. The workings of the international economy would be the primary emphasis of the third and final sphere.[34]

Lilley and Hunt's three-sphere approach appears to offer an opportunity to incorporate new scholarship on nonstate actors and agencies without abandoning a traditional emphasis on the centrality of state power. To date there has been very little effort to mesh the three separate spheres – to study, for example, the connections between nonstate actors, be they corporate or individual, and the foreign policy elite. Still, though very few late nineteenth-century specialists have attempted to combine areas of the three separate spheres, the Lilley-Hunt concept has opened the way for the next step: providing analyses of the areas in American foreign relations where the spheres overlap and, ultimately, synthesizing these analyses.[35]

33 Charles R. Lilley and Michael H. Hunt, "On Social History, the State, and Foreign Relations: Commentary on 'The Cosmopolitan Connection,'" *Diplomatic History* 11 (Summer 1987): 243–50.
34 Ibid., 248–50.
35 Examples of recent studies that deal with aspects of the Lilley-Hunt three-sphere approach are Sherman Cochran, *Big Business in China: Sino-Foreign Rivalry in the Cigarette Industry, 1890–1930* (Cambridge, MA, 1980); F. G. Notehelfer, *American Samurai: Captain L. L. Janes and Japan* (Princeton, NJ, 1985); Patrick J. Hearden, *Independence and Empire: The New South's Cotton Mill Campaign, 1865–1901* (DeKalb, IL, 1982); William H. Becker, *The Dynamics of Business-Government Relations: Industry and Exports, 1893–1921*

In theory the Lilley-Hunt model and the various other investigative proposals of the past decade, including John Lewis Gaddis's most recent call for an interdisciplinary perspective, are viable and suggestive guidelines for revitalizing the craft. But perhaps the simplest and most useful way to approach the mysteries of late nineteenth-century foreign relations is via the study of empire and imperial history. Coming to terms with American empire and the nation's imperial history would appear to be the key to understanding the United States' role in the world from the end of the Civil War to the dawn of the American century. The study of empire is fundamental to the craft because it enables scholars to explain motives and actions at the center of state power as well as at the periphery, where nonstate actors and private agencies at the cutting edge of American imperialism traverse the borders of empire.

Of all the calls for new approaches to the field of late nineteenth-century diplomacy, the call for "a new departure in the study of American imperialism" has been the most persistent. Robert Beisner made this plea in 1978 in his response to Field's "worst chapter" analysis, and his refrain has been echoed many times since by other scholars, including Robin Winks, who produced a thoughtful assessment of the question of empire in American history in 1980. In that essay Winks attempted to understand why the word "imperialism" has so frightened American scholars. He noted that the word had become so politicized and rife with pejorative connotations that Americanists preferred to use the more neutral word "expansionism." Americanists also operated on the assumption that their nation's brand of imperialism was exceptional and were generally convinced "that the historical formulations relevant to other nations' imperialisms had little relevance for an understanding of our own."[36]

(Chicago, 1982); David A. Lake, *Power, Protection, and Free Trade: International Sources of U.S. Commercial Strategy, 1887–1939* (Ithaca, NY, 1988); Thomas D. Schoonover, *The United States in Central America, 1860–1911: Episodes of Social Imperialism and Imperial Rivalry in the World System* (Durham, NC, 1991); and Steven C. Topik, *Trade and Gunboats: The United States and Brazil in the Age of Empire* (Stanford, 1996).
36 Robin Winks, "The American Struggle with 'Imperialism': How Words Frighten," in *The American Identity: Fusion and Fragmentation*, ed. Rob Kroes (Amsterdam, 1980), 143–

Winks recommended that his Americanist colleagues overcome their fear of "imperialism" and accept it as purely descriptive, not condemnatory. Imperialism was the natural and inevitable consequence of "the impact of high technology cultures on lesser technologies," Winks asserted. He also argued that unlike diplomacy, which was concerned with state-centered power among nations, imperialism was based on a system of commands intended to control and stabilize the empire. Uncertain that traditional diplomatic historians were up to the task, Winks nonetheless reiterated the need for a new history of American imperialism that was both comparative in design and free of ethnocentric and exceptionalist bias in practice.[37]

Over the next decade several other historians joined the chorus calling for reevaluations of American empire. In a fresh and timely review of a recent work on comparative imperial history, Emily Rosenberg strongly agreed with Winks about the politicized nature of the scholarly debate, which, spurred and shaped by Cold War assumptions about the evil Communist empire, had reached the point where the words "empire" and "imperialism" had become terms of opprobrium, labels "that no self-respecting liberal state would wish to claim." Rosenberg sensed, however, that by the late 1980s, just prior to the complete demise of the Cold War, there was a new intellectual atmosphere and that "the concept of American Empire" was back in vogue, "now suddenly beginning to gain once-unimaginable, even nostalgic, prominence." Although she was speaking specifically about the post-1945 period,

---

77. Beisner lamented that Field's essay "does not explain the historical phenomenon of American imperialism" ("Comment," 675).

37 Winks, "The American Struggle with 'Imperialism,'" 143–46. See also William A. Williams, *Empire as a Way of Life* (New York, 1980). For an effort by a non-American to explain the nature of American imperialism see Goran Rystad, *Ambiguous Imperialism: American Foreign Policy and Domestic Politics at the Turn-of-the-Century* (Lund, Sweden, 1975). For a discussion that emphasizes gender and historical fiction see Amy Kaplan, "Romancing the Empire: The Embodiment of American Masculinity in the Popular Historical Novel of the 1890s" *American Literary History* 2 (Winter 1990): 659–90. For a collection of insightful essays on cultural features of American empire see Amy Kaplan and Donald E. Pease, eds., *Cultures of United States Imperialism* (Durham, NC, 1993).

her comments were germane to the full sweep of U.S. empire from 1776 onward.[38]

In her review Rosenberg made it clear that she welcomed the opening of a new era of scholarly inquiry that would place the American imperial experience in a global tradition of imperium, and thus relegate the old, wearisome traditionalist/revisionist debates to the historiographic ash heap. She appeared to be seconding Winks's proposal that American diplomatic historians move beyond treating imperialism as morally reprehensible and begin studying it as a historical process "with manifest material benefits to both the dominant and dependent societies." To launch this return to the study of empire with a new emphasis on comparative analysis, Rosenberg recommended that members of the craft direct their future endeavors toward explaining the differences between the British and American imperial experiences. After all, as she and others before her have noted, British leaders gloried unabashedly in empire and imperialism, whereas "American imperialists, in sharp contrast, labored just as hard to *deny* the existence of empire."[39]

In a recent essay devoted to the proposition that the craft would benefit from adopting an interdisciplinary perspective, John Lewis Gaddis, the architect of Cold War postrevisionism, joined the comparative imperial history bandwagon. Gaddis asserted that the prevailing paradigms of American foreign relations all assumed that American actions decisively influenced other societies, "but other nations and people seldom affect what happens to Americans." He questioned the notion that in imperial relationships power flowed only in one direction, from the metropolitan center to the colonial periphery. This tendency to ignore a most persistent theme in imperial history, that influence may also flow from regions of weakness to those of strength, was especially prevalent, according to Gaddis, among historians of American foreign relations who defined the United States as an empire. What was needed to answer questions about the flow of power and influ-

---

38   Emily Rosenberg, "'The Empire' Strikes Back," *Reviews in American History* 16 (December 1988): 585.
39   Ibid., 588–90.

ence in imperial relationships was a comparative analysis of empires. In issuing this call for a comparative imperial history and in urging American diplomatic historians to come to terms with the concept of American empire, Gaddis followed Rosenberg, Winks, and Beisner. These prominent historians also appeared to agree that comparative imperial studies might help the craft come to terms with the costs as well as the benefits of empire.[40]

In building his case for a new imperial history that will help revitalize the craft of diplomatic history, Gaddis made some sweeping observations – some specialists might gleefully hail them as the concessions/confessions of a postrevisionist – about the nature of American empire. Not only did he acknowledge that the United States had been viewed as an empire by the Founding Fathers "without embarrassment," Gaddis also accepted that American "expansion in the nineteenth century took place on a scale sufficient to merit the adjective 'imperial' by any standard."[41] Thus, among historians trying to see the big picture there appears to be appreciable common ground and at least some agreement on the existence of American empire. Even within the ranks of late nineteenth-century specialists, areas of disagreement on the concept of empire have diminished. The ideological gap in interpretations of American imperialism, so prevalent and virulent in the late 1960s and early 1970s, appears to have closed as well. To paraphrase Emily Rosenberg's culturally perceptive depiction of current scholarly trends, the empire has indeed struck back.[42]

---

40   John Lewis Gaddis, "New Conceptual Approaches to the Study of American Foreign Relations; Interdisciplinary Perspectives," *Diplomatic History* 14 (Summer 1990): 411–16.
41   Ibid., 415–16.
42   Rosenberg, "Empire," 585. The field's four major textbooks exhibit this general agreement on late nineteenth-century imperialism. See Thomas G, Paterson, J. Garry Clifford, and Kenneth J. Hagan, *American Foreign Policy: A History to 1914*, 3d ed. (Lexington, MA, 1988), 155–215; Howard Jones, *The Course of American Diplomacy: From the Revolution to the Present*, 2d ed. (Chicago, 1988), 193–239; Walter LaFeber, *The American Age: United States Foreign Policy at Home and Abroad since 1750* (New York, 1989), 148–217; and Robert D. Schulzinger, *American Diplomacy in the Twentieth Century*, 2d ed. (New York, 1990), 16–38. Louis A. Perez, Jr., also has noted that "slowly the idea of empire is taking hold in American historiography, but this has been no easy process." See his review of David Healy, *Drive to Hegemony: The United States in the Caribbean, 1898–1917* (Madison, WI, 1988), in *Pacific Historical Review* 58 (November 1989): 518–19.

Recent scholarship on the post-Civil War era in American foreign relations supports another generalization about the period: the United States became a world power of the first rank by century's end. A number of scholars, especially generalists such as Walter Russell Mead, Paul Kennedy, Joseph Nye, and Tony Smith, have come to identify the three decades prior to the Spanish-American War as a crucial transitional phase leading to America's emergence as a major world power. Putting aside for the moment questions of intention and continuity in the late nineteenth-century foreign policy of the United States, how many Americanists, Europeanists, or for that matter advocates of international history would deny that the United States had become what world-systems analysts define as a core nation, having made the final successful leap from a position on the "semiperiphery" to the center of the world stage sometime in the 1890s? Precious few, I think. On two counts then, the existence of an American empire and the United States' attainment of major power status, there exists widespread scholarly agreement. One might add that those two areas of agreement surely fit Paterson's criteria for being "central and fundamental" to the field of diplomatic history.[43]

Late nineteenth-century specialists may generally agree that America emerged as a Great Power with an overseas empire won from Spain in 1898, but they continue to disagree as to how and why the United States achieved its imperial position and great-power status. In this longstanding dispute one of the basic points of contention has been whether or not the American empire was intentional, the product of systematic planning and sustained governmental and public support. As early as 1953, Robert Osgood, in his classic study, *Ideals and Self-Interest in America's Foreign*

---

43   Kennedy, *Rise and Fall of Great Powers*; Walter Russell Mead, *Mortal Splendor: The American Empire in Transition* (Boston, 1987); Joseph S. Nye, *Bound to Lead: The Changing Nature of American Power* (New York, 1990); Tony Smith, *The Pattern of Imperialism: The United States, Great Britain, and the Late-Industrializing World since 1815* (New York, 1981); Thomas J. McCormick, *America's Half-Century: United States Foreign Policy in the Cold War* (Baltimore, MD, 1989), 17–21; Fareed Zakaria, *From Wealth to Power: The Unusual Origins of America's World Role* (Princeton, NJ, 1998). See also Edward P. Crapol, "From Anglophobia to Fragile Rapprochement: Anglo-American Relations in the Early Twentieth Century," in *Confrontation and Cooperation: Germany and the United States in the Era of World War I, 1900–1924*, ed. Hans-Juergen Schroder (Oxford, 1993), 13–31.

Relations, presented the brief for unintentional expansion, arguing that the United States had a penchant for "acquiring an empire in a fit of absentmindedness." Ernest May followed suit,
claiming that no one foresaw that the events of 1898 would produce an empire and that the United States "had greatness thrust
upon it." Historians of this persuasion deny that there was a
calculated, sustained imperial drive for overseas bases or a consistent program of global economic expansion designed to capture foreign markets for America's surplus products. There may
have been an unceasing barrage of rhetoric from politicians, businessmen, and agrarians about the need for markets and overseas
expansion, but as David Pletcher has asserted, the rhetoric of economic expansion was not matched by concrete results. He charged
"that the historians who have developed this thesis have exaggerated the deliberate, systematic character of expansionist policies
and, at least by implication, the successful prosecution of these
policies before 1898." Presumably, the post-1898 period is another matter altogether.[44]

Skeptics such as Pletcher also exhibit a certain ambivalence
and defensiveness about the undeniable successes of American

44   Robert E. Osgood, *Ideals and Self-Interest in America's Foreign Relations: The Great
Transformation of the Twentieth Century* (Chicago, 1953), 42; Ernest R. May, *Imperial Democracy: The Emergence of America as a Great Power* (New York, 1961), 270; David M.
Pletcher, "Rhetoric and Results: A Pragmatic View of American Economic Expansion, 1865–
1898," *Diplomatic History* 5 (Spring 1981): 103–4. See also Pletcher, "1861–1898: Economic Growth and Diplomatic Adjustment," in *Economics and World Power: An Assessment
of American Diplomacy since 1789,* ed. William H. Becker and Samuel F. Wells Jr. (New
York, 1984), 119–71; and idem, *The Diplomacy of Trade and Investment: American Economic Expansion in the Hemisphere, 1865–1900* (Columbia, MO, 1998). Other historians
who share these doubts about the consistency of the imperial drive in the years before 1898
include Charles W. Calhoun, *Gilded Age Cato: The Life of Walter Q. Gresham* (Lexington,
KY, 1988); Justus D. Doenecke, *The Presidencies of James A. Garfield and Chester A. Arthur*
(Lawrence, KS, 1981); Richard E. Welch, Jr., *The Presidencies of Grover Cleveland* (Lawrence,
KS, 1988); Thomas J. Osborne, *"Empire Can Wait," American Opposition to Hawaiian
Annexation, 1893–1898* (Kent, OH, 1981); Tennant S. McWilliams, "James H. Blount, the
South, and Hawaiian Annexation," *Pacific Historical Review* 57 (February 1988): 25–46,
and idem, "James H. Blount, Paramount Defender of Hawaii," in McWilliams, *The New
South Faces the World: Foreign Affairs and the Southern Sense of Self, 1877–1950* (Baton
Rouge, LA, 1988), 16–46. McWilliams does stress, however, that there was a change in the
outlook of New South publicists at century's end as many came to accept the virtues of overseas expansion (*New South Faces the World,* 47–88). See also James M. Lindgren, "The
Apostasy of a Southern Anti-Imperialist: Joseph Bryan, The Spanish-American War, and Business Expansion," *Southern Studies* 2 (Summer 1991): 151–78.

imperial expansion and the nature of the empire both before and after 1898. This exercise in denial is clearly revealed in their descriptions of events and in the labels they employ to characterize the leaders of the imperial thrust. Their use of the more neutral word "expansionism" instead of "empire" or "imperialism" is indicative of evasion and denial. This fear of matters imperial, as Winks noted, means that at times even ostensibly neutral and innocuous labels and designations require additional qualification. Hence, post–Civil War expansion in Alaska is described as "tarnished," and expansionist presidents, particularly William McKinley, are referred to as "cautious," "reticent," and "reluctant."[45]

The apologetic tone, the pattern of evasion, and the implied uniqueness of American imperialism prevail as well in explanations of the United States' motives in initiating the war against Spain. The McKinley administration's actions have been described as owing "far more to the better side of American life than posterity has recognized"; hostilities with the Spanish began as a "humanitarian crusade" to free Cuba that unintentionally "left the United States with an overseas empire of sorts."[46] If by chance these historians concede that America gained an empire after 1898, they characterize its peculiar variety of imperialism as "protective," "preclusive," and "ambiguous." Its imperialists are "sen-

45 Paul S. Holbo, *Tarnished Expansion: The Alaska Scandal, the Press, and Congress, 1867–1871* (Knoxville, TN, 1983); Richard E. Welch, Jr., "William McKinley: Reluctant Warrior, Cautious Imperialist," in *Traditions and Values: American Diplomacy, 1865–1945,* ed. Norman A. Graebner (Landham, MD, 1985), 29–52; John Dobson, *Reticent Expansionism: The Foreign Policy of William McKinley* (Pittsburgh, 1988); David F. Trask, *The War with Spain in 1898* (New York, 1981), x; Stuart Creighton Miller, *"Benevolent Assimilation": The American Conquest of the Philippines, 1899–1903* (New Haven, 1982), 14; Ephraim K. Smith, "A Question from which We Could Not Escape: William McKinley and the Decision to Acquire the Philippine Islands," *Diplomatic History* 9 (Fall 1985): 374.
46 Lewis L. Gould, *The Spanish-American War and President McKinley* (Lawrence, KS, 1982), 53; Trask, *War with Spain,* 483; Pletcher, "Rhetoric and Results," 104. James C. Bradford recently argued that the United States went to war to end the chaos and "to maintain the principle of self-determination." See his edited volume, *Crucible of Empire: The Spanish-American War & Its Aftermath* (Annapolis, MD, 1993), xiii. See also Ivan Musicant, *Empire by Default: The Spanish-American War and the Dawn of the American Century* (New York, 1998); Richard H. Collin, *Theodore Roosevelt, Culture, Diplomacy, and Expansion: A New View of American Imperialism* (Baton Rouge, LA, 1985); and idem, *Theodore Roosevelt's Caribbean: The Panama Canal, The Monroe Doctrine, and the Latin American Context* (Baton Rouge, LA, 1990).

timental," motivated by "tutorial benevolence" and "a need to do good to others"; its policies in underdeveloped countries such as China are a hybrid of "selfish imperialism and selfless idealism." And on it goes.[47]

In a book published to mark the centenary of the Spanish-Cuban-American conflict, Louis A. Pérez, Jr., freshly examined the historiography of 1898. Pérez, the foremost scholar of the late nineteenth-century Cuban struggle for independence, concluded that American historical writing on the 1898 war was marked by ambiguity and from the beginning was "invested with the ideals by which Americans wished to define and differentiate their place in the international system." Pérez also discovered that American explanations of the origins and results of the war rarely were informed by Cuban historiography, and that the designation Americans commonly used for the conflict, the Spanish-American War, blatantly ignored the Cuban contribution to victory. American historical writing neglected to clarify as well that Cuban independence was neither the purpose of the U.S. intervention nor the result of the war. Although Pérez detected an increasing tendency to incorporate Cuban perspectives in historical accounts of the conflict, he believed the idea that empire was President McKinley's objective in the war "has not fit easily into the historiography of 1898."[48]

This lingering ambivalence and defensiveness among specialists on American imperialism should not obscure the point made previously, which is that over the past decade or so there has been

47   Schlesinger, *Cycles*, 143–44; Rystad, *Ambiguous Imperialism*; James C. Thomson, Jr., Peter W. Stanley, and John Curtis Perry, *Sentimental Imperialists: The American Experience in East Asia* (New York, 1981); David L. Anderson, *Imperialism and Idealism: American Diplomats in China, 1861–1898* (Bloomington, 1985), viii.

48   Louis A. Pérez Jr., *The War of 1898: The United States and Cuba in History and Historiography* (Chapel Hill, NC, 1998), x–xi, 36, 116. For another perceptive discussion of the American role "in the multinational 1898 war" see Thomas G. Paterson, "United States Intervention in Cuba, 1898: Interpretations of the Spanish-American-Cuban-Filipino War," *The History Teacher* 29 (May 1996): 341–61. For a recent synthesis see Joseph Smith, *The Spanish-American War: Conflict in the Caribbean and the Pacific 1895–1902* (London, 1994). For an innovative updating of the "crisis of confidence" interpretation of 1898 that stresses gender beliefs and cultural origins see Kristin L. Hoganson, *Fighting for American Manhood: How Gender Politics Provoked the Spanish-American and Philippine-American Wars* (New Haven, CT, 1998).

a gradual acceptance, particularly among historians who identify with Gaddis's postrevisionism, of the concept of American empire. But consensus, even on such a fundamental issue as the nature of that empire, eludes the craft. We are not yet all agreed, and it may seem only yesterday, as Lloyd Gardner reiterated in his 1988 SHAFR presidential address, "Lost Empires," that the American empire was still "the empire that dare not speak its name." It is probably correct, however, to say that the outlook of a majority of the craft on the concept of empire has changed. With or without consensus, diplomatic historians increasingly speak the dread word of late.[49]

The work of William Appleman Williams, long the profession's leading advocate of confronting empire and the consequences of America's imperial past, has become the basis for interpretations of the post-Civil War period presented in the field's major textbooks. His highly influential *The Tragedy of American Diplomacy*, originally published in 1959, was deservedly acclaimed twenty-five years later by a prominent member of the guild as a "stimulus and not a blueprint" for redirecting how we view American diplomatic history. Retrospectively, Williams has been acknowledged by a number of historians, including those, like Gaddis, who remain unconvinced by his open door analysis, as "the most influential diplomatic historian of his generation." Perhaps it also is time to extend Williams credit for disproving, or at the very least seriously challenging, Lenin's theory of imperialism by demonstrating that the roots of America's late nineteenth-century overseas empire were distinctly agrarian.[50]

Morgenthau?

---

49   Lloyd C. Gardner, "Lost Empires," *Diplomatic History* 13 (Winter 1989): 2. Arthur *introduce* Schlesinger, for one, accepted the concept of empire and wondered: "Yet who can doubt that there is an American empire? – an 'informal' empire, not colonial in polity, but still richly equipped with imperial paraphernalia: troops, ships, planes, bases, proconsuls, local collaborators, all spread across the luckless planet" (*Cycles*, 141).
50   Bradford Perkins, "'The Tragedy of American Diplomacy': Twenty-Five Years After," *Reviews in American History* 12 (March 1984): 1–18; Gaddis, "New Conceptual Approaches," 407 n.11; Gary R. Hess, "After the Tumult: The Wisconsin School's Tribute to William Appleman Williams," *Diplomatic History* 12 (Fall 1988): 499; William A. Williams, *The Roots of the Modern American Empire: A Study of the Growth and Shaping of Social Consciousness in a Marketplace Society* (New York, 1969). For a suggestive analysis of the American origins of "the surplus-capital theory of modern capitalist imperialism" see Carl P.

Evidence supporting this perceptible shift in the craft's thinking about the nature of American empire is continually coming to light and accumulates steadily. The work of two historians, Walter LaFeber and Joseph A. Fry, has particularly advanced our understanding of the nation's imperial past. LaFeber's *The American Search for Opportunity, 1865–1913*, which is the best recent synthesis of the period, relied upon his earlier definition of American overseas territorial expansion as a "new empire" that sought only "the minimum territory" necessary to capture the world's markets. But LaFeber's focus now has shifted to an emphasis on the United States' relentless search for commercial and economic opportunity, which he argued took precedence over concerns for order and stability, and instead promoted revolution and disorder in the world. Fry, in several excellent articles that provide interpretive overviews of the field, has honed and sharpened our understanding of American empire by providing cogent definitions of imperialism, including an insightful discussion of what he has labelled an "American-style" imperialism. Although Fry did not find evidence for a master plan of empire, he contended that the "key to understanding the course of late-nineteenth-century U.S. foreign relations" was "the ongoing evolution of different phases of empire."[51]

A number of other scholars, including this author, have responded affirmatively as well to the question of whether the foreign policy establishment consciously guided the transformation to major power status and tried to establish a permanent policy to further American expansionism. Specialized studies on late nineteenth-century politicians, naval officers, diplomats, world's

Parrini and Martin J. Sklar, "New Thinking about the Market, 1896–1904: Some American Economists on Investment and the Theory of Surplus Capital," *Journal of Economic History* 43 (September 1983): 559–78.

51   Walter LaFeber, *The American Search for Opportunity, 1865–1913* (New York, 1993); idem, *The New Empire: An Interpretation of American Expansion, 1860–1898*, 35th anniversary ed. (Ithaca, NY, 1998); Joseph A. Fry, "Phases of Empire: Late Nineteenth-Century U.S. Foreign Relations," in *The Gilded Age: Essays on the Origins of Modern America*, ed. Charles C. Calhoun (Wilmington, DE, 1996), 283. See also Fry, "Imperialism, American Style, 1890–1916," in *American Foreign Relations Reconsidered, 1890–1993*, ed. Gordon Martel (London, 1994), 52–70; and idem, "From Open Door to World Systems: Economic Interpretations of Late-Nineteenth-Century American Foreign Relations," *Pacific Historical Review* 65 (May 1996): 277–303.

fairs, and key diplomatic episodes by Frederick C. Drake, Michael J. Devine, Barry Rigby, Robert W. Rydell, Joyce S. Goldberg, Judson M. Lyon, and William Michael Morgan strengthen the case for continuity and intentionality. In addition, independent writer and film producer, Tom Coffman, has ably demonstrated the continuity of purpose that succeeded in tying the Hawaiian Islands to the United States with "hoops of steel," to use Secretary of State Hamilton Fish's apt description of the relationship, and that ultimately led to annexation of the islands in 1898.[52]

Recent works on the McKinley administration, especially those of John Offner, Richard E. Welch, Jr., and Robert C. Hilderbrand, also demonstrate a calculated, purposeful pursuit of empire and overseas commercial expansion. McKinley may have been "cautious" and "reluctant," but as Welch concluded in an excellent evaluation of the Ohioan's presidency, "it should be acknowledged that America acquired a colonial empire in the years 1898–99 not in a fit of absentmindedness nor as the result of popular demand or some vague psychic crisis, but by the conscious act and decision of William McKinley." Another McKinley scholar, Lewis Gould, grudgingly conceded much the same, although he characterized the twenty-fifth president's policy in the Caribbean

---

52   See Frederick C. Drake, *The Empire of the Seas: A Biography of Rear Admiral Robert Wilson Shufeldt, USN* (Honolulu, 1984); Michael J. Devine, *John W. Foster: Politics and Diplomacy in the Imperial Era, 1893–1917* (Athens, OH, 1981); Barry Rigby, "American Expansion in Hawaii: The Contribution of Henry A. Pierce," *Diplomatic History* 4 (Fall 1980): 353–69; Robert W. Rydell, *All the World's a Fair: Visions of Empire at American International Expositions, 1876–1916* (Chicago, 1984); Joyce S. Goldberg, *The "Baltimore" Affair* (Lincoln, 1986); Judson M. Lyon, "Informal Imperialism: The United States in Liberia, 1897–1912," *Diplomatic History* 5 (Summer 1981): 221–43; William Michael Morgan, "The Anti-Japanese Origins of the Hawaiian Annexation Treaty of 1897," *Diplomatic History* 6 (Winter 1982): 23–44; and Tom Coffman, *Nation Within: The Story of America's Annexation of the Nation of Hawai'i* (Kane'ohe, HI, 1998). For an analysis of Benjamin Harrison's advocacy of overseas expansion see Homer E. Socolofsky and Allan B. Spetter, *The Presidency of Benjamin Harrison* (Lawrence, KS, 1987). For an examination of James G. Blaine's pivotal role in shaping late nineteenth century American foreign relations see Edward P. Crapol, *James G. Blaine: Architect of Empire* (Wilmington, DE, 1999). See also Joseph A. Fry, *Henry S. Sanford: Diplomacy and Business in Nineteenth-Century America* (Reno, NV, 1982); and idem, *John Tyler Morgan and the Search for Southern Autonomy* (Knoxville, TN, 1992). Two documentary films on American expansion in Hawaii, both available on videocassette, also are insightful: "Hawaii's Last Queen," a production of "The American Experience" and WGBH, Boston (1997); and "Nation Within," a production of Tom Coffman and Hawaii Public Television (1998).

and the Pacific as being "somewhere between accident and design."[53]

The intentionality/continuity argument, however, tends to overlook a crucial aspect of America's late nineteenth-century imperial development. While historians have recognized that prior to 1898 the United States was both a continental empire and an overseas commercial empire of modest territorial ambitions, they have not thoroughly explored the relationship between these co-existent empires. The United States had always moved in both directions—across the continent and across the ocean – but in the aftermath of the Civil War the landed empire approached and met its limits. The overseas empire, which would stretch from the waters of the Caribbean to the shores of Asia, then arose in its wake. Perhaps one source of our disagreement about the last three decades of the nineteenth century is that in those years the United States had two distinct overlapping and changing empires. To end our analytical confusion we need a proper imperial history in which the study of the process of empire is of the scope and methodological sophistication recommended by Robin Winks, Emily Rosenberg, and John Gaddis. Such a commitment to imperial history might dispel the notion that the craft is a languishing backwater of scholarly inquiry and free us of the accusation that we are hopelessly parochial and ethnocentric. Imperial history also might serve to overcome the rigid periodization that too often marks studies of nineteenth-century foreign relations.

Walter L. Williams offered one line of inquiry that in my view qualifies as imperial history in an essay discussing American Indian policy and its implications for our understanding of Ameri-

---

53   John Offner, "The United States and France: Ending the Spanish-American War," *Diplomatic History* 7 (Winter 1983): 1–21; Welch, "William McKinley," 44; Gould, *Spanish-American War*, 62; Robert C. Hilderbrand, *Power and the People: Executive Management of Public Opinion in Foreign Affairs, 1897–1921* (Chapel Hill, NC, 1981), 3–51. For an excellent overview of McKinley scholarship see Joseph A. Fry, "William McKinley and the Coming of the Spanish-American War: A Study in the Besmirching and Redemption of an Historical Image," *Diplomatic History* 3 (Winter 1979): 77–97. For Offner's recent more nuanced appraisal of McKinley see *An Unwanted War: The Diplomacy of the United States and Spain over Cuba, 1895–1898* (Chapel Hill, NC, 1992). See also Louis A. Pérez, Jr., "The Meaning of the Maine: Causation and the Historiography of the Spanish-American War," *Pacific Historical Review* 58 (August 1989): 293–322; and idem, *Cuba and the United States: Ties of Singular Intimacy* (Athens, GA, 1990).

can imperialism at the close of the century. The nation's Indian policy revealed "a clear pattern of colonialism toward Native Americans" and "served as a precedent for imperialist domination over the Philippines and other islands occupied during the Spanish-American War." Williams defined colonialism as "the conquest and control of culturally different peoples, who are so dissimilar that they cannot be easily incorporated but must be ruled as subjects outside the political process." Despite this clearly identifiable historical pattern of colonialism, Williams believed that there was "a mistaken consensus, at least among many diplomatic historians, that the United States did not have a tradition of holding alien peoples as colonial subjects before 1898."[54]

Late nineteenth-century imperialists such as Henry Cabot Lodge and Theodore Roosevelt understood this facet of the American expansionist experience and consciously made the connection between that experience and American policy in the Philippines. Lodge explained that the United States had colonial subjects throughout most of its brief history and declared that if the anti-imperialists were correct in their denunciations of the annexation of the Philippines and the suppression of the Filipino insurrection, then "our whole past record of expansion is a crime." Roosevelt made the same argument in his 1900 speech accepting the Republican vice presidential nomination, when he compared the annexation of the Philippines to previous territorial acquisitions such as Florida. He told his fellow Republicans that "the Seminoles, who had not been consulted in the sale, rebelled and waged war exactly as some of the Tagals have rebelled and waged war in the Philippines." On another occasion the future president wrote that if Americans were "morally bound to abandon the Philippines, we were also morally bound to abandon Arizona to the Apaches."[55]

According to Lodge's and Roosevelt's interpretation of American imperialism, the events of 1898 were not a "new departure." Williams likewise maintained that America's annexation of the

54 Walter L. Williams, "United States Indian Policy and the Debate over Philippine Annexation: Implications for the Origins of American Imperialism," *Journal of American History* 66 (March 1980): 810–12.
55 Ibid., 817–27.

Philippines and its suppression of the Aguinaldo-led revolt should
be understood "as the last episode of the nineteenth-century pattern of territorial acquisition and direct political rule of subject
peoples." For the imperialists of 1898, "the precedents to govern
colonial subjects were clear and exact, based on the long road
from independence to wardship for American Indians."[56]

Just as there were antebellum precedents for the governing of
colonial peoples, there were also threads of continuity in American diplomacy and American territorial and commercial expansionism throughout the nineteenth century. It appears that the
chief obstacle to a recognition and understanding of this consistency and continuity has been the craft's aforementioned penchant
for periodization. All too frequently the Civil War has been identified as the watershed in American history, the clear dividing line
that ushered in a new era and marked a distinct break with the
diplomacy of antebellum America. Perhaps the years 1861–65
may be better understood as a transitional phase of temporary
delay and deferred activity that did not completely erase or oblit-
erate the ambitious "incipient imperialism" of the 1850s.

The Civil War, Australian historian David P. Crook has argued,
was a cataclysmic event in international history that momentarily
"diverted the career of American imperialism" but ultimately
enabled the United States "to continue its headlong rush into
superpowerdom." Because he found the concept of imperial mission to be "highly resilient" during the war and because "geopolitical ambitions featured persistently in the foreign policy outlook of both sections," Crook advised diplomatic historians who
contend that the "new imperialism" of 1898 was an aberration
from traditional American behavior to reconsider "the neglected

---

56   Ibid., 831. More than thirty years ago, Charles Vevier made the same point that "the
imperialism of McKinley and Roosevelt was not a new departure in American history." See
"American Continentalism: An Idea of Expansion, 1845–1910," *American Historical Review* 65 (January 1960): 334. On the Philippines see also Miller, *"Benevolent Assimilation"*;
David Howard Bain, *Sitting in Darkness: Americans in the Philippines* (Boston, 1984); Richard E. Welch, Jr., *Response to Imperialism: The United States and the Philippine-American
War, 1899–1902* (Chapel Hill, NC, 1979); Stanley Karnow, *In Our Image: America's Empire
in the Philippines* (New York, 1989); and Kenton J. Clymer, *Protestant Missionaries in the
Philippines, 1898–1916: An Inquiry into the American Colonial Mentality* (Urbana, IL, 1986).

1860s."[57]   Other historians similarly have identified the years between American independence and the war between the states as a seedbed for beliefs, ideas, and aspirations about the nation's destiny in the world. This cluster of ideas and beliefs became an imperial ideology that survived the turmoil of civil war, was nurtured by the North's victory, and ultimately produced the full flowering of overseas empire in the 1890s.[58]

In a suggestive essay that further exposed the fallacy of rigid historical periodization, antebellum specialist Kinley Brauer stressed that Americans were conscious and fearful of Great Britain's enormous colonial expansion in the years 1815–60. Brauer argued that American leaders, concerned about the challenges posed by Britain's expanding formal and informal empire, not only understood the nature of the British threat but offered responses to it. Some American leaders, to prevent Britain from engrossing the world's resources and markets, unsuccessfully recommended overseas territorial expansion and the establishment of a formal empire as an "equalizing" measure. Others sought to promote, also prematurely, an informal empire.

Brauer emphasized that the American response to the perceived British challenge in the antebellum period was wavering, muddled, and marked by the same ideological and constitutional reservations that surfaced in the great debate of 1898–1900. The quest for informal empire was also stymied in the antebellum period because the United States had not yet fulfilled the two basic requirements for imperial success: economic independence and surplus production. According to Brauer, however, by the eve of the Civil War the groundwork for an informal empire had been prepared. He concluded that "the concept had been fully developed

---

57   David P. Crook, *Diplomacy during the American Civil War* (New York, 1975), preface. For a recent collection of essays evaluating the importance of the Civil War as an international event see Robert E. May, ed., *The Union, the Confederacy, and the Atlantic Rim* (West Lafayette, IN, 1995). For a fine synthesis of the Anglo-American recognition issue see Howard Jones, *Union in Peril: The Crisis over British Intervention in the Civil War* (Chapel Hill, NC, 1992).

58   LaFeber, *American Age*, 122–50; Paul A. Varg, *America, from Client State to World Power: Six Major Transitions in United States Foreign Relations* (Norman, OK, 1990), 32–98.

and awaited only a more suitable time and opportunity for implementation" at the turn of the century.[59]

The work of Kinley Brauer, David Crook, and Walter Williams
suggests that the key to deciphering the phenomenon of American empire might be found in defining the 1865–1900 period as
one in which the first empire, a landed continental empire, reached
fruition, then quickly faded, to be superseded by a second, insular
empire that burst to the forefront and briefly became the dominant paradigm of American imperial history. As a host of specialists have noted, the 1890s were a period of convergence and
transition in American foreign relations. Few diplomatic historians, however, have sufficiently emphasized the process by which
a waning continental empire was replaced by a waxing overseas
empire. The experience of securing and governing the continental empire became the model for pacifying and controlling the
insular empire. In addition, the experience of oceanic commercialism in the antebellum years served the nation well in its
end-of-the-century transformation to overseas empire. These dual
traditions of colonialism and oceanic commercialism were
embedded in the national consciousness, to be recycled and redi-
rected as the basis of the 1890s transition. Current scholarship
may not support the proposition that a grand imperial design
guided this process, but it certainly verifies that the shift to global
empire entailed an accumulation of calculated decisions to extend American interests that were based on certain assumptions
about the nation's destiny.[60]

In structuring our approach to an imperial history of the United
States we should recognize the dual nature of the empire that had
been part of American national experience prior to the twentieth

59   Kinley J. Brauer, "The United States and British Imperial Expansion, 1815–1860," *Diplomatic History* 12 (Winter 1988): 19–37. See also Edward P. Crapol, "The Foreign Policy of
Antislavery, 1833–1846," in *Redefining the Past: Essays in Diplomatic History in Honor of
William Appleman Williams*, ed. Lloyd C. Gardner (Corvallis, OR, 1986), 85–103; and idem,
"John Tyler and the Pursuit of National Destiny," *Journal of the Early Republic* 17 (Fall
1997): 467–91.
60   Walter LaFeber, *The New Empire, An Interpretation of American Expansion, 1860–
1898* (Ithaca, NY, 1963); Charles S. Campbell, *The Transformation of American Foreign
Relations, 1865–1900* (New York, 1976); Robert L. Beisner, *From the Old Diplomacy to the
New, 1865–1900*, 2d ed. (Arlington Heights, IL, 1986).

century. America had always been a hybrid empire of continental expansion and oceanic enterprise. In his sweeping study of American imperialism the British historian V. G. Kiernan aptly dubbed the emergence of the overseas empire a "logical sequel," a "next chapter." In a seemingly natural process the Anglo-American settlement of the continent reached its final stages; "one frontier had closed, others were opening; some inferior races had to be quelled, the time had come for others to be disposed of." This late nineteenth-century "consolidation of the homeland" in the American West, argued Kiernan, meant that the nation ultimately learned "how to handle the interior colonies and its Amerindian subjects."[61]

Obviously Kiernan's analysis is not traditional diplomatic history, but it is suggestive as a form of imperial history that might open the way to what Beisner called for: "a new departure in the study of American imperialism." For members of our craft Kiernan's approach may serve as a bridge to the work of several historians of the American West who have documented how white settlers (temporarily) and Indians (permanently) suffered a fate similar to that later endured by indigenous peoples on the periphery of the overseas empire – they were treated as colonials and inferiors by the metropolis.[62] Although some practitioners of what has been dubbed the New Western History might dispute Kiernan's emphasis on old frontiers closing and new ones opening, they would agree with his concept of the trans-Mississippi West being composed of interior colonies. Patricia Limerick, among others, portrayed Western history as imperial conquest and argued that "conquest forms the historical bedrock of the whole nation, and the American West is a preeminent study in conquest and its consequences."[63]

---

61 Victor G. Kiernan, *America, the New Imperialism: From White Settlement to World Hegemony* (London, 1980), 17–111.
62 Richard Drinnon, *Facing West: The Metaphysics of Indian-Hating and Empire-Building* (New York, 1980); Robert M. Utley, *The Indian Frontier of the American West, 1846–1890* (Albuquerque, NM, 1984). See also Richard Slotkin, *Gunfighter Nation: The Myth of the Frontier in Twentieth Century America* (New York, 1992).
63 Patricia N. Limerick, *The Legacy of Conquest: The Unbroken Past of the American West* (New York, 1987), 27–28. See also Donald Worster, *Rivers of Empire: Water, Aridity, and the Growth of the American West* (New York, 1985); Richard White, *"It's Your Misfor-*

Kiernan and other historians who define the subduing of the native American population as an imperial process probably would mark the 1890 Wounded Knee episode (and, indirectly, the 1890 census) as at least the ostensible end of the first phase of imperial history and the beginning of the second, symbolically marking the end of one frontier/empire and foretelling the dawn of another. Clearly many contemporary observers, including Lodge and Roosevelt, explained American expansionism as an inevitable progression. As Kiernan observed, much of Roosevelt's political skill "lay in convincing Americans" that this shift to overseas territorial expansion "was not 'imperialism,' but simply a natural continuation of the country's previous growth." Arguably, Kiernan's logical sequel analogy and the interpretations offered by Williams, Crook, and others move us beyond the "overstated dichotomies" that have plagued the study of imperialism and the endless debate surrounding the significance of the events of 1898. The year 1898 may have been a "turning point" in that it ushered in a new chapter of imperial history, but it also provided evidence of the continuity of the imperial process and the duality of the American imperial experience.[64]

In his new study of the rise of American seapower, Kenneth Hagan perceptively demonstrated how changes in naval policy mirrored the transformation of the American empire. Traditionally the U.S. Navy had pursued a strategy of *guerre de course*, which meant its primary function was the protection of American commerce on the high seas. In wartime the navy confined itself to commerce-raiding and hit-and-run attacks on the enemy. In the period of transition from the continental to the overseas empire, the U.S. Navy shifted its overall strategy to one of *guerre d'escarde*, which was premised on the maintenance of a large

tune and None of My Own": A New History of the American West (Norman, OK, 1991); William Cronon, *Nature's Metropolis: Chicago and the Great West* (New York, 1991); William G. Robbins, *Colony and Empire: The Capitalist Transformation of the American West* (Lawrence, KS, 1994). For a suggestive proposal urging the adoption of an environmental approach to the study of American foreign relations see Mark H. Lytle, "An Environmental Approach to American Diplomatic History," *Diplomatic History* 20 (Spring 1996): 279–300.
64 Kiernan, *America*, 85.

battleship fleet and the "doctrine of challenging all rivals for command of the sea."[65]

In explaining this change in naval strategy, Hagan stressed the nonpartisan commitment to American navalism and the "striking continuity" of policy in both Republican and Democratic administrations in the transition period of the 1880s and 1890s. International factors also shaped the transition, Hagan noted, because "after 1885 fundamental changes in the world balance of power seemed to render a commercialistic American navy obsolete and impotent." The U.S. Navy responded to these changes by retooling its technology and revising its strategy "to make itself into a European-style force ready for combat with the navies of the other major powers." Hagan's brilliant analysis, which integrates naval and imperial history, is an example of how to escape the narrow confines of diplomatic history. It also points the way toward additional avenues of inquiry for comparative analysis of late nineteenth-century empires.[66]

The work of Hagan, Kiernan, and other scholars indicates that the study of empire, and the complex relationships it creates, enables diplomatic historians to be innovative and imaginative. Members of the craft should accept that there is no single right way to do imperial history. Various approaches to the subject are feasible. Winks has proposed we examine the "system of commands" within the imperial framework; Rosenberg has suggested that scholars focus on the process of empire and imperial control; and Gaddis has stressed that scholars need to look at how the imperial relationship affects both the colonizer and the colonized.

---

65   Kenneth J. Hagan, *This People's Navy: The Making of American Sea Power* (New York, 1991), xi.

66   Ibid., 185–229. Frederick Drake believed that Admiral Shufeldt's career was a perfect example of the links between "the territorial and continental expansion of the antebellum period and the postwar drive for commercial expansion." See Drake, *Empire of Seas*, xii. See also William N. Still, Jr., *American Seapower in the Old World: The United States Navy in European and Near Eastern Waters, 1865–1917* (Westport, CT, 1980); Stephen Howarth, *To Shining Sea: A History of the United States Navy, 1775–1991* (New York, 1991); Donald A. Yerxa, *Admirals and Empire: The United States Navy and the Caribbean, 1898–1945* (Columbia, SC, 1991); and Mark Russell Shulman, *Navalism and the Emergence of American Sea Power, 1882–1893* (Annapolis, MD, 1995).

Broader and more inclusive definitions of empire also might be helpful to this scholarly endeavor.

Warren Cohen's fine synthesis of American foreign relations in the 1920s and early 1930s is an example of a study that analyzes empire in an imaginative nontraditional way. Cohen used the term empire "to encompass two very different manifestations of American wealth and power." His first category was the traditional one pertaining to "territories controlled directly or indirectly by the government of the United States, including China, where the privileges of empire were shared with other powers through the multilateral imperialism of the treaty system." His second category, which involved the concept of informal empire, was less conventional and, as he admitted, "less than universally accepted." It included "cases in which the principal instruments for the control of other peoples or their resources are private, generally economic, and profit-motivated, in which the role of the U.S. government is secondary or nonexistent." In the practice of informal imperialism, Cohen perceptively observed, "those who are its objects rarely distinguish between the exercise of official and private American power." This observation is particularly important because, as some specialists have pointed out, in the nineteenth century it was private, individual Americans who, more than diplomats and the policymaking elite in Washington, shaped the U.S. role in underdeveloped areas of the world.[67]

Other useful definitions of empire and suggestive investigative approaches to the imperial-colonial relationship have been presented in two recent comparative imperial histories by Philip Darby and Michael W. Doyle. Darby, in his study of British and American activities in Asia and Africa since the 1870s, described imperialism as a process of domination that had "three faces," which he identified as an exercise in power politics, an expression of moral responsibility, and an attempt to secure economic benefit. This analytical framework was predicated on the assumption, also

67   Warren I. Cohen, *Empire without Tears: America's Foreign Relations, 1921–1933* (New York, 1982,) 8–9. See also Emily S. Rosenberg, *Spreading the American Dream: American Economic and Cultural Expansion, 1890–1945* (New York, 1982), 12; and Frederick F. Travis, *George Kennan and the American-Russian Relationship, 1865–1924* (Athens, OH, 1990).

held by other historians, including Gaddis, that imperialism cannot be "comprehended simply in terms of the interests and ideas of the dominant power." Darby also made it clear at the outset that in his discussion imperialism carried "no pejorative implications." This nonjudgmental approach would seem to be a sine qua non of imperial history and one diplomatic historians should take to heart if they are to put to rest the charges of ethnocentrism and provincialism.[68]

In his comparative study of empires Michael Doyle eschewed Darby's emphasis on viewing imperialism as a facet of global power politics. He did, however, stress the two-way exchange between metropole and periphery and the need to understand the weaknesses of the imperial rim along with the motives, ambitions, and strengths of the center. Doyle appeared to be in agreement with Winks when he pointed out that his concept of empire set it "apart from the types of power characteristic of domestic and international politics." Applied judiciously, the Darby and Doyle models offer new perspectives on the study of nineteenth- and early twentieth-century American imperialism.[69]

Cohen, Darby, and Doyle all provide fresh insights on how late nineteenth-century specialists might come to terms with empire and fashion a "new departure" in the study of American imperialism. At present we have not accomplished that, but we have created the outlines of an acceptable synthesis. At the moment, imperial history – studying the process of empire – appears to be the best analytical approach for reinvigorating diplomatic history.[70] It would allow for the meaningful incorporation of women's

68 Phillip Darby, *Three Faces of Imperialism: British and American Approaches to Asia and Africa, 1870–1970* (New Haven, CT, 1987), 1–3. For an insightful and thorough analysis of two competing capitalist imperialisms see Walter LaFeber, *The Clash: U.S.-Japanese Relations throughout History* (New York, 1997).
69 Michael W. Doyle, *Empires* (Ithaca, NY, 1986), 12–13. For a pathbreaking effort at coming to terms with the process of empire see "American Empire, 1898–1903," *Pacific Historical Review* 48 (November 1979): 467–605, which includes articles by Michael H. Hunt, Louis A. Pérez, Jr., Glenn May, Norman G. Owen, and Jorge I. Dominguez. See also Peter W. Stanley, ed., *Reappraising an Empire: New Perspectives on Philippine-American History* (Cambridge, 1984); and Serge Ricard, ed., *An American Empire: Expansionist Culture and Policies, 1881–1917* (Aix-en-Provence, 1990).
70 For two recent innovative explorations of the "process of empire" see Steven Conn, "An Epistemology of Empire: The Philadelphia Commercial Museum, 1893–1926," and Christo-

history and issues of gender into the field. It would also allow for the integration of social history methods into the discipline, particularly in studies of racism and colonialism.[71] Imperial history offers a format for the study of both the center of power, something that diplomatic historians traditionally have done well, and the periphery, an area of flourishing scholarly inquiry that to date has been inadequately integrated into our understanding of late nineteenth-century American foreign relations. To accomplish these goals and to overcome the various criticisms of the field as a languishing intellectual backwater, members of the craft must accept the concept of empire in a nondefensive, noncondemnatory manner. Only then may we begin to come to terms with the reality of American empire.

pher Endy, "Travel and World Power: Americans in Europe, 1890–1917," a Symposium on "Imperial Discourses: Power and Perception," *Diplomatic History* 22 (Fall 1998): 533–63, 565–94.

71   For a recent effort at synthesis that emphasizes racial ideology see Michael H. Hunt, *Ideology and U.S. Foreign Policy* (New Haven, 1987). The pioneering, but largely neglected, study by Willard B. Gatewood, Jr., *Black Americans and the White Man's Burden, 1898–1903* (Urbana, 1975), should also be consulted; as should Nell Irvin Painter, *Standing at Armageddon: The United States, 1877–1919* (New York, 1987); and Rydell, *All the World's a Fair*. For the racial outlook of the elite and the dominant white majority see Reginald Horsman, *Race and Manifest Destiny: The Origins of American Racial Anglo-Saxonism* (Cambridge, MA, 1981); and Stuart Anderson, *Race and Rapprochement: Anglo-Saxonism and Anglo-American Relations, 1895–1904* (Rutherford, NJ, 1981). Glenn A. May, *Social Engineering in the Philippines: The Aims, Execution, and Impact of American Colonial Policy, 1900–1913* (Westport, CT, 1980), demonstrates the continuity from continental to insular empire by revealing that educational policy for blacks and Indians at Hampton and Tuskegee institutes served as a model for the program designed for the Philippines.

5

Symbiosis versus Hegemony: New Directions in the Foreign Relations Historiography of Theodore Roosevelt and William Howard Taft

RICHARD H. COLLIN

Although this may not be a golden era in the historiography of Theodore Roosevelt and William Howard Taft, the field is active, the pot is simmering, and the possibility exists that a new paradigm might emerge. John Lewis Gaddis has recently judged William Appleman Williams's economics-oriented "Open Door" thesis to be the "dominant interpretive paradigm in American diplomatic history."[1] And while Gaddis might be correct in assessing the entire field of diplomatic history, a somewhat similar paradigm – what I will call the hegemony paradigm – has emerged as the consensus model in the literature on Roosevelt and Taft. The hegemony paradigm originated in the traditional emphasis on Roosevelt's "big stick" diplomacy. William Harbaugh modified it by integrating the idea of responsibility with Roosevelt's exercise of power. And David Healy used it in his recently published synthesis of Roosevelt's diplomacy.[2]

1   John Lewis Gaddis, "New Conceptual Approaches to the Study of American Foreign Relations: Interdisciplinary Perspectives," *Diplomatic History* 14 (Summer 1990): 407.
2   William H. Harbaugh, *Power and Responsibility: The Life and Times of Theodore Roosevelt* (New York, 1961); Thomas McCormick, "'Every System Needs a Center Sometimes': An Essay on Hegemony and Modern American Foreign Policy," in *Redefining the Past: Essays in Diplomatic History in Honor of William Appleman Williams*, ed. Lloyd C. Gardner (Corvallis, OR, 1986), 195–220; and idem, "World Systems," *Journal of American History* 77 (June 1990): 125–32; David Healy, *Drive to Hegemony: The United States in the Caribbean, 1898–1917* (Madison, WI, 1988). For a recent elaboration of the Open Door thesis, see Walter LaFeber, *The Cambridge History of American Foreign Relations*, vol. 2, *The American Search for Opportunity, 1865–1913* (New York, 1993).

The hegemony paradigm has identifiable weaknesses and deserves to be replaced by another concept, which I call "symbiosis," that is far more useful. Many scholars who use the hegemony paradigm recognize the importance of cultural relations between peoples, but they generally emphasize struggles among the great nations or between imperial powers and weaker ones. The symbiosis paradigm, by contrast, emphasizes cultural interaction and thus eliminates one of the shortcomings in the hegemony approach; in addition, it is well-suited to diplomatic historians who are sensitive to international approaches, allowing them to consider the international context of crisis and the great global changes that confronted both Roosevelt and Taft.³ Recent works by Michael Hunt and Warren Cohen on U.S.-Asian relations and my own studies of the Caribbean follow the symbiosis paradigm, which other scholars should also consider as a model for understanding Roosevelt's diplomacy.⁴

David Healy's *Drive to Hegemony: The United States in the Caribbean, 1898–1917* (1988), marks the high point of the hegemonic framework. Healy's book spans the years from the Spanish-American War to U.S. entry into World War I with such balance and nuance that reviewers as disparate as David Pletcher, Louis A. Pérez, and Robert Freeman Smith lavishly praised the work. In every phase of U.S.-Caribbean relations Healy summarizes, synthesizes, and balances the extremes. He treats the United Fruit Company with rare nuance, for example, and deftly assesses dependency theory while also noting its flaws.⁵ The United States,

---

3 Sally Marks, "The World According to Washington," *Diplomatic History* 11 (Summer 1987): 265–82; Michael H. Hunt, "Internationalizing U.S. Diplomatic History: A Practical Agenda," ibid. 15 (Winter 1991): 1–11.

4 Richard H. Collin, *Theodore Roosevelt, Culture, Diplomacy, and Expansion: A New View of American Imperialism* (Baton Rouge, LA, 1985); and idem, *Theodore Roosevelt's Caribbean: The Panama Canal, the Monroe Doctrine, and the Latin American Context* (Baton Rouge, 1990); Michael H. Hunt, *The Making of a Special Relationship: The United States and China to 1914* (New York, 1983); Warren I. Cohen, *East Asian Art and American Culture: A Study in International Relations* (New York, 1992). Japanese architect Kisko Kurokawa, *The Philosophy of Symbiosis* (London, 1994), uses a similar conept to explain modern architecture, which I discovered after my article was published. I am indebted to la librarie, Musée National d'Art Moderne – Centre National d'Art et de Culture Georges Pompidou, Paris for bringing it to my attention.

5 Some of the recent relevant literature includes Thomas F. O'Brien, "Dependency Revisited: A Review Essay," *Business History Review* 59 (Winter 1985): 663–69; William Glade,

he says, never thought of itself as hegemonic when it intervened in Cuba, compromised its control with the Platt Amendment protectorate, and then in 1906 intervened again, reluctantly, because the Cubans had refused to govern themselves. By 1917, however, it had become a hegemon in the Caribbean, and its hegemony "was the product of a remarkably consistent effort which ran uninterrupted from the administration of William McKinley through that of Woodrow Wilson."[6]

David Pletcher takes issue with the word "drive" in Healy's title and with his assumption of a united U.S. effort. According to Pletcher, "Healy gives the impression that the Roosevelt Corollary was planned, part of the 'drive,' whereas it was clearly in large part a reaction to foreign and domestic circumstances as they arose." Pletcher links Healy's unity of purpose with the writings of the New Left, which in turn rely "too heavily on the facile writings of jingoes." Instead of a consistent policy, Pletcher sees an ad hoc accretion of reactions to immediate crises that drew the United States "in deeper and deeper" and "created a sense of responsibility, which spread to the Dominican Republic via Venezuela and fostered a desire for some permanent, automatic mechanism of adjustment, and so forth."[7]

Robert Freeman Smith notes the other basic weakness of Healy's hegemony, one that the author himself gracefully recognizes. "A true picture of the interaction of United States hegemony and Caribbean nationalism is difficult to construct," Healy admits, "for the relationship was shifting and complex."[8] He is right that hegemony happened, and he notes the contributing factors: U.S.

"Latin America and the International Economy, 1870–1914," in *The Cambridge History of Latin America*, ed. Leslie Bethell (Cambridge, England), 1986, 4:46–56; Robert A. Packenham, *The Dependency Movement: Scholarship and Politics in Development Studies* (Cambridge, MA, 1992). Brian McKercher, "Reaching for the Brass Ring: The Recent Historiography of Interwar American Foreign Relations," in this volume, cites Canada as the best example of dependency. For a provocative reconceptualization of the question, see Immanuel Wallerstein, "Braudel on Capitalism, or Everything Upside Down," *Journal of Modern History* 63 (June 1991): 354–61.

6 Healy, *Drive to Hegemony*, 288

7 David M. Pletcher, "Caribbean 'Empire,' Planned and Improvised," *Diplomatic History* 14 (Summer 1990): 447–60.

8 Robert Freeman Smith, review of Healy, *Drive to Hegemony*, in *American Historical Review* 95 (October 1990): 1300.

fear of German intentions; Caribbean fear of Germany and other European interests; Caribbean desire for technological and financial help; divisions in the Caribbean between factions that pushed for outright annexation, Plattish protectorates, or complete independence; Europe's other priorities; U.S. confidence in its political and moral superiority; and the growth of Yankee enterprise. But the large number and the very complexity of these factors makes it difficult for the historian to paint a "true picture" of U.S.-Caribbean relations.

Pletcher worried that Healy's book was so well done that it would become the last word. In a sense Pletcher's concern was well grounded, but only, I think, because Healy's work has extended the framework of hegemony as far as it can go. It explains a great many of the changes that transformed the Caribbean into an American "empire without colonies," as Lester Langley put it. But there is still much to do; and it can only be done, I believe, by going beyond Healy's synthesis, beyond his overly determinist interpretation of empire, and beyond the concept of hegemony, with its emphasis on economic, strategic, and military factors, to what I call symbiosis.

José Martí offers some clues as to why symbiosis can explain what *hegemony* does not try to. In the 1880s, Martí made his cultural peace with the United States by introducing literate Latin Americans to the varied joys of American life: baseball, Jesse James, Buffalo Bill, Roscoe Conkling, Ulysses S. Grant, and even Fourth of July celebrations. But by 1889, Marti had become deeply concerned by James G. Blaine's Pan-Americanism, which he regarded as a thinly veiled effort at U.S. economic domination, and he began to attack "the other America," his term for the United States. As an adversary in exile "inside the monster," Martí, in this second and better known phase, may well have been the founding father of the dependency protest movement.[9]

Latin America was proud to share with the United States its republican ideals, its revolutionary split with European monarchy, its geographic distance from Europe, and its sense of unique-

9   See José Martí, *Inside the Monster: Writings on the United States and American Imperialism*, ed. Philip S. Foner, trans. Elinor Randall (New York, 1975).

ness. The relationship, as Michael Coniff observes, was in this sense naturally symbiotic.[10] Latin and North America were neighbors with some things in common. But by 1900, with the natural ties to Spain ending and with growing doubts about the midnineteenth-century alliance with French positivism and European-inspired liberalism, Uruguayan intellectual José Rodó felt the need to warn Latin American youth against emulating the North American culture of materialism. The Latin American symbiotic ambivalence is best expressed by Nicaraguan poet Rubén Darío, who wavered between fear of Theodore Roosevelt and immense admiration for the Protestant warrior-intellectual.[11]

Economics, strategy, and power explain much of the U.S.- Latin American relationship, but the explanation is incomplete and unsatisfying without some emphasis on the cultural dimension. Even that dimension, moreover, can be distorted, though not always by design. One can make Walt Disney's capture of the Latin American imagination a form of cultural imperialism, though I prefer to see it as a worldwide cultural Gresham's law in which a simplistic youth culture, like fast food, has international appeal.[12] It is impossible to dismiss the Caribbean love of baseball as the result of some Yankee plot. Like hegemony, Caribbean baseball happened without conscious design.[13] And like the idea of Republicanism and the Latin American reverence for American writers such as Walt Whitman and Ralph Waldo Emerson, the Latin American love of baseball is an example of cultural symbiosis. To be sure, not all symbiosis is as positive as baseball and poetry. Friction, too, is part of the symbiotic relationship between all odd

10   Michael L. Conniff, *Panama and the United States: The Forced Alliance* (Athens, GA, 1992).
11   Rubén Darío, *Selected Poems*, ed. and trans. Lysander Kemp (Austin, TX, 1965); José Enrique Rodó, *Ariel*, trans. Margaret Sayers Peden (Austin, TX, 1988).
12   Ariel Dorfman and Armand Mattleart, *How to Read Donald Duck: Imperialist Ideology in the Disney Comic*, ed. and trans. David Kunzle (New York, 1975); Dorfman, *The Empire's Old Clothes: What the Lone Ranger, Babar, and Other Innocent Heroes Do to Our Minds* (New York, 1983).
13   Alan M. Klein, *Sugarball: The American Game, the Dominican Dream* (New Haven, CT, 1991); Bob Ruck, *The Tropic of Baseball: Baseball in the Dominican Republic* (Westport, CT, 1991).

couples, including Protestant North America and Catholic Latin America.[14]

Panama Canal historiography may offer the best example of a new approach using symbiosis to revise the hegemonic interpretation. Until Frederick Marks's *Velvet on Iron* and my own recent work on Roosevelt, this historiography was almost universally condemnatory.[15] Even sympathetic Roosevelt historians such as Mowry, Harbaugh, and McCullough railed against the president. Allen Nevins in 1940 compared him to Hitler.[16] Joseph Arbena explains why blaming Roosevelt rather than the United States may have assuaged Colombian anger and wounded pride.[17] Popular imagery, including the image of Roosevelt wielding his big stick, encouraged this view, as did Roosevelt himself, who used his Panama diplomacy as a symbol of presidential strength, an emblem of the new American internationalism, and a way to win renomination and reelection in 1908.[18]

The big stick thus became the perfect hegemonic symbol. In the standard interpretation, Roosevelt and the United States wanted a canal, Colombia objected to giving up its rights in Panama, and so Roosevelt either encouraged or fomented a "revolution" in Panama, which then became "free" to negotiate its own canal treaty with the United States. The result gave the United States what it wanted, left Panama in a state of permanent dependency

14 See Fredrick B. Pike, *The United States and Latin America: Myths and Stereotypes of Civilization and Nature* (Austin, TX, 1992), an unusual comparative cultural history written by a Latin Americanist. Elizabeth A. Cobbs, "Why They Think Like Gringos: The Discourse of U.S.-Latin American Relations," *Diplomatic History* 21 (Spring 1997): 307–16, examines the persistence of myths and stereotypes.
15 Frederick W. Marks III, *Velvet on Iron: The Diplomacy of Theodore Roosevelt* (Lincoln, NE, 1979); idem, "Morality as a Drive Wheel in the Diplomacy of Theodore Roosevelt," *Diplomatic History* 2 (Winter 1978): 43–62.
16 Allan Nevins, Introduction to Dwight C. Miner, *The Fight for the Panama Route: The Story of the Spooner Act and the Hay-Herran Treaty* (New York, 1940); Nevins's apparent hatred of Theodore Roosevelt is documented in Richard Cleveland Baker, *The Tariff Under Roosevelt and Taft* (Hastings, NE, 1941).
17 Joseph L. Arbena, "The Image of an American Imperialist: Colombian Views of Theodore Roosevelt," *West Georgia College Studies in the Social Sciences* 6 (June 1967): 3–20.
18 See Frederick W. Marks III, "Theodore Roosevelt and the Righting of History," *Theodore Roosevelt Association Journal* 12 (Winter 1986): 8–12; Gary Pearle and Mel Marvin, *Tintypes*, original Broadway musical production, Richard Crinkley (American National Theater and Academy and ABC-TV, 1982); and Albert Shaw, *A Cartoon History of Roosevelt's Career* (New York, 1910).

as an American protectorate, and made Colombia an example of what happens to a small Latin American nation that tangles with the Colossus to the North.

My symbiosis framework leads to a radically different reading of events. I argue that the conflict was cultural and that it centered on Colombia's President José Marroquín, a shrewd religious ideologue who resisted Liberals and the kind of developmental capitalism that a Panama Canal represented.[19] The War of the Thousand Days devastated Colombia and was the main cause of the dissolution of the *menage à trois* that had defined the U.S.-Colombian-Panamanian relationship since the Bidlack-Mallarino Treaty of 1848. When Roosevelt concluded that Marroquín had reneged on a canal agreement in return for U.S. intervention to save Panama and end the civil war, he threw his support behind Panama's separatists and behind the Frenchman Philippe Bunau-Varilla, whose actions as a revolutionary provocateur and a principal in the Hay-Bunau-Varilla Treaty symbolized the "crime of Panama."[20]

But a symbiotic "no-fault" historiography also recognizes that popular anger over the loss of Panama may have helped the Colombians to focus on their real problems. Panama was a colony of Colombia before 1903 and a dependent of the United States afterward. The narrow isthmus defined Panama's subsidiary role, whether it was to a European, Latin American, or North American protectorate.[21] The United States under Roosevelt built a canal that was a technological triumph and an international advance in civilization, as the Saint-Simonians who promoted canals would have wished.[22] The moralistic emphasis may be a

19   Richard H. Collin, "The Big Stick as Weltpolitik: Europe and Latin America in Theodore Roosevelt's Foreign Policy," in *Theodore Roosevelt: Many-Sided American*, ed. Natalie A. Naylor, Douglas Brinkley, and John Allen Gable (Interlaken, NY, 1992), 296–316.
20   Gustave Anguizola, *Philippe Bunau-Varilla: The Man behind the Panama Canal* (Chicago, 1980).
21   Walter LaFeber, *The Panama Canal: The Crisis in Historical Perspective*, rev. ed. (New York, 1989), is especially strong on prerevolutionary Panamanian separatism.
22   See *Henri Saint-Simon, 1760–1825: Selected Writings on Science, Industry, and Social Organisation*, trans. and ed. Keith Taylor (London, 1975), for a summary of Saint-Simon's "improvement of civilization" belief, which influenced French canal building and contributed to Theodore Roosevelt's rationale for the Panama Canal's urgency.

cause of some of the caricature that Waldo Heinrichs notes, but James Vivian shows that Roosevelt's aggressive diction may have been misquoted and misunderstood in 1911: If he was attacking anybody, it was the U.S. Congress, not Colombia. John Major's revelation that John Hay, not Philippe Bunau-Varilla, was behind the dreadful Hay-Bunau-Varilla Treaty is not really surprising. John T. Morgan was a fearsome adversary, and U.S. domestic and partisan party politics consistently complicated foreign policy.[23]

Richard Lael may find it incredible that Marks and I refuse to denounce American diplomacy as arrogant, but his views may have more in common with ours than he thinks. I agree that U.S.-Colombian relations made for shrill exchanges, but the problems of Panama for both sides were difficult and fundamental. Lael's own book provides the best evidence of American attempts to heal the discord, and the arrogance worked both ways.[24] Even Colombians regarded Marroquín as arrogant, and it is impossible to deal reasonably with nations in the midst of a revolution. Lael's approach reveals one of the difficulties of using a hegemonic framework – an overemphasis on two nations in diplomatic conflict. In Charles Bergquist's excellent history of Colombia's problems, the United States enters only occasionally and often peripherally.[25] Roosevelt wanted to build a canal with as little diplomatic and political fuss as possible. When Colombian politics precluded an easy solution, the United States moved to Panama as a second choice, rejecting a Nicaraguan alternative that would have left a partly built canal as a temptation to European competitors and also led to a further Balkanization of Latin America. The old moralistic Panama Canal historiography is one of the many ghosts that my symbiotic framework can diminish, if not replace.

23   Waldo Heinrichs, "The Panama Canal in History, Policy, and Caricature," *Latin American Research Review* 17:2 (1982): 247–61; James F. Vivian, "The 'Taking' of the Panama Canal Zone: Myth and Reality," *Diplomatic History* 4 (Winter 1984): 95–100; John Major, "Who Wrote the Hay-Bunau-Varilla Convention?" ibid 8 (Spring 1984): 115–23: Joseph A. Fry, *John Tyler Morgan and the Search for Southern Autonomy* (Knoxville, TN, 1992).
24   Richard L. Lael, *Arrogant Diplomacy: U.S. Policy toward Colombia, 1903–1922* (Wilmington, DE, 1987).
25   Charles Bergquist, *Coffee and Conflict in Colombia, 1886–1910* (Durham, NC, 1978).

The religious character of the conflicts between the United States and Spain and of the subsequent conflicts in Latin America and the Philippines have been largely overlooked in the hegemonic historiography. But the sense of Latin American crisis in Rodó and Darío's writing and in Marroquín's fears reflects a culture in which church and state were indissoluble. The U.S. effort as a Protestant nation to protect the Catholic majority in the Philippines from a militant Muslim minority was perhaps naive progressive paternalism, but it was driven by more than simply economic or strategic expansionism. David Alvarez's important article puts the religious conflict at the center.[26] He is right that American colonial policy was a "combination of altruism, paternalism, and national interest." He shows Roosevelt and Taft trying, with some sensitivity, to replace a Catholic state with a disestablished civil government. Alvarez's attention to the Vatican-American negotiations, to Filipino anticlericalism, and to the legacy of the corrupt Spanish friars underscores the substantial recent changes in Philippine-American historiography, which is now more concerned with interaction than with a one-sided search for empire.

Stuart Creighton Miller's *Benevolent Assimilation* uses William McKinley's phrase with ironic disapproval; yet this highly critical account of U.S. involvement blames inept or willful acts by American military leaders on the scene, not a larger policy of empire.[27] On the Philippine side, Glenn May finds a localized rather than a mass-based ideological revolution with enormous differences among provinces and even in neighborhoods. Clymer's American Protestant missionaries were as atomized and divided as the Filipino revolutionaries.[28] Latin American fears of U.S. religious intolerance were not justified, but, as Schoonover and Coniff show, American racial insularity effectively maintained a

26 David Alvarez, "Purely a Business Matter: The Taft Mission to the Vatican," *Diplomatic History* 16 (Summer 1992): 357–69.
27 Stuart Creighton Miller, *Benevolent Assimilation: The American Conquest of the Philippines, 1899–1903* (New Haven, CT, 1982).
28 Glenn Anthony May, *The Battle for Batangas: A Philippine Province at War* (New Haven, CT, 1991); Kenton J. Clymer, *Protestant Missionaries in the Philippines, 1898–1916: An Inquiry into the American Colonial Mentality* (Urbana, IL, 1986).

colonial underclass.[29] Thomas Dyer's nuanced study of Roosevelt's neo-Lamarckianism demonstrates the complexity of American racial attitudes even among the highly educated.[30]

Cuba, with its abundance of economic, religious, and racial issues, is an ideal subject for the symbiosis framework. At present there is a frequently fierce dispute in the historiography between Latin Americanists, who see Cuba as the victim, and North Americanists, who do not. According to Jack Lane, however, the time has come

for a new approach to North America-South American relations, one that sees the Latin American people as not only responsible but also accountable for their own destiny, for their mistakes as well as their achievements, and not just as begrudging recipients of American largess or helpless victims of American hegemony.[31]

Much the same could be said of our approach to U.S.-Cuban relations, where the basic assumptions of the hegemonic school, as represented by Louis A. Pérez, hold that neither Germany nor Britain ever seriously threatened Cuba's new independence, that Cuba was capable of self-government, and that U.S. interest in Cuba was primarily economic. Unfortunately, as Marks notes, much of Pérez's own evidence contradicts these assumptions.[32]

Although the evidence for U.S. economic hegemony may be further modified by new historiography on sugar production and marketing, especially the literature that emerged from the Third World Economic History Group's Edinburgh conference in September 1982, there are already indications that Perez himself has modified his thinking.[33] In *Cuba and the United States: Ties of*

---

29   Thomas D. Schoonover, *The United States in Central America 1860–1911: Episodes of Social Imperialism and Imperial Rivalry in the World System* (Durham, NC, 1991); Michael L. Conniff, *Black Labor on a White Canal: Panama, 1904–1981* (Pittsburgh, PA, 1985).

30   Thomas G. Dyer, *Theodore Roosevelt and the Idea of Race* (Baton Rouge, LA, 1980).

31   Jack Lane, review of Jules R. Benjamin, *The United States and the Origins of the Cuban Revolution: An Empire of Liberty in an Age of National Liberation* (Princeton, NJ, 1990), in *Journal of American History* 77 (March 1991): 1386.

32   Frederick W. Marks III, review of Louis A. Pérez, Jr., *Cuba under the Platt Amendment, 1902–1934* (Pittsburgh, PA, 1986), in *Journal of American History* 74 (September 1987): 541–42.

33   Bill Albert and Adrian Graves, *Crisis and Change in the International Sugar Economy,*

Singular Intimacy, Pérez acknowledges that the Platt Amendment, imperfect though it was, "kept the *independenista* vision alive." Cubans learned how to manipulate the Americans and most of "the issues that had so concerned North Americans during the nineteenth century were adequately satisfied through the Platt Amendment early in the twentieth."[34] This represents a substantial softening of Pérez's opposition to Platt and perhaps a shift from outright hegemony to some form of symbiosis.

Pérez's contention that American capital flooded into the vacuum left by the removal of Spain is undisputable. But what other options were possible? Cuba had no investment capital of its own. It had to rely on foreign investment, which is not inherently hegemonic and which can be mutually beneficial. Rondo Cameron, discussing French colonial investment, may help us to understand the problem with U.S. investment in Cuba:

Capital is a necessity but not a sufficient condition for economic development. In the case of imported capital or foreign borrowing, it is important chiefly as a vehicle for the transmission of technology and entrepreneurial abilities that are prepared politically and socially for development. When capital went abroad unaccompanied by French entrepreneurs or technical personnel, as was the case with the majority of government loans, it frequently made no positive contribution whatever.[35]

If this was also the problem with U.S. investment in Cuba, who are we to blame? President Roosevelt was struggling to control railroads and monopoly in the United States and investors were not normally endowed with social conscience. Pérez is right on the effect of untrammeled foreign investment in Cuba, but

1860–1914 (Norwich and Edinburgh, 1984); Daniel Catlin, Jr., *Good Work Well Done: The Sugar Business Career of Horace Havemeyer, 1903–1956* (New York, privately printed, 1988), 1–59; J. H. Galloway, *The Sugar Cane Industry: An Historical Geography from Its Origins to 1914* (New York, 1989). See also John Alfred Heitmann, *The Modernization of the Louisiana Sugar Industry, 1830–1910* (Baton Rouge, LA, 1987); Lippert S. Ellis, *The Tariff on Sugar* (Freeport, IL, 1933); and William Arthur Lewis, "International Competition in Manufacturers," *American Economic Review* 47 (May 1957): 578–609.

34   Louis A. Pérez, Jr., *Cuba and the United States: Ties of Singular Intimacy* (Athens, GA, 1990).

35   Rondo E. Cameron, *France and the Economic Development of Europe, 1800–1914: Conquests of Peace and Seeds of War* (Princeton, NJ, 1961), esp. 507.

the cause was not hegemonic design by the United States. Both the Platt Amendment and the acquisition of a naval base at Guantánamo were conceived as compromises to safeguard U.S. interests from European encroachments.[36] The confluence of American investors eager to compete favorably with Europe in a new and nearby market and a Cuba newly liberated from a precapitalist colonial dependency on Spain is an example of a symbiotic relationship between two nations of vastly unequal size and wealth.

In my first book on Roosevelt, I argued that culture preceded diplomacy and that American cultural expansion was already well developed before diplomacy followed during and after the Spanish-American War.[37] Culture, however, is a broad and amorphous term with too many meanings, so let me use the more specific "imaginative culture," and place it at the center of the symbiosis paradigm. Imaginative culture complements and further focuses the culture and ideology concepts that Akira Iriye and Michael Hunt have urged diplomatic historians to explore in writing a more cosmopolitan and international history.[38] Indeed, cultural foreign relations offers an interactive goldmine for diplomatic historians and art historians, who rarely use each other's extensive research.

Fortunately, Robert M. Crunden's *American Salons: Encounters with European Modernism, 1885–1917* is an accessible guide to the cultural foreign relations that moved the United States from provincialism through cosmopolitanism and eventually to its role

36 Bradley M. Reynolds, "Guantánamo Bay, Cuba: The History of an American Naval Base and Its Relationship to the Formulation of United States Foreign Policy and Military Strategy Toward the Caribbean" (Ph.D. diss., University of Southern California, 1982). For a useful coinage of Roosevelt as an "Atlanticist," see Priscilla Roberts, "The Anglo-American Theme: American Visions of an Atlantic Alliance, 1914–1933," *Diplomatic History* 21 (Summer 1997): 333–34.

37 Collin, *Theodore Roosevelt, Culture, Diplomacy, and Expansion.*

38 Akira Iriye, "The Internationalization of History," *American Historical Review* 94 (February 1989): 1–10; idem, "Intercultural Relations," in *Encyclopedia of American Foreign Policy*, ed. Alexander DeConde (New York, 1978), 2:428–42; idem, "Culture," *Journal of American History* 77 (June 1990): 99–107; Michael H. Hunt, *Ideology and U.S. Foreign Policy* (New Haven, CT, 1987); idem, "Internationalizing U.S. Diplomatic History," *Diplomatic History* 15 (Spring 1991): 1–12; Hunt, "Ideology," *Journal of American History* 77 (June 1990): 108–15.

as the twentieth century's cultural leader and the successor to nine-teenth-century France.[39] The Quai d'Orsay in 1907 recognized modernist changes by establishing a cultural department to deal with the new world of Fauve painting, Bergson's time, Einstein's relativity, and Proust's prose.[40] Europeans took art diplomacy seriously, with the German government, for example, seriously debating which art would best represent it at the 1904 Louisiana Exposition World's Fair in St. Louis.[41]

Crunden's method of using biographical sketches to locate the major modernists in their original American places of birth makes the modernist transformation more comprehensible as well as more dramatic. Similarly, Steven Watson centers his study of the avant-garde in active urban centers.[42] By the time of Roosevelt's presi-dency, the U.S. cultural establishment was so entrenched in parts of Europe and Asia that Americans were leaders in patronage, collection, scholarship, and innovation. So many American art-ists took advantage of the French government's encouragement of contemporary art and art teaching that in the 1889 Exposition Universelle in Paris only French artists exceeded the number of equally academic Americans displaying and winning prizes.[43] Gertrude and Leo Stein from Baltimore were among Picasso's and Matisse's earliest advocates, and Americans also supported Cézanne before most French collectors would.[44]

---

39   Robert M. Crunden, *American Salons: Encounters with European Modernism, 1885–1917* (New York, 1993).
40   Paul Gordon Lauren, *Diplomats and Bureaucrats: The First Institutional Responses to Twentieth Century Diplomacy in France and Germany* (Stanford, 1976), esp. 34–44. See also Linda Henderson, *The Fourth Dimension and Non-Euclidian Geometry in Modern Art* (Princeton, NJ, 1983); Stephen Kern, *The Culture of Time and Space, 1880–1918* (Cambridge, MA, 1983); James D. Herbert, *Fauve Painting: The Making of Cultural Politics* (New Haven, 1992); and Judi Freeman, *The Fauve Landscape* (New York, 1990).
41   Peter Paret, *The Berlin Secession: Modernism and Its Enemies in Imperial Germany* (Cambridge, MA, 1980).
42   Steven Watson, *Strange Bedfellows: The First American Avant-Garde* (New York, 1991).
43   Annette Blaugrund, *Paris 1889: American Artists at the Universal Exposition* (New York, 1989); H. Barbara Weinberg, *The Lure of Paris: Nineteenth-Century American Painters and Their French Teachers* (New York, 1990); Lois Marie Fink, *American Art at the Nineteenth Century Paris Salons* (Cambridge, Eng., 1990); David Sellin and James K. Ballinger, *Americans in Brittany and Normandy, 1860–1910* (Phoenix, AZ, 1982).
44   Brenda Richardson, *Dr. Claribel and Miss Etta: The Cone Collection of the Baltimore Museum of Art* (Baltimore, MD, 1985); John Richardson, *A Life of Picasso*, vol. 1, *1881–1906* (New York, 1991); John Rewald, *Cézanne and America: Dealers, Collectors, Artists,*

In London, Americans Henry James, James Whistler, John Singer Sargent, and Ezra Pound were cultural leaders. Edith Wharton in her writings and travels linked the expatriates.[45] Bernard Berenson became the world's authority on Italian Renaissance art, took up residence outside Florence, and supplied Italian primitive art to American museum founders such as Isabella Stewart Gardner.[46] Boston biologist Edward Morse became the leading connoisseur of Japanese ceramics, Charles Freer a collector of Korean and Japanese art and of James Whistler, the leading American exponent of the influential *Japoniste* style. Freer's proposed gift to the Smithsonian involved Roosevelt in the art diplomacy that gave the United States its first national art museum, the Freer Gallery, with its preponderance of Asian art.[47] J. P. Morgan, also interested in the kind of cultural patrimony that Freer began, bought so many works of art that Europe began to impose export restrictions to prevent Americans from taking all the best works.[48]

Cultural and diplomatic history are congenial, and younger scholars will find a treasure trove of unexplored interrelations.

and Critics, 1891–1921 (Princeton, NJ, 1989); Frances Weitzenhoffer, *The Havemeyers: Impressionism Comes to America* (New York, 1986); Alice Cooney Frelinghuysen et al., *Splendid Legacy: The Havemeyer Collection* (New York, 1993).

45   R. W. B. Lewis, *The Jameses: A Family Narrative* (New York, 1991); R. W. B. Lewis and Nancy Lewis, eds. *The Letters of Edith Wharton* (New York, 1988); Stanley Olson, *John Singer Sargent: His Portrait* (New York, 1986).

46   Ernest Samuels, *Bernard Berenson: The Making of a Legend* (Cambridge, MA, 1987); Rollin Van N. Hadley, ed., *The Letters of Bernard Berenson and Isabella Stewart Gardner, 1887–1924* (Boston, MA, 1987); William L. Vance, *America's Rome: Classical, Catholic, Contemporary* (New Haven, CT, 1989); David Alan Brown, *Raphael in America* (Washington, 1983).

47   Robert Rosenstone, *Mirror in the Shrine: American Encounters with Meiji Japan* (Cambridge, MA, 1988); Cohen, *East Asian Art and American Culture*; Julia Meech and Gabriel Weisberg, *Japonisme Comes to America: The Japanese Impact on the Graphic Arts, 1876–1925* (New York, 1990); Guimet Museum, *Japon, la Tentation de L'Occident, 1868–1912* (Paris, 1988); Denys Sutton, ed., "Charles Lang Freer as a Connoisseur," *Apollo* 83, (August 1983); Thomas Lawton and Linda Merrill, *Freer: A Legacy of Art* (New York, 1993).

48   Linda Horowitz Roth, ed., *J. Pierpont Morgan, Collector: European Decorative Arts from the Wadsworth Atheneum* (Hartford, CT, 1987); Louis Auchincloss, *J. P. Morgan: The Financier as Collector* (New York, 1990). Richard H. Collin, "Art Tariffs, Old Masters, and Modern Art in Turn-of-the-Century America" (Paper presented to the Southern Historical Association, Atlanta, November 1992); and "American and French Art Diplomacy, 1890–1929" (Paper presented to the American Association of Teachers of French, San Diego, July 1993), are early versions of parts of my books in progress on the American art tariff and the making of an American cultural patrimony.

Lt. William Sims, who led the American naval intelligence operations against Spain from Paris in 1898, stayed on to supervise the
installation of American art at the 1900 Paris World's Fair. Sims
left extensive records of his European activities in the Library of
Congress and National Archives. Indeed, this was a golden age
of national expositions and world's fairs, as Robert Rydell and Jo
Ann Thompson have noted, and both John Findling and the
Smithsonian Institution have given us wonderful reference guides
to sources on the world's fair movement in less-crowded pre-Cold
War archives.[49]

Edward Crapol is encouraged by the trend to a less moralistic
historiography of imperialism. His essay summarizes the change
characterized by Philip Darby's *Three Faces of Imperialism* toward a holistic, nonpejorative examination that recognizes the
primacy of moral responsibility over strategic and economic considerations. Darby reflects the symbiotic rather than the hegemonic understanding of expansion, the same understanding that
is evident in my own work on Roosevelt and in Tony Smith's
work on imperialism.[50] Both works have provoked a skeptical
and heated response but both approach Roosevelt-era expansionism as Darby approaches British imperialism.[51] Emily Rosenberg
summarized this approach in her review of Darby's book. Between 1870 and 1914, she writes

power politics most frequently guided British policymakers, who were
preoccupied with the intricate jockeying for national advantage. Eco-

---

49   Robert W. Rydell, *All the World's a Fair: Visions of Empire at American International
Expositions, 1876–1916* (Chicago, 1984); JoAnn Marie Thompson, "The Art and Architecture of the Pan American Exposition, Buffalo, New York, 1901" (Ph.D. diss., Rutgers University, 1980); John E. Findling and Kimberly D. Pelle, eds., *Historical Dictionary of World's
Fairs and Expositions, 1851–1988* (New York, 1990); Smithsonian Institution, *The Books of
the Fairs: Materials about World's Fairs, 1834–1916, in the Smithsonian Institution Libraries*
(Chicago, 1992).
50   Edward P. Crapol, "Coming to Terms with Empire: The Historiography of Late Nineteenth-Century American Foreign Relations," *Diplomatic History* 16 (Fall 1992), 573–97;
Philip Darby, *Three Faces of Imperialism: British and American Approaches to Asia and
Africa, 1870–1970* (New Haven, CT, 1987).
51   Tony Smith, *The Pattern of Imperialism: The United States, Great Britain, and the Late-
Industrializing World since 1815* (New York, 1981), esp. 185; Collin, *Theodore Roosevelt,
Culture, Expansion, and Diplomacy.*

nomic advantage was sometimes assumed, but so little was known of peripheral areas that policymakers seldom thought systematically or calculatedly about the economics of empire. Moral responsibility for foreign lands also figured as an imperial rationale. Moralistic sentiments figured as public manifestations of the many private anxieties of the age and they certainly were ethnocentric, but they were nonetheless sincere, framed within prevailing beliefs about racial hierarchy, inevitable progress, and the sanctity of work and "duty."[52]

Michael Doyle, again reflecting on British colonies, even argues that national independence required a "mobilized, potential citizenry" that was often not present at the time of colonization. Indeed, "one of the greatest unintended gifts a metropole could give its periphery," he concludes, "was the refusal to grant 'easy' independence. Too easy an independence can set up peripheral conditions for neo-imperial rule."[53]

Crapol's hope that the new imperial history will invite new approaches to the study of American diplomacy is perfectly compatible with the symbiosis framework. The most substantial disagreements in Roosevelt era historiography center not on Africa and Asia, which the new imperial history examines, but on Latin America and Central America, where the memory of the big stick and the record of U.S. interventions has created a sense – and even a historiography – of victimization and martyrdom.[54] There is a consensus that the United States was paternalistic and frequently insensitive, and it is this Protestant sense of smug moral superiority that grates on the Latin American mind, the way the Monroe Doctrine enraged Metternich in 1823. Latin America was not North America, nor was it Europe, and Roosevelt's assurances to Europe that he would protect the world against "chronic wrongdoing" in poor Latin America, assurances he gave while he was using Bunau-Varilla as an agent provocateur in Panama's revolution, account for the unwillingness of most Latin

---

52 Emily S. Rosenberg, "'The Empire' Strikes Back," *Reviews in American History* 16 (December 1988): 585–90.
53 Michael W. Doyle, *Empires* (Ithaca, 1986), esp. 371–72.
54 J. Michael Hogan, *The Panama Canal in American Politics: Domestic Advocacy and the Evolultion of Policy* (Carbondale, IL, 1986).

Americanists to excuse the "crime of Panama," regardless of its beneficial or defensible consequences.

The Latin American resistance – particularly intellectual and cultural resistance – to any foreign domination is a reflection of the cultural exceptionalism that lies at the heart of any nationalism. Gordon Lewis compares the essence of Caribbean cries for cultural independence – what Gabriel Mistral called Martí's tropicality – to Ralph Waldo Emerson's 1837 "The American Scholar," which was an impassioned plea for Americans to be free of Europe.[55] It is the smugness and the moralistic certainty that make American exceptionalism objectionable, as Geir Lundestad makes clear in his critique of American policy.[56] Take away the moralistic element in American exceptionalism and the moralistic indictment of American hegemony, and it might be possible to work toward a historiography that is more inclusive, less adversarial, and does not treat inter-American conflicts as an us-versus-them debate.

There are already some promising signs that point to a reconciliation and to new approaches. James D. Cochrane cautions that what many Latin Americans and dependency theorists see as imperialism is "more reasonably interpreted as the results of the vast disparity in power and wealth between the Latin American countries, individually and collectively."[57] Stephen Randall praises the new pluralist, liberal interpretations of imperialism, which he captures in the subtitle of his recent book, *Colombia and the United*

---

55   Gordon K. Lewis, *Main Currents in Caribbean Thought: The Historical Evolution of Caribbean Society in Its Ideological Aspects, 1492–1900* (Baltimore, MD, 1983), esp. 300.
56   Geir Lundestad, "Moralism, Presentism, Exceptionalism, Provincialism, and Other Extravagances in American Writings on the Early Cold War Years," *Diplomatic History* 13 (Fall 1989): 527–45; Ian Tyrrell, "American Exceptionalism in an Age of International History," *American Historical Review* 96 (October 1991): 1031–72; idem, *The Absent Marx: Class Analysis and Liberal History in Twentieth-Century America* (Westport, CT, 1986), better reveals the Marxist strain of the argument; Michael Kammen, "The Problem of American Exceptionalism: A Reconsideration," *American Quarterly* 45 (March 1993): 1–43, is a balanced overview.
57   James D. Cochrane, "The Troubled and Misunderstood Relationship: The United States and Latin America," *Latin American Research Review* 28: 2 (1993): 234; James William Park, *Latin American Underdevelopment: A History of Perspectives in the United States, 1870–1965* (Baton Rouge, LA, 1995), is an overview.

States: Hegemony and Independence.[58]   John Johnson traces U.S.
policy in Latin America to a fear of British ambitions and domination that lasted well into the early twentieth century.[59]   Fear of
German encroachment, too, influenced Roosevelt's aggressive
rhetoric, but at the same time the Latin Americans were able to
play on U.S. fears of Britain and Germany – as they would later
play on U.S. fears of communism.   On the cultural side, Katherine
Manthorne's account of the North American artists painting Latin
American landscapes in the nineteenth century points to an "awak-
ening inter-American consciousness" too often blurred by moralistic exceptionalism on both sides.[60]

Alfred D. Chandler's newest work extends the symbiosis paradigm into economic history.   In *Scale and Scope: The Dynamics
of Industrial Capitalism*, Chandler traces the development of an
advanced industrial technology that revolutionized and internationalized the manufacture and distribution of goods.[61]   Chandler's
specific analysis – nation by nation and industry by industry –
shows that the main competition in the early twentieth century
was among developed industrial nations, especially the United
States, Great Britain, and France.

Chandler's emphasis on the gains in technology and innovation
dramatically revises the older emphasis on national rivalry for
Third World markets and the hegemonic emphasis of the Williams school.[62]   The unexpected growth in developed-world econo-

58   Stephen J. Randall, "Ideology, National Security, and the Corporate State: The Historiography of U.S.-Latin American Relations," *Latin American Research Review* 27:1 (1992):
205–17; idem, *Colombia and the United States: Hegemony and Interdependence* (Athens,
GA, 1992).
59   John J. Johnson, *A Hemisphere Apart: The Foundations of United States Policy toward
Latin America* (Baltimore, MD, 1990).
60   Katherine Emma Manthorne, *Tropical Renaissance: North American Artists Exploring
Latin America, 1839–1879* (Washington, 1989); John A. Britton, *Revolution and Ideology:
Images of the Mexican Revolution in the United States* (Lexington, KY, 1995).
61   Alfred D. Chandler, Jr., *Scale and Scope: The Dynamics of Industrial Capitalism* (Cambridge, MA, 1990).
62   Gardner, ed., *Redefining the Past*, is an excellent summary of the Williams school and its
origins.   See also William H. Becker, *The Dynamics of Business-Government Relations: Industry and Exports, 1893–1921* (Chicago, 1982); David M. Pletcher, "1861–1898: Economic
Growth and Diplomatic Adjustment," in *Economics and World Power: An Assessment of
American Diplomacy since 1789*, ed. William H. Becker and Samuel F. Wells, Jr. (New York,
1984), 119–71; and idem, "Rhetoric and Results: A Pragmatic View of American Economic
Expansion, 1865–1898," *Diplomatic History* 5 (Spring 1981): 93–105.

mies contributed to American friction with Europe over tariffs and trade. Recent attention to American concern with comparative world currency reflects our new awareness of increased U.S.-European trade.[63] Chandler's attention to the international development of capitalism across national boundaries is a major redirection of American economic history that can be accommodated in both the corporatist and symbiosis paradigms.[64]

Chandler's modernist industrial capitalist is a far different species from the European banking entrepreneurs who joined forces with Latin American political entrepreneurs to saddle countries as disparate as the Dominican Republic and Venezuela with unpayable international debts in the late nineteenth century. Hegemonic history emphasizes the American role in the series of interventions that began in Roosevelt's presidency.[65] But even under Roosevelt's activist foreign policy the United States at the beginning of the new century was a reluctant participant in Caribbean affairs. Symbiosis theory is better suited to understanding the complex and protean tripartite relationship between Germany (and Europe), Venezuela (and Latin America), and the rapidly changing United States.

The place to start is not in the United States, with its fundamentally defensive and reactive foreign policy, but in the individual Latin American countries, such as Venezuela. Holger Herwig's *Germany's Vision of Empire in Venezuela* is a persuasive economic, cultural, and diplomatic study of German ambitions and their ultimate futility. Germany's failure to establish an effective economic presence in Caribbean Latin America resulted from Venezuelan cultural and political resistance well before any

---

63 Emily S. Rosenberg and Norman L. Rosenberg, "From Colonialism to Professionalism: The Public-Private Dynamic in United States Foreign Financial Advising, 1898–1929," *Journal of American History* 74 (June 1987): 59–82; Emily S. Rosenberg, "Foundations of United States International Financial Power: Gold Standard Diplomacy, 1900–1905," *Business History Review* 59 (Summer 1985): 169–202; Carl P. Parrini and Martin J. Sklar, "New Thinking about the Market, 1896–1904: Some American Economists on Investment and the Theory of Surplus Capital," *Journal of Economic History* 43 (September 1983), 559–78.
64 See the review colloquium of Alfred D. Chandler's *Scale and Scope* in *Business History Review* 64 (Winter 1990): 736–58.
65 Lester Langley, *The Banana Wars: An Inner History of American Empire, 1900–1934* (Lexington, KY, 1983).

thought of possible American intervention.[66] Judith Ewell shows
a Venezuelan society especially adept at repelling outside influence, ready to mobilize against European threats, and armed to
the teeth as a result of the nation's constant civil wars. Miriam
Hood shows how the Venezuelans were also able to anger the
usually circumspect British.[67] And Wayne Guthrie's study of European cultural, naval, and political ineptitude illuminates the
foolhardiness of the European naval operation. The Eurocentric
character of the intervention is spelled out in Vernassa's account
of the late Italian participation in exchange for British concessions in the African Somaliland.[68] The American response was
only partly successful, but it did succeed in embarrassing Europe
and forestalling further clumsy interventions.[69]

Harry Hoetink's *The Dominican People* makes a compelling
case against stereotyping Latin America's nations into one model.
Victimized by corrupt deals between their own leaders and marginal European loansharks, the Dominican Republic was held
together by an efficient authoritarian dictator.[70] When Ulíses
Heureaux was assassinated in 1899, the tenuous social and political fabric disintegrated into total anarchy. Since defaulted
Dominican bonds were held by citizens of most developed countries, Europe constantly threatened intervention. Roosevelt used

---

66 Holger W. Herwig, *Germany's Vision of Empire in Venezuela, 1871–1914* (Princeton,
NJ, 1986).
67 Judith Ewell, *Venezuela: A Century of Change* (Stanford, 1984); Miriam Hood, *Gunboat Diplomacy: Great Power Pressure in Venezuela, 1895–1905* (London, 1983). See also
John V. Lombardi, *Venezuela: The Search for Order, the Dream of Progress* (New York,
1982).
68 Wayne L. Guthrie, "The Anglo-German Intervention in Venezuela, 1902–03" (Ph.D
diss., University of California, San Diego, 1983); Maurizio Vernassa, *Emigrazione, Diplomazia
e Cannoniere L'intervento Italiano in Venezuela, 1902–1903* (Livorno, 1980).
69 Collin, *Theodore Roosevelt's Caribbean*, 60–123. One hopes that Edmund Morris, "'A
Few Pregnant Days': Theodore Roosevelt and the Venezuelan Crisis of 1902," *Theodore
Roosevelt Association Journal* 15 (Winter 1989): 2–13, is the last word on the peripheral
debate over Roosevelt's veracity on when (or if) he delivered an ultimatum to the German
ambassador. When Germany replaced von Holleben with Roosevelt's friend Speck von
Sternburg on 11 December, Roosevelt had obviously won. Sternburg proved as inept as
Holleben. Nancy Mitchell, "The Venezuela Blockade. 1902–3," *Diplomatic History* 20 (Spring
1996): 185–210, is a balanced historiographical assessment.
70 H. Hoetink, *The Dominican People, 1850–1900: Notes for a Historical Sociology* (Baltimore, MD, 1982). See also Michiel Baud, "The Origins of Capitalist Agriculture in the
Dominican Republic," *Latin American Research Review* 22: 2 (1987): 135–53.

the Dominican crisis to develop the Caribbean policy he eventually enunciated in the Roosevelt Corollary in 1904, beginning with an ad hoc naval protectorate in 1904, which reassured the French that the United States was willing to assume power as well as respect French (and European) interests.[71]

The Dominican crisis resolution is a model for the symbiosis paradigm. The Russo-Japanese War played a significant role in distracting Europe from minor Caribbean adventurism.[72] It also destroyed Roosevelt's original arbitration strategy of deflecting European gunboat diplomacy by pressuring Europe to use the Hague World Peace Court (instituted in 1899) to resolve Latin American debt disputes. The bellicose Russian judge who heard the original Venezuela blockade case ruled in favor of naval intervention, and Roosevelt was forced to act independently. The Roosevelt Corollary was the result. Roosevelt may have added the Monroe Doctrine to his main policy of power and responsibility to make it more palatable to Congress, a strategy that badly backfired.[73]

Symbiosis identifies the idealistic progressivism that Roosevelt tried to export to the Dominican Republic as part of a world movement and not just a U.S. political phemenonon. James T. Kloppenberg's comparative world history of philosophical progressivism shows how widely this political and intellectual movement resonated throughout Europe.[74] Roosevelt's emissaries to the Dominican Republic were international progressives. Johns Hopkins economist Jacob Hollander, appalled by the victimization of the Dominican people, negotiated a highly favorable settle-

---

71 Richard H. Collin, "The 1904 Detroit Compact: U.S. Naval Diplomacy and Dominican Revolutions," *Historian* 52 (May 1990), 432–52; idem, "The Tage's Visit to New Orleans, Mardi Gras, 1903: Changing French Naval Strategy and Carnival Goodwill," *Louisiana History* 35 (Winter 1994): 51–66.

72 Richard H. Collin, "The Caribbean Theater Transformed: Britain, France, Germany, and the U.S., 1900–1906," *American Neptune* 52 (Spring 1992): 102–12; Ian Nish, *The Origins of the Russo-Japanese War* (London, 1985).

73 For the earlier domestic political dimensions of the Monroe Doctrine see Ernest R. May, *The Making of the Monroe Doctrine* (Cambridge, MA, 1975); Harry Ammon, "The Monroe Doctrine: Domestic Politics or National Decision?" *Diplomatic History* 5 (Winter 1981): 53–70; and Ernest R. May, "Response to Harry Ammon," ibid., 71–72.

74 James T. Kloppenberg, *Uncertain Victory: Social Democracy and Progressivism in European and American Thought, 1870–1920* (New York, 1986).

ment with the European and American creditors. George Colton, a Nebraska banker, worked hard to win tariff concessions for the Philippines and later worked affectionately for the Dominican Republic and Puerto Rico (as governor). A symbiosis analysis considers comparative domestic political pressures. Roosevelt's Dominican programs were defeated by Dominican domestic political pressures, as intense and as interest-driven as in the U.S. Congress.

Frank Ninkovich identifies Theodore Roosevelt's commitment to a symbiotic relationship with the concept of civilization that inspired the president's foreign policy.[75] For all his booster rhetoric, Roosevelt was a confirmed pessimist who constantly feared the kind of societal dissolution of today's ex-Yugoslavia and Somalia. Roosevelt understood the symbiotic relationship of Europe, Asia, and Latin America. He was certain that the United States had to think and act in globalist terms and that American internationalism was not at odds with narrow national interests. William Widenor's portrait of "Theodorus Pacificus" shows that Roosevelt's commitment to an orderly world was consonant with his intense nationalism.[76] William Tilchin shows Roosevelt's restraint in the face of insulting behavior by minor British officials in Jamaica in 1907 and at the London Olympic Games in 1908.[77]

Roosevelt's belief that maintaining civilization was his first priority, his understanding of the symbiotic nature of the modern world, and his awareness of the president's foreign policy powers enabled him to become the principal player in the Russo-Japanese War.[78] First he convinced the kaiser that the United States would resist any German-Russian alliance against Japan; alone of all Western leaders he recognized Japan's right to social equal-

---

75 Frank Ninkovich, "Theodore Roosevelt: Civilization as Ideology," *Diplomatic History* 10 (Summer 1986): 221–45.

76 William C. Widenor, *Henry Cabot Lodge and the Search for an American Foreign Policy* (Berkeley, 1980), 121–70.

77 William Tilchin, *Theodore Roosevelt and the British Empire: A Study in Presidential Statecraft* (New York, 1997); idem, "Theodore Roosevelt, Anglo-American Relations, and the Jamaica Incident of 1907," *Diplomatic History* 19 (Summer 1995): 385–405.

78 Raymond A. Esthus, *Double Eagle and Rising Sun: The Russians and Japanese at Portsmouth in 1905* (Durham, NC, 1988).

ity and its capacity for military equality; he mediated the end of the war at the Portsmouth Peace Conference; and he prevented the kaiser from using a Moroccan crisis to destabilize Europe.[79] Serge Ricard suggests that Roosevelt's second corollary might be "the right of the United States to interfere in European quarrels that were likely to compromise its security."[80]

Symbiosis is well demonstrated by the ripple effect of German change described in Otto Pflanze's recent biography of Bismarck, which graphically demonstrates how Germany's metamorphosis in leadership precipitated a naval race with Britain that Germany could not win. Wilhelm II's world ambitions forced Japan, France, and eventually the United States into new formal and informal alliances.[81] Symbiosis is especially effective in understanding the technological transformation that complemented the new German diplomacy. The same technology that fueled Alfred Chandler's new industrial capitalism made possible the astonishing growth of naval ship building.[82] Jon Sumida's study of the British response to the German threat is not only an account of naval technology and the problems of financing a naval race but also a case study in the modernist dilemma of how to deal with rapid, complex change.[83] The German naval threat became an economic and political problem to Britain that spread throughout the world.[84]

---

79 Peter Larsen, "Theodore Roosevelt and the Moroccan Crisis, 1904–1906" (Ph.D. diss., Princeton University, 1984).
80 Serge Ricard, "Theodore Roosevelt: Principles and Practice of a Foreign Policy," *Theodore Roosevelt Association Journal* 18 (Fall-Winter 1992): 2–6.
81 Otto Pflanze, *Bismarck and the Development of Germany*, 3 vols. (Princeton, NJ, 1990), esp. vol. 3, contrasts Bismarck's and the Kaiser's foreign policies; Raimund Lammersdorf, "Amerika und der Kaiser: Dur Perzeption Wilhelm II in Den Vereinigten Staaten, 1888–1909," *Amerikastudien* 31:3 (1986); Lamar Cecil, *Wilhelm II: Prince and Emperor, 1859–1900* (Chapel Hill, NC, 1989). Gordon A. Craig, "Review of Lamar Cecil, *Wilhelm II*," *Journal of Modern History* 63 (March 1990): 182–84, summarizes the recent historiography.
82 Gary E. Weir, *Building the Kaiser's Navy: The Imperial Naval Office and German Industry in the von Tirpitz Era, 1890–1919* (Annapolis, MD, 1992); Ivo Nikolai Lambi, *The Navy and German Power Politics, 1862–1914* (London, 1984).
83 Jon Tetsuro Sumida, *In Defense of Naval Supremacy: Finance, Technology, and British Naval Policy, 1889–1914* (Boston, 1989).
84 See Aaron L. Friedberg, *The Weary Titan: Britain and the Experience of Relative Decline, 1895–1905* (Princeton, NJ, 1988); and Rhodri Williams, *Defending the Empire: The Conservative Party and British Defense Policy, 1899–1915* (New Haven, CT, 1991). D. George Boyce, ed., *The Crisis of British Power: The Imperial and Naval Papers of the Second*

Germany's attempts to reassure the United States through a series of superficial initiatives are good examples of the indirect cultural diplomacy that symbiosis recognizes. Wilhelm II donated an art cast collection to the Germanic Museum of Harvard, began a University of Berlin Amerika Institute, and sent his brother Prince Henry on an American goodwill visit in 1902. These efforts were far outweighed by German threats to perceived American interests in the Philippines, Venezuela, Lower California, and the Danish West Indies and against American diplomacy to contain and end the Russo-Japanese War.[85] When Roosevelt sent the Great White Fleet toward Japan, he was making a significant gesture to Tirpitz and Germany as well as to Japan.[86]

To a large degree the failure of Taft's much more limited foreign policy lies in the narrowness of its conception. But the failure of Dollar Diplomacy in conception and practice may owe more to clumsiness than hegemonic expansiveness. And one cannot discount the simpler domestic motivation of Taft to change Roosevelt's way of doing things.[87] David Healy identifies the crux of Taft's problem, the "cold, formal, impassive, and impeccably dressed" five-foot five-inch secretary of state, Philander C. Knox. "Little Phil," as Roosevelt called him, enlisted as his aide the bright Francis M. Huntington-Wilson, who "had a genius for antagonizing people." Taft, Knox, and Huntington-Wilson abandoned Roosevelt's emphasis on containing Germany, which they did not see as a threat, and substituted "dollars for bullets" in their foreign policy. These were lawyers, not intellectual aristocrats like Roosevelt and Root, and they favored active intervention and American economic primacy. Knox and Huntington-Wilson were strident enough to offend many Americans, including most of the press, which gave dollar diplomacy its name.[88]

Earl of Selborne, 1895–1910 (London, 1990), is an especially telling collection of the Selborne Papers, which evoke the British sense of unavoidable impending disaster.

85 Manfred Jonas, *The United States and Germany: A Diplomatic History* (Ithaca, 1984).

86 James R. Reckner, *Teddy Roosevelt's Great White Fleet* (Annapolis, MD, 1988).

87 See Joseph A. Fry, "In Search of an Orderly World: U.S. Imperialism, 1898–1912," in *Modern American Diplomacy*, ed. John M. Carroll and George C. Herring (Wilmington, DE, 1986), 1–20.

88 Healy, *Drive to Hegemony*, 145–63. For a detailed overview and a postmodernist chal-

They made an even more striking impression on sensitive Central America, where their attempts to promote American economic interests confirmed the already strong distrust of Yanqui capitalism. Thomas Leonard details the sorry clumsiness that led to armed intervention by marines in Guatemala, mercenaries in Honduras, and British gunboats in Guatemala, all to support American banking schemes to restructure Central American debts.[89] Taft's and Knox's aggressive economic initiatives in China eventually offended Europe, China, Japan, and Russia without gaining any economic advantage for the United States.[90] By replacing Roosevelt's nuanced use of power and responsibility and his commitment to internationalism with open American economic motives, Taft and Knox obliterated much of Roosevelt's attempt to establish friendlier relations with Latin American countries. Root's goodwill mission in 1907 and the establishment, with Andrew Carnegie's help, of the Pan American Union were building blocks that went for naught when Taft's clumsy economic initiatives reinforced the Latin stereotypes of Yanqui materialism and insensitivity.[91]

Whitney T. Perkins, in *Constraint of Empire*, emphasizes the radical differences in succeeding American administrations and resists the temptation to paint all American foreign policy as an exercise in unbridled hegemony.[92] Thomas Dyer explains that Roosevelt, as a neo-Lamarckian and not a social Darwinist, believed that if political and economic reform could be established in Latin America and the Philippines, the seed would grow and replace the centuries-old authoritarian tradition.[93] Roosevelt's progressive paternalism may not have worked, but it was this

lenge to the term itself, see Emily S. Rosenberg, "Revisiting Dollar Diplomacy," *Diplomatic History* 22 (Spring 1998): 155–76.

89 Thomas M. Leonard, *Central America and the United States: The Search for Stability* (Athens, GA, 1991), 60–68.

90 John Allphin Moore, Jr., "The Conger Pledges and the Hukuang Railway Loan," *SHAFR Newsletter* 24 (March 1993): 5–22.

91 Joseph Smith, *Unequal Giants, Diplomatic Relations between the United States and Brazil, 1889–1930* (Pittsburgh, 1991); Collin, *Theodore Roosevelt's Caribbean*, 490–500.

92 Whitney T. Perkins, *Constraint of Empire: The United States and Caribbean Interventions* (Westport, CT, 1981).

93 Dyer, *Theodore Roosevelt and the Idea of Race*.

idealism and not economic expansion that fueled his initiatives. For a brief period during the Venezuelan crisis the American Monroe and Argentine Drago doctrines were unified.

In spite of Taft's efforts to transform Roosevelt's fundamentally altruistic and benign policy into one of economic advantage, Michael L. Krenn finds no significant links between the U.S. government and business until the late 1920s.[94] Benjamin Harrison cites Woodrow Wilson's "contempt for businessmen as greedy predators" as the controlling American attitude into the 1920s.[95] Robert Naylor's phrase "penny-ante imperialism" describes Britain's economic policies in nineteenth-century Central America, a kind of Alice-in-Wonderland approach without planning or cooperation – a process of bumbling through, similar to American efforts in new markets in Roosevelt's time.[96]

The imaginative cultural links between the two Americas are as significant as the economic. Rubén Darío's 1904 poem "To Roosevelt" dramatizes Latin American anguish over the disparity in fortunes between the two Americas but also expresses the hope that the American president's cultural affinities might transform a hegemonic into a symbiotic relationship.[97] Later Latin American writers have used the device of Magic Realism to celebrate Latin America's cultural uniqueness while dealing ironically with its inherent poverty.[98]

Symbiosis theory thrives on world events in which the international ripple effect is more significant than the specific conflict. The Mexican Revolution that began in 1910, the first of the monumental twentieth-century revolutions, fits better into Theodore

---

94 Michael L. Krenn, *U.S. Policy toward Economic Nationalism in Latin America, 1917–1929* (Wilmington, DE, 1990).
95 Benjamin T. Harrison, *Dollar Diplomat: Chandler Anderson and American Diplomacy in Mexico and Nicaragua, 1913–1928* (Pullman, WA, 1988), xii. See also Richard V. Salisbury, *Anti-Imperialism and International Competition in Central America, 1920–1929* (Wilmington, DE, 1989).
96 Robert Naylor, *Penny Ante Imperialism: The Mosquito Shore and the Bay of Honduras, 1600–1914: A Case Study in British Informal Empire* (Rutherford, NJ, 1989).
97 Rubén Darío, "To Roosevelt" in Darío, *Selected Poems*, ed. and trans. Lysander Kemp (Austin, 1965), 69–70.
98 Stephen Slemon, "Magic Realism as Post-Colonial Discourse," *Canadian Literature*, no. 116 (Spring 1988): 9–24.

Roosevelt's globalist stage than into Taft's more limited national interest foreign policies. John Mason Hart's account of the revolution, the global context he draws, and his attention to the modern revolutionary impulse, make his *Revolutionary Mexico* the essential text. "The Mexican Revolution," he writes,

comprised the same social forces and groups that carried forward the first massive popular uprisings of the twentieth century (between 1905 and 1911) in Iran, Russia, China. Peasants, industrial workers, *pequeña burguesîa*, and provincial elites mobilized, challenging the government, while meeting the threats presented by foreign intruders and one another. In all four of these early twentieth-century national revolutions, formally constituted political parties possessed little of the organizational strength and unity between peasants and industrial workers that characterized later struggles in Russia and China.

Only in the second phase of the revolution, characterized by "class confrontation, American intervention, and workers defeat," did American foreign policy directly enter the conflict.[99]

Though there is still some historical debate over the role, if any, that the United States played in the origins of the Mexican Revolution, the more interesting issues go beyond the peripheral national involvement to the monumental question of world change and revolution, issues that must be addressed by comparative international history. Frederick Katz's history of a tripartite relationship between Mexico, Europe, and the Mexican Revolution reveals Mexican discontent – not with American investment in Mexico but with the changes of investment intensity from middle-sized companies to large corporations.[100] William Beezley's social analysis of Mexico's revolutionary turmoil illuminates the uniqueness of the contradictory layers of Mexican society and how the elites and the poor became unified only in the desire for revolutionary change.[101] Symbiosis theory has no better example

---

99 John Mason Hart, *Revolutionary Mexico: The Coming and Process of the Mexican Revolution* (Berkeley, 1987), 12, 14.

100 Friedrich Katz, *The Secret War in Mexico: Europe, the United States and the Mexican Revolution* (Chicago, 1981).

101 William H. Beezley, *Judas at the Jockey Club and Other Episodes of Porfirian Mexico* (Lincoln, NE, 1987).

than the dissemination of Mexican imaginative culture after American capitalists became enamored of Mexican revolutionary muralist art. The influence of Diego Rivera's murals live on in American post offices and other artifacts of the American Depression and the New Deal art programs.[102]

In recent U.S. historiography corporatism, through its linkage of domestic, diplomatic, and economic policies in an internationalized context, has already moved away from hegemonic diction.[103] Corporatism's primary focus is still economic, however, whereas symbiosis concentrates on whatever defines the interactive elements at a particular time, including domestic politics, which are always an integral part of foreign policy but rarely evident in diplomatic records. For example, Alabama Senator John Tyler Morgan and the minority Democratic party, together with domestic Panamanian politics and the Colombian Liberal and Conservative political struggles, were all decisive in the Panama Canal disputes.[104] Domestic discontent with Queen Isabella's government, to give another example, and a widespread desire to change Spanish politics, may also help explain Spain's diplomatic reluctance to deal with the Cuban and Philippine problems and Spain's apparent military and naval ineptitude.[105]

Corporatism's interest in institutional economic change and symbiosis's view of modernism's significance are more compatibile than they might first appear. James Livingston's sweeping reexamination of the political and philosophical changes in American

---

102   See Irene Herner de Larrea, *Diego Rivera's Mural at the Rockefeller Center* (Mexico City, 1990); and Karal Ann Marling, *Wall-to-Wall America: A Cultural History of Post-Office Murals in the Great Depression* (Minneapolis, 1982).

103   Ellis Hawley, "The Discovery and Study of a 'Corporate Liberalism,'" *Business History Review* 52 (Autumn 1978): 309–20; Thomas J. McCormick, "Drift or Mastery? A Corporatist Synthesis for American Diplomatic History," *Reviews in American History* 10 (December 1982): 318–30; Michael J. Hogan, "Corporatism: A Positive Appraisal," *Diplomatic History* 10 (Fall 1986): 363–72; John Lewis Gaddis, "The Corporatist Synthesis: A Skeptical View," ibid., 357–62.

104   Helen Delpar, *Red against Blue: The Liberal Party in Colombian Politics, 1863–1899* (University, AL, 1981); Alex Perez-Venero, *Before the Five Frontiers: Panama, from 1821–1903* (New York, 1978).

105   David F. Trask, *The War with Spain in 1898* (New York, 1981), esp. 14–16. See also Donald L. Shaw, *The Generation of 1898 in Spain* (New York 1975); and John L. Offner, *An Unwanted War: The Diplomacy of the United States and Spain Over Cuba, 1895–1898* (Chapel Hill, NC, 1992).

capitalism fits into both frameworks.[106] The new examinations of American Progressive capitalism are essential to an understanding of the domestic economic and political institutions that are central to the symbiosis framework.[107] Thomas Schoonover's world systems theory and Lucien Pye's arguments for the triumph of modernization theory offer useful frameworks for incorporating wider perspectives into a diplomatic history that must become cosmopolitan and international to remain relevant.[108] Symbiosis can accommodate a wider cultural corporatism, internationalized not only in its economic focus but also in its eagerness to emphasize the domestic politics of all nations, imaginative culture, and intellectual change.

The symbiotic framework has already made a substantial impact. Michael Hunt's *The Making of a Special Relationship: The United States and China to 1914* is a masterful symbiotic history of the interrelations of two disparate cultures. Hunt shows how the Chinese used the American Open Door initiative for their own purposes and the American disappointment with China's resistance to modernization.[109] Frank Ninkovich also moves the Open Door from economic policy to ideology, which William Appleman Williams as defined as "a nation's cultural value system." Ninkovich argues that the Open Door policy was a structure (meta-

---

106   James Livingston, *Origins of the Federal Reserve System: Money, Class, and Corporate Capitalism, 1890–1913* (Ithaca, 1986); Gerald Berk, "Corporate Liberalism Reconsidered: A Review Essay," *Journal of Policy History,* no. 3 (1991): 70–84.

107   Emily S. Rosenberg, *Spreading the American Dream: American Economic and Cultural Expansion, 1890–1945* (New York, 1982); Morton Keller, *Regulating a New Economy: Public Policy and Economic Change in America, 1900–1933* (Cambridge, MA, 1990); Martin J. Sklar, *The Corporate Reconstruction of American Capitalism, 1890–1916: The Market, the Law, and Politics* (New York, 1988); Stephen Skowronek, *Building the New American State: The Expansion of National Administrative Capacities, 1877–1920* (New York, 1982); Naomi R. Lamoreaux, *The Great Merger Movement in American Business, 1895–1904* (New York, 1985).

108   Schoonover, *The United States in Central America;* Lucian Pye, "Political Science and the Crisis of Authoritarianism," *American Political Science Review* 84:1 (1990): 3–19. For the linkage of dependency and modernism in world systems theory, see Thomas J. McCormick, "Something Old, Something New: John Lewis Gaddis's 'New Conceptual Approaches,'" *Diplomatic History* 14 (Summer 1990): 425–32. Joseph A. Fry, "From Open Door to World Systems: Economic Interpretations of Late Nineteenth-Century American Foreign Relations," *Pacific Historical Review* 65 (May 1996): 277–303 is a recent overview.

109   Hunt, *The Making of a Special Relationship.*

phor?) for a new American internationalism.[110] These works support Warren Cohen's claim for East-Asian historiography as the cutting edge of diplomatic history. Cohen's *East Asian Art and American Culture* treats the influence of the world's fairs on U.S. culture and notes how American art collectors like Charles Freer suggested the use of imaginative culture as an instrument of foreign relations.[111] Roosevelt, who encouraged Freer's gift to a new national museum, used money from the Boxer Rebellion indemnity to encourage Chinese students to choose American universities over their customary Asian or European schools.[112]

Michael Hunt's optimism about "the broad parameters of the field" is tempered by the number of approaches he finds deficient. My plea for a new symbiosis framework is not another chapter in the diplomatic historian's "battle for interpretive preeminence."[113] I prefer for symbiosis to be inclusive, not exclusive. I disagree with Kinley Brauer's requirement that a new framework must "serve as a unifying and consistent framework for the entire span of American foreign relations."[114] Ernest May wisely observed that what works for one period does not necessarily work for another, and he uses pre-1930 history as his exemplar.[115]

Akira Iriye's proscription against making each national culture unique is another way of suggesting the cosmopolitanizing process; but we must also be careful not to denationalize what is unique in specific cultures, a problem the new Europe is facing now.[116] Hegemony well suited the Cold War era, but national-

---

110   Frank Ninkovich, "Ideology, the Open Door, and Foreign Policy," *Diplomatic History* 6 (Spring 1982): 185–208.
111   Warren I. Cohen, "The History of American-East Asian Relations: Cutting Edge of the Historical Profession," *Diplomatic History* 9 (Spring 1985): 101–12; idem, *East Asian Art and American Culture.*
112   Delber McKee, "The Boxer Indemnity Remission: A Damage Control Device?" *SHAFR Newsletter* 23 (March 1992): 1–19; Terence E. Brockhausen, "The Boxer Indemnity: Five Decades of Sino-American Dissension" (Ph. D. diss., Texas Christian University, 1981).
113   Michael H. Hunt, "The Long Crisis in U.S. Diplomatic History: Coming to Closure," *Diplomatic History* 16 (Winter 1992): 115–40.
114   Kinley Brauer, "The Great American Desert Revisited: Recent Literature and Prospects for the Study of American Foreign Relations, 1815–61," *Diplomatic History* 13 (Summer 1989): 411.
115   Ernest R. May, "Writing Contemporary International History," *Diplomatic History* 8 (Spring 1984): 103–13.
116   Akira Iriye, "Culture and International History," in *Explaining the History of Ameri-*

ism – not empire – may be the key for our depolarized post-Cold War world.[117]

Symbiosis is not reductionist. It looks for interaction, it welcomes inclusion, and it resists imposing the models of one age upon another. Modern art and physics were central to Theodore Roosevelt's age, as ideology was central to the Cold War conflicts. Imaginative culture was at the heart of the new modernizing internationalism of Theodore Roosevelt's era: it transformed the entire world. France led the way in using its art as an active diplomatic force in World's Fair competitions throughout the world. Germany debated what art should represent it at the St. Louis World's Fair in 1904. Latin American *modernissmo* was an artistic movement to free Latin America from its cultural dependency on Europe. The first American national art museum in Washington was a mixture of Oriental art and the paintings of expatriate American James Whistler. Symbiosis is a framework for the new internationalist modernist cultural community that began in earnest with Theodore Roosevelt's presidency and influenced more of the events and peoples in the world than the nineteenth century's nationalist economic conflicts. It is time for us to consider imaginative culture as one of the engines of change and influence and to integrate art, music, and culture with the politics and economics that we know so well. The new symbiosis paradigm offers diplomatic historians an opportunity for a richer, more inclusive, more accurate international history.

---

can Foreign Relations, ed. Michael J. Hogan and Thomas G. Paterson (New York, 1991), 219–20.

117   See Peter F. Sugar, "From Ethnicity to Nationalism and Back Again," in *Nationalism: Essays in Honor of Louis L. Snyder*, ed. Michael Palumbo and William O. Shanahan (Westport, CT, 1981), 67–84.

6

The Reclamation of Woodrow Wilson?

DAVID STEIGERWALD

Sitting on the Senate Foreign Relations Committee in 1989, Daniel Patrick Moynihan apparently could not resist baiting the witness. If it was now obvious that Russo-American relations were to be conducted by "the normal means of compromise and accommodation," what then, Moynihan mused, are we to make of Woodrow Wilson's legacy? "I was long skeptical about Wilson's vision," answered the witness. "But I begin today in the light of just what has happened in the last few years to think that Wilson was way ahead of his time."[1]

Moynihan's prey here was George Kennan, the dean of American realism and an initiator in the early 1950s of two generations of biting criticism of Woodrow Wilson, and his comments, accordingly, raise the possibility that much of what has been written on Wilson in the last half century is obsolete. Today's main currents – economic globalization and the momentum of political liberalization – appear to have ushered in a Wilsonian world. The end of the Cold War gutted Kennan's realist critique, because America's security has vastly improved as its national ideals have prevailed – quite the opposite from how Kennan thought about these matters. At the same time, the sting of New Left revisionism, which always rested heavily on the claim that Wilson's Open

---

1 George Kennan quoted in Daniel Patrick Moynihan, *On the Law of Nations* (Cambridge, MA, 1990), 151. As Thomas J. Knock has pointed out, Kennan has been warming up to Wilson for some time and there are strong affinities—as often is the case with opposites – between the two. See Thomas J. Knock, "Kennan Versus Wilson," in *The Wilson Era: Essays in Honor of Arthur S. Link*, ed. John Milton Cooper and Charles E. Neu (Arlington Heights, IL, 1991), 302–26. In response, Kennan wrote that his criticism of Wilson must be understood in the context of the early Cold War. That context having changed, Kennan writes, "I now view Wilson . . . as a man who like so many other people of broad vision and acute sensitivities, was ahead of his time, and did not live long enough to know what great and commanding relevance his ideas would acquire before this century was out" ("Comments on the Paper Entitled 'Kennan Versus Wilson'," in ibid., 330).

Door was a façade for the extension of American power, has worn off. Third World guerrillas, now in power, court Chicago School economists and bow to International Monetary Fund austerity demands – Franz Fanon has given way to financial prudence. N. Gordon Levin's *Woodrow Wilson and World Politics* no longer carries strength as a timely critique of neo-imperialism. Instead, it conjures up images of the cranky old Trotskyite in the back of the room who keeps blathering about "class struggle" while everyone else shifts impatiently. History itself has humbled George Kennan and William Appleman Williams.[2]

These new conditions have tempted writers in the last decade to vindicate Wilson. It is a telling indication of how much has changed that within a decade the attempts to define the Wilsonian tradition in American foreign relations have moved from Lloyd Gardner's highly critical *A Covenant with Power* to Thomas Knock's laudatory *To End All Wars*. The tendency to trace back to Wilson a tradition of economic self-seeking and arrogant interventionism has yielded to a new impulse to see Wilsonian diplomacy as having established "a new American agenda for world affairs," as Akira Iriye writes, built upon "the ideas of economic interdependence and of peaceful settlement of disputes."[3]

Fading Realism

The twentieth century appears to be ending on the same promising notes with which it began. The rise of genuine multilateralism and the United Nations, a thoroughgoing economic interdepen-

2   The well-known works that define these two interpretations are George Kennan, *American Diplomacy, 1900–1950* (Chicago, 1951); William Appleman Williams, *The Tragedy of American Diplomacy* (New York, 1959); and N. Gordon Levin, Jr., *Woodrow Wilson and World Politics: America's Response to War and Revolution* (New York, 1968).
3   Lloyd Gardner, *A Covenant With Power: America and World Order from Wilson to Reagan* (New York, 1984); Thomas J. Knock, *To End All Wars: Woodrow Wilson and the Quest for a New World Order* (New York, 1992); Akira Iriye, *The Globalizing of America, 1913–1945*, vol. 3, *The Cambridge History of American Foreign Relations*, ed. Warren Cohen (New York, 1993), 18. Perhaps the most important historiographical development in Wilsonian scholarship during the last fifteen years was the completion in 1993 of the published *Wilson Papers*. Every scholar working on Wilson is indebted to professors Arthur Link and David Hirst and the staff at the *Papers* for producing a series unique in breadth and

dence, the triumph of a human-rights rhetoric to which all nations apparently are called to answer – all these developments seem to fulfill the internationalist hope of an orderly, reasonably civil, mostly constitutional world where diplomacy prevails over force. No wonder so few writers of the last twenty years have attempted to defend the realist critique.

Most writers who address themselves to Kennan and his colleagues do so critically, a task that compels attention to wartime diplomacy in Europe and Russia. It was in the cause of countering Kennan, for example, that Arthur Link set down his most systematic view of Wilson's wartime diplomacy. Anyone familiar with Kennan's *American Diplomacy* can see Link's *Revolution, War, and Peace* as a blow-by-blow response to it: Link acknowledges Wilson's ideological and ethical commitments but argues that his policies were properly adjusted to means and ends. In 1914, neutrality acknowledged both public opinion and American economic interests; as Europe lumbered toward self-destruction, however, Wilson began to instruct the public in America's international responsibilities and to position himself among the belligerents as a mediator. Wilson understood the consequences of an ongoing war and worried that the American public "might drive him into war in sheer anger. Then they would be fighting blindly in defense of national rights, without any long-range objectives." By early 1917, Wilson had concluded that intervention was the only way to achieve "a reasonable peace settlement and the reconstruction of the world order." Once at Versailles, Wilson was far more determined to restore political and economic stability than any of the allies, but given the upheaval in central Europe, all he could do was "draw the least absurd boundaries possible." Far from the dreamy idealist, Wilson was, as John Milton Cooper, Jr., calls him in his artful reinforcement of Link, neither warrior nor priest; he was the Nietzschean "Superman."[4]

editorial competence. It may well be that the publication of the *Papers* has itself improved Wilson's reputation, not because they are selective and biased but because their thoroughness makes an objective reading of Wilson unavoidable. See Arthur S. Link, et al., eds., *The Papers of Woodrow Wilson* (PWW), 69 vols. (Princeton, NJ, 1966–93).

4 Arthur S. Link, *Woodrow Wilson: Revolution, War, and Peace* (Arlington Heights, IL., 1979), 53, 69–71, 95; John Milton Cooper, Jr., *The Warrior and the Priest: Woodrow Wilson*

Link plays on Kennan's turf here, arguing that Wilson was, indeed, a realist. He fails to address adequately just how Wilson acted in specifically realist ways. The most important issue in assessing Wilson's diplomatic performance, for example, concerns his leverage at Versailles, a point on which there should be more debate. The two main assumptions are, as Link has it, that Wilson expected to use American military participation as a wedge against allied diplomatic demands, or that he expected a prostrate Europe to accede to the Fourteen Points out of its desperate need for American economic aid. The first makes little sense after American forces were engaged, for Wilson could hardly bargain with them. The second assumption suffers from the lack of evidence that Wilson expected to bring economic pressure to bear at Versailles. It is possible that Wilson also expected to appeal to the European masses to pressure their respective national governments. This explanation has plausibility, because Wilson appealed "over the heads" of the Italian delegation during the Adriatic crisis. If public appeals were all Wilson had up his sleeve, however, he deserves serious criticism. I still think that Walter Lippmann got it right when, after the disillusionment of 1919 eased, he admitted that the president had lost all real leverage when he called the nation to war without insisting on the abrogation of the secret treaties. One could argue that Wilson could not have demanded the abrogation of agreements about which he knew nothing. Yet rumors of their existence were widespread. Wilson at least should have demanded an explication of allied war aims before asking Congress for a declaration. Let us assume that he knew nothing of these rumors. In mid-May 1917 the British sent copies of most of the treaties for Wilson's review. Apparently he passed them along without reading them. At this late date, perhaps what they contained was irrelevant. Still, a very modest recent book makes clear that particularly the French were in desperate need of everything from steel workers to soldiers in April 1917, and conceivably Wilson could have begrudged

and Theodore Roosevelt (Cambridge, MA, 1983), 321. Aside from differences in tone and emphasis, August Heckscher makes a similar case in his straightforward biography, *Woodrow Wilson* (New York, 1991).

them aid until an agreement was reached on war aims, but he would have had to assert this pressure in May and June 1917.[5]

In any event, the dismantling of the realist critique has not always yielded interpretations friendly to Wilson, for it can lead to claims that Wilson was not idealistic enough. In his study of neutrality law before the war, for example, John W. Coogan argues that Wilson accepted the British blockade even though it violated the Declaration of London. He and his advisors, giving in to "the most fervent pro-Allied sympathies" almost as soon as the war began, adopted a policy of "informal accommodation" that "made a mockery of neutrality." Kendrick Clements, on the whole a sympathetic biographer, concludes that if Coogan's argument is "overstated," it remains true that "the Americans had let trade reshape their neutrality so that it favored the Allies." Robert Ferrell bluntly states that Wilson never was neutral; he merely waited until public opinion and world events set loose the conditions under which he might lead the nation to war. If ideals drove Wilson in the abstract, Georg Schild argues, his ends in any given case were strongly influenced by realpolitik. Frederick Calhoun similarly blends these two influences by posing an ongoing dialectic within Wilson between ideals and a penchant to use force. Wilson's ideal was peace, yet "he had no principled aversion to compelling others to accept his views"; he sought democracy, but the means he employed – military intervention – denied others the opportunity to develop in their own way.[6]

In the face of such scholarship, defending realism is by no means easy. There are hints in Calhoun's work of a way to go about salvaging the realist critique, though they do not lie in his rigid

5 See Link, *Woodrow Wilson*, 78n., and 101; Cooper, *The Warrior and the Priest*, 338–39; Walter Lippmann, "The Intimate Papers of Colonel House," *Foreign Affairs* 4 (April 1926): 383–93; and David M. Esposito, *The Legacy of Woodrow Wilson: American War Aims in World War I* (Westport, CT, 1996), 100–107.

6 John W. Coogan, *The End of Neutrality: The United States, Britain, and Maritime Rights, 1899–1915* (Ithaca, NY, 1981), 176; Kendrick Clements, *Woodrow Wilson: World Statesman* (Boston, 1987), 154–55; Robert H. Ferrell, *Woodrow Wilson and World War I, 1917–1921* (New York, 1985), 7–12; Georg Schild, *Between Ideology and Realpolitik: Woodrow Wilson and the Russian Revolution, 1917–1921* (Westport, CT, 1995); Frederick Calhoun, *Power and Principle: Armed Intervention in Wilsonian Foreign Policy* (Kent, OH, 1986); idem, *Uses of Force and Wilsonian Foreign Policy* (Kent, OH, 1993), 53.

determination to detect a will to power in everything Wilson did. Here and there, Calhoun notes that the sort of democracy that Wilson attempted to impose on others was very narrow indeed, the democracy, he writes, of "ethnocentric humanitarianism."[7] This claim is similar to the one Lloyd Ambrosius ventures in his recent efforts to preserve what he can from the realist critique in which he was schooled, and the result has been two provocative books, *Woodrow Wilson and the American Diplomatic Tradition* and *Wilsonian Statecraft*, that puzzle out Wilson's position in an increasingly complex, paradoxical world. The fundamental problem with Wilsonianism, Ambrosius argues, was that it was poorly designed for dealing with the "pluralism" inherent in the world, and in place of the sluggish old distinction between realism and idealism, Ambrosius poses Wilson's universalist assumptions against the world's stubborn complexity. Wilson may have been of practical mind, but at issue is whether the policies he developed were well conceived for a world that was unwilling to conform to Wilsonian type.[8] Ambrosius concludes that they were not. The ideological inclinations of modernity were never uniform, and opponents of Wilson's attempts to make it so appeared not so much as antediluvian aristocrats or rabid radicals but as members of groups centered upon ethnic, nationalist, and racial claims.

Such is the conclusion Tony Smith comes to in his *America's Mission*, the most ambitious attempt to reformulate realism. Smith argues that if Wilson molded the liberal ideals of self-determination, free trade, and disarmament into internationalism, he did so "not for pietistic reasons but because it served national security." Liberal internationalism is a policy all the more important now that the Cold War has ended, but echoing Ambrosius, Smith cautions that potent ethnic and religious obstacles to internationalism remain.[9] Reading back into the Wilsonian tradition Kennan's

---

7 Calhoun, *Power and Principle*, 23, 258.
8 Lloyd Ambrosius, *Woodrow Wilson and the American Diplomatic Tradition* (New York, 1987); idem, *Wilsonian Statecraft: Theory and Practice of Liberal Internationalism during World War I* (Wilmington, DE, 1991). See especially the introduction to the latter for Ambrosius's historiographical claims.
9 Tony Smith, *America's Mission: The United States and the Worldwide Struggle for De-*

assumption that the world is a messy place alerts us to the continuing pitfalls in front of Wilsonianism. But by seeing Wilson's ideals as practical forms of policymaking, these works provide a clever means not so much of rescuing realism as of putting it honorably to rest.

The Obsolescence of Revisionism

Much as Link's *Revolution, War, and Peace* aimed at Kennan, so one might read Thomas J. Knock's *To End All Wars* as a counterpoint to the leading revisionist writer on Wilson, Lloyd Gardner. Whereas Gardner insists that Wilson sought to discipline and control revolution, Knock argues that he was consistently on the left, in many cases even left of his fellow Progressives. Emphasizing Wilson's political internationalism and not the pursuit of national economic interests, Knock maintains that Wilson drew from socialists and pacifists and in turn inspired them. At every instance, from the 1913 Mobile Address on Latin America through the Fourteen Points, where Gardner sees insidious designs Knock sees a statesman pressing progressive internationalism.[10] In contrast to Link, however, Knock attacks a body of thought that thrived well into the 1980s, thanks largely to Ronald Reagan's intensely ideological foreign policy, which lent continued credence and urgency to New Left interpretations.

Tracing American interventionism in the Western Hemisphere quite rightly draws writers to the Wilson era. Much of the recent work done on Latin America begins with the obligatory note that America's steadily growing economic involvement in Latin America was the point of departure for policy. By 1913, David Healy reports in *Drive to Hegemony*, one half of America's total foreign investments were in Latin America; that year the region consumed $135 million in U.S.-manufactured goods. According

---

mocracy in the Twentieth Century (Princeton, NJ, 1994), 329. Georg Schild ends *Between Ideology and Realpolitik* with a similar warning (pp. 130–31).

10 Knock, *To End All Wars*. See pp. 140–47 for a good example of Knock's method, in which he disputes the long-standing claim that the Fourteen Points was a political or ideological response to the Bolsheviks.

to Gardner, Americans were dominant throughout the Mexican economy at the outset of the great revolution, and their hold only increased, as a number of writers point out, when the Great War banished the Europeans from the hemisphere, leaving Americans supreme.[11]

The question, however, is what effect the hefty growth in American investment had on U.S. policy in the region. In the years before Wilson took office, American economic interests clearly translated into heavy-handed American imperialism. In Healy's view, Americans proceeded through a barely veiled racism with the intention to tame Latin America and establish the rule of law and property among people they deemed too incompetent to care for either. Like most imperialist thugs, Americans vigorously pursued self-interested "hegemony" while professing disinterested benevolence.[12] Such imperialism is easy to illustrate. One can look at Panama or Cuba for examples, but there was no more high-handed episode than when U.S. Ambassador to Mexico Henry Lane Wilson conspired with counterrevolutionaries to overthrow the liberal landowner, Francisco Madero, a coup that led to Madero's murder and unleashed the chaos of the Mexican Revolution.[13]

What of that other Wilson? As a scholar, Woodrow Wilson announced his support of a paternalistic imperialism, according to Healy and others. He was as interested in American economic advance as Taft or Roosevelt. During the 1912 presidential campaign he told audiences that "if prosperity is not to be checked in this country we must broaden our borders and make conquest of

---

11 Lloyd Gardner, "Woodrow Wilson and the Mexican Revolution," in *Woodrow Wilson and a Revolutionary World, 1913–1921*, ed. Arthur Link (Chapel Hill, NC, 1982), 4-5; Linda B. Hall, *Oil, Banks, and Politics: The United States and Postrevolutionary Mexico, 1917–1924* (Austin, TX, 1995), 13; David Healy, *Drive to Hegemony: The United States in the Caribbean, 1898–1917* (Madison, WI, 1988), 24, 166–68; Michael Krenn, *U.S. Policy Toward Economic Nationalism in Latin America, 1917–1929* (Wilmington, DE, 1990), 7–9; Mark Gilderhus, *Pan-American Visions: Woodrow Wilson in the Western Hemisphere, 1913–1921* (Tucson, AZ, 1986), 2–3.
12 Healy, *Drive to Hegemony*, 71.
13 See ibid., chaps. 3 and 5, for Cuba and Panama. Lloyd Gardner describes Ambassador Wilson's "Compact of the Embassy" in "Woodrow Wilson and the Mexican Revolution," 8–11, and in *Safe for Democracy: The Anglo-American Response to Revolution, 1913–1923* (New York, 1984), 47–50.

the markets of the world." The 1913 Federal Reserve Act, one of the grand "reforms" of his first term, permitted American banks to open up foreign branches, with Latin America as the practical target. He sought a respectable merchant marine. He did all this even though he "came into office with only the barest knowledge of recent events in Mexico," as Gardner writes. He showed "naive arrogance," one biographer concludes, and shrouded his policies in "glittering prattle," in the words of another. David Healy sums up the condemnation of Wilson in Latin America when he writes that, however much his "rhetoric of idealism and altruism . . . differentiated him from so many of his policy-making contemporaries," the end result was the same interventionist policy that had been conducted for decades, not least because of Wilson's "acceptance of so much of the mainstream consensus" that the United States was a benevolent father.[14]

All this vigorous writing should serve to sustain revisionism, except that the two most important critiques of Wilson's policy in Mexico reveal, through their considerable strengths, the challenge that faces that point of view. Lloyd Gardner's *Safe for Democracy* and Friedrich Katz's monumental *The Secret War in Mexico* hold that Wilson intended to prevent Mexico's radicalization in the interests of American capital. Yet Wilson comes off well in both books, in spite of the authors' efforts to the contrary. Both Gardner and Katz come to Wilson's Mexican policy through transnational studies that draw from European as well as American sources, and the more Wilson is compared to others, the more decent a man he appears.

Katz's *Secret War in Mexico* is simply the best work on the diplomacy of the Mexican Revolution. It is a sophisticated critique of dependency theory, that dreary old view of Latin Americans as powerless peons before the onslaught of metropolitan capital. To Katz, the Mexicans actively manipulated the powers for their own local interests, which was not difficult because there was no single "metropolis." Katz sees the Mexican Revolution

---

14 Gardner, *Safe for Democracy*, 26–27, 38–39, 51; Clements, *Woodrow Wilson*, 125; Jan Willem Schulte Nordholt, *Woodrow Wilson: A Life For World Peace*, trans. Herbert H. Rowen (Berkeley, 1991), 119; and Healy, *Drive to Hegemony*, 178–79.

as an early example of a new turn in Western diplomacy, whereby governments sought to extend and protect the business interests of their nationals by manipulating anti-imperialist movements within the societies they sought to exploit – the new diplomacy turned to old purposes, one might say. Meanwhile and among other things, Katz provides a panoramic understanding of Pancho Villa's 1916 raid in New Mexico and the infamous Zimmermann telegram. He scrutinizes English, German, Austrian, and even Japanese activity and reveals it to have been, if anything, more dangerous to the Mexican Revolution than Wilson believed it to have been.[15]

Katz's handling of the incredible twists and turns of great-power diplomacy within the equally complex revolution is nothing short of masterful. Yet he falters when it comes to Wilson. In the years before and after Wilson's presidency, American policy conformed to Katz's description. But he gets carried away by the intrigue and assumes that Wilson was as big a schemer as the Europeans. The great strength of the work, its transnational scope, encourages Katz to interpret Wilson through the cynical perspective of the European diplomatic corps – clearly bad strategy, inasmuch as the Europeans could not shake the assumption that Wilson's rhetoric about Latin American "dignity" and "self-respect" constituted so much smoke clouding over the desire for gain.[16] Determined to fit Wilson into his mold, Katz fails to appreciate just how "new" Wilson was. He exaggerates the administration's willingness to support the Huerta "regime" in 1913.[17] In Katz's handling, the administration "was pleased" to lend its support to Federico Gamboa, the regime's appointed candidate for the presidency in 1913, which Katz reads as recognition of the Huerta

15 Friedrich Katz, *The Secret War in Mexico: Europe, the United States, and the Mexican Revolution* (Chicago, 1981).

16 The British doubtless wondered, as Lloyd Gardner summed up their befuddlement, whether Wilson "did not know what he was doing . . . was naive, [was] bent on driving out all interests except purified American capitalists, or just playing for time" ("Wilson and the Mexican Revolution," 19).

17 Friedrich Katz, *The Secret War in Mexico*, 168–69. For the relevant correspondence see "Remarks at a Press Conference" and Bryan to Wilson, with enclosure, 25 September 1913, *PWW* 28:322–26; Bryan to Wilson, with enclosure, 28 September 1913, ibid., 339–42; and Wilson to John Bassett Moore, with enclosure, October 9, 1913, ibid., 381.

regime if not Huerta himself and, in turn, a repudiation of Carranza and the revolutionary Constitutionalists. A close reading of the correspondence regarding the proposed October election gives a much different impression. At first, Wilson and Secretary of State William Jennings Bryan (not House or Lansing) were willing to accept Gamboa only as a legitimate presidential candidate, on the grounds that they had demanded only that Huerta step down; otherwise, their main hope was that the elections tentatively scheduled for October would be fair and representative. Their position cannot be construed as having "clearly recognized" the Huerta regime, as Katz claims. Furthermore, there is little evidence that Wilson gave thought to defending or extending American oil interests, as Katz charges, or for that matter that he gave much consideration to the position of American economic interests at all. Thomas J. Knock counters that "for every sentence he uttered on commerce [and imperialism], he spoke two on the moral responsibility of the United States to sustain its historic idealism and render the service of its democracy."[18] To assume that Wilson did the bidding of American oil ignores everything that he had to say about private interests and foreign policy. It ignores, as Kendrick Clements has pointed out, that Wilson recognized Carranza in 1917, after the new Constitution, with its famous Article 27, was adopted, and that Wilson staunchly resisted continued pressure to take Mexican oil fields by force – a proposal he likened to the German invasion of Belgium. Even Lloyd Gardner admits that in dealing with Mexico Wilson unleashed "the most thoroughgoing critique of imperialism made by a leader of a capitalist nation before World War I."[19]

18 Katz flatly claims that "among the most important norms of Western society, as Wilson defended it and wished to spread it, was the concept of free enterprise," which presumably translated into a policy of defending property rights (*The Secret War in Mexico*, 156–57). See also Knock, *To End All Wars*, 10–11.
19 Knock calls attention to the 1914 Fourth of July speech, during which Wilson stated: "If American enterprise in foreign countries . . . takes the shape of imposing upon and exploiting the mass of people in that country, it ought to be checked and not encouraged. I am willing to get anything for an American that money and enterprise can obtain, except the suppression of the rights of other men" (*To End All Wars*, 28). See also Clements, *Woodrow Wilson*, 131–32; Hall, *Oil, Banks, and Politics*, 22; and Gardner, *Safe for Democracy*, 62.

If we take Gardner at his word here, then we must ask just how effective the revisionists' general critique of Wilsonian diplomacy can be, for Gardner argues that Wilson's actions in Mexico presaged his wider efforts in Asia and Europe to thwart radicalism. As he strains to follow Wilson into Europe and through Russia, Gardner is unable to develop a consistent portrait. He writes that "no one was more aware of the economic forces at work than Woodrow Wilson" but never clearly spells out just how those forces influenced Wilson as he led the nation to war.[20] Gardner is determined to cast Wilson as an interventionist, but that is no easy task, given Wilson's great reluctance to use force in Russia. He has a strong tendency to impute to Wilson views that came from others, Robert Lansing in particular. Gardner reads Wilson's disavowals of interventionist intent as having just those intentions; Wilson's "watchful waiting" over Russia was in truth a policy of incessant interventionism. How else, Gardner asks, to read Point 6 of the Fourteen Points? When Wilson called on the powers to respect Russian sovereignty, he was actually stating his opposition to the Bolsheviks. Point 6 "did not say that the United States would ever recognize a Bolshevik government, and was, in fact, a promise to turn over Russian territory to a government that thought in terms of Russian territory, as opposed to Marxist internationalism." In what has to be read as a direct answer to Gardner here, Betty Miller Unterberger reads Point 6 as a sign of Wilson's "determination to continue his crusade for a just peace"; here "he refused to abandon Russia's borderlands to the Central Powers."[21] Gardner's Wilson can't help himself. He might announce his desire to let the Russians "wallow in anarchy a while," but he "was too much a Calvinist to believe that anyone should be allowed to wallow very long," and so, presumably, he participated in the Siberian intervention. Leaving aside the presumption that "Calvinism" somehow predisposed Wilson to butt into others' affairs, Wilson's consistent reluctance to intervene in Russia hints that he was inclined to great patience. Gardner knows

20   Gardner, *Safe for Democracy*, 123, 240–41.
21   Ibid., 162; Betty Miller Unterberger, "Woodrow Wilson and the Bolsheviks: The 'Acid Test' of Soviet-American Relations," *Diplomatic History* 11 (Spring 1987): 72.

as much, for by 1919 he finds Wilson again resisting Entente pressures for outright anti-Bolshevik intervention in Russia and Hungary.[22] Thus Wilson, once the personification of liberal-capitalist neo-imperialism in the revisionist critique, now seems to have resisted the portrait successfully.

Just when revisionism seems bent into contortions, we have in David Foglesong's *America's Secret War against Bolshevism* a strenuous effort to straighten it out. Foglesong argues that the Wilson administration undertook a policy of hostile intervention against the Bolsheviks immediately after the October Revolution. The public commitment to self-determination, necessary to Wilson's diplomatic leverage among the allies, limited the means of that intervention and forced him to fall back to intervention through proxy. Compelled to rely on discrete methods, Wilson pioneered not in a new diplomacy but in Cold War secrecy.[23]

This provocative book ventures a series of specific new claims. Foglesong argues that Boris Bakhmeteff, the Kerensky government's ambassador to the United States, not only kept his portfolio well after the government he represented had ceased to exist but also was a conduit through whom money was poured into anti-Bolshevik activities.[24] In early 1918, Wilson agreed to channel U.S. funds through the English government to White armies in the south. Whereas Arthur Link sees this decision as a momentary aberration quickly reversed, Foglesong argues that it fit a developing pattern of indirect intervention that eventually included spy networks, active propaganda campaigns inside Russia, and the provision of food relief for anti-Bolshevik forces. The crucial document in question is a telegram that Lansing prepared recommending support for White armies under Gen. Aleksei Kaledin. "Without actually recognizing his group as a de facto government," Lansing wrote, "which is at present impossible since it has not taken form, this Government cannot under the law loan money to him to carry forward his movement. The only practicable course seems to be for the British and French Governments

---

22 Gardner, *Safe for Democracy*, 180, 234, 244.
23 David S. Foglesong, *America's Secret War against Bolshevism* (Chapel Hill, NC, 1995).
24 Ibid., 68–72.

to finance the Kaledine [sic] enterprise, . . . and for this Government to loan them the money to do so." Wilson apparently signed off on the telegram, saying that it "has my entire approval." Referring to this episode in the Introduction to Volume 46 of the *Wilson Papers*, Link writes that "after flirting with the idea of secretly supporting the Cossacks who are attempting to establish an independent regime in the Ukraine, Wilson decides to follow a policy of nonintervention in what is developing as a civil war in Russia and to attempt to establish informal relations with the Bolshevik government." Yet Foglesong contends that some money was indeed transferred in this scheme. Georg Schild, in yet another view, treats the episode as a moot point, since Kaledin's movement fell apart so quickly that the general committed suicide in February 1918.[25]

Foglesong disputes the long-standing view that Wilson agreed to the Murmansk intervention only at Trotsky's invitation. George Kennan held the older view, and Betty Miller Unterberger still does. Everyone agrees that Wilson was reluctant to participate with the British at Archangel in the absence of proof that "some body of opinion in Russia" supported it; everyone agrees as well that Trotsky and Lenin considered asking for allied help. It is also clear that Wilson tried to wiggle out of the intervention by arguing that Trotsky was unreliable. Foglesong maintains that Wilson's hostility to the Bolsheviks won out here; at least once he was persuaded that there was some military justification and that the local population would not be hostile. He notes that, regardless of the president's public stance, U.S. personnel in the north were convinced that they were there to fight the Bolsheviks. I am persuaded that the Trotsky "invitation" was not important in Wilson's thinking. There are other explanations, however, for his decisions. John W. Long argues that Wilson cracked under months of "relentless" allied pressure for action but chose to participate in the northern expedition because, aside from its marginal military justification, it had none of the complicating dangers associ-

---

25 See Lansing to Wilson, *PWW* 46:274–75; Link's introduction to *PWW* 46:vii; Foglesong, *America's Secret War*, 103; and Schild, *Between Ideology and Realpolitik*, 72–73.

ated with the proposed Japanese intervention in Siberia. In other words, Wilson chose the least of evils. Foglesong takes no note of the allied pressure on Wilson, which is an important omission and telling about how he makes his case. Foglesong does well to remind us that the allies engaged in a shooting war against the Bolsheviks in the north, but his position should be balanced against Benjamin D. Rhodes's, who in *The Anglo-American Winter War with Russia*, looks closely at allied military operations and finds rampant incompetence instead of persistent malevolence. If American troops knew they were fighting the Bolsheviks, they were hardly enthusiastic about it. They fought in a Russian winter, battled the deadly flu of that year, occasionally expressed ideological sympathy with Bolshevism, and hated being led by English officers – a hatred the British returned in kind.[26]

Audacity alone recommends Foglesong's book as one of the most important written on Wilsonian diplomacy in the last few years. Yet his charges add up to less than advertised; many of his most inflammatory contentions are neither new nor potent. No one should be surprised that Wilson was anti-Bolshevik; it is more surprising that he was so consistently opposed to intervention. Again and again, Foglesong notes that Wilson did not necessarily know – nor would he have approved – of anti-Bolshevik actions undertaken on the ground by American officials. Yet he nonetheless blames Wilson for what they did, and he does so in disregard for other good books on the Americans in Russia. Linda Killen, for example, in *The Russian Bureau*, comes to conclusions not far from Foglesong's but in much less heated fashion. Killen be-

---

26   George Kennan, *Soviet-American Relations*, 2 vols. (Princeton, NJ, 1956); Unterberger, "Woodrow Wilson and the Bolsheviks"; Foglesong, *America's Secret War*, 193–202; John W. Long, "American Intervention in Russia: The North Russian Expedition, 1918–19," *Diplomatic History* 6 (Winter 1982): 45–68; and Benjamin D. Rhodes, *The Anglo-American Winter War with Russia, 1918–1919: A Diplomatic and Military Tragicomedy* (Westport, CT, 1988). The narrative that unfolds in volumes 47 and 48 of *PWW* shows how relentless the Allied pressure on Wilson was; I have always been impressed by how long Wilson resisted. For a new twist on these issues see Victor M. Fic, *The Collapse of American Policy in Russia and Siberia, 1918: Wilson's Decision Not to Intervene* (New York, 1995), who argues that Wilson turned his back on the Russian people by not intervening aggressively to overthrow the Bolsheviks – an indication, perhaps, that the end of the Cold War invites some rather different interpretations of Wilson's Russian policies.

lieves the Americans at the bureau were supporters of the March Revolution, as distinguished from the Bolshevik Revolution, and they sought to help that Russian revolution along by funnelling aid and building economic ties. They were, she finds, a good deal more enlightened than State Department officials. But, in any case, they were given far too little resources to do either harm or good. Many of Foglesong's claims against Wilson, furthermore, are really charges against Robert Lansing, and it is clear that Lansing was not only aggressively anti-Bolshevik but also willing to undercut the president to get his way. Lansing's "treason," however, suggests quite the opposite of what Foglesong argues: it is more reasonable to assume that Wilson tuned out Lansing's advice. But still he charges that Wilson was responsible for creating the momentum for such actions.[27]

Like Gardner, Foglesong reads Wilson's general allusions of friendship with "the Russian people" as anti-Bolshevik because he never explicitly endorsed the regime. Yet he notes that Wilson refused to recognize the socialist Omsk regime in the fall of 1918 despite allied pressure to do so. The situation was too unstable, the Omsk regime far too wobbly. "The administration understandably hesitated to extend formal diplomatic recognition until a new government for *all* of Russia had been established." But if this were so for the Omsk regime, it ought to be applied to Wilson's dealings – or lack thereof – with the Bolsheviks as well.[28]

Even more than Gardner, Foglesong has a pronounced tendency to impute to Wilson beliefs that come from someone else, and much of the rhetorical thrust of the book links Wilson to all manner of odious assumptions, among them, racism, nativism, anti-Semitism, and "Puritanism." One example might illustrate this tendency. In regard to Wilson's endorsement of the Lansing scheme to aid Kaledin, Foglesong writes:

---

27 See Foglesong, *America's Secret War*, 270–71; Linda Killen, *The Russian Bureau: A Case Study in Wilsonian Diplomacy* (Lexington, KY., 1983); and, for the Lansing-Wilson tensions, Dimitri D. Lazo, "A Question of Loyalty: Robert Lansing and the Treaty of Versailles," *Diplomatic History* 9 (Winter 1985): 35–54.
28 Foglesong, *America's Secret War*, 146, 175.

What went through Wilson's mind as he contemplated Russia in chaos? Americans had long drawn parallels between Russia's "dark people," and African Americans, particularly since the nearly simultaneous emancipation of serfs and slaves in 1861 and 1863. In mid-November 1917 Russia's descent into "anarchy" led General Judson to write that the 180 million people in Russia were "mostly ignorant as plantation negroes." Did Wilson silently liken the disorder in Russia to the South during Reconstruction? There is no record of his making such a comparison. However, he certainly thought the situation in Russia called for strong measures to restore order.[29]

The passage is breathtaking. I know a little about turn-of-the-century cultural history, and I cannot recall any widespread tendency to equate serfdom with slavery. Frankly, I would like to be enlightened here. Does Foglesong want us to assume that this supposedly long-held notion was to be found among white supremacists? Had Radical Republicans seen themselves as part of a global emancipation? Or is he reading backward from, say, John Eastland's accusations that Martin Luther King, Jr., was a Communist? That Judson so remarked is indeed curious, but it would be helpful to have a little more context for understanding the comment. Not that it would matter, since Foglesong indicts Wilson even as he admits that he has no proof that Wilson saw the matter similarly. Clearly, Foglesong wants us to assume that Wilson "silently" brooded over a new Lost Cause. He was a Southerner, after all. He had lived through Reconstruction, after all. He had watched *Birth of a Nation* while in the White House, enthusiastically so by all accounts. Why not assume that Wilson drew from that long habit of mind that equated serfdom and slavery – though it apparently was a habit of mind that only Foglesong has yet discerned? One wonders why Foglesong stopped short of equating the White Russians with the Ku Klux Klan.

It is no secret that Wilson was a racist, but to jump from this point to the claim that his racism infused his policy toward the Russian Civil War strikes me as something of a reach. One could

---

29 Ibid., 90.

make the point much better by noting Wilson's reluctance to support a general protection for racial minorities in the League Covenant, though even here his motives were varied and complex. Wilson was not an anti-Semite; he advocated the protection of Eastern European Jews at Versailles, in part because he worried that anti-Semitism was a sign of political reaction in Poland.[30]

Seeking to sustain a proud tradition of scholarship, Foglesong presents material that is genuinely important and must be reckoned with. But the tendency to overreach and settle for trite swings at Wilson mar an otherwise valuable book. Thirty years ago, *America's Secret War* would have found its way onto every college student's reading list. Today the argument is so overwrought that it can only raise suspicions that the tradition it seeks to sustain is on its last legs.

Wilson and the Age of Nationalism

Given the present difficulties with realism and revisionism, it does not seem too bold to suggest that Wilson scholarship needs a paradigm shift. Indeed, there are indications that one is developing. A good deal of recent work recognizes that World War I was the "apogee of modern nationalism," the point at which corporate organization, mass production, mass politics, and state centralization merged to create the twentieth century. I draw here from E. J. Hobsbawm, who writes that "by 1913 capitalist economies were already moving rapidly in the direction of large blocs of concentrated enterprise, supported, protected, and even to some extent guided by governments. The war itself had greatly accelerated this shift towards a state-managed, even a state-planned capitalism."[31] At the same time, the nation-state at its height depended on an international economy to provide resources and markets, and this paradox between nationalism and internation-

---

30   On these issues see my *Wilsonian Idealism in America* (Ithaca, NY, 1994), 67–75.
31   E. J. Hobsbawm, *Nations and Nationalism since 1780: Programme, Myth, Reality* (Cambridge, England, 1990), 132.

alism provides not only the best framework for further work but
also a good way for reading much of the recent scholarship.

Republicanism — The related rise of corporate capitalism, mass politics, and state
centralization in the late nineteenth century blurred the public
and private worlds: the flip side of greater state regulation of
domestic economies was greater state promotion of wealth-tak-
ing abroad. Katz builds *The Secret War in Mexico* upon his strong
insights into this process. English policy in Mexico developed as
it did because the needs of state – oil for a navy just converted
from coal – coincided precisely with British oil magnate Lord
Cowdray's private interests. The identification of private with
public interests was even more blurred among the Germans. After Wilson's downfall, American policy moved in the same way.
Linda Hall's study of U.S. policy in Mexico during the 1920s
demonstrates a consistent governmental effort to do the bidding
of U.S. interests against the competition, not of other oil companies, but against the postrevolutionary Mexican state. Albert Fall,
the senator from New Mexico who served as Warren Harding's
interior secretary, led these systematic efforts with motives that
demonstrate the blurring of interests. "Although Fall certainly
had private gain in mind for himself and his friends," Hall writes,
"he did think more broadly in terms of the national interest . . .
[For] he had become acutely aware of the immense importance
that petroleum would play in the future power of nations."[32]

Christine A. White and David W. McFadden, in two closely
related books, show that similar elements were at work in Soviet
Russia. Like Mexico, Russia had seen a steady stream of foreign
investment enter in the last years of the nineteenth century; after
the revolution and in spite of the intervention, both English and
American interests elbowed for room, sometimes pushing their
governments more steadily toward frank dealing with the Bolsheviks than the politicians were otherwise prepared to go. Nor was
the relationship one way. McFadden, whose work equals Katz's
in richness, shows that the Bolsheviks courted American business
after their bid for political legitimacy collapsed at Versailles.

---

32   Hall, *Oil, Banks, and Politics*, 58, 72–74, 6.

Ludwig C. A. K. Martens, a Russian-born German who headed the New York Soviet Russian Information Bureau, did a land-office business enticing Americans to invest in Russia, and he did so in spite of the State Department's public warnings that he was not recognized in any official capacity.[33]

The blurring of private and public interests, of course, is the central focus of the "corporatist synthesis," and to draw attention to it here says nothing new. I merely would shift emphasis and language and argue that the creation of the consolidated state was but one of many essential parts of modern nationalism. Though they tell us nothing entirely new in this regard, Michael Pearlman's *To Make Democracy Safe for America* and the third volume in George H. Nash's enormous biography of Herbert Hoover demonstrate the old cliché that "war is the health of the state." In his study of the civilian advocates of preparedness, Pearlman demonstrates that universal military training had the nationalist intention of hastening the assimilation of new immigrants. Meanwhile, Nash's third volume finds Hoover presiding as food czar during the war, where, having lost all patience with that most decentralized of industries, agriculture, he pushed hard for centralized control.[34]

The consolidation of private and public interests was never purely a matter of doing the bidding of big business, nor did it create genuine national unity. Linda Hall shows that business interests were themselves divided over the best policy toward Mexico. More important, the process of state consolidation inherently introduced the messy element of mass politics into statecraft. The notion that foreign policies should be beholden to public opinion substantially begins with Wilson, an underappreciated development, for it involves momentous issues, among them the electoral survival of governments (extremely important at

33 Christine A. White, *British and American Commercial Relations With Soviet Russia, 1918–1924* (Chapel Hill, NC, 1992); David W. McFadden, *Alternative Paths: Soviet-American Relations, 1917–1920* (New York, 1993).
34 Michael Perlman, *To Make Democracy Safe for America: Patricians and Preparedness in the Progressive Era* (Urbana, IL, 1984); George H. Nash, *The Life of Herbert Hoover: Master of Emergencies, 1917–1918* (New York, 1996).

Versailles) and the ideological infiltration of foreign policy.[35] We
see in many recent works how organized labor and ethnic groups
weighed in on policy, sometimes as active proponents, often in
public opposition. Gregg Andrews's *Shoulder to Shoulder?* and
Elizabeth McKillen's study of Chicago labor groups explore the
uneven influence of organized labor on policy in the Wilsonian
period.[36] Andrews demonstrates that the modern industrial
economy compelled Samuel Gompers to see that the conditions
of American workers and the conduct of national foreign policy
were entwined. Gompers "tried to promote the integration of
AFL concerns into a national foreign policy agenda," Andrews
explains in a way that nicely catches the overlapping of interests,
"which would nurture a more progressive United States-led economic expansion into Latin America." Yet Gompers's commitment was to the American working class and not to the abstraction of international class solidarity, and he lent his support to
policies in which "U.S. hegemony took precedence over the principles of anti-imperialism." Gompers "demonstrated that his
brand of labor internationalism could be useful as an instrument
of American foreign policy." Andrews might have put it the other
way and pointed out that, so too, Gompers became convinced
that American foreign policy could be useful as an instrument of
labor.[37]

More interesting because less dogmatic, McKillen's *Chicago
Labor and the Quest for a Democratic Diplomacy* has two main
virtues: first, it notes how some labor activists saw the war as an
opportunity for democratic change, including the fundamental
alteration of property relations in their own lives; second, and
most important by my lights, it apprehends the importance of
ethnic and nationalist sentiments in the working-class view of the

35   John A. Thompson provides the most systematic attention to the issue in *Reformers and
War: American Progressive Publicists and the First World War* (New York, 1987), and
"Woodrow Wilson and World War I: A Reappraisal," *Journal of American Studies* 19 (1985):
325–48.
36   Gregg Andrews, *Shoulder to Shoulder? The American Federation of Labor, the United
States, and the Mexican Revolution, 1910–1924* (Berkeley, 1991); Elizabeth McKillen, *Chicago Labor and the Quest for a Democratic Diplomacy, 1914–1924* (Ithaca, NY, 1995).
37   Andrews, *Shoulder to Shoulder?* 12, 29, 49–57, 169–70.

war. McKillen's focus, wisely, is Chicago, where Polish and Irish loyalties were unquestionably pronounced. Wide differences between them notwithstanding, Irish and Polish working-class organizations, by virtue of their activism, tended to promote a process of foreign policymaking that was decentralized and democratic. Irish activists were vigorous internationally, and yet their activism shared much with the spirit of American isolationists such as William Borah. The sympathy between Borah, best thought of as a "peace progressive," according to Robert David Johnson, and Irish radicals in the Chicago Federation of Labor went well beyond their shared dismay over Wilson's war policy or the failure at Versailles. Opposition to Wilsonian diplomacy very often included far-reaching differences over political economy, which meshed domestic and international affairs together. If official policy was intensely ideological, so too was the opposition.[38]

In the United States, nationalism made strange bedfellows. Irish opposition to the League of Nations, which Wilson regarded as treasonous, brought them into the favor of the peace progressives as well as nationalists rallying around Henry Cabot Lodge, both of whom were quick to see the value of ethnic sentiment.[39] The Irish and Lodge: here at first glance was a strange relationship. As William Widenor argues in his formidable biography, Lodge was an American nationalist who considered himself heir to the Federalist-Whig tradition of seeking coherence and unity in national life. In this commitment, Lodge was very much like his fellow WASP, Wilson, who was likewise given to Whig ideals of

---

38 Robert David Johnson, *The Peace Progressives and American Foreign Relations* (Cambridge, MA, 1995). It is interesting, in this regard, to compare Johnson's peace progressives to Herbert F. Margulies's "mild reservationists," that small group of Republicans who supported the league in theory in 1919 but who sought small revisions in order to pacify or outmaneuver the treaty's opponents. Mild reservationists such as Porter McCumber and Irvine Lenroot entertained precious little of the midwestern radicalism of Borah and La Follette, and they offer evidence in contrast that support for Wilsonianism and support for the domestic status quo ran hand-in-hand. Herbert F. Margulies, *The Mild Reservationists and the League of Nations Controversy in the Senate* (Columbia, MO, 1989). See Johnson, *The Peace Progressives*, 111–12, 118, for examples of the differences between mild reservationists and peace progressives over political economy and foreign policy.
39 Ambrosius, *Woodrow Wilson and the American Diplomatic Tradition*, 168–69, 142–43.

political unity.[40] Yet Lodge and the Irish share a peculiar affinity. Both show how deep and enduring nationalist loyalties are and how potentially divisive they can be.[41]

There was, then, in the United States and, indeed, worldwide, a process that began to work during World War I in which the organization of consolidated nation-states, in contrast to the imperial states whose collapse started the war, proceeded just as ethnic and racial consciousness intensified. The two were joined in the idea that territorial nationhood should coincide with linguistic and racial homogeneity. This formulation, which E. J. Hobsbawm calls "Wilsonian nationalism," was the singular feature of war-era politics. During the war, the Entente exploited the yearnings for nationhood among subject peoples as a means to threaten Austria and Germany with dismemberment and at war's end to make irredentist demands for territory. These moves came back to haunt them when colonial peoples lobbied for recognition of their nationhood, as Hobsbawm writes, in "the language of European nationalism, which they had so often learned in or from the west." The only truly universalistic sentiment was, paradoxically, the yearning for separate nationhood based on race.[42]

But to what extent was Wilson responsible for a wave of nationalism that equated race with territory? Two important studies take up this question: Klaus Schwabe's study of the German appeal to Wilsonian war aims and Betty Miller Unterberger's *The United States, Revolutionary Russia, and the Rise of Czechoslovakia*.[43] Schwabe's close examination of German-American diplomacy from war's end through Versailles entertains many issues, but the latter half delves into the issue of self-determination

---

40   William C. Widenor, *Henry Cabot Lodge and the Search for an American Foreign Policy* (Berkeley, 1980). I make a case for Wilson's Whig inspirations in *Wilsonian Idealism in America*, chap. 2.

41   McKillen ruefully concedes as much: "The organic working-class internationalism promoted by the CFL leaders," she concludes, "ultimately shattered on the shoals of ethnic divisity" (*Chicago Labor and the Quest for Democratic Diplomacy*, 222).

42   Hobsbawm, *Nations and Nationalism*, 136.

43   Betty Miller Unterberger, *The United States, Revolutionary Russia, and the Rise of Czechoslovakia* (Chapel Hill, NC, 1989); Klaus Schwabe, *Woodrow Wilson, Revolutionary Germany, and Peacemaking, 1918–1919: Missionary Diplomacy and the Realities of Power*, trans. Rita and Robert Kimber (Chapel Hill, NC, 1985).

and nationhood. On the whole, Wilson sought only modest "revolution" within Germany, and he certainly did not want the nation dismembered. He essentially stumbled upon the utility of self-determination here. In contrast to the Inquiry's recommendations for territorial changes on historic, economic, and strategic grounds, Wilson, Schwabe reports, was far more willing to use ethnic and linguistic definitions for self-determining groups because he believed that this basis would prevent German dismemberment, given the breadth of German-speaking populations. A consistent application of the principle, moreover, would prevent Allied landgrabbing.[44]

In the case of Germany, Wilson used the principle of self-determination as a practical way to maintain the coherence of state structure in Europe. Something of the same conclusion comes through Unterberger's study of Wilson and Czechoslovakia. Well into the war, Wilson continued to assume that Austria-Hungary would be maintained as a state; it was hoped, after all, that the Dual Empire would strike a separate peace. But the "bohemian people" exhibited their animosity to imperial rule, not least by deserting the Austrian army in such numbers that they had to be collected in camps on the eastern front, where they constituted the infamously vexatious Czech Legion. Czechoslovakian nationalism had an able advocate in Thomas Masaryk, a matter of no small importance because Masaryk and Wilson were like-minded. The tension between Czech nationalism and the need for political structure in Europe would have forced Wilson's hand sooner or later. But the eruption of outright conflict on the Trans-Siberian Railway brought from Wilson, in the form of the Siberian intervention, a preliminary recognition of Czech nationhood.

Unterberger's account tells us much about how self-determination forced itself on Wilson but less about exactly what the principle entailed in Wilson's mind. One reasonable impression is that the meaning of self-determination was inchoate. Thus unfor-

---

44 Schwabe, *Woodrow Wilson, Revolutionary Germany, and Peacemaking*, 67–71, 112, 169–71, 174, 255. On how this issue worked out in Poland see Kay Lundgreen-Nielsen, "Woodrow Wilson and the Rebirth of Poland," in *Wilson and a Revolutionary World*, 105–26, where Wilson tried to apply a linguistic litmus test to Polish nationality in the east.

mulated, it meant in practice whatever a given group of people could demand by force of arms – and in this sense it was not a very edifying principle. Unterberger offers her own assessment of Wilson's thinking, which is as good as any: "At the core of his thought, self-determination meant government by consent of the governed – a moral necessity. This logic did not conceive of the implementation of the concept in its broader sense apart from the parallel existence of a league of nations." Wilson figured that once the league was established, once "states had become adjusted to working for the common welfare and without resorting to exploitation," then the causes of strife and division presumably would dampen demands for separatism and minority oppression at the same time.[45]

Still we have the question of who rules over whom and on what grounds in the Wilsonian order of things. Let me venture an answer here. Wilson was not a one-worlder who had in mind the diminution of national sovereignty. He was a nationalist of the nineteenth-century variety, whose "peace program," Jan Willem Schulte Nordholt rightly notes, "was an attempt to express the deepest dreams of the whole eighteenth and nineteenth centuries, the culmination of two centuries of belief in progress."[46] To put it less grandly, Wilson was committed to the cosmopolitan state, which inherently fused people in political union. It is useless to ask on what basis that fusion was to weld diverse peoples together. Wilson merely left that up to the mysterious process of organic development. He assumed that the movement of human beings was toward cosmopolitan political union. Questions of race, language, economics, so important to us today, were secondary.[47] Wilson would have agreed wholeheartedly with John Stuart Mill's terse formulation of nineteenth-century bourgeois nationalism: "Nobody can suppose that it is not more beneficial

---

45 Unterberger, *The United States, Revolutionary Russia, and the Rise of Czechoslovakia*, 90–91.
46 Schulte Nordholt, *Woodrow Wilson*, 251.
47 For a further discussion of the background of Wilson's understanding of self-determination see Sterling J. Kernek, "Woodrow Wilson and National Self-Determination along Italy's Frontier: A Study of the Manipulation of Principles in the Pursuit of Political Interests," *Proceedings of the American Philosophical Society* 126 (August 1982): 243–300.

for a Breton or a Basque in French Navarre to be . . . a member of the French nationality . . . than to sulk on his own rocks, revolving in his own little mental orbit, without participation or interest in the general movement of the world."[48]

Wilson, therefore, was not a "Wilsonian nationalist," as Hobsbawm defines that character. When he tried to align territory with race or language, it was for practical purposes, as in Poland or in Germany, where he sought to uphold the cosmopolitan state. Czechoslovakia was probably the ideal example of Wilsonian nationalism: not only were its foremost advocates liberal intellectuals but it was multiethnic, a quality which, Tony Smith speculates, is one possible explanation for why Czechoslovakia was a more successful democracy than the other new states of Europe.[49] This is just my point: to Wilson, it was inconceivable that the Breton, given free choice through self-determination, would prefer "to sulk on his own rocks, revolving in his own little mental orbit."

Wilson in the Age of One World

One might well argue that if Wilson was not a "Wilsonian nationalist" by this measure, neither were most of the major twentieth-century nationalists. Perhaps the Europeans were, but that fact leaves us with Hobsbawm's fairly torturous claim that Hitler "was in this respect a logical Wilsonian nationalist."[50] Most Third World nationalists were committed to leading independent, Western-style states that contained some mix of ethnic groups. This was true to some extent of Vietnam, surely of India; as Basil Davidson has taught us, it holds true for most African nationalism as well, even when cosmopolitan states made little sense in the African context.[51] And here, I think, is the most fertile ground

48 Mill quoted, conveniently, in Hobsbawm, *Nations and Nationalism*, 34.
49 Smith, *America's Mission*, 101.
50 Hobsbawm, *Nations and Nationalism*, 133.
51 See Basil Davidson, *Africa in Modern History: The Search for a New Society* (London, 1978).

for further writing about Wilsonianism. Today, the best work would be a global history of nationalism as it ran through and developed after the Great War. There is a great book of synthetic history waiting to be written that would demonstrate the effects of the war not just on Sun Yat Sen, Ho Chi Minh, W. E. B. Du Bois, and Jan Smuts, but also on Tilak in India, Kemal in Turkey, Aminoto in Indonesia, and Thomas Horatio Jackson in Nigeria, among many others.[52]

The trick to any new writing in this vein is to play the paradox. These new nation-states all struggled, as Michael Krenn shows us Mexico did, to control their own destinies by controlling their own economies, and yet the thrust of economic development has been away from economic nationalism. In balancing political nationalism against markets that defy boundaries, we may come to see Wilson's liberal internationalism not just as the best disposition for the United States but as a not unhealthy approach to the world as well. Moreover, it is less important to preoccupy ourselves with Wilson's motivations – whether he sought to spread American economic interests or give vent to a racist drive toward domination – than it is to see that the call for self-determination fired the imaginations of countless nationalists in the colonial world, many of whom understood that the best chances for survival in an interdependent world depended on the organization of Western-style states. Akira Iriye has something like this in mind when he writes that Wilson had to give "his blessing" to "the idea that each 'nationality' should have its own nation," lest the principle of self-determination "remain an abstraction."[53]

Even here, however, Wilson presents a problem. Liberal internationalism may well have been a decent way to settle the necessary balance between nationalism's domestic requirements and industrial capitalism's demand for access to global resources and markets. It may have been the best way feeble human beings

---

52   I have in mind a more compelling version of what, for example, Henri Grimal does in the first part of *Decolonization: The British, French, Dutch, and Belgian Empires 1919–1963*, trans. Stephan De Vos (Boulder, CO, 1965). For a more modest example see Kenton J. Clymer, "Jawaharlal Nehru and the United States: The Preindependence Years," *Diplomatic History* 14 (Spring 1990): 143–62.
53   Iriye, *Globalization of America*, 46–47.

could devise to adjust the relations between states of more or less equal nationalist ardor, as the finest writers on multilateralism and liberal internationalism – Tony Smith, Mark T. Gilderhus, and Thomas Knock – seem to suggest.

But it is important to remember that Wilson did indeed have a fairly narrow conception of what nationalism should be, and it was primarily based on the organization of and loyalty to the democratic state. It has not been the democratic state that has fused the nations together, but rather the marketplace, more specifically, the consumer marketplace, which not only has made the world more economically interdependent but culturally homogenous as well. The historical problem here is that the transformation of American commercial culture into global commercial culture marks not the ongoing strength of the democratic nation-state, as Wilson would have wanted it. It is closer to the truth to say that it marks the passing of the nation-state, democratic or otherwise. Global commercial culture did indeed arise out of America, but it is not inherently or irreducibly "American." There is no national content to the Nike swoosh. The spread of this culture, regardless of how many people across the southern hemisphere see it as "the American way of life," works through appealing to the lowest common denominator and the understandable desire for material comfort, but it neither advances the national characteristics of its progenitor nor honors the culture of its recipients. Simply as a matter of fact, Wilson ought not to be credited or criticized for having given shape to a world of which he could scarcely have imagined: one world with nations exploding outward into a bland global consumerism, while their polities implode into separatist enclaves of varying degrees of venality. If we can now look back at him with some admiration, I doubt we can see him as having been "way ahead of his time."

7

Reaching for the Brass Ring: The Recent Historiography of Interwar American Foreign Relations

BRIAN McKERCHER

In the period between 1918 and 1941, the years separating American involvement in the two world wars of this century, the United States emerged as the preeminent global power. Significantly, this occurred despite the supposed isolation of the United States from international political affairs in those two decades. Involvement in international economic and financial affairs, however, was another matter. Since the mid-1940s, America's rise to preeminence has been an issue of enduring interest to scholars of international history, in general, and of American foreign relations, in particular. And although recent international historians have focused most of their attention on the period since 1941 and especially on the Cold War, the interwar period has retained a fascination for a sizable group of scholars. Coupled with recent efforts to address criticisms made by social and economic historians and others of that ilk, this fascination has led to the emergence of a more rigorous analysis of these pivotal years in the history of American foreign relations.[1] As a consequence, older

I would like to thank the Social Sciences and Humanities Research Council of Canada, as well as the Academic Research Programme of the Department of National Defence, Ottawa, for their support in the preparation of this article.
1 Compare Michael Fry, "In Further Pursuit of Lloyd George: International History and the Social Sciences," in *Shadow and Substance in British Foreign Policy: Memorial Essays Honouring C. J. Lowe*, ed. Brian McKercher and David Moss (Edmonton, 1984), 249–80; Charles S. Maier, "Marking Time: The Historiography of International Relations," in *The Past Before Us: Contemporary Historical Writing in the United States*, ed. Michael Kammen (Ithaca, NY, 1980), 355–87; Michael Hunt et al., "Responses to Charles S. Maier, 'Marking

issues have been reexamined, newer ones have been assessed for the first time, and different interpretations, some at decided variance with one another, have emerged about how and why the United States achieved its preeminence. This is not to say that lacunae do not exist; they do. But American foreign relations in the interwar period are now recognized as more complex than previously imagined, and as integral to a distinct phase of historical development that was more than just prologue to what Henry Luce proclaimed in 1941 as the dawning of "the American century." The debate that has emerged since the late 1970s shows the vibrancy of not only this particular area of concern but also that of international history in general.

The crucial point to consider in this is that the study of American foreign relations in the interwar period is no longer the exclusive province of American scholars. Indeed, this aspect of modern American history knows no boundaries. As the United States achieved global power status by 1945, extra-American interest in American foreign relations increased markedly, especially among international historians in Britain and continental Europe and, within the remnants of the old British Empire, Australia and Canada. It is unfortunate that until recently American scholars have not made much use of the work of their non-American counterparts. This was a natural omission, for who better than Americans to write about their own history? Happily, this situation is

Time: The Historiography of International Relations'," *Diplomatic History* 5 (Fall 1981): 353–82; Christopher Thorne, "International Relations and the Promptings of History," in his *Border Crossings: Studies in International History* (New York, 1988): 12–28; and Donald Cameron Watt, *What About The People? Abstraction and Reality in History and the Social Sciences* (London, 1983). Scholarly journals have not been remiss in seeking to give greater precision to the field; for instance, *Diplomatic History*, *History Today*, and the *Journal of American History* have all recently published wide-ranging collections of articles to this end. See "Writing the History of U.S. Foreign Relations: A Symposium," *Diplomatic History* 14 (Fall 1990): 554–605; "What is Diplomatic History?" *History Today* 34 (July 1985): 33–42; and "A Round Table: Explaining the History of American Foreign Relations," *Journal of American History* 77 (June 1990): 93–180. The *Journal of American History* collection has been expanded and has appeared in Michael J. Hogan and Thomas G. Patterson, ed., *Explaining the History of American Foreign Relations* (Cambridge, England, 1991). Then see C. vM. Crabb, *American Diplomacy and the Pragmatic Tradition* (Baton Rouge, LA, 1989); G. Martel, ed., *American Foreign Relations Reconsidered, 1890–1993* (London, 1994); T. Smith, *America's Mission: The United States and the Worldwide Struggle for Democracy in the Twentieth Century* (Princeton, NJ, 1994).

now changing, though occasionally the tendency to downplay the work of non-American historians still receives tangible, if discreet, expression.[2] But the fact remains that non-Americans have produced and are producing shrewd analyses of U.S. foreign relations, particularly of the interwar period. What they offer is a perspective that, because it may differ from that of American historians, provides additional insight into the questions at hand. In fact, by coming to grips with different assessments of American foreign relations, especially ones that might be critical of U.S. policies and actions, American international historians can come to a more complete understanding of their country and its place in the world.

The historiography of American foreign relations in the interwar period originated in the aftermath of the Second World War when, fresh from Allied victory over the Axis Powers and Japan, the United States assumed leadership of the Western powers in the Cold War against Soviet Russia. To a large extent, the developmental historiographical typology of this work in the United States mirrors that of the Cold War: the evolution of a traditional or orthodox school, the emergence of a revisionism that questioned the methodology and basic assumptions of the older school, and the advent of recent postrevisionist analyses.[3]

Established during the early years of the Cold War and lasting until the late 1950s and early 1960s, the traditional school uti-

---

2   See, for example, the bibliographical essay in Warren Cohen, *Empire without Tears: America's Foreign Relations, 1921–1933* (New York, 1987), 129–32 which refers to the work of just one non-American. By the same token the "Selected Readings" for chaps. 14 to 17, which deal with the period from the end of the First World War to Pearl Harbor, in Howard Jones, *The Course of American Diplomacy from the Revolution to the Present*, 2d ed. (Chicago, 1988), 364–65, 385–86, 407–8, 434–35, contain references to the work of more than one hundred historians; less than five of these, including Winston Churchill and despite his American mother, are non-Americans. See C. Carlier and G. Pedroncini, eds., *Les États-Unis dans la première guerre mondiale, 1917–1918: actes du colloque international, Paris* [The United States in the First World War, 1917–1918: acts of the international colloquium] (Paris, 1992); and C. M. Santoro, *Diffidence and Ambition: the intellectual sources of U.S. foreign policy* (Boulder, CO, 1992) (originally published as *Pèrla e Ostrica: alle fonti della politica globale degli Stati Uniti* [Pearl and Oyster: the springs of United States global policy] [Milano, 1987]).

3   The developmental typology utilized here is that outlined in Donald Cameron Watt, "Britain and the Historiography of the Yalta Conference and the Cold War," *Diplomatic History* 13 (Winter 1989): 70–73.

lized approaches and methodologies for writing "diplomatic history" long established in Britain, Europe, and the United States.[4] Much of the work at this time was based on the memoirs and autobiographies published by statesman, diplomats, military men, and others who were part of the foreign policymaking process in the interwar period, as well as on the few published papers and available archives. Consequently, there was a heavy concentration on personality and strategy, on the wrangling between the executive and the legislature to produce policy, and on external pressures and events influencing the formal process of foreign policymaking. Proponents of this school held that after 1921 the Wilsonian idealism and internationalism that had characterized American foreign policy since 1918 were replaced by the narrow nationalism and isolationism of the Republican administrations of Warren G. Harding, Calvin Coolidge, and Herbert Hoover; and that, in turn, the Republican ascendancy was eroded in the aftermath of the Wall Street collapse of 1929 and replaced in 1933 by Franklin D. Roosevelt's Democratic administration.[5] Thus began a new era in American foreign policy that was circumscribed by the increasing isolation of the United States and codified in neutrality legislation, and that sought carefully to protect

4   Despite their obvious philosophical differences, the work of William Langer and Charles Beard is exemplary. See William L. Langer, *The Diplomacy of Imperialism, 1890–1902* (New York, 1935); and William L. Langer and S. Everett Gleason, *The Challenge to Isolation, 1937–1940* (New York, 1952); and Charles A. Beard and George H. E. Smith, *The Idea of National Interest: An Analytical Study in American Foreign Policy* (New York, 1934); Charles A. Beard, *American Foreign Policy in the Making, 1932–1940: A Study in Responsibilities* (New Haven, CT, 1946); and idem, *President Roosevelt and the Coming of the War, 1941* (New Haven, CT, 1948). Perhaps the classic pre-1941 traditional treatments of American foreign relations are Thomas A. Bailey, *A Diplomatic History of the American People* (New York, 1940); and Samuel F. Bemis, *A Diplomatic History of the United States* (New York, 1936).
5   Except where noted, the rest of this paragraph is based on the examples of Selig Adler, *The Uncertain Giant, 1921–1941: American Foreign Policy between the Wars* (New York, 1965); Robert A. Divine, *The Illusion of Neutrality* (Chicago, 1962); L. Ethan Ellis, *Frank B. Kellogg and American Foreign Relations, 1925–1929* (New Brunswick, NJ, 1961); Robert H. Ferrell, *American Diplomacy in the Great Depression: Hoover-Stimson Foreign Policy, 1929–1933* (New Haven, CT, 1957); idem, *Frank B. Kellogg and Henry L. Stimson* (New York, 1963); Arthur S. Link, *Wilson the Diplomatist: A Look at His Major Foreign Policies* (Baltimore, 1957); Allan Nevins, *The New Deal in World Affairs, 1933–1945* (New Haven, CT, 1950); Julius W. Pratt, *Cordell Hull, 1933–1944*, 2 vols. (New York, 1964); and, the quintessential work in this respect, Arthur M. Schlesinger, Jr., *The Age of Roosevelt*, vol. 1, *The Crisis of the Old Order, 1919–1933* (Boston, 1957).

American external interests and security in an ever-more dangerous world. Scholarship on this period was fraught with heated
debates about success and failure – and, in the case of Roosevelt,
with discussion of whether his policies reflected honest endeavors
or Machiavellian conniving[6] – because the net result was American involvement in the Second World War. This corpus of books
and articles essentially showed that the United States had risen to
international preeminence in the quarter century after 1918 by –
take your pick about which was most important – a combination
of skill, misadventure, and luck.

To a large degree, this historiography mirrored the contemporary situation in a United States conditioned by the first decade
and one half or so of the Cold War. An integral part of this was a
division among American historians over the question of the degree of "realism" in American foreign policy.[7] Searching for the

6 Consideration of this question was marked by vituperation, character assassination, conspiracy theory, and more; for a good cross section of the historiography of the initial period
see Harry Elmer Barnes, ed., *Perpetual War for Perpetual Peace: A Critical Examination of
the Foreign Policy of Franklin D. Roosevelt and Its Aftermath* (Caldwell, ID, 1953); Beard,
Roosevelt and the Coming of the War; Charles Callan Tansill, *Back Door to War: The Roosevelt
Foreign Policy, 1933–1941* (Chicago, 1952); and Robert A. Theobald, *The Final Secret of
Pearl Harbor: The Washington Contribution to the Japanese Attack* (New York, 1954), for
the anti-Roosevelt school; and for the pro-Roosevelt, Donald F. Drummond, *The Passing of
American Neutrality, 1937–1941* (Ann Arbor, MI, 1955); Langer and Gleason, *Challenge to
Isolation*; Basil Rauch, *Roosevelt from Munich to Pearl Harbor: A Study in the Creation of a
Foreign Policy* (New York, 1950); and Hans L. Trefousse, *Germany and American Neutral-
ity, 1939–1941* (New York, 1951). The question of Roosevelt and the Pearl Harbor attack
can be addressed by looking at the anti-Roosevelt school listed above and comparing it to
Robert H. Ferrell, "Pearl Harbor and the Revisionists," *Historian* 17:2 (1955): 215–33; John
McKechney, "The Pearl Harbor Controversy: A Debate among Historians," *Monumenta
Nipponica* 18:1 (1963): 45–88; R. S. Thompson, *A Time for War: Franklin D. Roosevelt and
the Path to Pearl Harbor* (New York, 1991); and Roberta Wohlstetter, *Pearl Harbor: Warning and Decision* (Palo Alto, CA, 1962).
7 The great tome in this matter is by the political scientist, Hans J. Morgenthau, *Politics
among Nations: The Struggle for Power and Peace* (New York, 1948). By 1960, this book
had been issued in a third edition. For historical treatments of "realism" in the early period,
see Edward H. Buehrig, *Woodrow Wilson and the Balance of Power* (Bloomington, IN, 1955);
Norman Graebner, *Cold War Diplomacy: American Foreign Policy, 1945–1960* (Princeton,
NJ, 1962); Louis Halle, *Dream and Reality: Aspects of American Foreign Policy* (New York,
1959); George F. Kennan, *American Diplomacy, 1900–1950* (Chicago, 1951); Walter
Lippmann, *U.S. Foreign Policy: Shield of the Republic* (Boston, 1943); Robert Osgood, *Ideals
and Self-Interest in America's Foreign Relations: The Great Transformation* (Chicago, 1953);
and Kenneth W. Thompson, "The Limits of Principle in International Politics: Necessity and
the New Balance of Power," *Journal of Politics* 20 (August 1958): 437–67. The best analysis
of the "realists" is in the intelligent and insightful Jerald A. Combs, *American Diplomatic
History: Two Centuries of Changing Interpretations* (Berkeley, 1983), 199–387, passim, which

supposed lessons that could be drawn from the appeasement of Hitler at Munich in 1938, historians of American foreign relations looked to the past for lessons that might be applied to meet the threat of Soviet Russian totalitarianism in the late 1940s and 1950s.

By the late 1950s and early 1960s, however, as American employment of the supposedly discredited methods of the old diplomacy blurred the moral certainties of the early Cold War, a reaction began to set in against the general purposes and practices of post-1945 American foreign policy. Put uncharitably but more accurately, there was a reaction against Washington's tendency to act in a supposedly un-American way by functioning as any great power would to protect its external interests. This led to the formation of the "revisionist" school. Arguing that American foreign policy had been expansionist since the early days of the Republic, in contradistinction to the avowed ideals of the American way of life, revisionist historiography increasingly gained practitioners and adherents among younger historians. This was particularly so as the Vietnam War went badly for the United States and supposedly exposed the tragedy brought about by an interventionist American foreign policy. The seminal proponent of this interpretation was William Appleman Williams who, with his disciples in the so-called Wisconsin school, offered a "paramarxist" interpretation of American external relations that sought to tie those relations into a framework of economic determinism.[8] Even more blinkered than the traditionalists had been in their defense of American actions, this disparaging view purposely ignored the human element in policymaking. Williams,

---

differentiates between the "hard" and "soft" realists. And on "realism" as an aspect of "idealism" – "Even realist and neorealist writing that claims to isolate those self-interested factors that allegedly determine all foreign policy-making can be deconstructed to reveal a subtext of 'political idealism'" – see Alan Cassels, *Ideology & International Relations in the Modern World* (London, 1996), 240–41.

8   See William Appleman Williams, *The Tragedy of American Diplomacy* (Cleveland, 1959). On the term "paramarxist" see Raymond Aron, *The Imperial Republic: The United States and the World 1945–1975* (London, 1974), xviii, esp. note 5. Of course, Williams did not suddenly spring his views on the academic community in 1959, but only did so after thinking long and hard on what he saw as the nature of American foreign policy; for instance, see his "The Legend of Isolationism in the 1920s," *Science and Society* 18 (1954): 1–20.

his adherents, and others endeavored to show that great continuities existed in American foreign relations from at least the mid-nineteenth century through the mid-twentieth century and beyond.[9] This continuity was seen in terms of the American elite's use of the state's political, military, and financial resources to exert American influence abroad so as to capture markets, undermine the existing preeminence of established imperial powers like Britain, allow for the easy penetration of excess American capital abroad, and cynically manipulate domestic public opinion by using external problems to reduce class tensions within the Republic. Tied to this, for the period after 1917, was increasing political reaction among American economic and political leaders who worked to counter the threat that Bolshevik Russia posed to the United States and international capitalism.[10]

For the revisionists, the course of American external relations in the interwar period was crucial. First and foremost, these historians saw little difference in the thrust of policy pursued by Wilson, the three Republicans, and Roosevelt.[11] They contended that the United States had emerged as the preeminent power in the world by the end of the First World War because of both the tremendous economic fillip the war had given to American industry and finance and the growing weakness of the old European great powers – the victors as much as the vanquished. Williams,

9 Walter LaFeber, *The New Empire: An Interpretation of American Expansion, 1860–1898* (Ithaca, NY, 1963); Howard B. Schonberger, *Transportation to the Seaboard: The "Communication Revolution" and American Foreign Policy, 1860–1900* (Westport, CT, 1971); Tom E. Terrill, *The Tariff, Politics, and American Foreign Policy, 1874–1901* (Westport, CT, 1973); Richard W. Van Alstyne, *The Rising American Empire* (New York, 1960); William Appleman Williams, "The Age of Mercantilism: An Interpretation of the American Political Economy, 1763–1828," *William and Mary Quarterly*, 3d ser., 15:9 (1958): 419–37; and idem, *The Roots of the Modern American Empire: A Study of the Growth and Shaping of Social Consciousness in a Marketplace Society* (New York, 1969).

10 Arno Mayer, the Luxembourg-born Princeton historian of modern Europe, set the tone for this by arguing that this element of modern American foreign policy was established by Woodrow Wilson in the Paris peace settlement. See his *Political Origins of the New Diplomacy, 1917–1918* (New Haven, CT, 1959); and *Politics and Diplomacy of Peacemaking: Containment and Counterrevolution at Versailles, 1918–1919* (New York, 1967).

11 See, for instance, Lloyd C. Gardner, *Economic Aspects of New Deal Diplomacy* (Madison, 1964); Robert F. Smith, "American Foreign Relations, 1920–1942," in *Towards a New Past: Dissenting Essays in American History*, ed. Barton J. Bernstein (New York, 1968), 232–62; and William Appleman Williams, *The Tragedy of American Diplomacy*, 2d rev. ed. (New York, 1972), 108–201.

Frank Costigliola, Gabriel Kolko, and Carl Parrini, among others, emphasized this economic determinist view of American foreign policy in the interwar period as counterpoint to their contention that the United States had become the greatest of the great powers by the 1920s.[12] This power was then directed toward Latin America, the Far East, and other regions of the world where the imperial United States competed for economic advantage and markets at the expense of the older imperial powers. This is not to say that uniformity of opinion existed among the revisionists. Some American scholars, for instance Michael J. Hogan, sought to show that there was a cooperative element in American economic diplomacy, in fact that a cooperative competition between the British and the Americans existed until as late as 1928 or 1929.[13] Still, in a dialectical sense, this softer revisionist view was to a large degree part and parcel of the same general interpretation.

Williams and the revisionists also tangentially offered a different approach to the study of American foreign relations. This involved a need to examine more closely the domestic roots of American foreign relations, a task made easier by the increasing availability of public and private archives. Essentially, this was an attack on the older methodologies of foreign policy analysis that concentrated rather heavily on external pressures and the formal policymaking processes. It was not, however, a uniquely American reaction. The work of the American revisionists corresponded to that being done in Germany about the same time by

---

12 Notable are Frank Costigliola, "The United States and the Reconstruction of Germany in the 1920s," *Business History Review* 50:4 (1976): 477–502; idem, "Anglo-American Financial Rivalry in the 1920s," *Journal of Economic History* 37:4 (1977): 911–34; Gabriel Kolko, "American Business and Germany, 1930–1941", *Western Political Quarterly* 15 (December 1962): 713–28; and Carl P. Parrini, *Heir to Empire: United States Economic Diplomacy, 1916–1923* (Pittsburgh, 1969).

13 Michael J. Hogan, *Informal Entente: The Private Structure of Cooperation in Anglo-American Economic Diplomacy, 1918–1929* (Columbia, MO, 1977). Interestingly, because he deviated from the hard revisionist line of thought, Hogan was taken to task in Carl Parrini, "Anglo-American Corporatism and the Economic Diplomacy of Stabilization in the 1920s," *Reviews in American History* 6 (September 1978): 379–87. Hogan's work was not unique in this respect. Joan Hoff Wilson, *American Business and Foreign Policy, 1920–1933* (Lexington, KY, 1971), had earlier questioned the hard revisionist line by arguing that while a complex relationship existed between government and business, the latter was too divided to permit a business-inspired program to determine foreign policy.

Fritz Fischer and his devotees on the primacy of domestic considerations over external ones in German foreign policymaking: the so-called *innenpolitik* versus *aussenpolitik* debate.[14] Along with the increasing academic prominence of the Annales school in France and the heavy concentration on social and economic history generally, the purely politicostrategic dimension of foreign policymaking came under a sustained attack. This led to a questioning in Europe and North America of the Rankean view of how and why the Great Powers created foreign policy, and an attempt to dismiss the older methods of analysing foreign policy. Although an antirevisionist school of thought quickly emerged in Europe to counter the *innenpolitik* advocates and the Annales apostles – the "new international history," which emphasized the amalgam of politicostrategic, economic, and financial elements in foreign relations, but stressed human agency rather than unseen forces[15] – the same did not happen in the United States, a consequence of the chancre of Vietnam. Indeed, by the mid-1970s, some reasonable American diplomatic historians – reasonable in that their work was not encumbered by the heavy ideological baggage of the revisionists – were even discussing whether the older analytical methodologies had been flawed and whether "diplomatic history" had perished beneath the onslaught of social and economic history.[16] While the study of foreign relations was still deemed to be valid, this discussion did conclude that some revi-

---

14   Fritz Fischer, *Griff nach der Weltmacht; die Kriegzeilpolitik des Kaiserlichen Deutschland 1914/18* [Grasp for world power: the war aims policy of Imperial Germany 1914–1918] (Düsseldorf, 1961). This book was subsequently published in English as *Germany's Aims in the First World War* (New York, 1967).

15   Jean-Baptiste Duroselle, of the Sorbonne, and Donald Cameron Watt, of the London School of Economics, were the seminal thinkers here. See J.-B. Duroselle, *La politique extérieure de la France de 1914 à 1945* [The foreign policy of France from 1914 to 1945] (Paris, 1965); idem, *La Décadence, 1932–1939* [Decadence, 1932–1939] (Paris, 1979); Donald Cameron Watt, *Personalities and Policies: Studies in the Formulation of British Foreign Policy in the Twentieth Century* (London, 1965); idem, *Too Serious a Business: European Armed Forces and the Approach of War* (Cambridge, England, 1975); and idem, "Foreward: the New International History," *International History Review* 9 (November 1987): 518–20.

16   See, for instance, Ernest R. May, "The Decline of Diplomatic History," in *American History: Retrospect and Prospect*, ed. George Billias and Gerald Grob (New York, 1971), 399–430.

sionist charges had merit and that the matters they raised about the wellsprings of foreign policy had to be addressed.[17]

Outside of the United States, chiefly in Britain and France, proponents of the "new international history" were already working to this end. More rigorous studies, some even relying on social science analytical methodologies, were being undertaken to show the interplay of people and ideas and the connection between politicostrategic and financial-economic issues in international history. Thus, in the early 1970s outside of the United States, traditional "diplomatic history" was quickly superseded by a new approach in "international history" that was at once more diffuse in its interpretations and less dogmatic.[18] As that decade ended, a similar "international history" of the interwar period also began to emerge in the United States, coincident with "postrevisionism" in Cold War studies. These developments occurred for the same reason. The shifting constellation of international power brought about by the end of the Vietnam war, by the barrenness of détente, and by increasing Soviet Russian involvement in sub-Saharan Africa, Central America, and Afghanistan – not to mention a seemingly more open Soviet Russian state after 1985 – created a changed world. At the same time, a new generation of historians uncontaminated by the political agenda of the revisionists and

17   Indeed, Professor May continued to produce balanced assessments of American foreign relations in the traditional mold that utilized new methodologies and came to grips with revisionist critiques. For instance, see his thought-provoking *"Lessons" of the Past: The Use and Misuse of History in American Foreign Policy* (New York, 1973). For examples of others who sought to meet the criticisms of the revisionists see Robert J. Maddox, "Another Look at the Legend of Isolationism in the 1920's," *Mid-America* 53:1 (1971): 35–43; Arnold A. Offner, "Appeasement Revisited: The United States, Great Britain, and Germany, 1933–1940," *Journal of American History* 64 (September 1977): 373–93; and David F. Trask, *Captains and Cabinets: Anglo-American Naval Relations, 1917–1918* (Columbia, MO, 1973).

18   See, for example, Denise Artaud, *La question des dettes interalliées et la reconstruction de l'Europe: 1917–1918* [The question of inter-allied debts and the reconstruction of Europe: 1917–1929], 2 vols. (Paris, 1978); Anthony Adamthwaite, *France and the Coming of the Second World War* (London, 1977); Sidney Aster, *1939, The Making of the Second World War* (London, 1973) which was subsequently published in French as *Les Origines de la Seconde Guerre Mondiale* (Paris, 1974); Michael G. Fry, *Illusions of Security: North Atlantic Diplomacy 1918–22* (Toronto, 1972); Christopher Thorne, *The Limits of Foreign Policy: The West, the League and the Far Eastern Crisis of 1931–1933* (New York, 1972); and Robert J. Young, *In Command of France: French Foreign Policy and Military Planning, 1933–1940* (Cambridge, MA, 1978).

too young to have been markedly affected by the moral certainties of the Cold War, began to look afresh at the interwar period. Although difficult to prove, there was probably also an understandable revulsion against the tyranny of social and economic historians in forcing other scholars to move from the large picture to the small in the study of all human phenomena. As P. G. Wodehouse said about cows, such a parochial approach "lacks sustained dramatic interest"[19] and cannot explain crucial issues in human affairs, like war and peace. States, not societies, pursue foreign policy. The result has been a recent historiography diverse in interpreting how and why the United States evolved as it did in the two decades after 1918.

This historiography is most easily considered by looking at developments within the chronological confines of the three general periods of U.S. political life between 1918 and 1941: the final phase of the Wilson administration; the twelve years of Republican power; and the period of Roosevelt's tenure to Pearl Harbor. In the case of Woodrow Wilson, historians in the last twenty years or so have concentrated on two principal concerns that preoccupied his administration in its later stages: American policies at the Paris Peace Conference and the nature of the U.S. relationship with the Latin American powers. The two are connected. Wilson went to Europe in December 1918 to ensure that a new international order, based on the moral precepts of "the Fourteen Points," would be created via the peace settlement. Ideals such as open diplomacy, freer trade, and national self-determination were to be the essence of an American rejection of isolationism and the entry of the United States into the political affairs of the great powers. Though traditional historians argued that Wilsonianism offered the basis for a new international order after the great war, they disagreed over whether Wilson betrayed his ideals at Paris to achieve the peace settlement.[20] Despite this division, they did agree that Wilson embodied an internationalist approach to Ameri-

---

19 P. G. Wodehouse, "The Custody of the Pumpkin," in *The World's 100 Best Short Stories*, ed. Grant Overstreet (New York, 1927), 10:43–68. The quotation is from p. 44.

20 For a traditionalist defense of Wilson see Link, *Wilson the Diplomatist*; and idem, *Woodrow Wilson: Revolution, War, and Peace* (Arlington Heights, IL, 1979), which revises

can foreign relations. Revisionists, on the other hand, contended that the idealistic Wilson had been out-maneuvered by the realists, David Lloyd George and Georges Clemençeau, at Paris. Adding to Wilson's unacceptability in their eyes was that in pursuing the economic interests of imperial America in Latin America, the president had employed a "dollar diplomacy" that was rarely constricted by morality and was thus no different than either his predecessors or his successors.[21] More recent historiography, despite the odd foray by traditionalists and revisionists, has seen the focus of the debate shift. It has endeavored to determine the level to which Wilson's ideals and moral approach to foreign policy were affected by domestic pressures and by the desire and the need to protect and extend America's external economic and strategic interests within both its own sphere of interest and the charmed circle of the great powers. Permeating all of this is the supposition that the United States had become the greatest of the great powers by 1918, a development that added piquancy to Wilson's failures at Paris.

To consider Latin America first, there is an emerging consensus about Wilson's policies in this region. The leading work in this respect is Mark Gilderhus's *Pan-American Visions: Woodrow Wilson in the Western Hemisphere 1913–1921*.[22] Building on his earlier work, Gilderhus breaks new ground by offering the compelling argument that Wilson's policies were part of "the ongoing efforts of the United States to manage the affairs of the western hemisphere and to bestow more orderly and predictable structures upon its relations with the countries of Latin America."[23]

---

to a degree the former. For a critique of Wilson – "with [his] tremendous contrasts of brilliant insight and appalling personal deficiencies" – see George F. Kennan, *Russia and the West under Lenin and Stalin* (Boston, 1961), 120–35 (the quotation herein is from p. 121). See also F. S. Calhoun, *Uses of Force and Wilsonian Foreign Policy* (Kent, OH, 1993; and D. M. Esposito, *The Legacy of Woodrow Wilson: American War Aims in World War I* (Westport, CT, 1996).

21 See N. Gordon Levin, Jr., *Woodrow Wilson and World Politics: America's Response to War and Revolution* (New York, 1968); and Robert F. Smith, *The United States and Revolutionary Nationalism in Mexico, 1916–1932* (Chicago, 1972).

22 Mark T. Gilderhus, *Pan American Visions: Woodrow Wilson in the Western Hemisphere, 1913–1918* (Tucson, AZ, 1986).

23 This quotation is from ibid., ix. For examples of Gilderhus's earlier work see his *Diplomacy and Revolution: U.S.-Mexican Relations under Wilson and Carranza* (Tucson, AZ,

Looking beyond American bilateral relationships with the Latin American powers, Gilderhus seeks to put the multifarious elements of American policy toward the region within an overarching framework. His essential argument is that Wilson and his advisers sought to establish a working network of trade and investment for the region and, at the same time, to coordinate a united hemispheric resistance to potential European intervention. This resistance entailed an active foreign policy that, in turn, necessitated American intervention in the hemisphere. The difficulty for Wilson lay with the Latin American perception of U.S. foreign policy. From Washington's perspective, American policy might well have been pursued for the benefit of both the United States and the Latin American powers; but to those powers, especially Mexico, there seemed to be little difference between intervening Americans and intervening Europeans.

Gilderhus's general ideas are supported by other more recent works that deal with specific instances of American intervention. David Healy, for instance, has sought neither to exonerate nor to condemn American policies in the Caribbean between the McKinley and Wilson administrations; rather, Healy takes great pains to explain how and why American policy evolved as it did.[24] Unlike the hard revisionists, who gleefully sought to show Wilson's apparent hypocrisy, Healy sees the president less as a solitary figure directing policy in somewhat contradictory ways and more as a representative of the American people, who themselves held contradictory views about the proper role of the United States as the dominant power in the Western Hemisphere. American leaders, especially Wilson, had to balance the ideals of a moral American foreign policy with domestic political and economic pressures and external strategic necessities, the latter being particularly important after August 1914. Although Wilson and other American leaders had a clear notion of how policy ought to de-

---

1977); "Pan-American Initiatives: The Wilson Presidency and 'Regional Integration', 1914–17," *Diplomatic History* 4 (Fall 1980): 409–23; and "Wilson, Carranza, and the Monroe Doctrine: A Question in Regional Organization," ibid. 7 (Spring 1983): 103–15.
24   David Healy, *Drive to Hegemony: The United States in the Caribbean, 1898–1917* (Madison, WI, 1988).

velop regarding Latin America, especially in a moral sense, sometimes morality had to be subordinated to the dictates of realpolitik. This might have resulted in increasing American intervention in Mexico, Cuba, or Santo Domingo (with all the unforeseen danger this created for American interests then and later because of the rise of anti-American sentiment), but the goal of American policy was to ensure stability. And an important corollary here, even for the Wilson administration, was that stability did not necessarily mean ensuring the export to Latin America of both American liberal democratic values and investment. Although the shades of interpretation vary concerning the economic and financial goals of American policies, additional case studies produced by Kendrick Clements, Friedrich Katz, Emily Rosenberg, and others underscore Healy and Gilderhus.[25] Indeed, Emily Rosenberg's analysis of the "spreading of the American dream," which covers the entire interwar period and more, makes the point that although special interest groups like missionaries and businessmen were fundamental to the expansion of U.S. international power in the half century before 1945, "the government gradually came to assist much of this private expansion, not so much because special interests demanded government support (though many did call for a stronger show of the flag) but because policy-makers began to accept expansionism as a fundamental condition of 'national interest' and international betterment."[26] This is a fitting testament

25 Kendrick Clements, "Emissary from a Revolution: Luis Cabrera and Woodrow Wilson," *Americas* 35 (January 1979): 353–71; idem, "Woodrow Wilson's Mexican Policy, 1913–1915," *Diplomatic History* 4 (Spring 1980): 113–36; Paul Henderson, "Woodrow Wilson, Victoriano Huerta, and the Recognition Issue in Mexico," *Americas* 41 (October 1984): 151–76; Friedrich Katz, *The Secret War in Mexico: Europe, the United States and the Mexican Revolution* (Chicago, 1981); Emily Rosenberg, "La Politica del Presidente Wilson en America Central: la lucha contra la inestabilidad economica" [The Policies of President Wilson in Central America: the struggle against economic instability], *Revista de Historia* 5 (1980): 33–58; and James A. Sandos, "Pancho Villa and American Security: Woodrow Wilson's Mexican Diplomacy Reconsidered," *Journal of Latin American Studies* 13 (November 1981): 293–311. I would like to thank my former colleague, David Dinwoodie, for directing me to Dr. Rosenberg's article.
26 Emily S. Rosenberg, *Spreading the American Dream: American Economic and Cultural Expansion, 1890–1945* (New York, 1982). The quotation is from pp. 230–31. Also telling in this respect is Emily S. and Norman L. Rosenberg, "From Colonialism to Professionalism: The Public-Private Dynamic in United States Foreign Financial Advising, 1898–1929," *Journal of American History* 74 (June 1987): 59–82; and, though it deals with West Africa, Emily

to the developing new approach to the nature of Wilsonian idealism, its connection to domestic opinion and external considerations, and the nature of American foreign policy toward Latin
America after the Great War.

The recent historiography focusing on Wilson's travails over
peacemaking after November 1918, the more important consideration, is not marked by the same sort of emerging consensus
that exists concerning Latin America. Wilson's endeavors at Paris
concentrated on several issues: territorial adjustments, the treatment of defeated Germany, the relationship of the United States
with the victorious Allied Powers, the Russian question, and the
creation of the League of Nations. Suffusing all of these was the
president's ultimate failure to secure the ratification of the Treaty
of Versailles. In seeking better to understand Wilson, recent historiography has been concerned with answering several questions
unresolved by the earlier debate between traditionalists and revisionists. How did Wilson's morality and idealism square with the
reality of competing great power interests in Europe and abroad?
Did the president understand the problems that confronted both
the victors and the vanquished in Europe and make policy accordingly? What were the precise domestic pressures that affected the nature and content of his diplomacy?

Wilson's principal concern at the peace conference entailed ensuring that a new international order would emerge from the war.
Here lies the matter of idealism versus realism in Wilson's diplomacy. It is interesting that a non-American historian was the first
to produce a new international history assessment of Wilson by
consciously synthesizing the traditional and revisionist interpretations that had emerged by the late 1960s. In 1971, responding
to the competing charges that Wilson had either forsaken his ideals or been outflanked by Lloyd George and Clemençeau, the
German historian, Klaus Schwabe, posited that Wilson, like St.
Peter, denied rather than betrayed his principles.[27] The key to his

---

S. Rosenberg, "The Invisible Protectorate: The United States, Liberia, and the Evolution of
Neocolonialism, 1909–40," *Diplomatic History* 9 (Summer 1985): 191–214.
27 Klaus Schwabe, *Deutsche Revolution und Wilson-Frieden: Die Amerikanische und
Deutsche Friedens-strategie Zwischen Ideologie und Machtpolitik, 1918–1919* [German revo-

argument is that the president may have been an idealist in external policy but, like any other leader, he also possessed the essential element of pragmatism in pursuit of his political goals. In 1985, Schwabe's work was published in a shortened English version – only 565 pages!!! – that utilized additional archival and secondary sources that had become available in the interim.[28] His argument was more compelling because it showed Wilson's mind to be more subtle than historians had argued previously. Wilson realized that he could not dictate to Lloyd George and Clemenceau; to achieve anything, he had to be willing to compromise. Hence, deals were struck and, despite what the traditionalists and the revisionists earlier contended, Wilson did not jettison his ideals, nor was he outfoxed by the "realist" Europeans. For example, Schwabe argues that Wilson consistently held Germany to be guilty for the war and, ignoring the unconvincing arguments of the Ebert government about the need for leniency because of the Bolshevik threat, worked consistently to ensure that Germany was punished for its transgressions. The only area in which Wilson was forced to retreat on principle involved reparations.[29] But this simply showed his pragmatism. Without concessions here, the peace conference would have broken up, with incalculable consequences for both the European powers and the United States.

Schwabe has not been the only recent historian to go beyond the dialectical strictures imposed by both the traditionalists and revisionists. Lloyd Ambrosius has worked to redefine the way in which Wilson's policies at the peace conference can be assessed.[30]

---

lution and Wilson-peace: the American and German peace strategy between ideology and power politics, 1918–1919] (Düsseldorf, 1971).

28 Klaus Schwabe, *Woodrow Wilson, Revolutionary Germany, and Peace-making, 1918–1919: Missionary Diplomacy and the Realities of Power* (Chapel Hill, NC, 1985).

29 Ibid., 370–74. See also Klaus Schwabe, "Woodrow Wilson and Germany's Membership in the League of Nations," *Central European History* 8 (March 1975): 3–22.

30 Lloyd E. Ambrosius, *Woodrow Wilson and the American Diplomatic Tradition: The Treaty Fight in Perspective* (New York, 1987). See also his "The Orthodoxy of Revisionism: Woodrow Wilson and the New Left," *Diplomatic History* 1 (Summer 1977): 199–214; "Ethnic Politics and German-American Relations after World War I: The Fight over the Versailles Treaty in the United States," in *Germany and America: Essays on Problems of International Relations and Immigration*, ed. Hans Trefousse (New York, 1980), 29–40; "Woodrow Wilson and the Quest for Orderly Progress," in *Traditions and Values: American Diplomacy, 1865–1945*, ed. Norman A. Graebner (Lanham, MD, 1985), 73–100; and *Wilsonian State-*

Deprecating the labels that Wilson's defenders and critics have employed to examine his diplomacy – "realism," "idealism," "internationalism," and "isolationism" – Ambrosius offers what he contends are the more precise terms of "interdependence and pluralism."[31] Ambrosius's argument centers on Wilson's personality, which, like Schwabe, he sees as too full of nuances to permit the simple black and white classifications that revisionists have loved and have used to heap criticism on the president. Wilson wanted to impose order on international anarchy, and he wanted to do it on American terms. The source of this desire was the domestic America that had surrounded Wilson in his prepresidential years. American society had adapted to industrialization and modernization through reform, not revolution. It was social control writ large and, despite a Republican Congress after November 1918, Wilson sought the same kind of control in peacemaking. Of course, he failed to impose an American solution at Paris. Unlike Schwabe, Ambrosius is not sympathetic to Wilson, nor does he see the president as a pragmatic diplomatist. Instead, with a degree of hindsight, he criticizes Wilson for not realizing that the United States could not unilaterally impose its will on other powers. This had nothing to do with being idealistic, realistic, internationalist, or isolationist. It had to do with Wilson's failure to appreciate that the world was increasingly interdependent and that a pluralism existed among the powers that did not allow for the kind of Americanized world that Wilson wished to create. Crucially, Wilson was not alone in this among Americans. In a wide-ranging concluding chapter, Ambrosius argues that Wilson established a tradition in American foreign policy built around the idea that, to avoid the kind of crises that marked the interwar period, American ideals had to be imposed unilaterally on allies and others. The consequence of this can be seen in the record of U.S. foreign policy thereafter, culminating in Vietnam and beyond.

Although Schwabe and Ambrosius seek to show the more human side of Wilson, admittedly from different perspectives, and

craft: Theory and Practice of Liberal Internationalism During World War I (Wilmington, DE, 1991).
31 Ambrosius, *Wilson and the American Diplomatic Tradition*, ix–xxi.

to place him in the context of the peace conference, the new approach in international historiography concerning Wilson the peacemaker, as mentioned earlier, lacks any sort of consensus. True to his revisionist credentials, Lloyd Gardner has argued that Wilson's idealism and morality were more apparent than real.[32] The litmus test was Wilson's attitudes toward the revolutions in China, Mexico, Germany, and Russia in the decade after 1913 and, in this, the Anglo-American relationship was crucial, because both Wilson and his British counterparts opposed revolutionary movements. Like Ambrosius, but with an unrepentant revisionism, Gardner sees much of Wilson's diplomacy directed toward winning acceptance of American notions about liberal international capitalism from other Powers, particularly Great Britain. But then Gardner diverges. He sees Lloyd George at Paris as more flexible on both Germany and Russia than Wilson. Showing revisionist purity of thought, Gardner is unwilling to accept the obvious criticisms of his school's shortcomings concerning the president. Thus, his stark view of Wilson contrasts sharply with the more subtle one suggested by Ambrosius and Schwabe.[33] It also contrasts with other recent works. For instance, Antony Lentin, in examining the war guilt question at Paris, makes no bones about the fact that on this matter Lloyd George was not only the more unyielding but also the more mercurial.[34] Admittedly, this view might be dismissed because, like Gardner and Wilson, Lentin has only coldness in his heart for Lloyd George and uses an acid-tipped pen to assert that the problems Europe confronted with the German question over the next twenty years, culminating in Munich, can be laid at the British premier's door and not at Wilson's. Less easy to discount are older historians

32   Lloyd C. Gardner, *Safe for Democracy: The Anglo-American Response to Revolution, 1913–1923* (New York, 1984).

33   See L. Ambrosius, "Franklin D. Roosevelt, National Self-Determination, and World Peace: A Comparison with Woodrow Wilson," and K. Schwabe, "Woodrow Wilson and the Problems of Peacemaking at the Paris Peace Conference of 1919," both unpublished papers delivered at the June 1998 SHAFR Conference, University of Maryland. See also M. L. Eiland, III, *Woodrow Wilson, Architect of World War II* (New York, 1991); D. Heater, *National Self-Determination: Woodrow Wilson and His Legacy* (New York, 1994).

34   Antony Lentin, *Lloyd George, Woodrow Wilson and the Guilt of Germany: An Essay in the Prehistory of Appeasement* (Baton Rouge, LA, 1985).

who can admit that their original assessments were flawed. Thus, Arthur Link, the staunchest of Wilson's traditionalist defenders, has revised his earlier assessments to address criticisms that arose after 1960.[35]

Apart from these analyses, recent historiography has wrestled with specific problems in Wilson's peacemaking. One of these, the president's role in Allied relations with Bolshevik Russia, stemmed from 1960s and 1970s revisionism, which concentrated rather heavily on interwar Russo-American relations, not because of their importance before 1941 but because of American policies toward Soviet Russia during the Cold War. Although Gardner not surprisingly sees a large degree of equivocation in Wilson's attitude toward Russia, Betty Unterberger leads a coterie of historians who argue seductively that the president approached the problem of Bolshevik Russia with caution and good sense whether one looks at the Allied intervention in Russia or at the territorial settlement along the ill-defined frontiers of the Bolshevik state.[36] Thus, although historians are divided over how clearly defined Wilson's goals on this issue were, they do see him as a leader who had to balance his advisers, his allies, and others, including expatriate Russians. Recent interpretations of Wilson's effort to se-

---

35 See Link's work cited in footnote 20.
36 Gardner, *Safe for Democracy*, 180–82, 234–35, 238–40, 244–54. See also W. Allison, *American Diplomats in Russia: Case Studies in Orphan Diplomacy, 1916–1919* (Westport, CT, 1997); D. S. Foglesong, *America's Secret War against Bolshevism: U.S. Intervention in the Russian Civil War, 1917–1920* (Chapel Hill, NC, 1995); Kay Lundgreen-Nielsen, "Woodrow Wilson and the Rebirth of Poland," in Link, ed., *Revolutionary World*, 105–26; idem, "The Mayer Thesis Reconsidered: The Poles and the Paris Peace Conference," *International History Review* 7 (February 1985): 68–102; D. W. McFadden, *Alternative Paths: Soviet-American Relations, 1917–1920* (New York, 1993); N. V. Salzman, *Reform and Revolution: The Life and Times of Raymond Robins* (Kent, OH, 1991); N. V. Salzman, ed., *Russia in War and Revolution: General William V. Judson's Accounts from Petrograd, 1917–1918* (Kent, OH, 1998); James Smallwood, "Banquo's Ghost at the Paris Peace Conference: The United States and the Hungarian Question," *East European Quarterly* 12 (Fall 1978): 289–307; and Betty M. Unterberger, "Woodrow Wilson and the Bolsheviks: The 'Acid Test' of Soviet-American Relations," *Diplomatic History* 11 (Fall 1987): 71–90. Linda Killen's work must be set off by itself; she sees Wilson as being somewhat contradictory in his approach to the Bolsheviks but determined to preserve "Russia" intact for what he thought would be the inevitable more moderate successors of Lenin. See her "The Search for a Democratic Russia: Bakhmetev and the United States," *Diplomatic History* 2 (Summer 1978): 237–56; "Self-determination vs. Territorial Integrity: Conflict Within the American Delegation over Wilsonian Policy Toward the Russian Borderlands," *Nationalities Papers* 10 (Spring 1982): 65–78; and *The Russian Bureau: A Case Study of Wilsonian Diplomacy* (Lexington, KY, 1983).

cure national self-determination, however, are generally fraught with intense debate between those who see him as hypocritical and those who conclude that he was a pragmatic leader who had to make some concessions for the good of a larger peace.[37] In any event, historians in Europe and the United States over the past twenty years support Ambrosius's argument that Wilson's unilateral actions at Paris, because they failed to deliver a golden era, resulted in disillusionment with the United States among "progressive" elements in Europe.[38]

The debate over Wilson's other efforts has also been a fundamental part of recent historiography and, given the importance of the subject to subsequent interwar history, has not produced a consensus. Like Inga Floto, Arthur Walworth continues to lay much of the blame for the president's problems on the doorstep of his chief adviser, Colonel Edward M. House.[39] Antony Lentin, who has his own anti-Lloyd George agenda, however, defends House with the argument that "his work was necessary, intelligent and on the whole beneficial."[40] George Egerton has written widely to demonstrate that over the creation of the League of Nations – about which Wilson did little except ensure that the quarrelsome Article Ten was encased in the Covenant – the president's policies lacked sensitivity toward Britain's postwar

37 For criticisms see Heater, *National Self-Determination*; Duane Myers, "The United States and Austria, 1918–1919: The Problem of National Self-determination," *Proceedings of the South Carolina Historical Association* (1975): 5–15; and for supportive views see F. W. Brecher, "Revisiting Ambassador Morgenthau's Turkish Peace Mission of 1917," *Middle Eastern Studies* 24 (July 1988): 357–63; and Joylon Girard, "Pierrepont Noyes and the Rhineland Agreement: A Case Study in Wilsonian Internationalism," *Maryland Historian* 18:2 (1987): 23–33.
38 Exemplary are G. R. Conyne, *Woodrow Wilson: British Perspectives, 1912–21* (New York, 1992); Shaul Ginsburg, "Du Wilsonisme au Communisme: l'itinéraire du pacifiste Raymond Lefebvre en 1919" [From Wilsonism to communism: the itinéraire du pacifiste Raymond Lefebvre in 1919], *Revue d'Histoire Moderne et Contemporaine* 23:4 (1976): 581–605; T. J. Knock, *To End All Wars: Woodrow Wilson and the Quest for a New World Order* (New York, 1992); David F. Schmitz, "Woodrow Wilson and the Liberal Peace: The Problem of Italy and Imperialism," *Peace and Change* 12:1–2 (1987): 29–44; Bruno Tobia, "Il Partito Socialista Italiano e la Politica di W. Wilson (1916–1919)" [The Italian Socialist Party and the policies of W. Wilson (1916–1919)], *Storia Contemporanea* 5:2 (1974): 275–303.
39 Arthur Walworth, *Wilson and His Peacemakers: American Diplomacy at the Paris Peace Conference, 1919* (New York, 1986).
40 Antony Lentin, "What Really Happened at Paris?" *Diplomacy and Statecraft* 1 (July 1990): 264–75; the quotation is from p. 271. See also Inga Floto, *Colonel House in Paris: A Study of American Policy at the Paris Peace Conference, 1919* (Copenhagen, 1973).

international security.[41] Indeed, Egerton has shown for the first
time precisely why Lord Grey's mission to find an Anglo-American condominium of interests at the time of the treaty fight in the
Senate was scuppered by Wilson's personal pique concerning a
social imbroglio involving Mrs. Wilson and a junior member of
the British Embassy in Washington.[42] In contradistinction to
Schwabe, Denise Artaud has charged that Wilson's lack of realism about British war debts and his antagonism toward British
financial power laid the basis for the flawed reparations settlement and the problems that plagued European reconstruction after Versailles.[43] But in a wide-ranging study of reparations from
Versailles to 1932, Bruce Kent holds Lloyd George and Clemençeau
to be more blameworthy, primarily because their policies were
dictated by the internal dynamics of British and French politics.
To a large degree David Stevenson's work on French war aims in
the Great War, Franco-American wartime relations, and the nature of international politics during the period of fighting sees the
Europeans as working hard to ensure that their essential national
interests were not imperiled by the American challenge implicit
in Wilsonianism.[44] Although Ambrosius's book, discussed earlier, concerns the peace settlement as it pertained to the treaty

41   Cf. George Egerton, "The Lloyd George Government and the Creation of the League of
Nations," *American Historical Review* 79:2 (1974): 419–44; idem, *Great Britain and the
Creation of the League of Nations: Strategy, Politics and International Organization, 1914–
1919* (Chapel Hill, NC, 1978); idem, "Britain and the 'Great Betrayal': Anglo-American Relations and the Struggle for the United States Ratification of the Treaty of Versailles, 1919–
1920," *Historical Journal* 21 (December 1978): 885–911; idem, "Collective Security as Political Myth: Liberal Internationalism and the League of Nations in Politics and History,"
International History Review 5 (November 1983): 496–524; and idem, "Ideology, Diplomacy, and International Organisation: Wilsonism and the League of Nations in Anglo-American Relations, 1918–1920," in *Anglo-American Relations in the 1920s: the struggle for supremacy*, ed. Brian McKercher (London, 1991), 17–54.
42   George Egerton, "Diplomacy, Scandal, and Military Intelligence: the Craufurd-Stuart
Affair and Anglo-American Relations, 1918-1920," *Intelligence and National Security* 2:4
(1987): 110–34.
43   Denise Artaud, "Sur L'Entre-Deux-Guerres: Wilson à la Conférence de la Paix" [On the
interwar period: Wilson at the peace conference], *Revue d'Histoire de la Deuxième Guerre
Mondiale* 31:124 (1981): 97–107.
44   David Stevenson, "French War Aims and the American Challenge, 1914–1918," *Historical Journal* 22 (December 1979): 877–94; idem, *French War Aims against Germany, 1914–
1919* (Oxford, England, 1982), esp. 120–47; and idem, *The First World War and International Politics* (Oxford, 1988), esp, 236–56, 266–95.

fight in the United States, those by Egerton, Kent, Lentin, Schwabe, and Walworth have sought to address Wilson's role and that of his adversaries, like Henry Cabot Lodge. As they see Wilson the diplomatist, they see Wilson the domestic politician. Therefore, the only consensus about Wilson the peacemaker is that there is no consensus, and conclusive answers to the questions about his idealism or realism, his understanding of the requirements of the other powers, and the domestic pressures on his foreign policies have yet to appear.

After the 1920 elections led to the defeat of the Democrats and the demise of Wilsonian foreign policy, Americans reverted to political isolation outside the Western Hemisphere during a dozen years of Republican control over the White House. Under Republican guidance, the might of the United States in international politics was directed into other areas. Recent historiography on this period has concentrated heavily on one of the most important of these areas: economic diplomacy. This is a direct result of the revisionist writings of Williams, Gardner, and others after 1959 who argued that imperial America, while it might have eschewed political commitments abroad, showed little restraint as far as exporting investment and collecting war debts were concerned. So strong was this revisionism that older studies of interwar American foreign relations, acknowledged as "objective, fair, and . . . well-documented,"[45] disappeared from bibliographies. The explicit assumption in this new historiography was that the United States emerged from the Great War unscathed and, because it was a creditor nation with the largest industrial base in the world and vast amounts of surplus capital, had become preeminent among the great powers. Nowhere has this general line of thought been expressed more forcefully than in Paul Kennedy's *The Rise and Fall of the Great Powers*.[46] The United States, he avows, "by

---

45   This is from the review of Jean-Baptiste Duroselle, *From Wilson to Roosevelt: Foreign Policy of the United States, 1913–1945* (Cambridge, MA, 1963) by Adolph Berle, which appeared in *New York Times Review of Books*, 6 October 1963.
46   Paul Kennedy, *The Rise and Fall of the Great Powers: Economic Change and Military Conflict from 1500 to 2000* (New York, 1987), 275–343.

1918 was indisputably the strongest Power in the world."[47] Here is economic determinism with a vengeance.

The core of this recent work on American economic diplomacy may be found in the scholarship of specialists in European history rather than American foreign relations. Charles S. Maier first looked at the reestablishment of order in wartorn Europe in terms of "the process of stabilizing institutions under attack."[48] His study only concerned the United States obliquely, but other historians directed their attention to the matters of reparations, war debts, and American relations with Britain, France, and Germany. Within ten years, Walter MacDougall, Stephen Schuker, Dan Silverman, Marc Trachtenberg, and others produced a series of studies that explored the extent of America's ability to force its economic and financial will on the European powers in the immediate postwar period.[49] There proved to be decided disagreement about how and why events happened as they did. For example, Dan Silverman, a strong Francophile, tried not always successfully to undercut the prevailing view that France played the spoiler in every prudent resolution of the war debt-reparations predicament proposed by the British and the Americans. But in terms of the thrust of the original revisionist assertions about American economic and financial strength, regardless of whether American leaders were successful in pursuing their policies, no one disputed the central propositions that American isolationism in the 1920s had been a myth and that the United States was clearly the dominant power in the world.

These core works provided the basis for specific analyses of U.S. foreign relations in the Republican era that focused on Ameri-

47   Ibid., xix.
48   Charles S. Maier, *Recasting Bourgeois Europe: Stabilization in France, Germany, and Italy in the Decade after World War I* (Princeton, NJ, 1975). The quotation is from p. 8.
49   For instance, Melvyn P. Leffler, *The Elusive Quest: America's Pursuit of European Stability and French Security, 1919–1933* (Chapel Hill, NC, 1979); Walter MacDougall, *France's Rhineland Diplomacy, 1914–1924* (Princeton, NJ, 1978); Hermann Rupieper, *The Cuno Government and Reparations, 1921–1923* (The Hague, 1979); Stephen Schuker, *The End of French Predominance in Europe: The Financial Crisis of 1924 and the Adoption of the Dawes Plan* (Chapel Hill, NC, 1976); Dan Silverman, *Reconstructing Europe after the Great War* (Cambridge, MA, 1982); and Marc Trachtenberg, *Reparations in World Politics: France and European Economic Diplomacy, 1916–1923* (New York, 1980).

can wealth and its translation into international power and influence. Two thoughtful lines of argument, which are best characterized as "soft revisionism," exemplify this recent work. Like Gilderhus's treatment of earlier relations with Latin America, they suggest an all-encompassing structure to examine the myriad of issues touching post-1918 U.S. external strength. The first strand derives from the work of Ellis W. Hawley and Michael J. Hogan. They have argued that to understand how and why American foreign relations evolved as they did after the Great War, it is essential "to construct an analytical framework that illuminates the internal and external sources of policy"; as an explanation for this evolution, they put forth the idea of "corporatism."[50] This theory avers that the nature of the burgeoning and highly competitive American economy in the period of the Great War and after saw a transformation of traditional socioeconomic structures, based on the individual, into new ones whereby the emergence of corporate entities, like organized labor, agriculture, and business, developed to ensure the economic survival of their members. At the same time, other powers were also evolving, making the international economy more competitive. Cognizant of this, and propelled by the desire to succeed, the new components within the United States worked to affect the development of public policy. Hawley's work appeared just as Maier was arguing that there was a transformation from a "bourgeois to [a] corporatist Europe."[51] Thus, in line with work in other fields and more dis-

---

50   Ellis W. Hawley, *The New Deal and the Problem of Monopoly* (Princeton, NJ, 1969); idem, "The Discovery and Study of a 'Corporate Liberalism,'" *Business History Review* 52 (Autumn 1978): 309–20; idem, *The Great War and the Search for a Modern Order: A History of the American People and Their Institutions, 1917–1933* (New York, 1979); Hogan, *Informal Entente*; idem, "Revival and Reform: America's Twentieth-Century Search for a New Economic Order Abroad," *Diplomatic History* 8 (Fall 1984): 287–310; idem, "Corporatism: A Positive Appraisal," ibid. 10 (Fall 1986): 363–72; and idem, "Corporatism," *Journal of American History* 77 (June 1990): 153–60. And in this context, R. D. Johnson, *The Peace Progressives and American Foreign Relations* (Cambridge, MA, 1995); E. McKillen, *Chicago Labor and the Quest for a Democratic Diplomacy, 1914–1924* (Ithaca, NY, 1995); B. G. Plummer, *Rising Wind: Black Americans and U.S. Foreign Affairs, 1935–1960* (Chapel Hill, NC, 1996); J. W. Roberts, *Putting Foreign Policy to Work: The Role of Organized Labor in American Foreign Relations, 1932–1941* (New York, 1995); and E.P. Skinner, *African Americans and U.S. Policy toward Africa: In Defense of Black Nationality, 1850–1924* (Washington, DC, 1992), are important.
51   Maier, *Recasting Bourgeois Europe*, 3–15. Indeed, Hogan, "Corporatism," 160 n.14,

criminating than the revisionism of Williams and his supporters, corporatist analysis held that over time the prevailing ideology, the structure of society, and the interplay among its component parts, among other things, affected the development of foreign relations. Imperial America might have pursued its policies after 1919 outside the Western Hemisphere, but these were not inherently interventionist or in conflict with other imperial powers. This is one of the reasons why Hogan could talk about "informal entente" for most of the 1920s between the roughly equal Britain and United States, as opposed to the view of Carl Parrini that the United States had inherited the British Empire by 1923.[52] Unfortunately, corporatism denigrates the human element and, more tellingly, sees broad economic, social, and other factors in foreign relations history as overwhelmingly narrow, and transitory, political issues. As Thomas J. McCormick, an imperious corporatist, has written, corporatist analysis will ensure that "the study of American foreign relations need not remain mired in circular debates or in narrow empiricism."[53] Although corporatism has been criticized precisely for these reasons, its utility as another research tool is now being examined by non-American historians.[54]

Equally thoughtful because it added the critical issue of cultural strength into the equation was Frank Costigliola's *Awkward*

---

acknowledges that "Maier's book is still the best example of transnational or comparative national history."

52 Parrini, *Heir to Empire*.

53 Thomas McCormick, "Drift or Mastery? A Corporatist Synthesis for American Diplomatic History," *Reviews in American History* 10:4 (1982): 329. See also T. J. McCormick and W. LaFeber, eds., *Behind the Throne: Servants of Power to Imperial Presidents, 1898–1968* (Madison, WI, 1993), especially the chapter by D. Healy, "Thomas W. Lamont: international banker as diplomat."

54 For criticisms of corporatism, see A. Cox, "Corporatism as Reductionism: The Analytic Limits of the Corporate Thesis," *Government and Opposition* 16 (Winter 1981): 78–95; and John L. Gaddis, "The Corporatist Synthesis: A Skeptical View," *Diplomatic History* 8 (Fall 1986): 357–62. On the use of the concept outside of the United States see A. Booth, "Corporatism, capitalism and depression in twentieth-century Britain," *British Journal of Sociology* 33 (June 1982): 200–23; A. Cawson, "Pluralism, Corporatism, and the Role of the State," *Government and Opposition* 13 (Winter 1977): 178–98; Nino Galloni, "Esperimenti di razionalizzazione e programmazione industriale negli USA: 1919–1929" [Experiments in rationalization and industrial programming in the United States: 1919–1929], *Italia Contemporanea* 146–47 (1982): 141–52; and Daniel Ritschel, "A Corporatist Economy in Britain? Capitalist Planning for Industrial Self-government in the 1930s," *English Historical Review* 106 (January 1991): 41–65.

Dominion.[55] "The United States emerged from the Great War," his first sentence asserts, "as the world's leading nation." Although arguing that American political and economic strength outside the country went into temporary eclipse by the early 1930s, Costigliola affirms that the cultural impact of the United States, particularly in Europe, remained vibrant. It is precisely for this reason that this study is crucially important to recent writing on interwar American foreign relations; it melds the broader political and economic elements of those relations with the spread of Coca-Cola, Ford motorcars, and the other accoutrements of American civilization. As Costigliola affirms: "Although Germans and other Europeans found it easy to criticize American culture, it was harder to deny that culture's pervasive influence in the Old World."[56] Just as prewar Europe had been the political and financial center of the world – and, hence, of world civilization – the impact there of American culture after 1918, as much as the more traditional considerations of political and economic foreign policies, bespoke the potency of the United States.[57] But, like Hogan, Costigliola differed from the hard revisionists by acknowledging that American preeminence among the powers did not translate into omnipotence. This is an important contribution of recent historians of U.S. economic diplomacy in the 1920s and early 1930s.

Although the work of Hawley, Hogan, and Costigliola constitutes the apotheosis of the most recent writing on economic diplomacy, other studies underpin the determinist bent of the revisionists. Work concentrating on the nature of American economic penetration in Latin America in the period of the Republican Ascendancy is typical. For instance, the U.S. relationship with

---

55   Frank Costigliola, *Awkward Dominion: American Political, Economic, and Cultural* *Relations with Europe, 1919–1933* (Ithaca, NY, 1984). The quotation is from p. 15.
56   Ibid., 171.
57   And here Rosenberg, *Spreading the American Dream*, is also important. More gener- ally see Robert Dallek, *The American Style of Foreign Policy: Cultural Politics and Foreign Affairs* (New York, 1983); Akira Iriye, "Culture," *Journal of American History* 77 (June 1990): 99–107; idem, "Culture and Power: International Relations as Intercultural Relations," *Diplomatic History* 3 (Spring 1979): 115–28; and Frank Ninkovitch, "Interests and Discourse in Diplomatic History," ibid. 13 (Spring 1989): 135–61.

Mexico continues to hold the attention of American historians of economic diplomacy. During the Harding and Coolidge administrations, concern over the rise of Mexican nationalism provoked American businessmen and others to lobby the State Department to intervene directly to protect their investments, particularly petroleum. But the work analyzing these events conforms to what Joan Hoff Wilson argued in one of the first soft revisionist studies that looked at the connection between government and business in the interwar period: that the latter did not have enough unity of opinion to force Washington to follow a business-inspired program in foreign policy.[58] Thus, whether the Republican administrations appeared to bring about a new approach to American political relations with the region,[59] found different means to ensure their investments,[60] or continued to use traditional methods of intervention,[61] there were limits to American economic diplomacy. And what was true about the Latin Americans was also true about U.S. economic competition with other imperial powers in this crucial region.[62] Nonetheless, for the economic determinists, the pecuniary and industrial vitality of the United States was undeniable and lay at the bottom of its relative superiority over the other great powers in the interwar period.

58   See Wilson's study in footnote 13, above; and George Beelen, "The Harding Administration and Mexico: Diplomacy by Economic Persuasion," *Americas* 41 (October 1984): 177–89; Benjamin T. Harrison, "The Business of America is Business – Except in Mexico: Chandler Anderson's Lobby Efforts in the 1920s," *Mid-America* 68 (1986): 79–97; James Horn, "Did the United States Plan an Invasion of Mexico in 1927," *Journal of Inter-American Studies and World Affairs* 15 (November 1973): 454–71; N. Stephen Kane, "Bankers and Diplomats: The Diplomacy of the Dollar in Mexico, 1921–1924," *Business History Review* 47 (1973): 335–52; and D. Sheinin, *Argentina and the United States at the Sixth Pan American Conference* (Havana 1928) (London, 1991).
59   See, for example, Gene Sessions, "The Clark Memorandum Myth," *Americas* 34 (July 1977): 40–58.
60   David Bain, "The Man Who Made the Yanquis Go Home," *American Heritage* 36:5 (1985): 50–61.
61   Bruce Calder, *The Impact of Intervention: The Dominican Republic during the U.S. Occupation of 1916–1924* (Austin, TX, 1984).
62   Jonathan C. Brown, "Why Foreign Oil Companies Shifted Their Production from Mexico to Venezuela during the 1920s," *American Historical Review* 90 (April 1985): 362–85; Werner Pade, "Die Expansionspolitik des deutschen Imperialismus gegenüber Lateinamerika, 1918–1933" [The expansion policy of German imperialism toward Latin America, 1918–1933] *Zeitschrift für Geschichtswissenschaft* 22:6 (1974): 578–90; and Stephen G. Rabe, "Anglo-American Rivalry for Venezuelan Oil, 1919–1929," *Mid-America* 58:2 (1976): 97–110.

Lately, however, the economic determinist interpretation of American strength in the interwar period, particularly in the 1920s, has been questioned. The focus of this critique centers on the definition of "power" in international politics and on precisely how "power" is translated into specific means to defend or extend national interests. The impetus for this reassessment of American foreign relations is the Duroselle-Watt new international relations history, even though its practitioners primarily study British foreign and defense policy. After all, the corollary to America's rise after 1918 was Britain's supposed decline. And, although all of this school's adherents do not necessarily share Donald Cameron Watt's particular views on the interwar Anglo-American relationship, they do owe a great deal both to his pioneering work respecting how foreign policy is made and to his notions, along with those of Professor Duroselle, about the human element in policymaking.[63] What results, in contrast to the other methods of analysis, like corporatism, is a system of inquiry that treats the evolution of foreign relations as the result of a massive series of discrete transactions carried out, and to a certain degree planned, within and among groups of individuals. These individuals occupy positions in governments, legislatures, and among competing bodies within what can broadly be defined as "public opinion." Collectively, they constitute a "foreign-policy-making elite" whose distinguishing features are the continuity of its membership over time, the comparative freedom of debate and discussion within its ranks, and the fashioning of public and private policies based on the ability of the groups to assert their ideas or to find a basis for compromise to achieve the desired ends. Moreover, given the nature of international relations and national foreign policies, this work has endeavored to tie the politico-strategic elements of foreign relations to the economic and financial ones. Significantly, the approach can be utilized whether

---

63 See Donald Cameron Watt, *Succeeding John Bull: America in Britain's Place, 1900–* *1975. A Study of the Anglo-American Relationship and World Politics in the Context of British and American foreign-policy-making in the Twentieth Century* (Cambridge, England, 1984), esp. 40–89. See also Donald Cameron Watt, "The Nature of the Foreign Policy-Making Élite in Britain," in idem, *Personalities and Policies*, 1–15; and idem, *What About the People?*

one is examining a single state's foreign relations or wider bilateral or multilateral relationships.

In terms of American foreign relations in the Republican period, the work being done from this new perspective is by a group of historians increasingly known as "the London school"; this is because its proponents, both American and non-American, cluster around the Institute of Historical Research at the University of London.[64] Arguing that economic and financial muscle is just one component in a power's ability to achieve its external goals, the London school asserts that equally vital are a nation's strategic preponderance, its ability to project national strength, its political influence pursued through traditional diplomacy, and the will of its leaders to use the resources of the state to satisfy policy objectives. For these historians, only Britain (and not the United States) had a foreign policy marked by all of these elements. This was not for lack of American trying. On the contrary, while the London school does not necessarily quarrel with the goals of Republican economic diplomacy as described by the revisionists – and the goals were not always attained – the three Republican administrations were unable to make positive contributions to extra-Western Hemispheric peace and security between 1921 and 1933. It follows, therefore, that the nature of American foreign relations was more multifaceted than the revisionists suggest and, perhaps more important, that American economic strength did not necessarily translate into political clout.

The focus of the London school on the 1920s is the interrelationship of economic potency, naval power, and diplomatic leverage. In his study of English – and, then, British – military history since 1688, David French has crystallized the London school's

---

64 This is not to say that some British historians are immune to the appeal of economic determinism in terms of the relative strengths of Britain and the United States in the 1920s. For an example of a strongly determinist view see Anne Orde, *British Policy and European Reconstruction after the First World War* (Cambridge, England, 1990); and idem, *The Eclipse of Great Britain: The United States and British Imperial Decline, 1895–1956* (New York, 1996); and for one that is more cautious Kathleen Burk, "Diplomacy and the Private Banker: The Case of the House of Morgan," in *Konstellationen internationaler Politik 1924–1932* [Constellation of international power, 1924–1932], ed. Gustav Schmidt (Bochum, 1983), 25–40; and idem, *Morgan-Grenfell, 1838–1988: The Biography of a Merchant Bank* (Oxford, 1989), 135–66.

assessment of U.S. international strength in a chapter on the inter-war period. Refuting Paul Kennedy's argument about imperial overstretch and economic determinism respecting Britain, French observes that: "In 1917/18, the balance of economic advantage did shift in favour of the USA but between the wars the USA failed to translate its economic potential into international political involvement."[65] This point is fundamentally important to the general lines of argument advanced by the London school about the nature of "power" in interwar international politics.

In considering the 1920s, French has relied on the work of Brian McKercher and John Ferris, who have explored the nature of British economic, foreign, and defense policies in terms of the naval question that policymakers pursued from the end of the Great War to the London Naval Conference of 1930.[66] Building on the work of a number of earlier historians who examined the naval issue in Anglo-American relations in this period, and utilizing more extensive archival sources, they maintain that British leaders possessed the resources and the will to protect Britain's external interests. These leaders took for themselves a prominent role in the League of Nations, ensured Britain a say in maintaining the European balance of power, safeguarded the paramountcy of the Royal Navy, and utilized the global strategic advantage afforded by the Empire both navally and economically. For them, American power was more potential than real. An example makes this clear. The Harding administration won a great success at the Washington conference in 1921–22 with the abrogation of the Anglo-Japanese alliance and the British concession of capital ship and aircraft carrier equality between the Royal and United States

---

65   David French, *The British Way in Warfare, 1688–2000* (London, 1990), 175–201. The quotation is from p. 175.

66   John Ferris, "A British 'Unofficial' Aviation Mission and Japanese Naval Developments, 1919–1929," *Journal of Strategic Studies* 5 (December 1982): 416–39; idem, "Treasury control, the Ten Year Rule, and British Service Policies 1919–1924," *Historical Journal* 30 (December 1987): 859–83; idem, *Men, Money, and Diplomacy: The Evolution of British Strategic Policy, 1919–1926* (Ithaca, NY, 1989); Brian McKercher, *The Second Baldwin Government and the United States, 1924–1929: attitudes and diplomacy* (Cambridge, England, 1984); idem, "Wealth, Power, and the New International Order: Britain and the American Challenge in the 1920s," *Diplomatic History* 12 (Fall 1988): 411–41; idem, *Esme Howard: A Diplomatic Biography* (Cambridge, England, 1989), 269–351.

Navies. But importantly, Coolidge, Frank Kellogg, and others could not subsequently force full equality in lesser warships, particularly cruisers. The British refused to buckle under the threat that the Americans had the economic resources to outbuild them; and, even when the London naval conference of 1930 led to formal Anglo-American equality in all warships (although Britain retained an advantage in the type of cruisers it required), the Americans, as the British suspected they would, failed to build to their allotted levels. But the British built to their limit – they had the will – thereby surrendering only the symbol of seapower not its substance.[67] "Seapower" is more than just the possession of warships, moreover. The merchant marine is also critical when judging national strength, and in this area, too, interwar Britain stole the march on the United States.[68]

Whether one looks at the Locarno treaty in 1925 or the work of the League of Nations to initiate arms limitation, the point for the London school is that American efforts to shape the course of these events were weak at best.[69] Indeed, a reluctance on the part of the Americans to do anything more than propose anodyne ideas like the Kellogg-Briand Pact to aid European security,[70] coupled

67 John Ferris, "The Symbol and the Substance of Seapower: Great Britain, the United States, and the One Power Standard, 1919–1921," in McKercher, ed., *Anglo-American Relations*, 55–80. Also germane are the collection of articles in the special issue of the *International History Review* 13 (November 1991), "Did Britain Decline as a Great Power Before 1940": Keith Neilson, "Greatly Exaggerated: The Myth of British Decline Before 1914"; John Ferris, "'The greatest world power on earth'? Britain during the 1920s"; and Brian McKercher, "The Reality of Power: Britain and the United States in the 1930s." Along different but parallel lines see P. Clarke and C. Trebilcock, eds., *Understanding Decline: Perceptions and Realities of British Economic Performance* (Cambridge, England, 1998).
68 See G. C. Kennedy, "Anglo-American Naval Relations in the Pacific, 1922–39" (Ph.D. diss., University of Alberta, 1997), chap. 2; G. C. Kennedy and K. E. Neilson, eds, *Far Flung Lines: Essays on Imperial Defence in Honour of Donald Mackenzie Schurman* (London, 1997); and K. Smith, *Conflict Over Convoys: Anglo-American Logistics Diplomacy in the Second World War* (Cambridge, England, 1996).
69 See, for instance, Costigliola, *Awkward Dominion*, 126–27, who argues that American pressures over Dawes Plan loans were crucial in forcing the Germans to make the Locarno treaty "a reality." This is not the German view. See Angela Kaiser, *Lord D'Abernon und die englishe Deutschlandpolitik 1920–1926* [Lord D'Abernon and the English German policy 1920–1926] (Frankfurt am Main, 1989), 408–81.
70 J. Kneeshaw, *In Pursuit of Peace: The American Reaction to the Kellogg-Briand Pact, 1928–1929* (New York, 1991); M. Krenn, J. P. Rossi, and D. Schmitz, "Under-Utilization of the Kellogg Papers," *SHAFR Newsletter* 14:3 (1983): 1–9; and J. R. M. Wilson, *Herbert Hoover and the Armed Forces: A Study of Presidential Attitudes and Policy* (New York, 1993).

with British, French, and Italian distaste over the war debt issue, reduced American leverage with the other great Powers. Outside of Europe, particularly in the Far East, a region where the United States had a sizable economic and humanitarian investment, American strength was not enough to dislodge the British. Roberta Dayer has made this point in her work on the competitive Anglo-American relationship in China.[71] In fact, her most recent book considers a single question: "Why after the First World War did the United States not succeed in supplanting the British influence in China, when such was the intention of the State Department, which possessed the financial muscle to enforce its will?"[72] Her answer is that one powerful member of the British foreign-policy-making elite, Sir Charles Addis, who dominated the Hong Kong and Shanghai Bank throughout the 1920s, pursued aggressive policies toward American economic interests that, even though they at times ran counter to the policies of the Foreign Office at London, had the net effect of ensuring Britain's paramountcy in China. American leverage was minimal because the power resources supporting U.S. policy were minimal.

Hence, the historiography of American foreign relations in the Republican period seems to be entering a period of flux, as the effort of the London school to oust the more-established economic determinism is just beginning. On one side are arguments where matters of personality and policy are subsumed by the social and economic structure of the state and where American wealth and cultural strength are seen as dominant in the evolution of events. On the other side is a school that goes further by linking the economic and financial elements of American foreign relations with the politico-strategic ones in terms of the U.S. relationship with other great powers, all within the framework of human skill

---

71　Roberta Allbert Dayer, "Strange Bedfellows: J. P. Morgan & Co., Whitehall and the Wilson Administration during World War I," *Business History* 18:2 (1976): 127–51; idem, "The British War Debts to the United States and the Anglo-Japanese Alliance, 1920–1923," *Pacific Historical Review* 45 (November 1976): 569–77; idem, *Bankers and Diplomats in China, 1917–1925: The Anglo-American Relationship* (London, 1981); idem, *Finance and Empire: Sir Charles Addis, 1861–1945* (New York, 1988); idem, "Anglo-American Monetary Policy and Rivalry in Europe and the Far East, 1919–1931," in McKercher, ed., *Anglo-American Relations*, 158–86.
72　Dayer, *Finance and Empire*, xviii.

and frailty. A historiographical consensus here is unlikely to emerge for some time to come.

With Wall Street's collapse in 1929 and the advent of the Great Depression, Herbert Hoover's administration faced increasing dissatisfaction within the United States. The result was the debasing of Republican political capital and, by 1932, Franklin Roosevelt's rise to the presidency. Roosevelt took office at a difficult time. The American economy seemed unable to improve; the war debt and reparations settlements negotiated in the 1920s were collapsing; and the situation in Europe and the Far East was darkening because of the rise to power of Hitler in Germany and the Japanese-provoked Manchurian crisis in China. With League-sponsored arms limitation talks languishing, international trade slumping, and nationalism and isolationism stronger than ever in the United States, American foreign policy confronted a series of internal and external pressures with which the new American leadership had to contend.

In 1964, Lloyd Gardner produced the classic revisionist study of New Deal diplomacy by arguing that economics and finance influenced all facets of Roosevelt's foreign policy.[73] While correctly pointing out obvious weaknesses in the traditional school, which tended to disregard these aspects of foreign policymaking, Gardner's overweaning economic determinism obscured the realities of international politics in the 1930s and American responses to them. By the early 1970s, however, revisionist works relating to American foreign relations during the period of the Roosevelt presidency up to December 1941 tended to concentrate on U.S. "dollar diplomacy" and Latin America. This region had been the traditional American sphere of interest. Moreover, the collapse of the European war debt settlements, the end of German loan payments, and the breakdown of the reparations agreements, all in 1932 and 1933, saw whatever leverage Washington might have had beyond the Western Hemisphere diminish. Studies by both Americans and non-Americans showed that economic and financial competition among the United States, Britain, and Germany

---

73   Gardner, *New Deal Diplomacy*.

for advantage in Latin America was persistent in the decade before the war and straddled the Hoover and Roosevelt administrations.[74] Latin American powers like Brazil and Mexico were at
times able to exploit this rivalry to their advantage, so that initiatives like the Good Neighbor policy brought mixed results for
U.S. interests.

At the same time that these historians were laboring away, however, another group, including some revisionists, was assessing
equally critical issues in American foreign relations during the
Roosevelt period to 1941. Because the Second World War erupted
in September 1939, and because the United States became em-
broiled in this struggle two years later, the examination of American foreign relations after 1933 has been shaped by the vital considerations of war and peace – though the specific question of
Roosevelt's policies and the historiographical controversy about
the origins of the war are beyond the purview of this essay. Consequently, Warren Cohen, Wayne Cole, Geoffrey Smith, and others scrutinized the debates between the isolationists and their interventionist opponents over whether it was in American interests
to remain cocooned from the increasingly dangerous situations in
Europe and the Far East.[75] Dorothy Borg, James Compton, Arnold
Offner, and their confederates explored the nature of American

---

74   See Stanley Hilton, *Brazil and the Great Powers, 1930–1939: The Politics of Trade
Rivalry* (Austin, TX, 1975); A. F. Repko, "The Failure of Reciprocal Trade: United States-
German Commercial Rivalry in Brazil, 1934–1940," *Mid-America* 60:1 (1978): 3–20; Hans-
Jürgen Schröder, *Deutschland und die Vereinigten Staaten, 1933–1939: Wirtschaft und Politik
in der Entwicklung des Deutsch-Amerikanischen Gegensatzes* [Germany and the United States,
1933–1939: economics and politics in the development of German-American antagonism]
(Wiesbaden, 1970); idem, "Das Dritte Reich, die USA und Lateinamerika, 1933–1941" [The
Third Reich, the USA and Latin America, 1933–1941], in *Hitler, Deutschland und die Machte:
Materialien zur Aussenpolitik des Dritten Reiches* [Hitler, Germany and power: materials on
the foreign policy of the Third Reich], ed. Manfred Funke (Düsseldorf, 1976), 339–64; Dick
Steward, *Trade and Hemisphere: The Good Neighbor Policy and Reciprocal Trade* (Columbia, MO, 1975); Paul Varg, "The Economic Side of the Good Neighbor Policy: The Reciprocal Trade Program and South America," *Pacific Historical Review* 45 (February 1976): 47–72.
75   See, for instance, Warren Cohen, *The American Revisionists: The Lessons of Intervention in World War I* (Chicago, 1967); Wayne Cole, *America First: The Battle Against Intervention, 1940–1941* (New York, 1971); Manfred Jonas, "The United States and the Failure of
Collective Security in the 1930s," in *Twentieth-Century American Foreign Policy*, ed. John
Braeman, Robert Bremner, and David Brody (Columbus, OH, 1971), 241–93; and Geoffrey
Smith, *To Save a Nation: American Countersubversives, the New Deal and the Coming of
World War II* (New York, 1973), 75.

relationships with the great powers in Europe and the Far East in studies that considered appeasement, the search for stability, and that sort of thing.[76] And, given the importance of Soviet-American rivalry in this period, a sizable amount of work was also done on relations with Russia.[77]

As a consequence, by the mid-1970s, the historiography of American foreign relations in the period 1933–41 was wider in volume and scope than that for the Republican period. Despite the enormous amount of work done, however, nagging questions about the nature of American foreign relations remained, all hinging on Roosevelt and his attitudes toward the worsening international situation and how the United States should respond to it. Because Roosevelt dominated foreign policymaking during his entire administration, most work since the late 1970s concerning the final phase of the interwar period has concentrated on the president: his thoughts, personality, and actions. Hence, his towering presence forms the basis for this recent historiography, a development that has undercut the revisionist tendency to downplay personality and policy.

Robert Dallek's massive examination of Roosevelt's foreign policy, published in 1979, is the starting point for this historiography, although not all recent work on the 1933–41 period stems from it. With all of the controversy that had surrounded this president's peacetime diplomacy, which began even before Pearl Harbor,[78] Dallek undertook "to meet the need for a comprehensive one-volume study of Franklin Roosevelt's foreign policy, and to wrestle anew with the many intriguing questions about that subject."[79] In the way that Schwabe and Ambrosius produced

---

76 See, for instance, Dorothy Borg and Shumpei Okamoto, eds., *Pearl Harbor as History: Japanese-American Relations, 1931–1941* (New York, 1973); James Compton, *The Swastika and the Eagle: Hitler, the United States and the Origins of World War II* (Boston, 1967); Richard Dean Burns and Edward M. Bennett, eds., *Diplomats in Crisis: United States-Chinese-Japanese Relations, 1919–1941* (Oxford, 1974); and Arnold Offner, *American Appeasement: United States Foreign Policy and Germany, 1933–1938* (Cambridge, MA, 1969).

77 Edward Bennett, *Recognition of Russia: An American Foreign Policy Dilemma* (Waltham, MA, 1970); and Joan Hoff Wilson, "American Business and the Recognition of the Soviet Union," *Social Science Quarterly* 52 (September 1971): 349–68.

78 See Charles Beard, *A Foreign Policy for America* (New York, 1940); and Raymond Moley, *After Seven Years* (New York, 1939). See also the sources cited in footnote 6, above.

79 Robert Dallek, *Franklin D. Roosevelt and American Foreign Policy, 1932–1945* (Ox-

more complete pictures of Wilson the man by going beyond the unadorned depictions of the traditionalists and revisionists, Dallek synthesized the welter of emotive and contradictory works that had appeared by the late 1970s to do the same for Roosevelt. The result is a "warts and all" treatment that argues that Roosevelt was an internationalist, that he had clear ideas on the place of the United States in the world (although these were sometimes based on misperceptions and an imperfect understanding of the international situation), and that he was an exceedingly ambitious man who would change his policy, but not necessarily his goals, to meet new domestic and foreign political conditions.

Dallek's Roosevelt was not universally accepted[80] – how could it be with such a man as Roosevelt? But the net result of this important book was to provoke a renaissance in the study of American foreign relations under this president. Based on expanding archival sources in the United States and abroad, the new historiography has shown that New Deal diplomacy had more at its base than narrow financial and economic considerations. Naturally, trade, investment, and the desire for profits stood as essential parts of American foreign relations between 1933 and 1941. But also important were the domestic American milieu, the general international situation, and the relationship of the United States with the other great powers. In toto, these various strands of American foreign relations are being woven by recent historians into a new, more subtle assessment of Roosevelt and American foreign relations at a time in international history when the United States was transforming rapidly from a regional power into a global one.

As in so much recent historiography on interwar American foreign relations, examinations of economic diplomacy after 1933

---

ford, 1979). The quotation is from p. vii. A revised edition of Dallek's book appeared in 1995. Also see W. S. Cole, *Determinism and American Foreign Relations during the Franklin D. Roosevelt Era* (Lanham, MD, 1995); R. Dallek, *Franklin D. Roosevelt as World Leader: An Inaugural Lecture Delivered Before the University of Oxford on 16 May 1995* (Oxford, 1995). W. F. Kimball, *The Juggler: Franklin Roosevelt as Wartime Statesman* (Princeton, NJ, 1991); and C. van Minnen and J. F. Sears, eds., *FDR and His Contemporaries: Foreign Perceptions of an American President* (New York, 1992).
80   Watt, *Succeeding John Bull*, 76–84.

continue to focus on U.S. activities in Latin America. In the same year that Dallek's book appeared, Irving Gellman looked specifically at the "good neighbor" policy in Latin America after 1933.[81] His essential thesis conformed to the general precepts laid out by Dallek when looking at overall foreign policy. First and foremost, the personality of the president markedly influenced U.S. policies, as revealed by Roosevelt's unique ideas about the precise American role in Latin America, the salutary affect of American civilization on indigenous populations, the expediency of appearing to meet the nationalist aspirations of Latin American governments, and the necessity of weakening potential adversaries. In addition, given the competing interests of the other major powers, notably Nazi Germany, Roosevelt's Good Neighbor policy was not pursued separately from diplomatic strategies relating to other parts of the world. On the contrary, the Good Neighbor policy was integral to the general diplomacy pursued by Roosevelt the internationalist to protect and extend American economic, political, and strategic interests on a global scale.

A range of subsequent studies, though admittedly containing some divergences of opinion and emphasis, correspond to the view that the Roosevelt administration initiated policies that differed from those of its Republican predecessors because the president, and his senior advisers like Cordell Hull and Sumner Welles, were different men than those who came before them.[82] A desire to

---

81 Irving Gellman, *Good Neighbor Diplomacy: United States Policies in Latin America, 1933–1945* (Baltimore, MD, 1979). See also his *Roosevelt and Batista: Good Neighbor Diplomacy in Cuba, 1933–1945* (Albuquerque, NM, 1973).

82 See B. Welles, *Sumner Welles: FDR's Global Strategist: A Biography* (New York, 1997); F. W. Graff, *Strategy of Involvement: A Diplomatic Biography of Sumner Welles* (New York, 1988): G. Hodgson, *The Colonel: The Life and Wars of Henry Stimson, 1867–1950* (New York, 1990). Then see David Haglund, "'Gray Areas' and Raw Materials: Latin American Resources and International Politics in the Pre-World War II Years," *Inter-American Economic Affairs* 36 (Winter 1982): 23–51; John Knape, "British Foreign Policy in the Caribbean Basin 1938–1945: Oil, Nationalism and Relations with the United States," *Journal of Latin American Studies* 19 (November 1987): 279–94; Marcin Kula, "Another Face of the President (Franklin D. Roosevelt and Latin America)," *Hemispheres* 2 (1986): 55–64; idem, "The United States Policy vis-à-vis the Cuban Revolution of 1933," ibid. 3 (1986): 97–113; John Major, "F.D.R. and Panama," *Historical Journal* 28 (June 1985): 357–77; and Friedrich Schuler, "Germany, Mexico and the United States during the Second World War," *Jahrbuch für Geschichte von Staat, Wirstschaft und Gesellschaft Lateinamerikas* 22 (1985): 257–76. Also of interest is Michael Francis, "The United States at Rio, 1942: The Strains of Pan-American-

ensure adequate supplies of raw materials and safety for American investments was there, as it was for the leaders of any power who thought in terms of maintaining the national interest. But such maintenance also involved protecting the continental United States and American extraterritorial possessions. What this meant in Latin America after 1933, in one example, was Roosevelt's all-out effort to ensure American strategic dominance in Panama. More critically, David Haglund has demonstrated Latin America's importance in the development of U.S. strategic thought after 1936. "It is impossible to understand why the United States abandoned its policy of noninvolvement in European political and military affairs and entered into a de facto alliance with Great Britain during the summer of 1940," he argues, "without taking account of the important role that Latin America occupied in the international strategic calculations of policymakers at Washington."[83] But where Gellman and Dallek argue that Roosevelt was consistently an internationalist after 1933, Haglund paints the portrait of a man who shifted from isolationism to internationalism as the 1930s progressed. As Roosevelt underwent this odyssey because of the shifting international balance of power, his thinking began to consider geopolitical strategies in foreign policy. In getting away from narrow economic determinism, recent work shows that American foreign relations connected with Latin America contained political and strategic dimensions as much or more as financial and economic ones.

The domestic American milieu between 1933 and 1941 was dominated increasingly by divisions over the position of the United States in the wider world and the role it should arrogate for itself. In what is now probably the definitive study on the subject, Wayne Cole has recently dealt directly with Roosevelt and isolationist

---

ism," *Journal of Latin American Studies* 6 (May 1974): 77–95; and Gerald K. Haines, "Under the Eagle's Wing: The Franklin Roosevelt Administration Forges an American Hemisphere," *Diplomatic History* 1 (Fall 1977): 373–88. For a treatment – uninspired and workmanlike – of American strategic relations with its northern neighbor see G. R. Perras, *Franklin Roosevelt and the Origins of the Canadian-American Security Alliance, 1933–1945: Necessary, But Not Necessary Enough* (Westport, CT, 1998).

83 David Haglund, *Latin America and the Transformation of U.S. Strategic Thought, 1936–1940* (Albuquerque, NM, 1984). The quotation is from p. 1. Then see F. B. Pike, FDR's *Good Neighbor Policy: Sixty Years of Generally Gentle Chaos* (Austin, TX, 1995).

opinion.[84] He shows that this opinion played heavily on the president, as it did on Hull and the others, in furthering and shielding what they reckoned to be American external interests. In doing so, Cole concurs with Dallek's thesis that Roosevelt was an internationalist who had to align himself with isolationist legislators in his first term to ensure the passage of critical New Deal domestic legislation. Although Cole concentrates rather heavily on the midwest, downplaying the role of isolationists in other parts of the country and even within the administration,[85] he demonstrates that by Roosevelt's second term the alliance with the isolationists, never firm, had weakened because of perceived external threats to American strategic interests, particularly in Europe. Then, after his election to a third term, and with the outbreak of war in Europe, Roosevelt worked assiduously to destroy isolationism as a political force by any means possible, including less than honest ones. Cole's central point is that although Roosevelt's foreign policy for most of the period before 1941 was constrained by isolationism, the president played the key role in responding to this sentiment in order to achieve his domestic and foreign policy goals. The destruction of isolationism as a credible force within American domestic politics after 1941, doggedly pursued by Roosevelt, helped pave the way for America's preeminent international position after 1945.

This and other recent work on internal pressures and foreign relations in the United States between 1933 and 1941 suggest that domestic opinion had varying ideas about what constituted the

---

84 Wayne Cole, *Roosevelt and the Isolationists, 1932–1945* (Lincoln, NE, 1983). See also his *America First: Senator Gerald P. Nye and American Foreign Relations* (Minneapolis, MN, 1962); and *Charles A. Lindbergh and the Battle against American Intervention in World War II* (New York, 1974); as well as Selig Adler, *The Isolationist Impulse: Its Twentieth-Century Reaction* (New York, 1965); Alexander De Conde, *Isolation and Security* (Durham, NC, 1957); Justus Doenecke, "Non-Intervention of the Left: The Keep America out of the War Congress," *Journal of Contemporary History* 12:2 (1977): 221–36; J. N. Schacht, ed., *Three Faces of Midwestern Isolationism: Gerald P. Nye, Robert E. Wood, John L. Lewis* (Iowa City, 1981); and M. Stenehjem, *An American First: John T. Flynn and the America First Committee* (New Rochelle, NY, 1976). Two older books have recently been reissued: J. Doenecke and J. E. Wilz, *From Isolation to War, 1931–1941* (1968; rev. ed. Arlington Heights, IL, 1991); and M. Jonas, *Isolationism in America, 1935–1941* (1966; Chicago, 1990).
85 Interesting counterpoint is provided by Warren Kuehl, "Mid-Western Newspapers and Isolationist Sentiment," *Diplomatic History* 3 (Summer 1979): 283–306.

national interest and how it should be protected. As a diplomatist in office because of the sufferance of voters, Roosevelt had to balance among competing interests. Though lacking widespread support for much of the 1930s, American internationalists were the other half of the debate involving the isolationists. Robert Accinelli and Gilbert Kahn have chronicled an aspect of this in terms of the World Court fight and the American League of Nations Association's efforts to commit the United States to the international organization.[86] The difficulty here was that this constituency lacked political effectiveness, particularly in Congress, where Roosevelt needed support for New Deal legislation. While doing what he might to encourage internationalism in his first term, Roosevelt understood the political reality, and this meant maneuvering closer to the isolationists. Hence, the American people were a force with which to be reckoned. Later in the decade, when individuals sympathetic to the Japanese endeavored to convince the public at large, as well as influential members of the administration, to look favorably on Japanese actions in East Asia, entrenched attitudes critical of the Tokyo government ensured that such appeals fell on deaf ears.[87] Conversely, those who were pro-Chinese seemed to enjoy success.[88] Other recent historiography suggests that whether considering religious minorities abroad, the matter of American relations with the other great powers, and even defeated France after June 1940,[89]

---

86 Robert Accinelli, "The Hoover Administration and the World Court," *Peace and Change* 4 (Fall 1977): 28–36; idem, "The Roosevelt Administration and the World Court Defeat, 1935," *Historian* 40:3 (1978): 463–78; idem, "The Militant Internationalists: The League of Nations Association, the Peace Movement, and U.S. Foreign Policy, 1934–38," *Diplomatic History* 4 (Winter 1980): 19–38; and Gilbert Kahn, "Presidential Passivity on a Nonsalient Issue: President Franklin D. Roosevelt and the 1935 World Court Fight," ibid. 4 (Spring 1980): 137–59.

87 See J. W. Morley, ed., *The Final Confrontation: Japan's Negotiations with the United States, 1941* (New York, 1994); Sandra Taylor, "Japan's Missionary to the Americans: Sidney L. Gulick and America's Interwar Relationship with the Japanese," *Diplomatic History* 4 (Fall 1980): 387–407; idem, *Advocate of Understanding: Sidney Gulick and the Search for Peace with Japan* (Kent, OH, 1984); Jonathan Utley, "Diplomacy in a Democracy: The United States and Japan, 1937–1941," *World Affairs* 193:2 (1976): 130–40; and idem, *Going to War with Japan, 1937–1941* (Knoxville, TN, 1985).

88 See, for example, Warren Cohen, *The Chinese Connection: Roger S. Greene, Thomas W. Lamont, George E. Sokolsky, and American-East Asian Relations* (New York, 1978).

89 See John Bratzel and Leslie Rout, Jr., "FDR and the 'Secret Map,'" *Wilson Quarterly* 9

Roosevelt and his advisers could not neglect the attitudes of the American public. How far the president was led by public opinion in constructing his foreign policies and how much he exploited these feelings are moot questions. Nonetheless, little doubt exists that public opinion counted for much in determining the course of American foreign relations after 1933, this because Roosevelt the politician had to weigh it in the diplomatic balance. Any foreign policy, particularly one for an emerging global power, had to reflect the diverse nature of the society that gave it birth.

The last two strands of recent historiographical study of Rooseveltian foreign relations – the general international situation confronting the United States after 1933 and the American relationship with the other Great Powers – are intertwined. Moreover, they derive from a single question: What was Franklin Roosevelt's view of the world and of the United States' place in it? One aspect of this involves the degree of Roosevelt's isolationism. On one side is the Dallek view, supported by historians like Gellman. On the other is that epitomized by David Haglund (who owes much to the earlier work of Robert Divine[90]) and others. If Roosevelt perceived the international situation after 1933 as one from which the United States and Latin America could remain isolated, particularly if a second European war broke out, then choosing the side to which the United States should attach itself was not significant until after September 1939. But if the president consistently held internationalist beliefs and was earlier convinced about threats to the United States and American interests outside the Western Hemisphere – in 1935, say, when Ger-

(1985): 167–73; Henriette Louis, "Réactions Américaines à la défaite française de 1940: témoignages et enseignement" [American reactions to the defeat of France in 1940: eyewitnesses and lessons learned], *Revue d'Histoire de la Deuxième Guerre Mondiale* 30:119 (1980): 1–16; Leo Kanawada, *Franklin D. Roosevelt's Diplomacy and American Catholics, Italians, and Jews* (Ann Arbor, 1982); William Nawyn, *American Protestantism's Response to Germany's Jews and Refugees, 1933–1941* (Ann Arbor, MI, 1981); Joseph Rosenberg, "The 1941 Mission of Frank Aiken to the United States: An American Perspective," *Irish Historical Studies* 22:86 (1980): 162–77; and James Weinberger, "The British on Borah: Foreign Office and Embassy Attitudes toward Idaho's Senior Senator, 1935–1940," *Idaho Yesterdays* 25:3 (1981): 2–14.

90   See, for instance, Robert Divine, "Franklin D. Roosevelt and Collective Security, 1933," *Mississippi Valley Historical Review* 48 (June 1961): 42–59; idem, *Illusion of Neutrality*; and idem, *Roosevelt and World War II* (Baltimore, MD, 1969), 90.

many began to rearm in violation of Versailles, or in 1937, when Japan moved south of the Great Wall of China – his hand was not forced. He simply maneuvered to ensure the best possible conditions for the United States economically, diplomatically, and strategically before it was drawn into the deadly game of great-power rivalry. Although these issues have much to do with the controversy about Roosevelt and the origins of the Second World War, they are just as important in determining how and why the United States was emerging as the preeminent global power by 1941. Recently, the Dallek line is dominating.

Roosevelt's handling of Anglo-American relations, chiefly as they reflected on the problems posed by Germany and Japan, is telling. Richard Harrison is at the forefront of an international group of historians holding that on a wide range of questions in Europe and the Pacific before 1937, Roosevelt looked for a condominium of interests with the British.[91] While cooperation in this period confronted several difficulties, particularly differing views at London and Washington over how to achieve peace and security, the evidence points strongly toward Roosevelt's internationalism. Some historians quarrel with the degree of this internationalism vis-à-vis the British, criticizing Roosevelt for hamhandedness.[92] Regardless of whether the American president was successful or not – a question that had much to do with his handling isolationist sentiment in the United States – he did perceive

---

91 S. O. Agbi, "The British Foreign Office and the Roosevelt-Hugessen Bid to Stabilize Asia and the Pacific in 1937," *Australian Journal of Politics and History* 26:1 (1980): 85–95; Richard Harrison, "A Presidential Démarche: Franklin D. Roosevelt's Personal Diplomacy and Great Britain, 1936–37," *Diplomatic History* 5 (Summer 1981): 245–72; idem, "The Runciman Visit to Washington in January 1937: Presidential Diplomacy and the Non-Commerical Implications of Anglo-American Trade Negotiations," *Canadian Journal of History* 19 (August 1984): 217–39; idem, "Testing the Water: A Secret Probe Towards Anglo-American Co-operation in 1936," *International History Review* 7:2 (1985): 214–34; idem, "A Neutralization Plan for the Pacific: Roosevelt and Anglo-American Cooperation, 1934–1937," *Pacific Historical Review* 57 (February 1988): 47–72; André Kaspi, "Angleterre, États-Unis: le réveil des démocraties" [England, the United States: the awakenening of the democracies], *Histoire* 58 (1983): 115–22; Hans-Jürgen Schröder, "Economic Appeasement: Zur Britischen und Amerikanischen Deutschlandpolitik vor dem Zweiten Weltkrieg" [Economic appeasement: British and American policy toward Germany before the Second World War], *Vierteljahrshefte für Zeitgeschichte* 30:2 (1982): 82–97.
92 See, for instance, Watt, *Succeeding John Bull*, 69–89 passim.

threats to American interests outside of the Western Hemisphere
and moved to neutralize them. A large amount of recent historiography also shows that after Roosevelt won his second term in
November 1936, the pace of the American desire to cooperate
with Britain quickened. James Leutze, Malcolm Murfett, David
Reynolds, and William Rock are at the fore in this respect, and
their writing indicates that, in Reynolds's apt phrase, the years
from 1937 to 1941 saw "the creation of the Anglo-American alliance."[93] Significantly, Anglo-American cooperation found expression in both Europe and the Far East. The path to cooperation
was not smooth. Roosevelt harbored anticolonial attitudes which
boded ill for the survival of the British Empire.[94] Until the political demise of Neville Chamberlain and the rise of Winston
Churchill after September 1939, in fact, senior levels of the British Cabinet entertained suspicions of Roosevelt.[95] These and other
problems limited cooperation. Nevertheless, recent scholarship

93   James Leutze, *Bargaining for Supremacy: Anglo-American Naval Relations, 1937–1941*
(Chapel Hill, NC, 1977); Malcolm Murfett, *Fool-Proof Relations: The Search for Anglo-
American Naval Cooperation during the Chamberlain Years, 1937–1940* (Singapore, 1984);
David Reynolds, *The Creation of the Anglo-American Alliance, 1937–1941: A Study in Com-
petitive Cooperation* (Chapel Hill, NC, 1982); idem, *Lord Lothian and Anglo-American Re-
lations, 1939–1940* (Philadelphia, 1983); and William Rock, *Chamberlain and Roosevelt:
British Foreign Policy and the United States, 1937–1940* (Columbus, OH, 1988).
94   Although not much on this question has been done for the pre–1941 period, the general
tendancy can be seen in Kenton Clymer, "Franklin D. Roosevelt, Louis Johnson, India, and
Anticolonialism: Another Look," *Pacific Historical Review* 57 (August 1988): 261–84; S. M.
Habibuddin, "Franklin D. Roosevelt's Anti-Colonial Policy towards Asia: Its Implications for
India, Indo-China, and Indonesia (1941–45)," *Journal of Indian History* 53:3 (1975): 497–
522; I. H. Malik, *US-South Asian Relations, 1940–47: American attitudes towards the Paki-
stan Movement* (Basingstoke, 1991); G. T. Mollin, *Die USA und der Kolonialismus: Amerika
als Partner und Nachfolger der belgischen Macht in Afrika 1939–1965* [The United States
and colonialism: partner and successor of Belgian power in Africa, 1939–1965] (Berlin, 1996);
and M. S. Venkataramani and B. K. Shrivastava, *Roosevelt, Gandhi, Churchill: America and
the Last Phase of India's Freedom Struggle* (New Delhi, 1983). For the classic wartime
treatments of this question see William Roger Louis, *Imperialism at Bay: The United States
and the Decolonization of the British Empire, 1941–1945* (Oxford, 1978); and Christopher
Thorne, *Allies of a Kind: The United States, Britain, and the War against Japan, 1941–1945*
(London, 1978), 94.
95   The Churchill-Roosevelt relationship is fundamentally important. For the period from
October 1933 to December 1941 see Warren F. Kimball, ed., *Churchill and Roosevelt: The
Complete Correspondence*, vol. 1, *Alliance Emerging, October 1933–November 1942*
(Princeton, NJ, 1984), 23–281. See also Warren F. Kimball and Bruce Bartlett, "Roosevelt
and Prewar Commitments to Churchill: The Kent Tyler Affair," *Diplomatic History* 5 (Fall
1981): 291–311; and James Leutze, "The Secret of the Churchill-Roosevelt Correspondence:
September 1939–May 1940," *Journal of Contemporary History* 10:3 (1975): 465–91.

clearly shows that Roosevelt did what he could to facilitate opposition to the totalitarian powers in Europe and the Far East after 1937.[96]

None of this is to suggest that controversy concerning Roosevelt is waning. Tied to the controversy about Pearl Harbor and whether Roosevelt misled the American people is an intense debate over the degree of the president's internationalism versus interventionism after 1939;[97] in addition, there have yet to be satisfactory conclusions drawn about the degree to which American foreign policy can be tarred with the brush of "appeasement";[98] and, finally, studies of America's relationships with the other major powers are far from yielding anything like a harmony of opinion.[99]

96 See, for instance, Robert Herzstein, *Roosevelt & Hitler: Prelude to War* (New York, 1989), who goes as far as to say that Roosevelt took the lead in challenging "Germany's bid for global hegemony" (p. xiii). To do this justifiable thing, he was forced "to manipulate Americans, most of whom wanted to avoid war, by guile" (p. xiv). Compare this interpretation with Patrick Hearden, *Roosevelt Confronts Hitler: America's Entry into World War II* (DeKalb, IL, 1987).

97 See Frederick W. Marks III, "The Origin of FDR's Promise to Support Britain Militarily in the Far East—A New Look," *Pacific Historical Review* 53 (November 1984): 447–62; idem, "Six between Roosevelt and Hitler: America's Role in the Appeasement of Nazi Germany," *Historical Journal* 28 (December 1985): 969–82; and idem, *Wind Over Sand: The Diplomacy of Franklin Roosevelt* (Athens, GA, 1988).

98 See, for instance, K. S. Davis, *FDR, Into the Storm, 1937–1940: A History* (New York, 1993); Ralph DeBedts, *Ambassador Joseph Kennedy, 1938–1940: An Anatomy of Appeasement* (New York, 1985); George Eisen, "The Voices of Sanity: American Diplomatic Reports from the 1936 Berlin Olympiad," *Journal of Sport History* 11:3 (1984): 56–78; B. R. Farnham, *Roosevelt and the Munich Crisis: A Study of Political Decision-making* (Princeton, NJ, 1997); John McVickar Haight, Jr., "Franklin D. Roosevelt, l'Aviation Européenne, et la Crise de Munich" [Franklin D. Roosevelt, European aviation, and the Munich crisis], *Revue d'Histoire de la Deuxième Guerre Mondiale* 33:132 (1983): 23–40; Robert Keyserlingk, "Anschluss oder Besetzung: Der Anschluss Österreichs 1938–1945 aus der Sicht der USA" [Annexation or occupation: the Austrian Anschluss of 1938–1945 in the view of the United States], *Zeitgeschichte* 9:4 (1982): 126–40; Callum Macdonald, *The United States, Britain, and Appeasement, 1936–1939* (New York: 1981); W. R. Rock, *Chamberlain and Roosevelt: British Foreign Policy and the United States, 1937–1940* (Columbus, OH, 1988); D. F. Schmitz and R. D. Challener, eds., *Appeasement in Europe: A Reassessment of U.S. Policies* (New York, 1990); B. Sullivan, "Roosevelt, Mussolini, e la guerra d'Etiopia: una lezione sulla Diplomazia Americana" [Roosevelt, Mussolini, and the Ethiopian war: a lesson in American diplomacy], *Storia contemporanea* 19 (1988): 85–105; and Jane Karoline Veith, "Joseph P. Kennedy and British Appeasement: The Diplomacy of a Boston Irishman," in *U.S. Diplomats in Europe, 1919–1941*, ed. Kenneth Paul Jones (Santa Barbara, CA, 1981), 165–82.

99 For instance, Michael Barnhart, *Japan Prepares for Total War: The Search for Economic Security, 1919–1941* (Ithaca, NY, 1987); Edward Bennett, *Franklin D. Roosevelt and the Search for Security: American-Soviet Relations, 1933–1939* (Wilmington, DE, 1985); David Crowe, "American Foreign Policy and the Baltic State Question, 1940–1941," *East European Quarterly* 17 (Winter 1983): 401–15; Valdo Ferretti, "Fra Inghilterra e Germania: un

Still, it is clear from recent work on the Roosevelt period that American foreign relations involved far more than financial and economic considerations. These were important but so, too, were domestic constraints, the U.S. strategic response to the evolving pattern of international power, and American bilateral and multilateral relationships. The United States was no longer a regional power by 1941, and its position in world politics had changed markedly. In this respect the words of William Appleman Williams about the United States in 1929 can be modified to fit more accurately the situation eleven years hence: "A visitor from afar might have concluded in 1941 that the foundations and superstructure of the Pax Americana, so candidly avowed by Secretary of State Charles Evans Hughes in 1924, were firmly established. And so they were, a truth demonstrated by America's ability to meet the challenge of the Second World War and emerge as the first nuclear superpower in world history."[100]

It is clear that the recent historiography of interwar American foreign relations has not been one where historians have simply been "marking time." Significant efforts have been made to understand better these two fundamentally important decades in

aspetto delle origini della seconda guerra mondiale secondo la recente storiografia giapponese" [Between England and Germany: an aspect of the origins of the Second World War according to recent Japanese historiography], *Storia Contemporanea* 13 (1982): 1029–44; Douglas Little, *Malevolent Neutrality: The United States, Great Britain, and the Origins of the Spanish Civil War* (Ithaca, NY, 1985); idem, "Anti-Bolshevism and American Foreign Policy, 1919–1939: The Diplomacy of Self-Delusion," *American Quarterly* 35:3 (1983): 376–90; Frank Mintz, *Revisionism and the Origins of Pearl Harbor* (Lanham, MD, 1985); Gordon Prange et al., *Pearl Harbor: The Verdict of History* (New York, 1985); and M. J. J. Smith, "'Renovationists' and 'Warhawks': The Japanese-American Diplomatic Crisis of 1940," *Michigan Academician* 16 (Winter 1984): 145–56. And there is the debate about when the United States replaced Britain as the world's leading power: see B. Martin, "Amerikas Durchburch zur politischen Weltmacht: Die Interventionistische Globalstrategie der Regierung Roosevelt, 1933–1941" [America's breakthrough to world power: the interventionist global strategy of the Roosevelt administration, 1933–1941], *Militargeschichtliche Mitteilungen* 2 (1981): 57–98; B. J. C. McKercher, *Transition of Power: Britain's Loss of Global Preeminence to the United States, 1930–1945* (Cambridge, England, 1998); P. Melandri, "L'Apprentissage du Leadership Occidental: Le États-Unis et le Monde, 1941–1949" [The apprenticeship for leadership of the west: the United States and the world, 1941–1949], *Relations internationales* 22 (1980): 175–92; and R. B. Woods, *A Changing of the Guard: Anglo-American Relations, 1941–1946* (Chapel Hill, NC, 1990).
100   For the original quote see Williams, *Tragedy*, 164.

American history by going beyond the older debates engendered by the traditionalists and the revisionists. This does not mean that these earlier efforts have been ignored. Quite the contrary. They have provided a valuable basis for recent studies in that they asked penetrating questions not only about the role of the United States in twentieth-century international politics but also about the wellsprings and essential purposes of American policies. For instance, Williams and the revisionists (as well as Fritz Fischer in Germany) endeavored to correct traditional methodologies in diplomatic history by making pertinent (impertinent?) queries about the structure of the society that produced foreign policy and the economic bases underpinning it. No one would now ignore such fundamental issues when examining the foreign relations of the United States or any other Power in any slice of time. But American revisionists, in one instance, were blinded by a political agenda largely influenced by their intellectual revulsion against American foreign policy during the first phases of the Cold War and by the crisis of Vietnam. It is interesting that questions about the survival of diplomatic history would be raised in the early 1970s, just when the revisionist wave reached its apogee.

The changing international situation confronting the United States after the mid-1970s helped transform "diplomatic history" into "international history." So, too, did the emergence of newer historians largely immune to the political polarisation that had marked the 1960s and early 1970s; and they were joined by older ones who saw merit in the need to change. Although some unreconstructed traditionalists and revisionists have continued to write and publish, most recent historiography has come from historians employing in varying degrees and combinations the methodological approaches that have mushroomed in the past decade and one half: corporatism, personality and policy, cultural analysis, geopolitics, and more. Old issues are being reassessed; others never considered have recently been examined; and some have yet to offer themselves. And, more important, the interwar period is emerging as a distinct period in the transformation of the United States from a regional power to a global one: hence the vibrancy of the study of American foreign relations, in particular, and international history, in general.

To consider what directions the historiography of interwar American foreign relations might take, it is necessary only to observe that there are more questions than answers. For instance, one of the analytical methodologies that has recently emerged is "dependency theory."[101] Concentrating on U.S. relations with Latin America, it has addressed a host of issues, and more will undoubtedly appear. But it would seem that the "dependency theorists" have been rather narrow in their analysis. It is amazing that historians of American foreign relations, particularly dependency theorists and economic determinists, have largely neglected the one country in the Western Hemisphere where the largest slice of American investment capital has been directed since 1918, where the United States has created a "branch plant" economy, where American corporations, especially those in oil, have faced stiff indigenous left-wing criticism, and where American political influence is significant because the country is heavily dependent on trade with the United States to survive: Canada. Of course, Canada offers particular problems for dependency theorists: It is predominantly white; it is culturally similar to the United States; it possesses a capitalist economy; and, until the Second World War, it was firmly within the British Empire. But American scholars should not allow Canadian nationalists to distort the historical reality by writing, unchallenged, pernicious little studies that give the American side of the question short shrift.[102] This and other problems in interwar American foreign relations, like the division in American leadership between Europhiles and East Asianists or the impact of gender on policy, are all in need of

---

101   See Louis A. Perez, Jr., "Dependency," *Journal of American History* 77 (June 1990): 133–43, esp. the footnotes citing secondary studies.

102   When this piece first appeared in 1991, the pernicious study I referred to was Jack Granatstein, *How Britain's Weakness Forced Canada into the Arms of the United States* (Toronto, 1989), which used imagery that deliberately suggested the ravishing of Miss Canada by Uncle Sam. For subsequent examinations see R. Bothwell, *Canada and the United States* (New York, 1992); B. J. C. McKercher and L. Aronsen, eds., *The North Atlantic Triangle in a Changing World: Anglo-American-Canadian Relations, 1902–1956* (Toronto, 1996); and G. T. Stewart, *The American Response to Canada since 1776* (East Lansing, MI, 1992).

more profound study if we are to understand the United States and the rise of its cultural, diplomatic, economic, political, and strategic strength between 1918 and 1941. The result will only be a more complete understanding by both Americans and non-Americans of the United States and its place in the world in this century.

8

The United States and the European War, 1939–1941: A Historiographical Review

JUSTUS D. DOENECKE

Few periods in history have been as crucial as the years 1939–41, particularly the interval between Germany's invasion of Poland and the Japanese strike on Pearl Harbor. Contemporaries realized that at stake was nothing less than the course the world would take for decades to come. During this time, Western Europe was subjected to a German occupation that gave every indication of becoming permanent, the Soviet Union stood in mortal danger, and Japan appeared to be poised for lasting domination of all Asia. Under the presidency of Franklin D. Roosevelt, the United States was moving ever closer to an undeclared naval war against Germany and economic confrontation with Japan.

This essay focuses on current trends in the historiography of this period, with particular attention to U.S. policy between 1 September 1939, when Germany invaded Poland, and 7 December 1941, when Japan attacked Pearl Harbor. Several articles have covered the literature up to this point.[1] This article takes as

The author expresses much gratitude to several scholars whose comments have immeasurably strengthened this essay: Wayne S. Cole, Warren F. Kimball, Leo Ribuffo, Mark A. Stoler, and Gerald A. Wheeler. J. Garry Clifford deserves special mention.

1   By far, the most comprehensive listing is Richard Dean Burns, ed., *Guide to American Foreign Relations since 1700* (Santa Barbara, 1983). See also Wayne S. Cole, "American Entry into World War II: A Historiographical Appraisal," *Mississippi Valley Historical Review* 43 (March 1957): 595–617; Justus D. Doenecke, "Beyond Polemics: An Historiographical Re-Appraisal of American Entry into World War II," *History Teacher* 12 (February 1979): 217–51; Ernest C. Bolt, Jr., "Isolation, Expansion, and Peace: American Foreign Policy between the Wars, " in *American Foreign Relations: A Historiographical Review*, ed. Gerald K. Haines and J. Samuel Walker (Westport, CT, 1981), 133–57; Jerald A. Combs, *American*

its launching pad one of these, Gerald K. Haines's "Roads to War: United States Foreign Policy, 1931–1941," published in 1981.[2] Of necessity it occasionally refers to works published earlier. In order to harmonize this essay with Michael Barnhart's subsequent essay on the origins of the war in Asia, discussion is limited to works covering U.S. policies vis-à-vis Europe.[3]

To understand the significance of current research, one must begin the story much earlier. Originally, the historiography of American foreign policy concerning these years was characterized by bitter polemics. At issue was President Roosevelt himself: FDR's critics were "revisionists," his defenders "court historians." Although much of the attack on FDR centered on his supposed complicity in the Pearl Harbor attack, his critics connected his European policy to the crisis with Japan. Harry Elmer Barnes, for example, claimed that "Roosevelt lied us into war, from the destroyer-bases deal of September 1940, to Secretary Hull's ultimatum of November 26, 1941." Basil Rauch, in discussing American policy in the fall of 1941, replied to such accusations, writing that "the last thing Roosevelt wanted to do was to 'provoke' war."[4] The polemics surrounding Roosevelt spilled over to attacks on the historians themselves. The pro-administration historian Samuel Eliot Morison savaged FDR critic Charles A. Beard in an essay pointedly subtitled "History through a Beard." According to Morison, Beard was inferring that World War II centered on "a dim figure named Hitler," who was involved "in a limited sort of war to redress the lost balance of Versailles." Barnes responded by calling Beard's critics "jackals and hyenas hovering about the body of a dead lion."[5]

Diplomatic History: Two Centuries of Changing Interpretations (Berkeley, 1983); and J. Garry Clifford, "Both Ends of the Telescope: New Perspectives on FDR and American Entry into World War II," *Diplomatic History* 13 (Spring 1989): 213–30.

2   Gerald K. Haines, "Roads to War: United States Foreign Policy, 1931–1941," in *American Foreign Relations*, 159–85.

3   Michael A. Barnhart, "The Origins of World War II in Asia and the Pacific," *Diplomatic History* 20 (Spring 1996): 241–60.

4   Harry Elmer Barnes, "Summary and Conclusions," in *Perpetual War for Perpetual Peace: A Critical Examination of the Foreign Policy of Franklin Delano Roosevelt and Its Aftermath*, ed. Barnes (Caldwell, ID, 1953), 652; Basil Rauch, *Roosevelt, from Munich to Pearl Harbor: A Study in the Creation of a Foreign Policy* (New York, 1950), 421.

5   Samuel Eliot Morison, "Did Roosevelt Start the War? History through a Beard," *Atlantic*

In order to comprehend much of the bitterness of this fight, one fact must be noted. The first historiographical battles usually involved individuals who had themselves often participated in the original "Great Debate" over Roosevelt's foreign policy. In other words, in the late forties and early fifties, the interventionist/isolationist struggle was being refought, and this time the contestants were armed with documents and footnotes. Even the impassioned historiographical debate over the Vietnam War did not produce this kind of acrimony.[6] Pro-interventionist historians were not always of one mind, differing among themselves over such matters as Roosevelt's ability to lead effectively. These differences were particularly apparent in administration discussions of the spring of 1941, when the president refused to provide naval escorts for convoys bound for Britain. Those historians who found the president far too vacillating echoed certain voices within Roosevelt's own administration, among them such hawkish cabinet members as Henry L. Stimson, Harold L. Ickes, and Henry Morgenthau, Jr. Similarly, anti-interventionist scholars were not united on certain matters, such as FDR's direct role in the Pearl Harbor attack and the wisdom of later American Cold War involvements.[7] Yet, until about 1960, most historians who addressed themselves to American policy in 1939–41 could be placed in either the Roosevelt or the anti-interventionist camp.[8]

---

182 (August 1948): 91–97; Harry Elmer Barnes, "The Struggle Against the Historical Blackout," pamphlet (1951), 26.

6   Among Roosevelt's critics, Charles A. Beard had testified before the Senate against the lend-lease bill, Charles Callan Tansill had backed the arch-isolationist No Foreign War Committee, Harry Elmer Barnes had written an anti-interventionist column for the *New York World-Telegram*, and William Henry Chamberlain had addressed a rally of the Keep America Out of War Congress. During World War II, William L. Neumann had been a conscientious objector. Some of FDR's defenders in Clio's ranks had themselves been part of the Roosevelt administration: Herbert Feis as economic adviser to the State Department; William L. Langer as chief of research and analysis for the Office of Strategic Services; S. Everett Gleason as staffer for the Office of Strategic Services and the State Department; and Samuel Eliot Morison as official historian of U.S. naval operations. Others had made no secret of their pre-Pearl Harbor interventionism: Walter Millis, for example, was a staunch backer of the Fight for Freedom Committee.

7   For a description of the early revisionists and the differences among them see Justus D. Doenecke, *Not to the Swift: The Old Isolationists in the Cold War Era* (Lewisburg, PA, 1979), chap. 5.

8   A descriptive analysis of this early conflict is found in Cole, "American Entry into World War II."

During the 1960s, much of the old polarity ended. The graduate schools were training a generation of historians to whom World War II was at best a childhood memory. The demise of the anti-interventionist right, a group best represented by Robert A. Taft and the *Chicago Tribune*, marked the passing of old-style "isolationism" and much of the revisionism that went with it. To defend the claims of conspiracy surrounding so much of the revisionist argument became an impossible burden. Most historians acknowledged the gain in Soviet strength resulting from the war but found the Axis the more immediate and proximate enemy during 1939–45.

A major account of Roosevelt's wartime presidency, James MacGregor Burns's *Roosevelt: The Soldier of Freedom* (1970), undoubtedly expressed a massive scholarly consensus on one matter: a clear sympathy with the president's interventionist policies. At the same time, according to Burns, FDR was too cautious in the spring of 1941. Finding that the president's dilatory strategy was really "no strategy," the political scientist/historian wrote: "He seemed beguiled by public opinion, by its strange combinations of fickleness and rigidity, ignorance and comprehension, by rapidly shifting optimism and pessimism."[9]

If any of the traditional debate remained by the 1970s, it centered on the president's possible duplicity. Certainly disillusionment with the Vietnam War was the determining factor. To such a longtime Roosevelt defender as Joseph P. Lash, FDR's conduct in the Greer incident bore an uneasy resemblance to Lyndon Johnson's in the Tonkin Gulf affair.[10] Other scholars, however, still felt it incumbent to justify the president. In their book *Hitler vs. Roosevelt: The Undeclared Naval War* (1979), Thomas A. Bailey and Paul B. Ryan defended major Roosevelt measures, including the deployment of U.S. destroyers against German U-boats, on the grounds of presidential prerogative: "The President, not the

---

9   James MacGregor Burns, *Roosevelt: The Soldier of Freedom* (New York, 1970), 101, 66.
10   Joseph P. Lash, *Roosevelt and Churchill, 1939–1941: The Partnership That Saved the West* (New York, 1976), 421.

windy body known as Congress, is the final judge of what constitutes the national interest at a given time."[11]

Nevertheless, radically different assessments of Rooseveltian diplomacy were already in the offing. One interpretation, represented by Robert A. Divine and Arnold A. Offner, finds FDR's diplomacy permeated by isolationism and appeasement. To Divine, Roosevelt imperiled national security by continually surrendering initiatives to Germany and Japan. Only at the end of 1938, that is, just after the Munich conference, did FDR break with confirmed isolationism. In fact, Divine claims it was "quite possible that Roosevelt never committed himself to American involvement prior to Pearl Harbor."[12]

Offner sees "American appeasement" in a host of policies: support for German rearmament, approval of the Anglo-German naval agreement of 1935, limited action in the Ethiopian crisis, and backing of Munich. In elaborating on the U.S. rationale, he finds that Germany's case against the Versailles treaty was often justified but that American diplomats made mistakes that went beyond any justifiable appeasement. Hence, the United States sought to alleviate the concerns of Hitler's Reich through arms limitation, tariff reduction, and access to raw materials and markets. For Offner, FDR's conversion to interventionism came with the German assault on Western Europe, and even then the president remained most reluctant to lead openly.[13]

---

11   Thomas A. Bailey and Paul B. Ryan, *Hitler vs. Roosevelt: The Undeclared Naval War* (New York, 1979), 272.
12   Robert A. Divine, *The Reluctant Belligerent: American Entry into World War II* (New York, 1965), and idem, *Roosevelt and World War II* (Baltimore, MD, 1969), 48. In the second edition of *Reluctant Belligerent* (Baltimore, MD, 1979), Divine softened his indictment, while still maintaining that the passive nature of U.S. foreign policy contributed to the coming of the war, p. ix.
13   Arnold A. Offner, *American Appeasement: United States Foreign Policy and Germany, 1933–1938* (Cambridge, MA, 1969); idem, *The Origins of the Second World War: American Foreign Policy and World Politics, 1917–1941* (New York, 1975); idem, "Appeasement Revisited: The United States, Great Britain, and Germany, 1933–1940," *Journal of American History* 64 (September 1977): 373–93; idem, "The United States and National Socialist Germany," in *The Fascist Challenge and the Policy of Appeasement*, ed. Wolfgang J. Mommsen and Lothar Kettenacker (London, 1983), 413–27. For differences between Offner and Divine see Divine's review of *American Appeasement*, in *Journal of American History* 56 (December 1969): 709–10.

To a second school, rooted in the teachings of William Appleman Williams, it is impersonal "structures," not the individual choices of policy elites, that determine U.S. diplomacy. To this school, American entry into World War II centered on retaining economic opportunity overseas. Williams called the conflict "the war for the American frontier," declaring that the Americans believed that their "own prosperity and democracy depended upon the continued expansion of their economic system under the strategy of the open door." For both Lloyd C. Gardner and Hans Jürgen-Schröder, U.S. planners saw German competition in Europe and Latin America as threats to American capitalism. The Roosevelt administration, therefore, sought to steer Germany away from economic autarchy and bilateral agreements based on barter. When Hitler balked, war became inevitable.[14]

In 1979, Robert Dallek contributed a major study that has become a takeoff point for many scholars: *Franklin D. Roosevelt and American Foreign Policy, 1932–1945*. Not since William L. Langer and S. Everett Gleason's two-volume work, *The World Crisis and American Foreign Policy* (1952–53), had there been such a comprehensive account. Dallek combines massive research with an articulate defense of most FDR actions. What Divine and Offner would call appeasement and isolationism, Dallek portrays as necessary compromise, the president being limited by congressional pressures, public opinion, and international constraints. In covering the spring of 1941, when the British were experiencing heavy losses, Dallek sees the president privately concluding that the defeat of the Axis required American naval and air power. In discussing the undeclared naval war with Germany and the issue of administration honesty, he writes, "In light of the national unwillingness to face up fully to the international dan-

---

14 William Appleman Williams, *The Tragedy of American Diplomacy*, rev. and enl. ed. (New York, 1962), 200; Lloyd C. Gardner, *Economic Aspects of New Deal Diplomacy* (Madison 1964); Hans-Jürgen Schröder, *Deutschland und die Vereinigen Staaten, 1933–1939: Wirtschaft und Politik in der Entwicklung des deutsch-amerikanischen Gegensatzes* (Weisbaden, 1970); idem, "The Ambiguities of Appeasement: Great Britain, the United States and Germany, 1937–9," in *The Fascist Challenge*, 390–99.

gers confronting the country, it is difficult to fault Roosevelt for building a consensus by devious means."[15]

An even fresher generation of historians has come to the fore since the 1980s. Not surprisingly, Franklin D. Roosevelt remains subject to almost exhaustive scrutiny. Nevertheless, despite the plethora of research, there is no generally accepted view of the president. The sources, abundant as they are, offer more confusion than certainty.

Several new works present FDR as both wise and skillful. The first, Waldo Heinrichs's *Threshold of War: Franklin D. Roosevelt and American Entry into World War II* (1988), has met with almost universal praise. Heinrichs draws on countless sources unavailable to Langer and Gleason, including official records in London, German U-boat messages deciphered by British ULTRA units, and deck logs of U.S. naval craft. Unlike those historians who find FDR far too vacillating, Heinrichs depicts Roosevelt as an active, purposeful policymaker, "the only figure with all the threads in his hands." By August 1941, Heinrichs writes, Roosevelt was ready to risk war, doing so by directly entering the Battle of the Atlantic. To the president, such a move became essential, for only then could he assure the delivery of lend-lease supplies to both Britain and the Soviet Union. The president could not move faster on convoys to Britain because he did "not want to overreach in the Atlantic while a crisis brewed in Southeast Asia." Unlike the Williams school, which stresses economic factors, Heinrichs emphasizes the military threat posed by the Axis. He sees Hitler already well on his way to world domination; if the British were defeated, "a very real possibility existed that the Americans could find themselves an island in a world dominated by the Axis." One of Heinrichs's interpretations is particularly original: his assertion that Roosevelt's concern with maintaining the Russian front became the linchpin of his global strategy.[16]

---

15 Robert Dallek, *Franklin D. Roosevelt and American Foreign Policy, 1932–1945* (New York, 1979), 289.
16 Waldo Heinrichs, *Threshold of War: Franklin D. Roosevelt and American Entry into World War II* (New York, 1988), vii, 9–10, 117. See also idem, "President Franklin D.

Similarly, Warren F. Kimball presents Roosevelt as a skillful leader, though at times downright "disingenuous, deceptive, and devious." True, the FDR portrayed in Kimball's well-received work *The Juggler: Franklin Roosevelt as Wartime Statesman* (1991) is by no means the comprehensive planner described by Heinrichs. Kimball finds the president often muddling through, never developing his thoughts in any logical manner, and "sweeping obstacles under the rug in the hope that they would go away in time." Yet Kimball asserts that in 1941, FDR had a genuine foreign policy, one that centered on "the containment of Hitler, the survival of Britain, and the elimination of any need for large-scale American intervention." In a sense, Kimball's Roosevelt is fighting a proxy war, hoping that the British, and after June 1941 the Russians, would do the real fighting for him.[17]

While *The Juggler* does not center on U.S. entry into the war per se, it deals at some length with related issues. Kimball analyzes FDR's decision to aid the Soviets, a move he finds quite defensible. If successful, the measure would expedite one of the president's major goals: the exhaustion of German forces on the Russian front, a circumstance that would decrease the need for a commitment of U.S. ground troops to the European continent. Furthermore, according to Kimball, the Roosevelt administration hoped that such aid would foster general Allied cooperation once the conflict was over. Had Roosevelt not acted as he did, the postwar world might have been even more frightening.[18]

Kimball, however, does not find the Roosevelt administration perceptive on all matters, some of them quite major ones. In covering the lend-lease negotiations (a subject on which he has

---

Roosevelt's Intervention in the Battle of the Atlantic, 1941," *Diplomatic History* 10 (Fall 1986): 311–32; idem, "The United States Prepares for War," in *The Secrets War: The Office of Strategic Services in World War II*, ed. George C. Chalou (Washington, 1992), 8–18; and idem, "FDR and the Entry into World War II," *Prologue* 26 (Fall 1992): 119–30, where he also stresses the president's decisiveness.
17 Warren F. Kimball, *The Juggler: Franklin Roosevelt as Wartime Statesman* (Princeton, NJ, 1991), 7, 8, 12.
18 Ibid., 21–41. For Kimball's study on lend-lease see *The Most Unsordid Act: Lend-Lease, 1939–1941* (Baltimore, MD, 1969). For another appreciative account of FDR's statecraft see Harvey Leroy Young, "Franklin D. Roosevelt and Big Three Diplomacy, 1941–1945" (Ph.D. diss., Washington State University, Pullman, 1993).

written an entire book), Kimball sees U.S. negotiators vastly exaggerating the importance of cracking Britain's imperial preference system. American policymakers were remarkably eager to destroy what they themselves saw as the economic cornerstone of their own ally.[19]

Six years later, Kimball offered *Forged in War: Roosevelt, Churchill, and the Second World War* (1997). Here the Rutgers historian reiterates his claim that FDR sought "a limited war – with only naval and air forces engaged against the Germans." At the same time, he challenges an entire group of historians – including Bailey, Dallek, and Arthur M. Schlesinger, Jr. – who find the president's evasiveness rooted in the desire to gain time so as to "educate" the American public as to the perils they faced. Rather, claims Kimball, all elements concerned, from pollsters to administration figures to the public itself, sought "to be lied to"; that is, they willingly went along with the president's subterfuges in order to avoid hard decisions. Kimball praises the destroyers-for-bases deal but thinks the Atlantic Charter put Roosevelt perilously close to the "credibility gap" that Woodrow Wilson faced with the American people in 1919. He also stresses Churchill's threat, made in late spring 1940, of British negotiations with Hitler. Churchill's boast after the Newfoundland conference that FDR would soon enter the war was wishful thinking; the prime minister read more into Roosevelt's comments than the president intended.[20]

One ardently pro-Roosevelt book has been less well received: Robert Edwin Herzstein's *Roosevelt & Hitler: Prelude to War* (1989). To Herzstein, the crux of the president's foreign policy lay in his sympathy with Europe's persecuted Jews. In fact, writes Herzstein, "[i]n the center of [the] battle over intervention and neutrality stood the Jewish issue." So concerned was Roosevelt that he became the virtual architect of Germany's defeat. Herzstein claims that FDR's "entire European policy was predicated upon a commitment to destroying Hitler and all his works. There might

19 Kimball, *The Juggler*, 43–62.
20 Warren F. Kimball, *Forged in War: Roosevelt, Churchill, and the Second World War* (New York, 1997), pp. 7, 8, 100, 103.

have been no war in Europe had it not been for Roosevelt's pressure on London, Paris, and Warsaw." Accepting recent scholarship that stresses FDR's indifference to the fate of Jewish refugees, Herzstein concedes that Roosevelt "did abandon many refugees, and in a shameful manner." Given the public's own anti-Semitism, however, the president was involved in a necessary trade-off: FDR would not revise immigration laws or engage in massive rescue efforts, his refusal rooted in a desire to prevent an anti-Semitic backlash within the United States. Even if – as Herzstein claims – the president manipulated a confused and often hostile public opinion and blasted opponents unfairly, Roosevelt's victory over Nazism makes him "the giant figure of his age."[21]

Doris Kearns Goodwin is almost as flattering. In her joint biography of Franklin and Eleanor, she praises the president for a "magnificent sense of timing." Often FDR waited for events to unify the nation, and Goodwin gives as examples his handling of the military draft in the summer of 1940 and the lend-lease bill six months later. When necessary, however, Roosevelt displayed real courage, as in his overruling of his own military advisers over immediate aid to Britain and Russia.[22]

---

21   Robert Edwin Herzstein, *Roosevelt to Hitler: Prelude to War* (New York, 1989), xiv (emphasis in original), xv, xvi. Few reviewers have failed to take issue with Herzstein's analysis. Robert Dallek sees little to Herzstein's claim that FDR was the prime creator of the English-French-Polish coalition that resisted Hitler in 1939 (*New York Times Rook Review*, 28 January 1990, 17). Wayne S. Cole finds the research spotty and uneven, the framework polemical (*Journal of American History* 77 [March 1991]; 1408). Arnold A. Offner, devoting an entire essay to the book, contests a number of Herzstein's claims, among them assertions that Roosevelt was primarily roused by Hitler's treatment of the Jews, that domestic fascism was a serious threat to 1930s America, that FDR was a lifetime Germanophobe, that the United States could ever be subject to an anti-Jewish pogrom, and that the Welles mission to Europe, undertaken in February 1940, was merely "a failed bluff." In disputing Herzstein's defense of FDR's "fear tactics" and the president's labeling of opponents as subversives, Offner argues that the president should have contested opposition claims on their merits. See Offner, "Misperception and Reality: Roosevelt, Hitler, and the Search for a New Order in Europe," *Diplomatic History* 15 (Fall 1991): 607–19. There is a large literature on the Roosevelt administration and the Holocaust. Major works include David S. Wyman, *Paper Walls: America and the Refugee Crisis, 1938–1941* (Amherst, MA, 1968); idem, *The Abandonment of the Jews: America and the Holocaust, 1941–1945* (New York, 1984); Henry L. Feingold, *The Politics of Rescue: The Roosevelt Administration and the Holocaust, 1938–1945* (New Brunswick, 1970); and Richard Breitman and Alan M. Kraut, *American Refugee Policy and European Jewry, 1933–1945* (Bloomington, IN, 1987).

22   Doris Kearns Goodwin, *No Ordinary Time: Franklin and Eleanor Roosevelt: The Home Front in World War II* (New York, 1994), 609.

In an analysis of Roosevelt's general picture of Europe, John Lamberton Harper depicts the president as a neo-Jeffersonian who found the continent corrupt and the United States the sanctuary of civilized values. Even FDR's feelings toward Britain were "always a fluid mixture of resentment, rivalry, and regard." By June 1941, however, Roosevelt probably saw American entry into the European war as inevitable, a fact made clear by his shoot-on-sight orders that September. According to Harper, the president still adhered to his vision of a morally superior America, but he believed that only U S. participation could ensure an Allied victory and give America a dominant role in any peacemaking.[23]

Not all historians see FDR as a strong leader. To some historians, Roosevelt sought to avoid irrevocable decisions, and bureaucratic interests were successful in protecting their own turf.[24] Mark M. Lowenthal goes even further, using categories from B. H. Liddell Hart's *Strategy* (2d rev. ed., 1967). Liddell Hart had differentiated between "fundamental policy," that is, the goals, ends, and objectives of a nation, and "grand strategy," which involves the development, coordination, and utilization of all of a nation's resources to implement this fundamental policy. Roosevelt, Lowenthal writes, was unwilling to make the precise, definite decisions needed to execute fundamental policy, hence making life difficult for anyone seeking to plan grand strategy. Until May 1940, U.S. fundamental policy centered on return to the prewar status quo without any American commitment. After that date, the United States sought an Allied victory while avoiding full-scale entry into war. Nevertheless, FDR refused to give specific guidelines to his chiefs of staff. Instead, he operated in fits and starts, with every concrete step from the destroyers-for-bases deal to the shoot-on-sight orders simply a failed expedient. Frustrated military leaders were always forced to plan grand strategy in a vacuum of fundamental policy, a factor reflected in FDR's vagueness concerning Rainbow 5 and the 1941 Victory Plan. At the

23   John Lamberton Harper, *American Visions of Europe: Franklin D. Roosevelt, George F. Kennan, and Dean G. Acheson* (New York, 1994), 36.
24   See, for example, Jonathan G. Utley, *Going to War with Japan, 1937–1941* (Knoxville, TN, 1985).

same time, when the interventionists in the president's cabinet virtually rebelled over U.S. reluctance to implement convoys, FDR skillfully appeased his hawkish critics by announcing expanded patrols and moving part of the Pacific fleet to the Atlantic.[25]

Several scholars argue that Roosevelt could have been far more successful in forging a domestic consensus on his foreign policy. According to J. Garry Clifford, FDR played down his ability to lead. Noting that a president's power to persuade is greatest during an international crisis, such as the one that took place in 1940, Clifford writes, "One suspects that FDR led circuitously and deviously because he preferred it that way."[26] Thomas N. Guinsburg claims that an effort to educate the American public between 1933 and 1935 would have resulted in a more effective leadership in 1939–41.[27] Justus D. Doenecke and John E. Wilz accuse Roosevelt of appearing "to make an absolute virtue out of government by improvisation."[28] D. Cameron Watt finds merit in the accusation that FDR's policymaking involved "procrastination modified by indiscretion" but sees a more serious problem in Roosevelt's inability to handle Congress and his "uncanny gift for picking the worst possible man for a diplomatic appointment." Although Watt directly refers to such wartime emissaries as Patrick J. Hurley to China and Spruille Braden to Argentina, his comments could equally apply to William E. Bullitt to France and Joseph P. Kennedy to Britain.[29]

One historian, Frederick W. Marks III, continues the interpretation begun by Divine and Offner, namely, that the pre–1940 FDR was an appeaser. Marks's highly debated *Wind over Sand: The Diplomacy of Franklin Roosevelt* (1988) offers a major indictment: In the realm of foreign policy, "FDR accumulated the

---

25 Mark M. Lowenthal, *Leadership and Indecision: American War Planning and Policy Process, 1937–1942* (New York, 1988); idem, "Roosevelt and the Coming of the War: The Search for United States Policy," *Journal of Contemporary History* 16 (July 1981): 413–40.
26 Clifford, "Both Ends," 229.
27 Thomas N. Guinsburg, "The Triumph of Isolationism, " in *American Foreign Policy Reconsidered, 1890–1993*, ed. Gordon Martel (New York, 1994), 90–105.
28 Justus D. Doenecke and John E. Wilz, *From Isolation to War: 1931–1941*, 2d ed. (Arlington Heights, IL, 1991), 157.
29 D. Cameron Watt, *Succeeding John Bull: America in Britain's Place, 1900–1975* (Cambridge, England, 1984), 79–80.

largest overseas credibility gap of any president on record." His chapter "From the Potomac to the Rhine" contains accusations that FDR sought to be the architect of Munich, then prodded Britain and France to hold firm. At the same time, the president refused to build American armaments to "a level commensurate with the nation's national defense." Unlike such recent multiarchival books as Donald Cameron Watt's *How War Came* (1989), *Wind over Sand* argues that the United States – by encouraging both sides to hold fast – helped to precipitate the European war. "One is bound," writes Marks, "to be troubled by the president's apparent drifting, by his lack of any clearly defined strategy."[30]

Williams's "open door" interpretation has been somewhat recast by Thomas J. McCormick, who sees the United States of the 1930s embodying the drive of the capitalist world-system for global hegemony. Challenged by Germany and Japan, the United States first sought by appeasement to integrate these budding empires into a Wilsonian world order, one based on freedom of the seas, the open door, arms reduction, political self-determination, and an end to colonialism. When the appeasement effort failed, "living space for Germany and Japan" meant "dying space for American private enterprise." By the end of 1941, the United

---

30 Frederick W. Marks III, *Wind over Sand: The Diplomacy of Franklin Roosevelt* (Athens, GA, 1988), 167, 287. See also idem, "Six between Roosevelt and Hitler: America's Role in the Appeasement of Nazi Germany," *Historical Journal* 28 (December 1985): 969–82. For Watt see *How War Came: The Immediate Origins of the Second World War, 1938–1939* (London, 1989). Marks's work has been subject to much argument. Fraser Harbutt sees the book "a welcome spur to deeper thought," particularly in its use of foreign sources and prodigious notes (*Journal of American History* 76 [September 1989]: 643). Gary B. Ostrower calls it "a very important book," as it "intelligently challenges ideas and assumptions that usually go unchallenged" (*Presidential Studies Quarterly* 19 [Winter 1989]: 218–20). Other historians, however; stress major weaknesses. J. Garry Clifford finds fault with Marks for neglecting major research on Anglo-American policy and treating the 1933-45 period as seamless ("Both Ends," 216–18). Warren F. Kimball denies Marks's claim that the Welles mission was "an outgrowth of FDR's seven-year-exercise in appeasement" (*American Historical Review* 95 [April 1990]: 614; Marks's quotation on Welles mission, *Wind over Sand*, xi). While not directly addressing himself to Marks's argument, Wayne S. Cole denies that Roosevelt was ever an appeaser: Although the president hoped that Chamberlain's policies might bring peace, he did not really believe that they would. Cole also rejects the claim that FDR ever expected the Welles mission to result in a negotiated peace. See Cole, "American Appeasement," in *Appeasement in Europe: A Reassessment of U.S. Policies*, ed. David F. Schmitz and Richard D. Challener (New York, 1990), 1–20.

States was engaged in a full-scale war that would make it "global workshop and banker, umpire and policeman, preacher and teacher."[31]

Patrick J. Hearden's *Roosevelt Confronts Hitler: America's Entry into World War II* (1987) offered detailed supporting evidence for McCormick's thesis, as it, too, sees U.S. involvement as rooted in market anxieties. According to Hearden, American policymakers feared that major conflict with Germany would result in the Bolshevization of Europe. Therefore, they sought to ward off any such strife. Fear of radicalism led to a dual diplomacy, one based on the carrot and the stick – material inducement and military intimidation. Once these tactics proved unsuccessful, "American leaders were primarily concerned about the menace that a triumphant Germany would present to the free enterprise system in the United States." Faced with "the fundamental problem of domestic overproduction," government and business leaders were "terrified by the thought that the world might be closed to American commerce." They chose war, therefore, doing so to keep foreign markets open and thereby to preserve entrepreneurial freedom within the United States itself. Hearden certainly highlights the economic thinking of FDR and leading State Department personnel; he is, however, so myopic in his concentration on commercial factors that he neglects domestic political restraints and bureaucratic politics, much less the very real sense of military threat manifested after the fall of France.[32]

In addition to the more specialized books on FDR's diplomacy – Heinrichs, Kimball, Herzstein, Marks, and Hearden – general

31   Thomas J. McCormick, *America's Half-Century: United States Foreign Policy in the Cold War* (Baltimore, MD, 1989), 31, 33.
32   Patrick J. Hearden, *Roosevelt Confronts Hitler: America's Entry into World War II* (DeKalb, IL, 1987), x. Not surprisingly, Hearden's argument brought forth strong responses. To Manfred Jonas, the study is so narrow that ideological aspects never emerge. According to Jonas, FDR – like Woodrow Wilson – sought to make the world safe for democracy, by which the president meant "representative government, freedom, and capitalism" (*American Historical Review* 93 [June 1988]: 792–93). Warren F. Kimball writes, "To ignore Roosevelt's belief in Wilsonian liberalism (democratic capitalism, liberal democracy, Americanism – choose your label) would be reckless and wrong" ("Isolationism as Intervention: FDR in the Prewar Years," *Reviews in American History* 16 [September 1988]: 470).

works on FDR still abound. Frank Freidel, for example, summarizes a lifetime of research in *Franklin D. Roosevelt: A Rendezvous with Destiny* (1990). According to Freidel, by early 1941, Roosevelt believed that a huge American expeditionary force, engaged in massive combat with the Germans, was needed for victory.[33] Arguing to the contrary, Patrick J. Maney suspects that until Pearl Harbor day, Roosevelt still had hopes, however slim, that the United States could confine war participation to supplying Britain and Russia. Even if the United States entered the conflict, it could limit its involvement to air and sea power. All initiative for war or peace, writes Maney, remained with Hitler. Maney even argues that Roosevelt's eagerness to discredit the isolationists led him to brush aside the significant questions that they raised.[34]

Commenting on FDR's personal role leads directly to a related matter, the United States's relation to Britain. As noted in a new bibliographical work, since 1980 the thrust of much writing has radically changed.[35] Whereas earlier scholarship emphasized convergence and community of interest between the powers, today's historians uncover diversity and discord. The opening of fresh archives, particularly in Britain, severely modifies – if not undercuts – the picture of concord so carefully built up, for example, in Winston Churchill's magisterial six-volume work *The Second World War* (1948–53). When the Churchill memoirs were published, the former prime minister deliberately omitted certain wartime clashes, doing so in order to help continue the alliance with the United States amid early Cold War crises.[36] Although

---

33   Frank Freidel, *Franklin D. Roosevelt: A Rendezvous with Destiny* (Boston, 1990). For an excellent reference work see Otis L. Graham, Jr., and Meghan Robinson Wander, eds., *Franklin D. Roosevelt: His Life and Times, An Encyclopedic View* (Boston, 1985). Ted Morgan, *FDR: A Biography* (New York, 1985), and Kenneth S. Davis, *FDR, Into the Storm, 1937–1940: A History* (New York, 1993), are well-written accounts usually lacking fresh conclusions.

34   Patrick J. Maney, *The Roosevelt Presence: A Biography of Franklin Delano Roosevelt* (New York, 1992), 134–35.

35   David A. Lincove and Gary R. Treadway, comps., *The Anglo-American Relationship: An Annotated Bibliography of Scholarship, 1945–1985* (New York, 1988).

36   Winston S. Churchill, *The Second World War*, 6 vols. (Boston, 1948–53). See also Lash, *Roosevelt and Churchill.*

much of the new literature focuses on the thirties, the period 1939–41 receives ample treatment.

A milestone came in 1981 with the publication of David Reynolds's *The Creation of the Anglo-American Alliance, 1937–1941: A Study in Competitive Cooperation.* Drawing on both British and American archives, Reynolds challenges Churchill's long-stated claim that the alliance rested on latent cultural unity; rather, argues Reynolds, it reflected geopolitical interests. Until April 1940, when the Phony War ended, neither power saw a full-scale commitment to the other as necessary or desirable. At first, so Reynolds claims, FDR envisioned a strong Britain and France as deterrents to German expansion. In fact, Roosevelt was confident that British strategic bombing would preclude the need for another American Expeditionary Force. To Reynolds, the Welles mission of February 1940 had one major goal: to mobilize neutral Europe behind a compromise peace before an inevitable spring offensive and Allied defeat. Reynolds also claims that FDR's Charlottesville speech was more inspirational than substantive, and he stresses that the president – doubting Britain's ability to survive – hesitated six weeks before offering substantial aid. Even after the destroyers-for-bases deal was made in September 1940, Roosevelt hedged his bets. When lend-lease was passed in March 1941 – Reynolds notes in what must be a deliberate effort to be provocative – it was not outstandingly novel, notably attractive, or particularly important. After the Newfoundland conference, when Churchill told his war cabinet that Roosevelt had promised to provoke full-scale war with Germany, the president envisioned America's contribution as naval and air power alone, that is, "arms not armies." As the United States edged toward war, policymakers in Washington suspected the British of conspiring to keep their empire; conversely, the British found Americans stingy, unreliable, and plodding. Perhaps because he is so steeped in the British records, Reynolds – like so many of the newer multiarchival historians – describes a somewhat hesitant FDR, a man who felt he was blocked by isolationists and a reluctant military.[37]

---

37   David Reynolds, *The Creation of the Anglo-American Alliance, 1937–1941: A Study in Competitive Co-operation* (Chapel Hill, NC, 1981), 288. It should be noted that David G.

In 1984, Warren F. Kimball made a signal contribution in his edition of the complete Roosevelt-Churchill correspondence. The tally: 1,161 messages from Churchill, 788 from Roosevelt, a rate of more than one per day. Included in Kimball's collection are various drafts of unsent messages, the identity of original drafters, telephone transcripts, and means of transmission. In a lengthy preface, Kimball warns against overromanticizing the relationship between the two leaders. He stresses that Roosevelt drove a hard bargain over lend-lease while Churchill refused to promise that a defeated Britain would transfer its fleet to the United States. Here, for the first time, Kimball makes his claim that the president hoped that American participation in the war would be limited to naval and possibly air forces.[38]

The publication in 1991 of an extensive revision of Theodore A. Wilson's account of the Newfoundland conference, originally published in 1969, marked another step forward. In this new edition of *The First Summit: Roosevelt and Churchill at Placentia Bay, 1941*, Wilson uses materials recently available from the Public Record Office to shatter what he calls "the Churchillian paradigm"; that is, the assertion that the prime minister and the president shared a unique friendship devoid of all differences. In the first edition, Wilson had stressed that the informal meeting of British and American leaders far transcended any concrete agreements made, which were of limited importance and soon modified by the demands of war. Now, in an extensively rewritten

Haglund had already stressed one of Reynolds's most significant points: In May and June 1940, the Roosevelt administration believed that England was finished. See Haglund's "George C. Marshall and the Question of Military Aid to England, May–June 1940," *Journal of Contemporary History* 5 (October 1980): 745–60. In a separate article, Reynolds tackles Churchill's decision, made in the summer of 1940, to continue fighting rather than seek a negotiated peace. The prime minister, writes Reynolds, had reasoned incorrectly. He mistakenly assumed that the German economy could not sustain continued war and that within months the United States would be a belligerent. At the same time, he lacked any knowledge of the one factor that ultimately did save Britain – Hitler's coming attack on Russia. See Reynolds, "Churchill and the British 'Decision' to Fight On in 1940: Right Policy, Wrong Reasons," in *Diplomacy and Intelligence during the Second World War: Essays in Honour of H. Hinsley*, ed. Richard Langhorne (Cambridge, England, 1985), 147–67.

38   Warren F. Kimball, ed., *Churchill & Roosevelt: The Complete Correspondence*, 3 vols. (Princeton, NJ, 1984). Students will still find a similar volume helpful, in part because of its perceptive introduction. See Francis L. Loewenheim, Harold D. Langley, and Manfred Jonas, eds., *Roosevelt and Churchill: Their Secret Wartime Correspondence* (New York, 1975).

account, Wilson offers fresh material on the British decision to reinforce the Middle East, FDR's belief in the strategic bombing/ "arsenal of democracy" role for the United States and his apathy toward production priorities, and bureaucratic rivalries in the War and State departments. To Wilson, Roosevelt "was unwilling to face the risks that accompany aggressive leadership." Yet, given the Axis threat, "allowing oneself to drift with the tide of events embodies irresponsible if not downright idiotic behavior."[39]

The fiftieth anniversary of the Atlantic Charter brought forth a special anthology on the topic. Theodore A. Wilson sees the Eight Points as embodying a real if informal alliance between the United States and Britain, though he finds it likely that FDR saw American participation in the war limited to the production of weapons and the dispatch of naval and air forces.[40] Warren F. Kimball presents the charter as a genuine touchstone for the Roosevelt administration.[41] David Reynolds finds Churchill having to be satisfied with a common exposition of war aims when he hoped that the Newfoundland meeting would result in direct U.S. entry into the war.[42]

Specialized works, particularly by British scholars, offer supplementary detail on the 1939–41 period. Pursuing a line of inquiry initiated in 1977 by James R. Leutze, Malcolm H. Murfett shows how naval cooperation with the United States took place even before Churchill came to power.[43] William R. Rock, in a general study of Anglo-American relations from May 1937 to May 1940, sees FDR retaining suspicions of the British Empire while exaggerating its ability to restrain Germany.[44] Robert W. Matson's

---

39   Theodore A. Wilson, *The First Summit: Roosevelt and Churchill at Placentia Bay, 1941*, rev. ed. (Lawrence, KS, 1991), 230, 235.
40   Theodore A. Wilson, "The First Summit: FDR and the Riddle of Personal Diplomacy," in *The Atlantic Charter*, ed. Douglas Brinkley and David Facey-Crowther (New York, 1994).
41   Warren F. Kimball, "The Atlantic Charter: With All Deliberate Speed," ibid, 83–104.
42   David Reynolds, "The Atlantic 'Flop': British Foreign Policy and the Churchill-Roosevelt Meeting of August 1941," in ibid, 129–50.
43   James R. Leutze, *Bargaining for Supremacy: Anglo-American Naval Collaboration, 1937–1941* (Chapel Hill, NC, 1977); Malcolm H. Murfett, *Fool-Proof Relations: The Search for Anglo-American Naval Cooperation during the Chamberlain Years, 1937–1940* (Singapore, 1984).
44   William R. Rock, *Chamberlain and Roosevelt: British Foreign Policy and the United States, 1937–1940* (Columbus, OH, 1988).

study of the "navicert" controversy, whereby the British directed American shipping to their own ports for examination, supplements W. N. Medlicott's work of the fifties. Matson shows severe U.S. protest forcing Ambassador Lothian, Foreign Secretary Halifax, and Prime Minister Churchill to make some alterations in their economic blockade.[45] In a study that includes U.S. lend-lease aid to Britain, Alan P. Dobson exaggerates the part played by economic diplomacy but offers some excellent research. Like Kimball, he finds the program more magnanimous in conception than execution.[46]

Scholars have also examined Lords Lothian and Halifax, British ambassadors to Washington. In a small monograph, David Reynolds finds Lothian a skillful ambassador, a major player in working out the destroyer deal, though the diplomat's neglect of details and desire for U.S. cooperation occasionally impaired his effectiveness.[47] Conversely, Rhodri Jeffreys-Jones sees Lothian as out of touch with American life and values.[48] Andrew Roberts's life of Halifax shows Lothian's successor as an envoy ignorant of the American political system and at best lukewarm toward FDR; the "holy fox" only became popular in the United States after Pearl Harbor, at which point he turned into a skillful negotiator.[49]

Certain American scholars have also explored specific aspects of Anglo-American relations. Fred E. Pollock notes how skillfully FDR linked the Ogdensburg defense agreement with Canada to U.S. control of any remnants of the British fleet seeking refuge in Canadian waters.[50] The Tyler Kent affair, dealing with a young

---

45   Robert W. Matson, *Neutrality and Navicerts: Britain, the United States, and Economic Warfare, 1939–1940* (New York, 1994); W. N. Medlicott, *The Economic Blockade*, 2 vols. (London, 1952, 1959). See also Matson, "The British Naval Blockade and U.S. Trade, 1939–40," *Historian* 53 (Summer 1991): 743–63.
46   Alan P. Dobson, *US Wartime Aid to Britain, 1940–1946* (London, 1986).
47   David Reynolds, "Lord Lothian and Anglo-American Relations, 1939–1940," *Transactions of the American Philosophical Society* 73 (1983).
48   Rhodri Jeffreys-Jones, "The Inestimable Advantage of Not Being English: Lord Lothian's American Ambassadorship, 1939–1940," *Scottish Historical Review* 63 (April 1984): 105–10; idem, "Lord Lothian and American Democracy: An Illusion in Pursuit of an Illusion," *Canadian Review of American Studies* 17 (Winter 1986): 411–22.
49   Andrew Roberts, *"The Holy Fox": A Biography of Lord Halifax* (London, 1991).
50   Fred E. Pollock, "Roosevelt, the Ogdensburg Agreement, and the British Fleet: All Done with Mirrors," *Diplomatic History* 5 (Summer 1981): 203–19.

U.S. code clerk arrested by the British, still attracts its share of spy buffs. Warren F. Kimball and Bruce Bartlett have shown that Kent never had any of the truly incriminating cables between FDR and Churchill that he claimed to possess.[51] In his thoroughly researched study of the destroyers-for-bases deal, grounded in archival research, journalist Robert Shogan shows how American policy elites skirted the law to cement a bargain that shortchanged the British while setting the U.S. on the road to war.[52] Two writers posit that the British doctored the "secret" German map that FDR flourished in October 1941 to "prove" Hitler's designs on the Western Hemisphere.[53] Thomas Fleming suspects the British of leaking the War Department's Victory plan to the isolationist *Chicago Tribune* three days before the Pearl Harbor attack, doing so with FDR's own authorization.[54]

Extensive work has been done on the relationship between British policy and the American public. John E. Moser finds Anglophobia persisting well into the 1940s.[55] Nicholas John Cull, by immersing himself in British records, shows how closely English propagandists worked with American interventionists to entice the United States to enter the conflict as a full-scale ally.[56] Thomas Earl Mahl describes the covert efforts of British intelligence to undermine the anti-interventionist movement.[57]

51   Warren F. Kimball and Bruce Bartlett, "Roosevelt and Prewar Commitments to Churchill: The Tyler Kent Affair," *Diplomatic History* 5 (Fall 1981): 291–311. See also John Costello, *Ten Days to Destiny: The Secret Story of the Hess Peace Initiative and British Efforts to Strike a Deal with Hitler* (New York, 1991); and Ray Bearse and Anthony Read, *Conspirator: The Untold Story of Tyler Kent* (New York, 1991).

52   Robert Shogan, *Hard Bargain: How FDR Twisted Churchill's Arm, Evaded the Law, and Changed the Role of the American Presidency* (New York, 1995).

53   John F. Bratzel and Leslie B. Rout, Jr., "FDR and the 'Secret Map,'" *Wilson Quarterly* 9 (New Year's 1985): 167–73.

54   Thomas Fleming, "The Big Leak," *American Heritage* 38 (December 1987): 65–71.

55   John E. Moser, *Twisting the Lion's Tail: The Persistence of Anglophobia in American Politics, 1921–1948* (New York, 1988).

56   Nicholas John Cull, *Selling War: The British Propaganda Campaign against American "Neutrality" in World War II* (New York, 1995). For more on British propaganda see David Lloyd Jones, "Marketing the Allies to America," *Midwest Quarterly* 29 (Spring 1988): 266–83.

57   Thomas Earl Mahl, *Desperate Deception: British Covert Operations in the United States, 1939–44* (Washington, DC, 1998).

Not surprisingly, U.S.-German relations continue to receive attention. In able treatments of the subject, Hans W. Gatzke and Manfred Jonas find some elements of rationality in Hitler's declaration of war on the United States. In this regard, Gatzke notes that the Führer believed that German U-boats could greatly damage the American fleet, while Jonas stresses Hitler's assumption that the United States could be forced to concentrate its attention on the Pacific.[58] Arguing to the contrary, Andreas Hillgruber interprets Hitler's move as a tacit admission that the German leader no longer controlled the direction of the war.[59] Holger H. Herwig sees the German dictator taking a calculated risk: Without an immediate German threat, Hitler feared, the United States would be able to defeat Japan quickly, then turn its full fury toward Europe.[60]

According to Gerhard L. Weinberg's formidable history of World War II, *A World at Arms* (1994), Hitler welcomed war with the United States. Weinberg, a specialist in Nazi foreign policy, has engaged in extensive research in German, American, and British archives and concludes that the Führer could draw upon the full-scale participation of the Japanese navy, therefore compensating for his own weakness at sea. Furthermore, a full-scale war with America would give his U-boats the chance to impose crippling strikes. One should realize that Hitler was always biding his time, awaiting the day when the Russian campaign had ended and he had built sufficient battleships to attack the United States. Weinberg denies that FDR ever sought to enter the conflict. Even the shoot-on-sight orders, issued on 11 September 1941, were aimed more at frightening German submarines than provoking them.[61]

58   Hans W. Gatzke, *Germany and the United States: "Special Relationship"?* (Cambridge, MA, 1980); Manfred Jonas, *The United States and Germany: A Diplomatic History* (Ithaca, NY, 1984).
59   Andreas Hillgruber, *Germany and the Two World Wars* (Cambridge, MA, 1981).
60   Holger H. Herwig, "Miscalculated Risks: The German Declaration of War against the United States, 1917 and 1941," *Naval War College Review* 39 (Autumn 1986): 88–100.
61   Gerhard L. Weinberg, *A World at Arms: A Global History of World War II* (New York, 1994), 86–87, 238–63. See also idem, *World in the Balance: Behind the Scenes of World War II* (Hanover, NH, 1981), 75–95; and idem, "Pearl Harbor: The German Perspective," in *Germany, Hitler, and World War II* (New York, 1995), 194–204.

Yet the issue of national security remains debated. Contrary to most historians, Melvin Small sides with Bruce M. Russett in finding no "clear and present danger" from Germany in 1941. Germany, claims Small, did not even have the technical capacity to invade a defenseless Latin American country. As far as German atomic research is concerned, "[m]any things could have happened to Hitler before he obtained the means to rain terror on us from the skies." The United States had even less to fear from Germany on economic grounds: The quantity of its foreign trade was unimpressive; some U.S. trade was with nations – Canada, for example – that could never be controlled by Berlin; synthetic substitutes could replace needed rubber and tin.[62]

Similarly, we have fresh studies of U.S.-Soviet relations. Hugh De Santis examines the careers of thirty diplomats from the European and Soviet divisions of the foreign service. Such specialists, De Santis finds, were always strongly hostile to Soviet ideology. Once Russia entered the war, however, Washington felt forced to prevent a German victory to the east.[63] Thomas R. Maddux finds Roosevelt ignoring the State Department's Soviet specialists, who sought a quid pro quo for any bargaining. Even in 1941, when the Soviet Union came under German siege, FDR refused to make demands concerning territorial issues, which gave Stalin the impression that he was weak and vacillating.[64] Similarly, Edward M. Bennett accuses Roosevelt of pursuing "crisis-to-crisis" diplomacy and continually shifting between short- and long-range goals.[65] John Daniel Langer defends American generosity once Russia was under attack. True, the Cold War marks the failure of this policy, but – like Warren F. Kimball – Langer finds it difficult to fault Roosevelt and Churchill for seeking a sincere and lasting

---

62   Bruce M. Russett, *No Clear and Present Danger: A Skeptical View of the U.S. Entry into World War II* (New York, 1972); Melvin Small, *Was War Necessary? National Security and U.S. Entry into War* (Beverly Hills, 1980), 261.
63   Hugh De Santis, *The Diplomacy of Silence: The American Foreign Service, the Soviet Union, and the Cold War, 1933–1947* (Chicago, 1980).
64   Thomas R. Maddux, *Years of Estrangement: American Relations with the Soviet Union, 1933–1941* (Tallahassee, FL, 1980).
65   Edward M. Bennett, *Franklin D. Roosevelt and the Search for Victory: American-Soviet Relations, 1939–1945* (Wilmington, DE, 1985).

friendship.[66] Recent studies of diplomats with Soviet experience, such as George F. Kennan, say little directly about the State Department's attitude toward U.S. entry into war, but they are essential for grasping the mentality of those either enthusiastic about or suspicious of the Soviets.[67]

Related to U. S.-Soviet affairs is American policy in the Finnish war, a topic coming under reexamination. In a major work titled *America and the Winter War, 1939–1940* (1981), Travis Beal Jacobs finds American diplomacy almost an adventure in blunder. Although Jacobs denies that U.S. arms sales would have altered the outcome of the conflict, he does argue that American military aid might have profoundly affected general U.S. policy by drastically weakening the forces of anti-interventionism. Jacobs presents Roosevelt as a great procrastinator, one who permitted a leadership vacuum to develop. Had FDR tapped widespread anti-Soviet sentiment, the president could have mustered considerable congressional support for the principle of aiding victims of aggression.[68]

We do not have new detailed studies of Roosevelt's policy toward France in the early years of World War II, though some authors perceptively comment on the 1939–41 period. Marvin R. Zahniser has called upon historians to be far more aware of the radical shift in global power relations engendered by France's fall.[69] Julian G. Hurstfield denies that FDR ever saw his French

---

66 John Daniel Langer, "The Harriman-Beaverbrook Mission and the Debate over Unconditional Aid for the Soviet Union, 1941," *Journal of Contemporary History* 14 (July 1979): 463–82.

67 H. W. Brands, *Inside the Cold War: Loy Henderson and the Rise of the American Empire, 1918–1961* (New York, 1991); George W. Baer, ed., *A Question of Trust: Origins of U.S.-Soviet Diplomatic Relations: The Memoirs of Loy W. Henderson* (Stanford, 1986); Elizabeth Kimball MacLean, "Joseph Davies and Soviet-American Relations, 1941–1943," *Diplomatic History* 4 (Winter 1980): 73–93; idem, *Joseph F. Davies: Envoy to the Soviets* (Westport, CT, 1992); David Mayers, "Ambassador Joseph Davies Reconsidered," *SHAFR Newsletter* 23 (September 1992): 1–16; idem, *George Kennan and the Dilemmas of US Foreign Policy* (New York, 1988); Walter L. Hixson, *George F. Kennan: Cold War Iconoclast* (New York, 1989); Anders Stephanson, *Kennan and the Art of Foreign Policy* (Cambridge, MA, 1989).

68 Travis Beal Jacobs, *America and the Winter War, 1939–1940* (New York, 1981). For a similar indictment against FDR's role in the Finnish war see David L. Porter, *The Seventy-sixth Congress and World War II, 1939–1940* (Columbia, MO, 1979), 125–26.

69 Marvin R. Zahniser, "Rethinking the Significance of Disaster: The United States and the Fall of France in 1940," *International History Review* 14 (May 1992): 252–76.

policy, which included recognition of the Vichy government, as either morally awkward or inconsistent: "The political ideals were reserved for the postwar world, with details to be worked out then."[70] Mario Rossi notes that even before June 1940, FDR had become disillusioned by much of France's interwar leadership. The president was bitterly disappointed by the French surrender, and he exaggerated the degree of Vichy's independence from Germany.[71] Henry Blumenthal stresses that when war broke out, French leaders naively hoped that FDR would immediately come to their aid.[72]

Professional historians are finally focusing on U.S.-Italian relations. In an extended treatment of American policy toward Mussolini's regime, David E. Schmitz sees U.S. policy rooted in "a European peace based upon the Open Door, political stability, and the isolation of the Soviet Union." Hence, during the "phony war," Roosevelt sought to capitalize on Mussolini's nonbelligerent status in order to split the Axis, thereby limiting the fighting to northern Europe and helping to ensure an Allied victory. To Schmitz, FDR's diplomacy reveals one thing above all: "It was Nazi Germany's economic nationalism and military aggression that the Roosevelt administration opposed, and not Fascism as an ideology or a system."[73] James Edward Miller, in his history of U.S.-Italian diplomacy during the entire 1940s, portrays American internationalists as divided. Conservatives among them wanted to eliminate the Fascist regime while retaining traditional class and social structures; liberals sought to destroy the power of the Italian right.[74]

---

70   Julian G. Hurstfield, *America and the French Nation, 1939–1945* (Chapel Hill, NC, 1986), 239.
71   Mario Rossi, *Roosevelt and the French* (Westport, CT, 1993).
72   Henry Blumenthal, *Illusion and Reality in Franco-American Diplomacy, 1914–1945* (Baton Rouge, LA, 1986).
73   David F. Schmitz, *The United States and Fascist Italy, 1922–1940* (Chapel Hill, NC, 1988), 211–12. In a generally friendly review essay on Schmitz's book, James Edward Miller finds Schmitz neglecting domestic pressures on the president and ignoring differences between Nazism and Fascism. See "'That Admirable Italian Gentleman': The View from America (and from Italy)," *Diplomatic History* 13 (Fall 1989): 547–56.
74   James Edward Miller, *The United States and Italy 1940–1950: The Politics and Diplomacy of Stabilization* (Chapel Hill, NC, 1986).

In covering American relations with Canada, J. L. Granatstein notes that in early 1941 Canada was the Roosevelt administration's most valued ally. But after Congress passed lend-lease and the United States grew closer to Britain, Canada's importance sharply declined.[75] Both Granatstein and James Eayrs stress the bitterness of Prime Minister Mackenzie King, who was excluded from the Atlantic conference.[76]

New studies on Latin America focus on the controversy over Axis penetration. Irwin F. Gellman claims that FDR deliberately exaggerated the potential of the Nazi movement in the Americas to secure aid for the Allies.[77] Conversely, David G. Haglund sees the hemispheric anxieties of the entire Roosevelt administration as quite sincere. FDR, he writes, was genuinely opposed to intervention until the mid-1930s. Anxious over the security of Latin America, however, the president became globally conscious, in the late summer of 1940 going so far as to enter into a de facto alliance with Britain. Haglund himself believes that had Hitler attained victory in Europe, he might well have been in a position eventually to challenge the physical security of the United States.[78] According to William E. Kinsella, Jr., Roosevelt believed that Germany sought world domination. Hitler's Reich would first attempt to gain economic control of Latin America, then use the area as a military launching pad.[79] John A. Thompson denies that the United States was forced into war out of any need for self-defense. Rather it was motivated by the belief that "only American power stood between Hitler and victory."[80]

---

75 J. L. Granatstein, "The Man Who Wasn't There: Mackenzie King, Canada, and the Atlantic Charter," in *The Atlantic Charter*, 115–28.

76 James Eayrs, "The Atlantic Conference and Its Charter: A Canadian's Reflections," in ibid., 151–71.

77 Irwin F. Gellman, *Good Neighbor Diplomacy: United States Policies in Latin America, 1933–1945* (Baltimore, MD, 1979).

78 David G. Haglund, *Latin America and the Transformation of U.S. Strategic Thought, 1936–1940* (Albuquerque, NM, 1984).

79 William F. Kinsella, Jr., "The Prescience of a Statesman: FDR's Assessment of Adolf Hitler before the World War, 1933–1941," in *Franklin D. Roosevelt: The Man, the Myth, the Era, 1882–1945*, ed. Herbert D. Rosenbaum and Elizabeth Bartelme (New York, 1987), 73–84.

80 John A. Thompson, "Another Look at the Downfall of 'Fortress America,'" *Journal of American Studies* 26 (December 1992): 408.

A focus on geographical areas is not the only category of analysis, and for some aspects of U.S. policy it is not the best one. The Roosevelt leadership can also be approached by examining leading policymakers, the decision-making process, and public debate.

In *American Visions of Europe*, John Lamberton Harper divides FDR's foreign policy establishment into four major groups. First, the "Hullian" liberals, represented by Secretary Hull, Norman H. Davis, Leo Pasvolsky, and to some degree the president himself. Their program: disarmament, exports, and the elimination of European imperialism. Second, the advocates of "protocontainment," seeking above all the weakening of the Soviet Union, even at the risk of making common cause with Germany. Diplomats Joseph P. Kennedy, Breckinridge Long, John Cudahy, and Robert Kelley all articulated such sentiments, usually without Roosevelt's backing. Third, a school calling for what Harper terms "Europhobic-hemispherism" (which he finds more accurate than "appeasement"), with its stress on the integration of the Western Hemisphere and alleviation of "legitimate" German economic grievances. Represented by Adolf Berle, William C. Bullitt, and Sumner Welles, this school was dominant through the spring of 1940. Fourth, a pro-British party that linked U.S. security to the continental balance of power, friendly control of the Atlantic, and the defeat of Nazi Germany. Frank Knox, Henry L. Stimson, and Felix Frankfurter embodied such thinking. By the summer of 1940, this fourth school had gained the ascendancy.[81]

Historians have understandably given attention to FDR's reliance upon special emissaries. In his biography of Harry Hopkins, George McJimsey stresses how skillfully FDR's troubleshooter gathered a White House inner circle – the so-called Hopkins Shop – aimed at aiding Britain even before the United States had completed its own major military buildup. Hopkins was not above manipulating Roosevelt on behalf of the British.[82] Dwight Will-

81 Harper, *American Visions*, 48–73.
82 George McJimsey, *Harry Hopkins: Ally of the Poor and Defender of Democracy* (Cambridge, MA, 1987).

iam Tuttle, who concentrates on Hopkins as diplomat, presents him not simply as Roosevelt's alter ego but as a sophisticated innovator in his own right. In the middle of 1941, Tuttle claims, Hopkins called for caution on the Atlantic. He was originally skeptical of aid to the Soviet army and misled Churchill as to the imminence of U.S. entry into the war.[83]

As the State Department often served as a brake on FDR, its top leadership is especially important. Irwin F. Gellman portrays Cordell Hull during 1939–41 as an aging and frail man, stricken with tuberculosis. He was, therefore, often an absentee secretary of state and one often bypassed by his commander-in-chief. Gellman offers little credence to the Hull memoirs (1948), which were ghostwritten by journalist Andrew Berding; the account describes "the way he [Hull] would have liked events to have taken place rather than they actually did."[84]   Certainly we are looking forward to Jonathan G. Utley's study of Hull, particularly in light of the tremendous new material found in State Department and British archives over the past several decades.

Major work has begun on Sumner Welles, whose closeness to FDR made his diplomatic role often more important than that of Secretary Hull. In examining Welles in the early period of the war, Frank Warren Graff sees the undersecretary of state as pursuing an expediential policy toward the Soviets, remaining suspicious of Vichy France, and sharing much of Hull's economic vision. Unlike Hull, however, Welles was far from enthusiastic concerning international organization. Graff notes that Welles took his famous mission to Europe, made in February 1941, with the utmost seriousness; the emissary believed he might possibly be able to stop the conflict.[85]

In a major study of the Welles-Hull-FDR relationship, Irwin F. Gellman presents the undersecretary as a troubled homosexual,

83   Dwight H. Tuttle, *Harry L. Hopkins and Anglo-American-Soviet Relations, 1941–1945* (New York, 1983).
84   Irwin F. Gellman, *Secret Affairs: Franklin Roosevelt, Cordell Hull, and Sumner Welles* (Baltimore, MD, 1995), 385; *The Memoirs of Cordell Hull*, 2 vols. (New York, 1948).
85   Frank Warren Graff, *Strategy of Involvement: A Diplomatic Biography of Sumner Welles* (New York, 1988).

so close to Roosevelt that he saw the president daily. Welles's enemies not only included Hull but diplomat William Bullitt. Ironically Hull and Welles differed little on fundamental policy; their rivalry was a bureaucratic one that the president irresponsibly allowed to fester. As far as the Welles mission of early 1940 goes, Gellman finds the man naive concerning his authority to act as mediator. The entire idea was "poorly conceived, planned, and prepared."[86] Benjamin Welles's biography of his father is an appreciative account of the man whom he calls, with some exaggeration, "FDR's global strategist," but whom he portrays as a tragic figure.[87]

Other diplomats have also been studied. Jordan A. Schwarz's biography of Adolf A. Berle ably conveys the anti-British outlook and hemispheric focus of a powerful assistant secretary of state.[88] In their coverage of Roosevelt's mercurial emissary William C. Bullitt, Will Brownell and Richard N. Billings give credence to the accusation made in the *German White Book* of 1940, namely, that FDR's ambassador to France – an anti-interventionist until Munich – encouraged the British and French to support Poland against Germany. The Bullitt Papers remain in family hands.[89] Rudy Abramson's life of W. Averell Harriman shows how the multimillionaire-turned-diplomat went beyond the legal limits of lend-lease legislation in aiding the British.[90]

In a class by himself is Joseph P. Kennedy, and in recent years a number of historians have retold his story. Continually reiterated is the ambassador's anti-interventionism, based upon his fears of general devastation, the spread of Bolshevism, and injury to his family. The accusations are familiar. Kennedy promoted Chamberlain's policies more than Roosevelt's, frequently presented his personal views as official government policy, and favored

86   Gellman, *Secret Affairs*, 200.
87   Benjamin Welles, *Sumner Welles: FDR's Global Strategist* (New York, 1997).
88   Jordan A. Schwarz, *Liberal: Adolf A. Berle and the Vision of an American Era* (New York, 1987).
89   Will Brownell and Richard N. Billings, *So Close to Greatness: A Biography of William C. Bullitt* (New York, 1987).
90   Rudy Abramson, *Spanning the Century: The Life of W. Averell Harriman, 1891–1986* (New York, 1992).

German predominance in Eastern Europe. Michael R. Beschloss finds FDR skillfully immobilizing "the founding father," allowing Kennedy to preserve "the fiction that he could serve Roosevelt faithfully, advance his own career, and oppose intervention at the same time."[91] Ralph E. De Bedts shows how Kennedy often pushed his anti-interventionist alternatives as U.S. government policy, thereby becoming a diplomatic albatross to the Roosevelt administration.[92] Doris Kearns Goodwin and Jane K. Vieth repeat a familiar indictment.[93] One must note that the Kennedy family has only granted certain scholars – Beschloss and Goodwin – access to the ambassador's papers. Nigel Hamilton, whose study of the young John F. Kennedy was published in 1992, was denied use.[94]

Far more, however, is needed on other major figures of the Roosevelt administration. We do have several studies of Harold L. Ickes, both describing an arch-interventionist often in deep conflict with FDR, though relatively few historians have used the full unpublished manuscript diaries.[95] Work is particularly vital on Treasury Secretary Henry Morgenthau, Jr., not to mention such diplomats as William Phillips, John Cudahy, Jay Pierrepont Moffat, John Winant, and Lawrence Steinhardt.[96] Fortunately,

---

91 Michael R. Beschloss, *Kennedy and Roosevelt: The Uneasy Alliance* (New York, 1980), 276.

92 Ralph F. De Bedts, *Ambassador Joseph Kennedy, 1931–1940: An Anatomy of Appeasement* (New York, 1985).

93 Doris Kearns Goodwin, *The Fitzgeralds and the Kennedys: An American Saga* (New York, 1987); Jane Karoline Vieth, "Joseph P. Kennedy and British Appeasement: The Diplomacy of a Boston Irishman," in *U.S. Diplomats in Europe, 1910–1941*, ed. Kenneth Paul Jones (Santa Barbara, 1983), 165–82; idem, "Munich Revisited through Joseph P. Kennedy's Eyes," *Michigan Academician* 18 (Winter 1986): 73–85; idem, "Munich and American Appeasement," in *Appeasement in Europe*, 51–74.

94 Nigel Hamilton, *JFK: Reckless Youth* (New York, 1992), 801–2.

95 Graham White and John Maze, *Harold Ickes of the New Deal: His Private Life and Public Career* (Cambridge, MA, 1985); T. H. Watkins, *Righteous Pilgrim: The Life and Times of Harold L. Ickes, 1874–1952* (New York, 1990); Jeanne Nienaber Clarke, *Roosevelt's Warrior: Harold L. Ickes and the New Deal* (Baltimore, MD, 1996).

96 There has been preliminary work on some of these figures. Patrick J. Hearden demolishes many stereotypes by showing that until 1941, Cudahy combined his belief in German access to world markets with calls for U.S. military preparedness. Cudahy's anti-interventionism surfaced in June 1941 after his *Life* interview with Hitler. See Hearden, "John Cudahy and the Pursuit of Peace," *Mid-America* (April–June 1986): 99–114. A general study of Winant is found in Nina Davis Howland, "Ambassador John Gilbert Winant: Friend of an

there is finally a study on a prominent dissent from New Deal foreign policy, retired diplomat William R. Castle, Jr., whose provocative diary has long been mined by historians.[97]

In examining the role of the State Department, certain questions become obvious. To what degree did the department's cultural milieu lead to long-sustained efforts to accommodate Germany and Italy while overreacting to Soviet moves? Turning to the matter of overt and covert anti-Semitism within the department, how much did this attitude affect not only refugee policy but other matters as well? Conversely, a recent study by Richard Breitman and Alan M. Kraut finds Breckinridge Long more fearful of "fifth column" subversives than of Jews per se.[98]

If anything, military factors are even more crucial. Much of the military bureaucracy was most cautious about U.S. entry into the war, though in 1941 the Navy was eager to convoy across the Atlantic and the air force anxious to send planes to the Philippines. Donald Cameron Watt finds the ideology of the pre–Pearl Harbor army centering on fear of Bolshevism, distrust of Britain, and respect for German military professionalism.[99] Michael S. Sherry, in an account that contains much cultural history, notes how a belief in air power transcended the isolationist-interventionist debate. Both FDR and his anti-interventionist foes were enamored by its use.[100] In a comprehensive account of the Victory Plan of 1941, drafted by Major Albert C. Wedemeyer, Charles Kirkpatrick sees the blueprint as embodying an astute meshing of political and military aims, an appreciation of U.S. economic power, and a delineation of objectives that suited national goals – the elimination of totalitarianism from Europe and denial of the western Pacific to the Japanese. Drawbacks included gross over-

---

Embattled Britain, 1941–1946" (Ph.D. diss., University of Maryland, 1983). For the British left's influence on Winant's appointment as U.S. ambassador see David Reynolds, "Roosevelt, the British Left, and the Appointment of John G. Winant as United States Ambassador to Britain in 1941," *International History Review* 4 (August 1982): 393–413.

97 Alfred E. Castle, *Diplomatic Realism: William R. Castle, Jr., and American Foreign Policy, 1919–1953* (Honolulu, 1998).

98 For the Breitman-Kraut reference see footnote 19.

99 Watt, *Succeeding John Bull*, 93.

100 Michael S. Sherry, *The Rise of American Air Power: The Creation of Armageddon* (New Haven, CT, 1987).

estimation of the number of divisions needed, misunderstanding the type of weapons desired, and lack of provision for replacement.[101] Thanks to Steven T. Ross, we have access to other major war plans as well.[102] Stephen D. Wesbrook has shown how low Army morale had fallen in the summer of 1941 and the abortive efforts of a *New York Times* journalist to raise it.[103]

When it comes to military biography, however, our coverage is again spotty. In his treatment of Roosevelt and such commanders as George C. Marshall and Ernest J. King, Eric Larrabee credits the president with ably exercising initiative. This quality Larrabee finds particularly pivotal, for he claims that in December 1941 Hitler came within an ace of winning, or at least forcing a stalemate.[104] Godfrey Hodgson's life of Henry Stimson neglects major manuscript collections and exaggerates the influence of "the colonel."[105] Somewhat more scholarly is Kai Bird's life of Stimson's deputy, John J. McCloy, whom Bird implies was overly obsessed with sabotage matters.[106] Turning to George C. Marshall, Forrest C. Pogue's biography – with its stress on the general's effort to mobilize the United States – remains definitive.[107] In fresh accounts, both Mark A. Stoler and David G. Haglund stress the initial reluctance of the army chief of staff to aid Britain, an attitude also revealed in the recent edition of the Marshall Papers. Marshall feared that Roosevelt was dangerously overcommitting

---

101   Charles Kirkpatrick, *An Unknown Future and a Doubtful Present: Writing the Victory Plan of 1941* (Washington, 1990).
102   Of Steven T. Ross's *American War Plans, 1919–1941,* 5 vols. (New York, 1992), the most crucial volumes are vol. 3, *Plans to Meet the Axis Threat, 1939–1940,* vol. 4, *Coalition War Plans and Hemispheric Defense Plans, 1940–1941,* and vol. 5, *Plans for Global War: Rainbow–5 and the Victory Program, 1941.*
103   Stephen D. Wesbrook, "The Railey Report and Army Morale, 1941: Anatomy of a Crisis," *Military Review* 60 (June 1980): 11–24.
104   Eric Larrabee, *Commander in Chief: Franklin Delano Roosevelt, His Lieutenants, and Their War* (New York, 1987).
105   Godfrey Hodgson, *The Colonel: The Life and Wars of Henry Stimson, 1867–1950* (New York, 1990).
106   Kai Bird, *The Chairman: John McCloy, The Making of the American Establishment* (New York, 1992). Walter Isaacson and Evan Thomas, *The Wise Men: Six Friends and the World They Made – Acheson, Bohlen, Harriman, Kennan, Lovett, McCloy* (New York, 1986) does little with McCloy, or for that matter, several important subjects in the crucial 1939–41 period.
107   Forrest C. Pogue, *George C. Marshall: Ordeal and Hope, 1939–1942* (New York, 1966).

the country.[108]   George Q. Flynn finds surprising isolationism in selective service director Lewis B. Hershey, as does Mark A. Stoler in a top Marshall aide, Stanley D. Embick.[109]   Robert Hessen and J. Garry Clifford note the pessimistic views of one anti-interventionist officer close to Marshall, Colonel Truman Smith.[110]

Intelligence leadership is also coming under scrutiny. Anthony Cave Brown and Thomas F. Troy offer scholarly accounts of William ("Wild Bill") Donovan.   While Brown concentrates on Donovan's colorful personality, Troy describes a bureaucratic entrepreneur par excellence.   He shows how Donovan converted an agency established to coordinate information into one conducting espionage and military operations.   We are just beginning to gain information on the super-sleuth's liaisons with British intelligence, particularly given the "revelations" of H. Montgomery Hyde and William Stevenson ("the man called Intrepid").[111]

In examining Naval biographies, we face the same problems. True, we have recent studies by B. Mitchell Simpson III on Harold R. Stark and Thomas B. Buell on Ernest J. King, the former work showing Stark's wholehearted support for convoys to Britain.[112]

---

108   Mark A. Stoler, *George C. Marshall: Soldier-Statesman of the American Century* (Boston, 1989); David G. Haglund, "George C. Marshall and the Question of Military Aid to England"; Larry I. Bland, ed., *The Papers of George Catlett Marshall*, vol. 2, *"We Cannot Delay," July 1, 1939–December 6, 1941* (Baltimore, MD, 1986). Several new popular biographies of Marshall have been written: Leonard Mosley, *Marshall: Hero for Our Times* (New York, 1982); Thomas Parrish, *Roosevelt and Marshall: Partners in Politics and War* (New York, 1989); and Ed Cray, *General of the Army: George C. Marshall, Soldier and Statesman* (New York, 1990). Of these popular accounts, Cray's is by far the most scholarly.
109   George Q. Flynn, *Lewis B. Hershey, Mr. Selective Service* (Chapel Hill, 1985); Mark A. Stoler, "From Continentalism to Globalism: General Stanley D. Embick, the Joint Strategic Survey Committee, and the Military View of American National Policy during the Second World War," *Diplomatic History* 6 (Summer 1982): 303–21.
110   Robert Hessen, ed., *Berlin Alert: The Memoirs and Reports of Truman Smith* (Stanford, 1984); J. Garry Clifford, "A Connecticut Colonel's Candid Conversation with the Wrong Commander-in-Chief," *Connecticut History* 28 (November 1988): 25–38.
111   Anthony Cave Brown, *The Last Hero: Wild Bill Donovan* (New York, 1982); Thomas F. Troy, *Donovan and the CIA: A History of the Establishment of the Central Intelligence Agency* (Frederick, MD, 1981); idem, *Wild Bill and Intrepid: Bill Donovan, Bill Stevenson, and the Origins of CIA* (New Haven, CT, 1996); H. Montgomery Hyde, *Room 3603: The Story of the British Intelligence Center in New York during World War II* (New York, 1962); William Stevenson, *A Man Called Intrepid: The Secret War* (New York, 1976); Timothy J. Naftali, "Intrepid's Last Deception: Documenting the Career of William Stevenson," *Intelligence and National Security* 8 (July 1993), 72–92.
112   B. Mitchell Simpson III, *Admiral Harold R. Stark: Architect of Victory, 1939–1945*

In a fresh biography of Undersecretary of the Navy James V. Forrestal, Townsend Hoopes and Douglas Brinkley see the "driven patriot" as an excellent administrator and skilled infighter.[113] Yet it is almost scandalous that we lack a published biography of Frank Knox.[114] And despite Kenneth J. Hagan's able general history of the U.S. Navy, no one has given sea power the same kind of "cultural" scrutiny that Michael S. Sherry has given air power.[115]

In the heated debates over U.S. policy, Congress played an essential role, and we are finally getting in-depth coverage of many debates. In a highly significant study, based on many congressional manuscripts and roll call analyses, David L. Porter describes the battles in 1939–40 over cash and carry, aid to Finland, and selective service and claims that Congress was no rubber stamp for FDR. There was surprising Democratic defection on the draft just as there was equally surprising Republican sentiment favoring aid to Finland.[116]

In their specialized work on the 1940 conscription controversy, J. Garry Clifford and Samuel R. Spencer, Jr., fault Roosevelt for allowing the debate over conscription to endanger major aid to Britain. "An improviser at heart," they write, "the president preferred to move in a forward direction but without any predetermined destination." Clifford and Spencer find the draft the result of a group within the "eastern establishment," the so-called Plattsburgers; the hesitant FDR kept hands off while the Army preoccupied itself with hemispheric defense. Yet the summer of 1940 marked a major turning point: The United States made commitments to allies overseas and chose a method, conscription, that could raise the forces needed to defend overseas ramparts

---

(Columbia, SC, 1989); Thomas B. Buell, *Master of Sea Power: A Biography of Fleet Admiral Ernest J. King* (Boston, 1980).

113 Townsend Hoopes and Douglas Brinkley, *Driven Patriot: The Life and Times of James Forrestal* (New York, 1992).

114 For Knox, one should consult Steven MacDonald Mark, "An American Interventionist: Frank Knox and United States Foreign Relations" (Ph.D. diss., University of Maryland, College Park, 1977).

115 Kenneth J. Hagan, *This People's Navy: The Making of American Sea Power* (New York, 1991). For Sherry see footnote 84.

116 Porter, *The Seventy-sixth Congress and World War II*.

and rescue nations abroad.[117]   One might push the findings of Clifford and Spencer even further.   Was not the Plattsburg experience, indeed the experience of the Great War in general, more influential on many eastern interventionists than various Wall Street ties?   Perhaps World War II offered a "second chance" to rectify the defeat of Wilsonianism.

We do have recent studies of some congressional figures, but not nearly enough.   Betty Glad's biography of Key Pittman upgrades the reputation of the Nevada senator, better known for his heavy drinking and obsession with the price of silver than for any hardheaded realism.[118]   Rorin M. Platt offers a collective biography of the Virginia political elite, finding its militant interventionism rooted in concerns over democracy, security, and trade, plus a shared British heritage.[119]   Fortunately, scholarship has begun on such administration stalwarts in Congress as James F. Byrnes, Alben Barkley, and Claude Pepper.[120]   The same holds true for certain leading anti-interventionists – David I. Walsh, Burton K. Wheeler, and Hamilton Fish, Jr.[121]   Robert E. Burke's edition of the diary letters of Hiram Johnson well captures the volatile personality of the California senator, while the biography by Richard Coke Lower shows why the old maverick could no longer lead a major battle.[122]

117   J. Garry Clifford and Samuel R. Spencer, Jr., *The First Peacetime Draft* (Lawrence, KS, 1986), 230.

118   Betty Glad, *Key Pittman: The Tragedy of a Senate Insider* (New York, 1986).

119   Rorin M. Platt, "The Triumph of Interventionism: Virginia's Political Elite and Aid to Britain, 1939–1941," *Virginia Magazine of History and Biography* 100 (July 1992): 343–64; idem, *Virginia in Foreign Affairs, 1933–1941* (Lanham, MD, 1991).

120   Ric A. Kabat, "From New Deal to Red Scare: The Political Odyssey of Senator Claude A. Pepper" (Ph.D. diss., Florida State University, Tallahassee, 1995); Polly Ann Davis, *Alben W. Barkley: Senate Majority Leader and Vice President* (New York, 1979); David Robertson, *Sly and Able: A Political Biography of James F. Byrnes* (New York, 1994). For a first-hand memoir see Claude Denson Pepper with Hays Gorey, *Pepper: Eyewitness to a Century* (San Diego, 1987).

121   Until we have published biographies available, we must rely on the doctoral theses by John Thomas Anderson, "Senator Burton K. Wheeler and United States Foreign Relations" (University of Virginia, Charlottesville, 1982); Richard Kay Hanks, "Hamilton Fish and American Isolationism, 1920–1944" (University of California at Riverside, 1971); and Anthony C. Troscone, "Hamilton Fish, Sr., and the Politics of American Nationalism, 1912–1945" (Rutgers University, New Brunswick, NJ, 1993).

122   Robert E. Burke, ed., *The Diary Letters of Hiram Johnson*, 7 vols. (New York, 1983); Richard Coke Lower, *A Bloc of One: The Politics and Career of Hiram W. Johnson* (Stanford,

Of course the congressional debate over U.S. intervention spilled over into the public at large, a topic that continues to attract historians. As this subtopic is worth an article in itself, only a few of the more prominent themes and personalities can be covered here. The various action groups – such as the William Allen White Committee, Fight for Freedom, and the America First Committee – have long since been investigated.[123]

Other aspects of the intervention debate, however, have been subject to fresh scrutiny. John M. Muresianu, in covering the arguments among the nation's opinion elite, sees "potent moral reasons for contemporary intellectuals to oppose American intervention in the European crisis."[124] James C. Schneider offers a thoughtful focus on the debate in one major city, Chicago. Schneider finds that most interventionists in the Windy City could not bring themselves to accept the need for outright war. But rather than face the issue directly, Schneider claims, they concentrated on discrediting their opponents, thereby precluding any consensus at a time when the United States most needed to be united. Schneider's work could serve as a model for similar research elsewhere.[125] Far more is needed on grassroots sentiment throughout the nation. John W. Roberts has examined the foreign policy attitudes of American labor, in the process covering the role of isolationist John L. Lewis and the more interventionist Sidney Hillman, but the role of business needs more attention.[126]

1993). See also Peter Gerard Boyle, "The Study of an Isolationist: Hiram Johnson" (Ph.D. diss., University of California, Los Angeles, 1970), and Howard Arthur DeWitt, "Hiram W. Johnson and American Foreign Policy, 1917–1941" (Ph.D. diss., University of Arizona, Tucson, 1972).

123 For classic accounts of the major action committees see Walter Johnson, *The Battle against Isolation* (Chicago, 1944); Mark Lincoln Chadwin, *The Hawks of World War II* (Chapel Hill, NC, 1968); and Wayne S. Cole, *America First: The Battle against Intervention, 1940–41* (Madison, WI, 1953).

124 John M. Muresianu, *War of Ideas: American Intellectuals and the World Crisis, 1938–1945* (New York, 1988), 160.

125 James C. Schneider, *Should America Go to War? The Debate over Foreign Policy in Chicago, 1939–1941* (Chapel Hill, NC, 1989).

126 John W. Roberts, *Putting Foreign Policy to Work: The Role of Organized Labor in American Foreign Relations, 1932–1941* (New York, 1995). For a study of business leaders who cooperated with the president, see Richard Earl Holl, "The Corporate Liberals and the Roosevelt Administration's Preparedness Program, 1939–1941" (Ph.D. diss., University of Kentucky, Lexington, 1996).

Work has also begun on women as a distinct category. Margaret Ann Paton examines those women who found U.S. entry into war preferable to German victory.[127] Anne Marie Pois, Carrie A. Foster, and Margaret Hope Bacon all have reexamined the United States Section of the Women's International League for Peace and Freedom, in the process showing dissent over anti-interventionism within the league's ranks.[128] Glen Jeansonne, Laura McEnaney, and Kari Frederickson focus on women of the extreme right, Frederickson arguing that the rightists might have been more influential than the liberal women's groups.[129] To what degree was there a "sisterhood" among such mainstream anti-interventionists as Ruth Sarles, director of research for the America First Committee, or pacifist lobbyist Dorothy Detzer? Students also are now researched as a group, but focus here is usually limited to leftist and pacifist groups.[130]

Some recent biographies of those individuals who backed the interventionist position are extremely perceptive. Ronald Steel's study of Walter Lippmann notes that the columnist was far more hawkish in Europe than in Asia, something also revealed in his more recently published correspondence.[131] Biographies of Reinhold Niebuhr, Henry R. Luce, Dorothy Thompson, Ralph Ingersoll, Lewis W. Douglas, Freda Kirchwey, and Lewis Mumford

127   Margaret Ann Paton, "'Brave Women and Fair Men': Women Advocates of U.S. Intervention in World War II" (Ph.D. diss., University of Washington, Seattle, 1966).
128   Anne Marie Pois, "The Political Process of Organizing for Peace: The United States Section of the Women's International League for Peace and Freedom" (Ph.D. diss., University of Colorado, Boulder, 1988); Carrie A. Foster, *The Women and the Warriors: The U.S. Section of the Women's International League for Peace and Freedom, 1915–1946* (Syracuse, NY, 1995); Margaret Hope Bacon, *One Woman's Passion for Peace and Freedom: The Life of Mildred Scott Olmsted* (Syracuse, NY, 1993).
129   Glen Jeansonne, "Furies: Women Isolationists in the Era of FDR," *Journal of History and Politics* (1990): 67–96; idem, *Women of the Far Right: The Mothers' Movement and World War II* (Chicago, 1996); Laura McEnaney, "He-Men and Christian Mothers: The America First Movement and the Gendered Meanings of Patriotism and Isolationism," *Diplomatic History* 18 (Winter 1994): 47–57; Kari Frederickson, "Catherine Curtis and Conservative Isolationist Women, 1939–1941," *Historian* 58 (Summer 1996): 825–39.
130   Eileen Eagan, *Class, Culture, and the Classroom: The Student Peace Movement of the 1930s* (Philadelphia, 1981); Robert Cohen, *When the Old Left Was Young: Student Radicals and America's First Mass Student Movement, 1929–1941* (New York, 1993).
131   Ronald Steel, *Walter Lippmann and the American Century* (Boston, 1980); John Morton Blum, ed., *Public Philosopher: Selected Letters of Walter Lippmann* (New York, 1985).

all show how intensely personal the battle became.[132] Most writing on Wendell Willkie is still too sporadic and journalistic.[133]

Scholars are also examining FDR's opponents. Justus D. Doenecke, Charles F. Howlett, and Glen Zeitzer have contributed extensive bibliographies of anti-interventionism, including pacifism.[134] Thirty-five years of research on FDR's critics is embodied in Wayne S. Cole's *Roosevelt & the Isolationists, 1932–45* (1983), a work that has drawn upon many congressional manuscripts, over ten thousand FBI documents, and materials in the British Public Record Office. Concentrating (though not exclusively) on Senate leaders, Cole notes that these figures usually backed New Deal measures while the president – to Cole always a genuine internationalist – acquiesced in the neutrality legislation they proposed. Once war broke out, however, relations became so strained that Roosevelt met legitimate political opposition with wiretaps and federal probes."[135] A study is now needed on those isolationists who were conservative from the outset, especially those who came from the worlds of business and journalism. Justus D. Doenecke has made a start in this direction, combining a variety of anti-interventionist perceptions with contemporary sources.[136]

---

132   Richard Wightman Fox, *Reinhold Niebuhr: A Biography* (New York, 1985); Justus D. Doenecke, "Reinhold Niebuhr and His Critics: The Interventionist Controversy in World War II," *Anglican and Episcopal History* 64 (December 1995): 459–81; Robert E. Herzstein, *Henry R. Luce: A Political Portrait of the Man Who Created the American Century* (New York, 1994); Peter Kurth, *American Cassandra: The Life of Dorothy Thompson* (Boston, 1990); Roy Hoopes, *Ralph Ingersoll: A Biography* (New York, 1985); Robert Paul Browder and Thomas G. Smith, *Independent: A Biography of Lewis W. Douglas* (New York, 1986); Sara Alpern, *Freda Kirchwey: A Woman of the Nation* (Cambridge, MA, 1987); Donald L. Miller, *Lewis Mumford: A Life* (New York, 1989).

133   See, for example, Steve Neal, *Dark Horse: A Biography of Wendell Willkie* (Garden City, 1984). More scholarly treatments are found in James H. Madison, ed., *Wendell Willkie: Hoosier Internationalist* (Bloomington, IN, 1992); and David Alan Bathe, "Wendell L. Willkie: A Political Odyssey from Realism to Idealism" (Ph.D. diss., Illinois State University, Normal, 1991).

134   Justus D. Doenecke, *Anti-Intervention: A Bibliographical Introduction to Isolationism and Pacifism from World War I to the Early Cold War* (New York, 1987); Charles F. Howlett and Glen Zeitzer, *The American Peace Movement: History and Historiography* (Washington, 1985); Howlett, *The American Peace Movement: References and Resources* (Boston, 1991).

135   Wayne S. Cole, *Roosevelt & the Isolationists, 1932–45* (Lincoln, NE, 1983). For some speculation on Cole's part see his "What Might Have Been," *Chronicles: A Magazine of American Culture* 15 (December 1991): 20–22.

136   Justus D. Doenecke, *The Battle Against Intervention, 1939–1941* (Malabar, FL, 1997).

Several studies deal solely with Senate anti-interventionists. Thomas N. Guinsburg stresses their lack of cohesion and warns against exaggerating anti-interventionist sentiment in either Congress or the public."[137] An analysis of Senate progressives by Ronald L. Feinman shows why some remained firm opponents of FDR's foreign policy, some not.[138] Some general themes of anti-interventionism are currently being researched. In preliminary work on a broader study, one centering on changing attitudes of FDR's foes as the initial stages of the war progressed, Justus D. Doenecke has stressed the desire for a negotiated peace and continual hostility toward the Soviet Union. In his edition of the unpublished position papers and internal memorandums of the America First Committee, he offers fresh material on the economic and strategic rationale for avoiding even the risk of war.[139]

Certain individual foes of intervention have been subject to renewed study. Ellen Nore's life of Charles A. Beard offers the most thorough treatment of the prominent historian and one that is surprisingly sympathetic to his revisionism.[140] Ronald W. Pruessen presents by far the best treatment of the early views of a somewhat equivocal anti-interventionist, Wall Street lawyer John Foster Dulles.[141] Dorothy Herrmann's biography of Anne Morrow Lindbergh, while accurate on her earlier life, fails to do justice to the sensitive poet, a woman revealed in her diaries as being deeply torn between her abhorrence of bloodshed and her sympathy for

---

137 Thomas N. Guinsburg, *The Pursuit of Isolationism in the United States Senate from Versailles to Pearl Harbor* (New York, 1982).
138 Ronald L. Feinman, *Twilight of Progressivism: The Western Republican Senators and the New Deal* (Baltimore, MD, 1981).
139 Justus D. Doenecke, "Germany in Isolationist Ideology, 1939–1941: The Issue of a Negotiated Peace," in *Germany and America: Essays on Problems of International Relations and Immigration*, ed. Hans L. Trefousse (New York, 1981), 215–26; idem, "Rehearsal for Cold War: United States Anti-Interventionists and the Soviet Union, 1939–1941," *International Journal of Politics, Culture and Society* (Spring 1994): 375–92; idem, ed., *In Danger Undaunted: The Anti-Interventionist Movement of 1940–1941 as Revealed in the Papers of the America First Committee* (Stanford, 1990).
140 Ellen Nore, *Charles A. Beard: An Intellectual Biography* (Carbondale, IL, 1983); Ronald W. Pruessen, *John Foster Dulles: The Road to Power* (New York, 1982); Dorothy Herrmann, *Anne Morrow Lindbergh; A Gift for Life* (New York, 1993); Anne Morrow Lindbergh, *War Within and Without: Diaries and Letters, 1939–1944* (New York, 1980).
141 Pruessen, *John Foster Dulles.*

occupied peoples.[142] Walter L. Hixson roots Charles A. Lindbergh's stance in his belief that intervention would erode democratic idealism both at home and abroad.[143] Justus D. Doenecke roots the anti-interventionism of business leader Robert E. Wood in fear of economic dislocation, "fascist" theorist Lawrence Dennis in balance-of-power "realities," and legal scholars John Bassett Moore and Edwin M. Borchard in an absolutist belief in international law.[144]

Researchers continually find new dimensions in America's most prominent anti-interventionist, Herbert Hoover. In Gary Dean Best's *Herbert Hoover: The Post-Presidential Years, 1933–1964* (1983), the author shows that Hoover was more moderate than many anti-interventionists. The former chief executive sought "defensive" munitions to the Allies, a loan for invaded Finland, and – in lieu of lend-lease – a congressional loan of several billion dollars to Britain.[145] Richard Norton Smith, although often sympathetic to Hoover, finds that "his moral antennae seemed strangely insensitive to evil abroad." Comparing Hoover to Neville Chamberlain, Smith presents Hoover as "a decent man undone by his own equanimity."[146] Justus D. Doenecke calls for interpreting Hoover in light of the former president's continual fear that war only bred radical revolution.[147]

Fortunately we now have studies, long overdue, on Hoover's plan to feed occupied Europe. James H. George, Jr., challenges

142   Herrmann, *Anne Morrow Lindbergh*; Lindbergh, *War Within and Without*.
143   Walter L. Hixson, *Charles A. Lindbergh: Lone Eagle* (New York, 1996).
144   Justus D. Doenecke, "The Isolationism of Robert E. Wood," in *Three Fates of American Isolationism*, ed. John N. Schacht (Iowa City, 1981), 11–22; idem, "The Isolationist as Collectivist: Lawrence Dennis and the Coming of World War II," *Journal of Libertarian Studies* 3 (Summer 1979): 191–207; idem, "Edwin M. Borchard, John Bassett Moore, and Opposition to American Intervention in World War II," ibid. 6 (Winter 1982): 1–34.
145   Gary Dean Best, *Herbert Hoover: The Post-Presidential Years, 1933–1964*, 2 vols. (Stanford, 1983). Since 1980, works on Hoover include Mark O. Hatfield, ed., *Herbert Hoover Reassessed: Essays Commemorating the Fiftieth Anniversary of the Inauguration of Our Thirty-First President* (Washington, 1981); and John Lukacs, "Herbert Hoover Meets Adolf Hitler," *American Scholar* 62 (Spring 1993): 235–38.
146   Richard Norton Smith, *An Uncommon Man: The Triumph* (New York, 1984), 272. See also idem, "On the Outside Looking In: Herbert Hoover and World War II," *Prologue* 26 (Fall 1994): 141–51.
147   Justus D. Doenecke, "The Anti-Interventionism of Herbert Hoover," *Journal of Libertarian Studies* 8 (Summer 1987): 311–40.

the former president's own claim that FDR rejected his plans for personal and partisan reasons. Hal Elliott Wert sees Hoover fighting German duplicity, British hostility, and the growing apathy of the American people.[148]

Both Geoffrey S. Smith and Leo P. Ribuffo reveal that the Roosevelt administration deliberately linked mainstream anti-interventionists to the lunatic fringe. Indeed, Ribuffo sees a "Brown Scare" at work, one quite similar to the "Red Scare" of the McCarthy era.[149] A number of historians note Roosevelt's efforts to silence his opponents, tactics that include the political use of the Federal Bureau of Investigation.[150] Richard W. Steele also examines administration propaganda efforts, so persuasive and diverse, he argues, that they numbed the public's resistance to war.[151] Francis MacDonnell puts "the Fifth Column panic" into the context of what Richard Hofstadter once called "the paranoid style of American politics."[152] In a portrait of FDR that does not lack appreciation, Wayne S. Cole sees the interventionists stifling honest dissent.[153]

148   James H. George, Jr., "Another Chance: Herbert Hoover and World War II Relief," *Diplomatic History* 16 (Summer 1992): 389–407; Hal Elliott Wert, "The Specter of Starvation: Hoover, Roosevelt, and Aid to Europe" (Ph.D. diss; University of Kansas, Lawrence, 1991). For more on general relief see Wert, "U.S. Aid to Poles under Nazi Domination, 1939–1940," *Historian* 57 (Spring 1995): 511–24.

149   Geoffrey S. Smith, *To Save a Nation: American Countersubversives, the New Deal, and the Coming of World War II*, updated ed. (Chicago, 1992); idem, "Isolationism, the Devil, and the Advent of the Second World War: Variations on a Theme," *International History Review* 4 (February 1982) 55–89; Leo P. Ribuffo, *The Old Christian Right: The Protestant Far Right from the Great Depression to the Cold War* (Philadelphia, 1983).

150   See, for example, Kenneth O'Reilly, "A New Deal for the FBI: The Roosevelt Administration, Crime Control, and National Security," *Journal of American History* 69 (December 1982): 638–58; Charles E. Croog, "FBI Political Surveillance and the Isolationist-Interventionist Debate, 1931–1941," *Historian* 54 (Spring 1992): 441–58; Douglas M. Charles and John P. Rossi, "FBI Political Surveillance and the Charles Lindbergh Investigation, 1939–1944," ibid. 59 (Summer 1997): 831–47.

151   Richard W. Steele, "Franklin D. Roosevelt and His Foreign Policy Critics," *Political Science Quarterly* 94 (Spring 1979): 5–35 (including rejoinder by Arthur M. Schlesinger, Jr.); idem, "The Great Debate: Roosevelt, the Media, and the Coming of War, 1940–1941," *Journal of American History* 71 (June 1984): 69–92; idem, *Propaganda in an Open Society: The Roosevelt Administration and the Media, 1933–1941* (Westport, CT, 1985).

152   Francis MacDonnell, *Insidious Foes: The Axis Fifth Column and the American Home Front, 1938–1942* (New York, 1995); Richard Hofstadter, *The Paranoid Style in American Politics* (New York, 1965).

153   Wayne S. Cole, *Determinism and American Foreign Relations during the Franklin D. Roosevelt Era* (Lanham, MD, 1995).

In conclusion, we find that the "revisionist-court historian" debate has long since died, that the argument over "FDR-as-appeaser" is quite muted, but that the dispute over William Appleman Williams's "open door" interpretation is still much alive. New controversy has arisen in a number of matters, and it is hardly surprising that Roosevelt remains at the center.

After half a century of research, it must be noted that there is still no scholarly consensus as to whether the president sought full-scale intervention in the European war. Undoubtedly the use of still-untapped sources would increase our understanding of this matter. The Bullitt Papers, recently opened Soviet archives, and FDR's conversations with such foreign diplomats as Canadian prime minister Mackenzie King and Australian Ambassador Richard Casey might all be most revealing.

Had Roosevelt desired, could he have led the United States into war (which might not have involved a commitment of ground troops) as early as the spring of 1941, doing so by manifesting the candor that Stimson, Knox, and the Fight for Freedom Committee desired? Would the bureaucracies – military and diplomatic – have cooperated? Would Congress or the public have followed him? Did he have the option of converting some of the more moderate anti-interventionists to his side – say a Robert E. Wood or a Robert A. Taft? Did FDR exaggerate anti-interventionist strength and underestimate his own leadership powers? Or did he use both correctly? Would greater boldness and candor have left him at the head of a more united America or a more divided one?

In examining other American policymakers, one can be pleased by the progress made but appalled by the gaps remaining. Few doctoral theses are devoted to this period, and perhaps three-fourths of the writing in diplomatic history deals with events after 1945. Often the historians most productive on this era have personal memories either of the war or its immediate wake.

Much connected to presidential decision making is the matter of corporatism. In examining the period 1939–41, did various economic and political elites seek to restructure the world system along lines similar to the corporative order then emerging in the

United States? In short, the corporatist school forces us to ask anew: What was the driving impetus behind American policy – strategic concerns centering on military security, ideological concerns focusing on democracy, or economic concerns revolving around the structural dynamics of American capitalism and the world economy?

In this context, the 1939–41 debates appear more relevant than ever. In 1986, John Lewis Gaddis, in emphasizing the limits of the corporatist model, found it inadequate to explain the debate over U.S. entry into the European war. Michael J. Hogan concedes that the corporatist school has not examined certain debates closely, including obviously the one over U.S. intervention in World War II. Yet Hogan infers that the corporatist model can well apply to such divisive times, particularly given his assertion that the New Deal coalition expanded upon the corporatist design envisioned by Republican leaders in the 1920s.[154]

In his work on the early Cold War, Melvyn P. Leffler sees the basis of U.S. Cold War thinking as lying in the early 1940s: Potential adversaries must never again be allowed to gain control of the resources of Eurasia through autarchical economic practices, political subversion, and/or military aggression. The acquisition of such resources allowed potential foes to augment their military capabilities, encouraged them to penetrate the Western Hemisphere, tempted them to attack the United States, and enabled them to wage a protracted struggle."[155]

True, Thomas J. McCormick has made initial efforts at outlining a general corporatist schema, and the data uncovered by Patrick Hearden supports a corporatist interpretation for the decade before Pearl Harbor. Were the leading policymakers of 1939–41 simply carrying through on a long-articulated corporatist vision? Some historian should make a conscious effort to apply the corporatist analysis to the entire interventionist coalition, a group

---

154 John Lewis Gaddis, "The Corporatist Synthesis: A Skeptical View," *Diplomatic History* 10 (Fall 1986): 357–62; Michael J. Hogan, "Corporatism: A Positive Appraisal," ibid., 363–72; idem, "Corporatism," in *Explaining the History of American Foreign Relations*, ed. Michael J. Hogan and Thomas G. Paterson (New York, 1991), 226–36.
155 Melvyn P. Leffler, *A Preponderance of Power: National Security, the Truman Administration, and the Cold War* (Stanford, 1992), 23

that included conservative internationalists like Lippmann, old-time Wilsonians like Hull, New Deal loyalists like Pepper, and liberal ideologues like Niebuhr.

Similarly, did not the anti-interventionists have a corporatist vision of their own, one centering on closed markets and national autarchy? This group of economic nationalists drew upon the thought of administrators from the first New Deal (for example, George Peek), old-time progressives (for example, William F. Borah), McKinley Republicans (for example, Arthur Vandenberg), middle western corporation executives (for example, Robert E. Wood), labor leaders (for example, John L. Lewis), and democratic socialists (for example, Norman Thomas). And, after all, has not anti-interventionist Herbert Hoover gone down as the archetypical corporatist of the 1920s? All shared a consensus that intervention would destroy, not preserve, the American economy. Even if the Germans sought to dominate the markets of the world, the United States remained in the more advantageous position.[156]

Needed now is some synthesis of what far too often remains piecemeal analysis. Only Heinrichs's *Threshold of War* approaches the kind of integrated view we see in such works as Michael J. Hogan's on the Marshall Plan and Bruce Cumings's on the Korean War, much less the work of Arno J. Mayer or Christopher Thorne.[157] Hence this article ends with the plea that historians take full advantage of the public attention given to the fiftieth anniversary of World War II. War anniversaries will shortly be at an end, and even younger participants in the struggle will soon no longer be with us. True, we should realize that there is only so much to be said about FDR's correspondence, State Department

156 See, for example, America First Committee Research Division, Bulletin #6, "Buy or Die," 5 July 1941, in Doenecke, ed., *In Danger Undaunted*, 159–63; and Lawrence Dennis, "The Economic Consequences of American Intervention," n.d. [1941], ibid., 200–205.
157 Michael J. Hogan, *The Marshall Plan: America, Britain, and the Reconstruction of Western Europe, 1947–1952* (New York, 1987); Bruce Cumings, *The Origins of the Korean War*, 2 vols. (Princeton, NJ, 1981, 1990); Arno J. Mayer, *Politics and Diplomacy of Peacemaking: Containment and Counterrevolution at Versailles, 1918–1919* (New York, 1967); and Christopher Thorne, *Allies of a Kind: The United States, Britain, and the War against Japan, 1941–1945* (New York, 1978).

memorandums, British documents, and congressional debates. But we can still do much to probe the motives and policies of the historical actors, especially given the amount of scholarly disagreement shown in this essay. At stake is nothing less than an understanding of the behavior of the world's greatest power in two of the most momentous years of this century.

9

The Origins of the Second World War in Asia and the Pacific: Synthesis Impossible?

MICHAEL A. BARNHART

Scholars studying the origins of the Second World War in Asia are almost universally agreed on two points. A new synthesis is required to cover new work, especially new work for players besides the United States and Japan. For this very reason, a more satisfactory name for the conflict would be in order, since "Pacific War" seems inadequate. Unfortunately, this agreement exists despite international efforts at scholarly cooperation and exchange spanning decades and unparallelled in comparison to any other topic in the history of American foreign relations.

In fact, the first generation of scholarship on the war's origins was itself characterized by team studies. William Langer and Everett Gleason's classic two-volume work has stood the test of time.[1] On the Japanese side, a team of scholars collaborated to produce a five-volume *History of the Pacific War*, a deliberate attempt at a broad synthesis of the origins and course of the war in terms of the social, economic, and political conditions that resulted from Japan's incomplete adjustment to the challenges of Western capitalism.[2] Both of these broad syntheses, perhaps because they were syntheses, focused on the global environment of the path to Pearl Harbor. Both portrayed a United States and a Japan that considered each other distinctly secondary to more

---

1 William L. Langer and S. Everett Gleason, *The Challenge to Isolation, 1937–1940* (New York, 1952), and *The Undeclared War, 1940–1941* (New York, 1953).
2 Rekishigaku kenkyukai, ed., *Taiheiyo sensoshi*, 5 vols. (Tokyo, 1953–54).

pressing concerns, America's in Europe and Japan's in Asia. In addition, because both were written at a time when it was hardly clear that Japan would emerge from deep economic difficulties, or that a Japanese-American partnership would amount to much in the coming decades, attention to the Pacific conflict, while certainly present, was indirect.

Unhappily, the first burst of direct attention to that conflict was concerned with anything but wider issues. The controversy over the American disaster at Pearl Harbor generated a publishing industry unto itself, one with a remarkably long lifespan. These books fall into two groups, those blaming Roosevelt for engineering a "back door" to war at a frightful cost of American lives in Hawaii, and those blaming anyone but Roosevelt for incompetence, pettiness, and plain stupidity.[3] The latter may be passed over with scant loss. They apportion blame differently but, read as a whole, argue sufficiently well that there was plenty of blame to apportion. None is greatly interested in placing American unpreparedness at Pearl Harbor, much less Japan's decision to attack Hawaii, within the context of the origins of the Pacific war.[4] Rather more surprisingly, none bothers to illustrate the relevance of the "Pearl Harbor syndrome" that dominated a great deal of American strategic thought throughout the postwar era.

The "back door" books are another matter, for they take as their central premise the secondary nature of the Pacific war, at least on the American side. Several of these are thinly veiled attacks against Roosevelt's supposed tendency to tyranny.[5] But

---

3   One exception, which blames Winston Churchill instead, is James Rusbridger and Eric Nave, *Betrayal at Pearl Harbor: How Churchill Lured Roosevelt into World War II* (New York, 1991). The latest and most extreme (to date) rendition of this sort is Thomas E. Mahl and Roy Godson, *Desperate Deception: British Covert Operations in the United States, 1939–1944* (London, 1998). More useful than any of these "Pearl Harbor studies" is a collection of essays, written primarily for undergraduates, Hilary Conroy and Harry Wray, eds., *Pearl Harbor Reexamined: Prologue to the Pacific War* (Honolulu, 1990).

4   An interesting departure, however, that explores Japanese plans for Hawaii, can be found in John J. Stephan, *Hawaii under the Rising Sun: Japan's Plans for Conquest After Pearl Harbor* (Honolulu, 1984).

5   For example, Charles A. Beard, *President Roosevelt and the Coming of the War, 1941: A Study in Appearance and Realities* (New Haven, CT, 1948) and Harry E. Barnes, *Perpetual War for Perpetual Peace: A Critical Examination of the Foreign Policy of Franklin Delano Roosevelt and Its Aftermath* (Caldwell, ID, 1953).

Paul Schroeder's *The Axis Alliance* stood the "back door" thesis on its head, provoking an extended debate on the true reasons for America's refusal to come to terms, at least temporarily, with Japan over Asian and Pacific issues.[6] Schroeder argued that the United States' chief interests were indeed in Europe, and that Roosevelt and Cordell Hull, his secretary of state, were rightly concerned with the Tripartite Alliance that Japan had signed with Germany and Italy in September 1940. But this concern ought to have been short lived. It should have been clear, Schroeder argues, that by the summer of 1941 Japan was prepared to abandon whatever obligations it might have had under that alliance to intervene in the European war if the United States engaged German forces. Further, by that time Japan was ready to foreswear any further advance into British or Dutch possessions in the Southwest Pacific, another matter of European concern to Washington. Roosevelt and Hull easily could have had peace with Japan, but they foolishly elected to discard their chance by insisting upon a Japanese evacuation of China, a primary concern to Tokyo that its leaders could not possibly agree to. Why did their American counterparts insist upon the impossible and make war unavoidable? Schroeder's answer is an American obsession with morality and principle that could not see China abandoned, even if abandonment was in America's true interests. Bitterly, he concluded that America saved China from Japan, only to preserve it for the more despicable forces of international communism nearly a decade later.

Whatever else one might think of Schroeder's essay, it had the virtues of placing the central issues of the origins of the war in the Pacific and Asia on the table. Washington's primary interest clearly was in Europe. Roosevelt and Hull surely were correct to become alarmed when the Axis alliance and Japan's moves to the south endangered America's de facto allies in Europe. But Schroeder maintained that the United States was sufficiently tied to China, albeit with ropes of morality and delusion, to justify a

6 Paul W. Schroeder, *The Axis Alliance and Japanese-American Relations, 1941* (Ithaca, NY, 1958).

war with Japan under this independent compulsion. The next task appeared obvious enough: to gauge the strength of America's commitments to China before the final months of 1941.

Studies of this subject had their own intellectual baggage to labor under. If an examination of American-Japanese relations before the Pacific War strained to see through the smoke of Pearl Harbor, studies of Sino-American ties were seldom allowed to forget the collapse of Republican China and the bloodletting in Korea that followed, events that deflected attention from the seemingly less vital years of the mid-1920s to the start of the Pacific War. This relative inattention was remedied by the appearance of two lengthy studies by Dorothy Borg[7] and the first of many influential works by Akira Iriye.[8] Borg found an American government quite cautious in its commitments to China, even within the context of the new Pacific and Asian system forged at the Washington Conference of 1921–22, a position reinforced by Iriye's rich study in American, Chinese, Japanese, and other sources. The principles of international conduct embodied in that system were important to Washington, but for global reasons, not anything specific to China. Borg's study of the 1930s, as respect for those principles waned, portrayed a United States even less willing to extend even slight commitments to China at Japan's expense. Although Borg was reluctant to extend her analysis past 1938, it seems clear from her work that if America was willing to go to war with Japan in 1941, China could not have been the sole, or even primary, cause.

In Japan, however, scholarly work in the early 1960s demonstrated just how important China had become – to Japan – as a sufficient cause to justify war with America. Unsurprisingly, the keystone of this work came in a multivolume series, *The Road to the Pacific War*, authored by leading Japanese scholars.[9] Despite

---

7   Dorothy Borg, *American Policy and the Chinese Revolution, 1925–1928* (New York, 1947), and *The United States and the Far Eastern Crisis of 1933–1938: From the Manchurian Incident Through the Initial Stage of the Undeclared Sino-Japanese War* (Cambridge, MA, 1964).

8   Akira Iriye, *After Imperialism: The Search for a New Order in the Far East, 1921–1931* (Cambridge, 1965).

9   Nihon kokusai seiji gakkai, ed., *Taiheiyo senso e no michi*, 7 vols. (Tokyo, 1962–63). The

the series's title, its volumes, especially the earlier ones, focused upon continental questions. Japan's treaty rights in Manchuria, the legacy of the victory over Russia in 1905, had become of critical importance not to Japan at large, but to an Imperial Japanese Army that had emerged, certainly by 1931, as the key player in Japan's continental policy. Within that army, the garrison force along the South Manchurian Railway, by 1919 known as the Kwantung Army, had become powerful enough to enforce its militant version of maintaining those treaty rights.[10] The rise of the Chinese Nationalists posed the most immediate threat to those rights. But as the authors of *Taiheiyo senso e no michi* made clear, the Imperial Army viewed them as essential not in preventing the eventual reunification of Chinese territory, but in containing the growing power of the Soviet Union. China was to be enlisted into the anti-Communist cause if possible – a theme of Japanese diplomacy throughout the interwar period – but suborned into it otherwise. Some recruiters were to be Japanese business leaders, either in the semipublic South Manchurian Railway Company or in other enterprises in China, and Chinese who had been educated in Japan.[11]

But the spearhead was always the army. The authors of *Taiheiyo senso e no michi* presented the first glimpses of the debates within the army that pitted those desiring a consolidation of Japan's dominance of all north China before confronting the Soviet Union against others who felt that the time for confrontation had arrived in the mid-1930s.

English translations, all edited by James W. Morley, are *Japan Erupts: The London Naval Conference and the Manchurian Incident, 1928–1932* (New York, 1984), *The China Quagmire: Japan's Expansion on the Asian Continent, 1933–1941* (New York, 1983), *Deterrent Diplomacy: Japan, Germany, and the U.S.S.R., 1935–1941* (New York, 1976), *The Fateful Choice: Japan's Advance into Southeast Asia, 1939–1941* (New York, 1980), and *The Final Confrontation: Japan's Negotiations with the United States, 1941* (New York, 1994).

10   See Leonard A. Humphreys, *The Way of the Heavenly Sword: The Japanese Army in the 1920's* (Stanford, 1995). Although it discusses army politics in general excellently, this book is especially valuable for the Kwantung Army's role in Manchuria during these years.

11   William Miles Fletcher III, *The Japanese Business Community and National Trade Policy, 1920–1942* (Chapel Hill, NC, 1989). There is still no good study of Chinese educated in Japan who later collaborated with the Japanese in Manchuria and north China in the early 1930s, though for a later period see John H. Boyle, *China and Japan at War 1937–1945: The Politics of Collaboration* (Stanford, 1972).

The findings of *Taiheiyo senso e no michi*, and of another American-trained Japanese scholar, Sadao Asada, also discovered militants inside the Imperial Navy. In many respects, this was a more interesting finding, at least in terms of the origins of the Pacific War, because the Navy had good reason to find the United States the source of its torments and justification for its budgets for nearly two decades. Indeed, one of the central contributions of Asada's early work and a core idea of his later writings has been the existence of a bitterly anti-American "Fleet Faction" in the Navy long before the explosive debates over the ratification of the London Naval Treaty in 1930.[12] A decade later, that faction had come to dominate the Navy so completely that that service, far from acting as a brake upon Japan's eventual collision with the United States, actually served as an accelerator, especially during the crucial high-level discussions of the summer of 1941.[13]

The recognition that there were extreme militants inside the Japanese military was hardly a discovery of the early 1960s, of course. The multiple assassinations of the early 1930s were quite public at the time, and well covered by early histories of Japan's road to war.[14] But the Naval side was new. So also was an argument, raised most directly by James Crowley, that the assassins did not represent the entirety of army opinion, or even very much of it.[15] Crowley agreed that the Army favored an aggressive foreign policy, but its senior army officers were more interested in alliance with civilian elites to ensure that policy's success. Moreover, that policy was entirely reasonable given Japan's difficult position as it entered the 1930s; it was hardly the byproduct of an atavistic and irrational deathwish on the part of young

12 Sadao Asada, "Japan and the United States, 1915–1925" (Ph.D. diss., Yale University, New Haven, CT, 1962). Asada's latest is *Ryo taisenkan no Nichi-Bei kankei: Kaigun to seisaku kettei katei* [Japanese-American relations between the wars: Naval policy and the decision-making process] (Tokyo, 1993). It is possible that this work will appear in English.
13 An interesting discussion of Naval politics somewhat earlier, along the lines of Asada's interpretation, is Gerhard Krebs, "Admiral Yonai Mitsumasa as Navy Minister (1937–1939): Dove or Hawk?" in *Western Interactions with Japan: Expansion, the Armed Forces & Readjustment, 1859–1956*, ed. Peter Lowe and Herman Moeshart (Sandgate, 1990).
14 Richard Storry, *The Double Patriots: A Study of Japanese Nationalism* (London, 1957).
15 James B. Crowley, *Japan's Quest for Autonomy: National Security and Foreign Policy, 1930–1938* (Princeton, NJ, 1966).

fanatics who had managed to intimidate their seniors, civilian and military alike.

Such findings set the stage for the next multivolume synthesis of *Pearl Harbor as History*.[16] The product of a 1969 conference at Lake Kawaguchi, this collection provided sets of mirrored studies: of the role of the Imperial Japanese Navy and United States Navy, of the Foreign Ministry and State Department, and so on, all focused on the decade prior to the Japanese attack on Pearl Harbor. The chapters on Japan extended the arguments of *Taiheiyo senso e no michi*, not surprising since some of the authors had participated in that earlier project, but also broke new ground. Asada's study of the Imperial Navy contributed to the overall assessment of most Japanese authors that their government had chosen courses that made war with America difficult to avoid by 1941. Katsuro Yamamura's study of the Finance Ministry, Hideichiro Nakamura's of the Japan Economic Federation (*Nihon Keizai Renmeikai*), and a joint chapter by Shigeo Misawa and Saburo Ninomiya on the Diet and political parties showed how weak the opposition was (when it existed) to the aggressive programs of the Army and its civilian allies. Akira Fujiwara pointed out that the Army barely considered the United States in its calculations before 1939, and not very much thereafter.[17]

The American chapters often represented new ways of thinking about Washington's role in the origins of the Pacific War. Russell Weigley and Waldo Heinrichs made clear how little influence the American Army and Navy had over foreign policymaking prior to Pearl Harbor. James Thomson's excellent study of internal divisions within the Department of State concluded that its most senior adviser, Stanley Hornbeck, misunderstood many fundamental features and workings of the Japanese government. A common theme, in fact, of nearly all the American essays was ignorance, and the American authors tended to blame Washington for

16   Dorothy Borg and Shumpei Okamoto, eds., with the assistance of Dale K. A. Finlayson, *Pearl Harbor as History: Japanese-American Relations, 1931–1941* (New York, 1973). The Japanese-language version, which includes additional materials, is a four-volume work.
17   This point is reinforced in my contribution to Ernest R. May, ed., *Knowing One's Enemies: Intelligence Assessment Before the Two World Wars* (Princeton, NJ, 1984); and Mark R. Peattie, *Ishiwara Kanji and Japan's Confrontation with the West* (Princeton, NJ, 1975).

permitting a drift toward war until collision became unavoidable.

Despite its outstanding scholarship, original contributions, and binational representation and archival research, *Pearl Harbor as History* drew criticism, especially in Japan.[18] Ironically, the chief point of attack was that the studies were much too binational, making the war in Asia and the Pacific appear entirely too narrow. What of Great Britain, the Soviet Union, or Germany, much less China? How could historians assess the influence of Japan's drive to the south without examining British, French, and even Dutch archives? How could it be possible to determine the role of the Axis alliance without an inspection of German and Italian records? And how could a reasoned examination of the role of China be completed without Chinese studies? A truly comprehensive synthesis appeared more distant than ever to these critics.

Yet much of the scholarship in the decade that followed ignored these calls for unity and built on *Pearl Harbor as History*, usually in studies on Japan or the United States. This turned out to be no bad thing, for a comprehensive synthesis appeared to be emerging, unforced, from these specialized works. James Herzog reinforced Thomson's view that senior policymakers were rarely in thrall to their East Asian specialists, and that those specialists did not always hold sophisticated views of Japan, though Herzog's institution was the Navy, not the State Department.[19] A delightfully innovative book by Irvine Anderson examined the role of multinational oil companies, primarily Standard-Vacuum, in American-Japanese relations. It is regrettable that no one has pursued his focus in other industries, and doubly so that new scholarship appearing in the mid-1990s does not extend itself very often to Asian concerns.[20]

18 See, for example, Takeshi Matsuda, "The Coming of the Pacific War: Japanese Perspectives," *Reviews in American History* 14 (December 1986): 629–52.

19 James H. Herzog, *Closing the Open Door: American-Japanese Diplomatic Negotiations, 1936–1941* (Annapolis, MD, 1973).

20 See, for example, Gregory Nowell, *Mercantile States and the World Oil Cartel, 1900–1939* (Ithaca, NY, 1994). Nowell's approach is deliberately transnational and stimulating, but East Asia is largely absent.

On the Japanese side, Ben Ami Shillony's *Revolt in Japan* provided a detailed examination of the fanatical young officers during their abortive coup of February 26, 1936.[21] Their antiliberal, hence anti-Western, sentiments emerge with great clarity, but it is not so certain whether those sentiments would have led to war with the United States. Such a connection is much more apparent in the excellent study by Mark Peattie of that driven eccentric, Kanji Ishiwara.[22] Ishiwara was a young officer in 1931, a crucial cog in the Kwantung Army's decision to force the Manchurian issue that year. He was nearly unique in the Imperial Army in arguing that the United States was the Army's real enemy and it, not Asia, should be the focus of Army attention, a stance that baffled his fellow officers. It was also a stance that led to Ishiwara's vigorous, unsuccessful, and ultimately career-ending attempts to block the expansion of fighting with China after the Marco Polo Bridge Incident of July 1937. Ishiwara was finished, but his pan-Asianist ideas would survive long after the war they had helped foster had concluded.

Appearing shortly after Peattie's book was *Parties out of Power in Japan, 1931–1941*, by Gordon M. Berger.[23] Japan's political parties, it turns out, were not so far out of power as earlier accounts had supposed, nor were they uniformly composed of civilian moderates anxious to prevent the military's aggressive actions abroad. Instead, Berger paints a much more complex mural of the Army's repeatedly unsuccessful efforts to create a broad civil-military consensus in favor of aggression abroad, which most party leaders were willing to tolerate, and fundamental economic and political change within Japan in order to sustain that aggression, which they were not. No account is better in showing the terrific ambivalence of Prince and frequent Prime Minister Fumimaro Konoe, upon whom the army pinned so much of its

---

21 Ben Ami Shillony, *Revolt in Japan: The Young Officers and the February 26, 1936 Incident* (Princeton, NJ, 1973).
22 Peattie, *Ishiwara*.
23 Published in 1977 by Princeton University Press.

hopes only to be disappointed time after time, last and most famously in Konoe's resignation of mid-October 1941.[24]

Also in the mid-1970s came two genuinely multinational studies. Both were written along the lines of *Pearl Harbor as History*'s cross-institutional comparison instead of attempting a new grand synthesis. In many respects, Robert J. C. Butow's exhaustive *The John Doe Associates* is a tale of institutional confusions, if not outright breakdowns. Butow's judgments are harsh but well grounded. Bishop James E. Walsh and Father James M. Drought were well-intentioned amateurs whose efforts for peace made real diplomatic solutions less likely. Ambassador Nomura failed in the most basic respects of his office. Hull is faulted for not putting his "Four Principles" and a reasonable proposal on the table long before he managed only the former.[25]

Race to Pearl Harbor incorporates Britain into a three-way examination of naval rivalry and racing.[26] Its author, Stephen Pelz, maintains somewhat ironically that the Royal Navy did not much matter in the end, but that it, and its American counterpart, might have helped avoid war if they had built with more steadiness in the mid-1930s and less panic as they entered the new decade. The American program of 1940 in turn led to desperation in the Imperial Navy. In this fashion, the naval race contributed to the cause, and timing, of the Pacific War.

The British connection itself led to a London conference of Japanese and British scholars in 1979 on the theme of *Anglo-Japanese Alienation*.[27] Although most of the papers dealt with wartime and postwar aspects of that alienation, many provide key insights into the origins of the Pacific War. Chihiro Hosoya and D. C. Watt had hoped to sponsor studies that would deemphasize the

24 More focused upon Konoe himself is Yoshitake Oka, *Konoe Fumimaro: A Political Biography* (Tokyo, 1983).
25 Robert J. C. Butow, *The John Doe Associates: Backdoor Diplomacy for Peace, 1941* (Stanford, 1974). See also his most recent addition to the literature on the negotiations, "Marching off to War on the Wrong Foot: The Final Note Tokyo Did Not Send to Washington," *Pacific Historical Review* 63 (February 1994): 67–79; and Ikuhiko Hata, "Going to War: Who Delayed the Final Note?" *Japan Echo* 19 (Spring 1992): 53–65.
26 Stephen E. Pelz, *Race to Pearl Harbor: The Failure of the Second London Naval Conference and the Onset of World War II* (Cambridge, MA, 1974).
27 Ian Nish, ed., *Anglo-Japanese Alienation, 1919–1952* (New York, 1982).

Tokyo-Washington connection in order to provide a more international view of those origins. In fact, Watt went so far as to term much American scholarship on the subject the result of American fixations upon contemporary American concerns, from the height of the Cold War to the depths of Vietnam. He joined Hosoya in arguing that the Pacific War was, at base, a war between Japan and Britain. The United States intervened only because the Imperial Navy believed that the American fleet had to be neutralized to permit victory over Britain in Asia and because Roosevelt viewed such a victory as possibly leading to Britain's collapse in Europe.[28] Apparently, Schroeder had been right all along, at least from the American angle.

Then again, most of the chapters were considerably more ambiguous on this count. Every Japanese study emphasized the long-term connection between London and Washington in the eyes of Japan's leaders, dating at least from Prince Konoe's famous public article of 1918, "Down with the Anglo-American peace principles."[29] No mere strategic consideration of 1940 here. And as Watt himself pointed out, it was not so much Britain's colonies as its Commonwealth that compelled it, year after year and decade after decade, to ignore the tactical advantages of arrangements with Japan that might offend the Commonwealth and, by the same token, the Americans. In so doing, Watt ensured that no true synthesis of the origins of the Pacific War would be complete without an understanding of how Canada, the Antipodes, or even South Africa influenced relations between London and Washington. For good measure, he reminded scholars that there still were no studies on the role of economics and finance, certainly from the European side. What effect did growing British imperial protectionism have upon Japan in the early and middle 1930s? And what of the rift between the sterling and dollars blocs during those same years?[30]

---

28 Ibid., 288–89.
29 Ibid., 77.
30 As Watt acknowledged, there were a few such studies. Rather interestingly, they focused upon Britain's stake in China, not Southeast Asia. See Ann Trotter, *Britain and East Asia, 1933–1937* (New York, 1975); and Stephen L. Endicott, *Diplomacy and Enterprise: British China Policy, 1933–1937* (Vancouver, 1975).

Watt and Hosoya are joined in their emphasis on the war as primarily Anglo-Japanese by three studies appearing nearly a decade later. Richard J. Aldrich's tightly focused work places Thailand alongside a Japan interested in weakening the Western empires.[31] Nicholas Tarling cast a wider net. In doing so, he made plain how "Southeast Asia" was anything but a monolith. Malaya and Borneo alone were an incredible hodgepodge of ethnic satrapies, such as the Sarawak of the (British) Brooke family. Burmese leaders – with a new constitution in 1937 – were bold enough to challenge the extent to which they were to pay, in money and possibly blood, for wider imperial interests. In the Philippines, a wary Manuel Quezon toyed with the idea of entering the British Commonwealth after achieving independence from the United States. Yet the pivot of the region remained Singapore. Its central importance in the nineteenth century as an economic center had compelled British interests in the surrounding areas and, ironically, had led London by the 1930s to view Singapore as a "fortress" to protect those surroundings, an ironic turnabout.[32]

Tarling portrayed British diplomacy as exceptionally active in Southeast Asia in the years before Pearl Harbor, an activity he surmised due primarily to British military weakness there. Anthony Best's study likewise sees a great deal of activity, but argues more widely that British diplomats, because they were British, had to juggle the nationalist aspirations of China, the schemes of the Soviet Union, and of course the growing complications from Nazi Germany's drive to power. Best argues that there was nothing foreordained about an Anglo-Japanese war; in fact, there were compelling reasons for a rapprochement in the late 1930s, as advocated by Ambassador to Tokyo Robert Craigie. Craigie's frustrations with Washington's refusal to consider compromise and London's easy assumptions of the rightness of Britain's pre-eminence in East Asia form an important part of an important work.[33]

---

31 Richard J. Aldrich, *The Key to the South: Britain, the United States, and Thailand during the Approach of the Pacific War, 1929–1942* (New York, 1993).
32 Nicholas Tarling, *Britain, Southeast Asia and the Onset of the Pacific War* (Cambridge, England, 1996).
33 Anthony Best, *Britain, Japan and Pearl Harbor: Avoiding War in East Asia* (London, 1995).

Some of Watt's wider questions were addressed by yet another international group of scholars meeting in the early 1980s. One result of their collaboration was *American, Chinese, and Japanese Perspectives on Wartime Asia, 1931–1949.*[34] Three chapters discuss economic and business affairs at considerable length. Wang Xi, elaborating upon an argument first broached by Borg, noted how America's silver purchasing policy of mid-decade "played into the hands of Japan."[35] Washington swiftly cast aside the vaunted Open Door principles whenever domestic considerations required it. The ubiquitous and prolific Hosoya sounded a similar tune. He maintained that an opportunity to improve American-Japanese relations existed after the crises of 1931–33 but was quashed by a hastily conceived but much debated cotton and wheat loan from Washington to Nanking. The result was further dismay among moderates in Japan's Foreign Ministry, who believed that America had undercut their position against the fire-eaters. Sherman Cochrane boldly asserted that "war in China" was the "main event" in East Asian-American relations for the two decades after 1931. He also argued that American policy was greatly affected by private businesses, including Chinese business leaders who strongly supported the cotton and wheat loan, the South Manchurian Railway's struggle to limit the Kwantung Army's encroachments upon its domain, and Standard-Vacuum's vigorous defense of its market and market rights on the Asian mainland, which Washington steadily, if not always strongly, supported. Stanvac also made an appearance in Gary R. Hess's consideration of American influence in Southeast Asia, though Hess is inclined to discount much importance for that region in the coming of the Pacific War. In his view, Roosevelt sought to "stabilize" the region without sacrificing "priorities elsewhere."[36]

Institutional studies proliferated in the 1980s, proving that a good deal could be learned about the broad questions of war ori-

---

34 Akira Iriye and Warren Cohen, eds., *American, Chinese, and Japanese Perspectives on Wartime Asia, 1931–1949* (Wilmington, DE, 1990).
35 Ibid., 9.
36 Ibid., 195. The role of business leaders in China, whether Chinese, Japanese, British, or American, remains largely unexplored.

gins from narrowly focused examinations of key players. One of
the best on the American side was Jonathan Utley's *Going to War
with Japan*.[37] Utley establishes that the State Department, particularly Cordell Hull, quite firmly kept control of American policy
toward Japan, with one rather crucial exception.[38] Dismissing
the Schroeder-realist critique, Utley argues that neither Hull nor
his senior advisers were idealists. They were perfectly aware that
words alone would not restrain Japan. But they did want Japan
restrained.[39] Hull believed precisely what he said he believed in
his memoirs: Japan was untrustworthy because it was in the hands
of ruthless militarists aiming for hegemony over all East Asia by
use of force whenever necessary. These militarists intended to
create a self-sufficient trading bloc that would be a mockery of
the American principles of the Open Door. As importantly, that
creation would make it very nearly impossible for the Open Door –
free international trade – to exist anywhere in the world. All nations, including the United States, would have to pass up the chance
for shared prosperity in exchange for an existence less vulnerable
to foreign interference, to be sure, but far less commodious as a
result. Militarist Japan, therefore, had to be restrained because it
sought to impose poverty upon all and to do so using the tools of
violence. Both invited a return to the scabrous carnage of 1914–
17 and further deterioration of the human condition everywhere.

These certainly seemed strong grounds for opposing Japan, but
public memories of that carnage ruled out any military means for
doing so. Roosevelt intermittently toyed with the idea of using
America's economic leverage over Japan as a tool, or at least as a
threat. Utley makes clear, however, that Hull fended off such
exercises as much too provocative, even in the aftermath of Japan's
unprovoked attack on the *Panay* and the Stanvac barges she was

---

37 Jonathan G. Utley, *Going to War with Japan, 1937–1941* (Knoxville, TN, 1985).
38 The exception was the asset freeze that became an oil embargo, which Utley first examined in "Upstairs, Downstairs at Foggy Bottom: Oil Exports and Japan, 1940–1941," *Prologue* 8 (Spring 1976): 17–28.
39 That is, most officials in the State Department wanted Japan restrained. Hugh Wilson,
Adolf Berle, and Jay Pierrepont Moffat, for example, acutely aware of the storm rising in
Europe, consistently maintained that Asia was worthless to the United States and ought to be
ignored, if not appeased. Hull, Welles, the department's Asianists, and of course most importantly, Roosevelt, rejected this view.

escorting on the Yangtze River. By the same token, Hull was disinclined to appease. After Ambassador Joseph C. Grew obtained, or believed he had obtained, a meaningful concession from the Japanese military, Hull refused to reciprocate with any goodwill gesture of his own.[40] He, and most of his advisers in Washington, felt that Japan could not defeat China. In its failure, its military leaders would be discredited and fall from power without any active American opposition. On the other hand, American encouragement of the militarists had to be avoided. Better to let them overreach themselves.

But what if, in overreaching, they reached for Southeast Asia? A Japanese declaration of interest in continuing oil shipments from the Netherlands East Indies triggered marathon sessions for Hull and his staff and a shift in the American fleet's base for Pacific operation from California to Hawaii. Utley makes clear that this new attention had more to do with the new crisis in Europe than the intrinsic value of Southeast Asian resources to the United States. But resources were not completely irrelevant.[41] To Hull and Roosevelt, the crises in Europe and East Asia were increasingly of one piece, one threat to the liberal world order that they saw as critical to American well-being.[42] Japan would not be provoked, but its leaders would be shown the stick.

As it turned out, Japan was shown two sticks, one not fully within Hull's control. A central theme, and original contribution, of Utley's study is his careful examination of the evolution of an economic control bureaucracy arising from the July 1940 passage of the National Defense Act, itself a direct result of Germany's stunning triumphs in Europe. This bureaucracy, embodied in such agencies as the Office of Production Management, was primarily concerned with conserving materials for America's re-armament, exactly the materials that Japan required to continue its military efforts. As well, it provided fertile ground for

---

40 The concession was rights for American vessels to navigate the Yangtze as far as Nanking.
41 A vigorous, though to this author unpersuasive, argument that Southeast Asian resources mattered a great deal to the United States is found in Jonathan Marshall, *To Have and Have Not: Southeast Asian Raw Materials and the Origins of the Pacific War* (Berkeley, 1995).
42 Utley, *Going to War*, 85.

hardliners, both outside the State Department, such as Henry Morgenthau and Harold Ickes, and inside, such as Hornbeck and Herbert Feis, to put the screws on Tokyo inch by inch.

Hull resisted these efforts, remaining the central figure in Utley's account. The secretary of state entered 1941 certain that he wanted no confrontation with Japan over China or Southeast Asia until the situation in Europe had improved. Unfortunately, Hull was also certain, it seems, that American entry into the war against Germany would be necessary for that improvement, and that for Japan to encroach further upon British and Dutch possessions in Southeast Asia would lead instead to deterioration in the mother countries. A further complication was Tokyo's alliance with Berlin, which might require Washington to fight on two fronts if it acted against Germany.

The preferred solution was obvious. Hull wanted to nullify the alliance and stop any encroachment. How to do either eluded him, as concessions to Japan remained repulsive. At this juncture Utley introduces the John Doe Associates. In his interpretation, Hull and Roosevelt were nearly as skeptical of the associates' claims as the chorus of doubters in the State Department, but elected to proceed on a gamble that at least some time might be purchased (as Roosevelt emphasized) or that a genuine and comprehensive settlement might be reached (as Hull desired). So the Hull-Nomura discussions began.

Utley forcefully shows that they were Hull's discussions all the way. Hull wanted the German alliance nullified and Japan to leave Indochina and China (but not necessarily Manchuria). Yet these demands were only means, not ends, Utley argues. Hull sought nothing less than his primary goal all along: to "regenerate" Japan by shaking militarism to its core.[43] That goal emerged most clearly in his "Four Principles" of mid-April and virtual insistence, two months later, that pro-German elements such as Foreign Minister Yosuke Matsuoka be purged from the Japanese government.[44] Hull's problem was Germany's success. So long

43 Ibid., 145-46.
44 Butow argues that Hull, upon seeing that Nomura had nothing official to offer, ought to have placed something like the Four Principles on the table in February or March (*John Doe,*

as Berlin's star was rising, it would be difficult to weaken those pro-German elements in Japan. There was not much Hull could do to influence Germany's latest attack, against the Soviet Union.[45] But he was willing to show Japan the two sticks after learning that the Imperial Army would occupy the remaining, southern half of French Indochina in late July. American reinforcements were moved to the Philippines, and the United States froze all Japanese assets, a move that quickly escalated into a full embargo, including oil.

At this point Hull begins to fade from Utley's account. Hull himself was taking a badly needed vacation. He was not on hand for implementing the freeze. That task fell to Welles, who in turn entrusted it to Dean Acheson. Welles loosened Acheson's tough initial procedures regarding export licenses for goods bound for Japan but was unable to moderate the Treasury Department's insistence upon exceedingly strict conditions for the unfreezing of funds to pay for those goods. The implications of this hard freeze dawned upon Prime Minister Konoe by early August, leading him to propose a summit meeting with Roosevelt. According to Utley, Hull opposed the summit because he feared a loss of control over American relations with Japan. This motive cannot be discounted, though it seems as likely that Hull feared that Roosevelt would sacrifice his overarching goal of regenerating Japan in favor of an informal agreement to buy more time, the sort of improvisation that the president was occasionally partial toward.[46] Hull also believed that Konoe was untrustworthy, all the more reason to insist upon a fundamental and comprehensive agreement, or at least agreement in principle, before any summit. Hull would receive such a proposal in late November, labeled "Plan A." Again

316). Utley does not address this point directly, but it seems to this author that Hull thought he was preparing Nomura for just such a comprehensive statement during the early discussions.

45   But see discussion of Waldo H. Heinrichs, *Threshold of War: Franklin D. Roosevelt and American Entry into World War II* (New York, 1988).

46   The degree of Roosevelt's eagerness for a summit is in debate. Robert Dallek believes that Roosevelt was much more cautious, even reluctant to attend. Robert Dallek, *Franklin D. Roosevelt and American Foreign Policy, 1932–1945* (New York, 1979).

differing with the thrust of Schroeder's analysis, Utley maintains that Hull saw little that was attractive, or even new, in that proposal, and he successfully dismissed "Plan B," a modest modus vivendi, as a betrayal of China.

Utley concludes with a somewhat startling attack upon the fundamentals of Hull's diplomacy as he examines the actual origins of the Pacific War. The United States was foolish to permit "its diplomatic goals [to exceed] its military means, thus forcing it to depend too much upon China."[47] This dependence was created by America's need to protect Southeast Asia out of European concerns, and thus America's need to keep China in the fight to protect Southeast Asia. But it was also created by Hull's stubborn insistence on a comprehensive settlement with Japan. A modus vivendi would probably not have led to a Chinese collapse; it almost certainly would have bought invaluable time for the United States. Finally, Hull's inability to control the re-armament bureaucrats ultimately led to his inability to control America's drift toward war.

These are stinging indictments of American diplomacy, and Utley is hardly alone in making them. Yet they raise the obvious question of whether a modus vivendi, along the lines of "Plan B" or any other, really would have been acceptable to Japan, which is to say whoever was in control in Japan. Shortly after Utley's book, two studies of Japan's most powerful institution, the Imperial Army, appeared, Alvin Coox's *Nomonhan* and this author's *Japan Prepares for Total War.*[48]

Both are cautionary tales for those who would believe that even a temporary solution to American-Japanese differences was possible by 1940–41, much less likely. Coox's massive study is highly focused upon the intense war (a lesser term for that struggle would be incorrect) between the Soviet Union and the Imperial Army in the summer of 1939. As such, it was not written to directly address the origins of the Pacific War. Nevertheless, Coox provides

---

47 Utley, *Going to War*, 177.
48 Alvin D. Coox, *Nomonhan: Japan against Russia, 1939* (Stanford, 1985); Michael A. Barnhart, *Japan Prepares for Total War: The Search for Economic Security, 1919–1941* (Ithaca, NY, 1987).

a devastating portrait of an Imperial Army led by remarkably inflexible senior officers determined to have their way in the most irrational of circumstances. Some officers, appalled at the army's slaughter at the hands of the Red Army, openly wondered how their service could even consider conflict with the even better armed West.[49] They were ignored.[50] Perhaps worse, the army permitted its experience at Nomonhan to incline it to oppose an attempt against the Soviet Union in the summer of 1941. Instead, it would move south to take on the (even better armed) West![51]

This author's book is more broadly based, but likewise places the Imperial Army at its center. Many officers, middle-level and senior, had concluded shortly after the First World War that Japan could not cope with a second. The country had an impossibly slim base of resources and was not much better off in terms of its industry, yet both materials and the means to make them into engines of war were crucial to any nation's survival. These "total war" officers dedicated themselves to a two-pronged program of reform: securing resources in Manchuria, northern China, and possibly the Southwest Pacific, and constructing a broad, modern industrial economy for Japan under the army's direct or indirect control. Only in this way – the way of autarky – could Japanese security be guaranteed.

As Berger's and other prior studies have noted, the officers encountered few obstacles to their program outside Japan and very substantial ones in it, especially to their mechanisms for controlling the economy.[52] The result was swift difficulty when the "total war" officers proved completely unable to control their hot-

---

49 Over eight thousand Japanese died at Nomonhan.

50 Coox, *Nomonhan*, 1027–29.

51 Coox has extended his grim portrait in a trenchant article on the matter of the army and Japan's surrender in 1945. It should be required reading for any believing that surrender could have been swiftly or easily arranged. See Coox, "The *Enola Gay* and Japan's Decision to Surrender," *Journal of American-East Asian Relations* 4 (Summer 1995): 161–67.

52 As well as subsequent studies. See Fletcher, *Japanese Business Community*, cited above. It is unfortunate that Mark Mason's splendid study of multinational business in Japan elected not to make connections to contemporary political and military concerns (*American Multinationals and Japan: The Political Economy of Japanese Capital Controls, 1899–1980* [Cambridge, MA, 1992]). Some quite interesting work was done by Kenichi Goto, Takafusa Nakamura, Peter Duus, Carter Eckert, and Ramon Myers for a conference held at the Hoover Institution in 1991, though it has not yet been published.

headed counterparts in the field during the summer of 1937. Ironically, Ishiwara of 1931 fame led the "total war" officers six years later in arguing that any escalation of the fighting around the Marco Polo Bridge would simply sap Japan's strength and render it more dependent upon the West, especially the United States. They lost their fight but lived to see their dire predictions fulfilled all too well. The army was experiencing difficulties supplying its campaign by the spring of 1938. At the same time, the advocates of autarky hoped to use civilian allies such as Konoe to overthrow the existing political and economic order now that wartime needs and, presumably, fervor, were at high pitch. Konoe disappointed in 1938 and again two years later, by which time it is fair to say that the Japanese economy overall was in quite serious trouble. Then came Germany's great successes in Europe.

Those successes offered twin rescue to a beleaguered Imperial Army. First, the colossal drain of the China "incident" might at last be ended by an occupation of French Indochina that would nearly sever the remaining flow of Western aid to Chiang Kai-shek. Second, the fall of Holland and besieging of the British home islands might open access, by diplomatic or military routes, to their rich colonies to the south. It was a perversion of the "total war" officers' original attempt to achieve autarky, of course. That attempt had relied upon good relations with the West while Japan acquired the wherewithal to finally ignore and, if necessary, confront the Anglo-American powers. This new one required immediate confrontation in order to solve outstanding problems in China and then create conditions of relative self-sufficiency after the confrontation had been resolved in Japan's favor.

The obvious finesse was to assume that any southward advance, even by force, would not involve the United States. Not surprisingly, that is exactly what the army argued until early August 1941. This exercise in fantasy was checked only by the Imperial Navy's insistence that America had to be involved, in fact attacked, as part of any "Southward Advance." But the Navy's argument was not based on any sounder understanding of Washington's disposition. Instead, the navy insisted upon the United States as an opponent to ensure itself adequate funding

and materials for warship construction even as Japan was beginning to run short of iron, steel, alloys, and practically everything
else needed for such construction.

The lone exception was oil. Washington's cutoff of early April
compelled the Army to agree to a Southward Advance of the
Navy's design, ensuring American belligerency by deliberate act
of Japan.[53] Utley's book makes clear that Roosevelt's attempt to
fine-tune the flow of oil to Tokyo went awry, but Waldo Heinrichs's
most recent book maintains that the asset freeze was a carefully
considered part of a global plan of the administration, and one
that, in the end, worked rather well for American interests.

Heinrichs deliberately attempts a new synthesis, observing that
literature on American entry into the Second World War is "rich
and abundant but mostly segmented."[54] His study centers squarely
on a Roosevelt who had an outstanding grasp of the global
diplomatic situation and the intricacies of power politics.
Unsurprisingly, Roosevelt followed Germany's wartime fortunes
in extraordinary detail. Putting relations with Japan within the
global context of Roosevelt's policies provides insights that are
new and persuasive. Moreover, those insights make clear that
Japan was an important but secondary consideration in Roosevelt's
calculations. For example, Hull informed Nomura of his "Four
Principles" just as Yugoslavia was collapsing under German attack and Roosevelt was moving to extend the hemispheric defense zone to include Greenland and the Azores. Defense of the
Americas grew more urgent through May as German successes in
North Africa and a coup in Iraq triggered fears about the future
of French West Africa, Portugal, Spain, and eventually Iceland.

---

53 Although it was clear by mid-August that the Southward Advance would feature an
assault upon the Philippines, the "Hawaiian Operation" was the subject of bitter debate for
nearly three more months. In English see Gordon W. Prange, *At Dawn We Slept: The Untold
Story of Pearl Harbor* (New York, 1981); idem, *Pearl Harbor: The Verdict of History* (New
York, 1986); Hiroyuki Agawa, *The Reluctant Admiral: Yamamoto and the Imperial Navy*
(New York, 1979); and Michael A. Barnhart, "Planning the Pearl Harbor Attack: A Study in
Military Politics," *Aerospace Historian* 29 (December 1982): 246–52.
54 Heinrichs, *Threshold*, vii.

Yet Roosevelt and Hull were reluctant to permit the weakening of the Pacific Fleet and quite adamant about maintaining a very hard line with Japan. Neither was prepared to break off Hull's discussions with Nomura, hoping that the talks themselves would irritate Berlin (as they did) without dismaying London and Chungking (but they did). Hull's message of 21 June came quite close to a break, however. He remained determined to regenerate Japan, even after the first days of Germany's attack on the Soviet Union convinced nearly everyone that the Russians were doomed. Roosevelt agreed with Hull's stance, Heinrichs reminds us. But the president also moved to restore balance in July. He increased American assistance to China just enough, he noted, to replace aid lost from the Soviet Union and to counter defeatist sentiment in Chiang's latest capital. He pressed hard for more and faster help for the Russians.[55] He met with Churchill and agreed to warn Japan away from the Southwest Pacific. But, aware of the Japanese buildup in Manchuria along the Soviet border, he did not warn Tokyo too much against moving southward, and he supported the asset freeze and sharp reduction of oil shipments to Japan at least in part to frustrate any plans to attack the Russians.

The Russian angle colors Heinrichs's subsequent discussion of American-Japanese relations. The Americans read Tojo's appointment as prime minister in mid-October as a sign of renewed Japanese interest in attacking the Soviet Union, as Germany launched its offensive against Moscow.[56] Washington increased its military presence in the Philippines, and London its in Singapore, in response. As the Soviet defenses stiffened, Roosevelt became more interested in a *modus vivendi* with Japan, since a northern attack had become less likely and peace with Tokyo would buy time to aid the Soviet Union and Britain.

Why did Roosevelt, in the end, reject Japan's "Plan B" and refuse to offer a modus vivendi of his own? Heinrichs supplies

---

55 Ibid., 132–41.
56 Ibid., 217. This impression was completely wrong. The Imperial Army had dismissed any thought of a Northward Advance in 1941 by October, and Tojo, at the emperor's request, was completely reexploring Japan's options toward the Americans and the south.

three answers. American code-breaking operations, known as
MAGIC, reinforced already strong impressions of Japanese bad
faith. Apparently Hull's suspicions had been right all along.
Germany recommenced a push to Moscow in mid-November, just
as "Plan B" was under consideration, with good initial success.
Roosevelt had fresh worries about a possible northward attack if
he consented to any temporary accord in the south. Finally, Britain and China were wary of any American-Japanese deal. To
damage relations with Britain was unthinkable to Roosevelt, who,
on December 1, at last assured London that the United States
would intervene even if Japan avoided American territory.[57] Permitting defeatism to triumph in China would almost certainly
permit the Japanese assault against Russia that Roosevelt had
tried so hard to prevent since July. Heinrichs reminds his readers
that Roosevelt had had very few cards in his hand for much of
1941, but he played them quite well. America entered the war,
globally, with an international coalition built in no small part by
Roosevelt and capable of victory if maintained, as he so well
understood.

In Tokyo, by contrast, there was little appreciation of the usefulness of coalitions. In part this myopia was the result of the
"total war" officers' desire for autarky, which hardly lent itself to
alliance building. But Akira Iriye's overview of the origins of the
war in Asia and the Pacific demonstrates that that war was the
result of Japan's failure to prevent its conflict with China from
escalating into a wider struggle and, conversely, China's diplomatic success in precisely this regard.[58] As well, Iriye traces the
roots of that conflict to Japan's initial challenge to the Washington treaty system in 1931, not simply to the outbreak of widespread fighting six years later.

At first, Japan enjoyed the fruits of its bilateral approach to
differences with China as the West shied from a direct challenge
to Tokyo, although the Soviet Union, closer and thus more con-

---

57   Ibid., 217. It was a pledge that need not have been made, since interservice politics had
compelled the inclusion of American territory in any Southward Advance.
58   Akira Iriye, *The Origins of the Second World War in Asia and the Pacific* (New York,
1987).

cerned, moved to align itself with Chinese resistance.[59] By mid-1935, Moscow's Comintern was showing keen interest in containing the fascist powers. The resulting Anti-Comintern Pact of 1936 might have signaled Japan's end of isolation in the global arena. Instead, Japan so badly misplayed its position that when war commenced in Europe in 1939 it was utterly alone and virtually without compass. The stunning Nazi-Soviet Pact was only the most obvious indication that Japan was adrift. Iriye comments that the Russians signed it – deciding to meet Germany halfway (or more) in Europe – even as their army was ripping Japanese forces to shreds at Nomonhan. As for the West, Nomura, the new foreign minister who inherited the war in Europe and disaster at Nomonhan, understood that Japan's dickering with Germany and burnt bridges to accommodation with China limited options rather severely. Under these circumstances, it was no surprise that Konoe and the army thought themselves and their country rescued by German successes the next spring and a neutrality pact, though more had been hoped for, with the Soviets a year later.

In fact, both of these initiatives badly backfired. The Axis alliance was a godsend to China and instrumental in forming a grand anti-Japanese "ABCD" coalition. The neutrality pact was useless within months as Germany attacked the Soviet Union. By that time, Iriye judges, only a Japanese renunciation of the "Southward Advance" or an American betrayal of ABCD could have avoided a Pacific war. Konoe was strong enough to oust the newly anti-Soviet Matsuoka Yosuke as his foreign minister, but he could not prevent the Army and Navy from agreeing to proceed minimally with the advance by occupying the remainder of French Indochina. Iriye argues at length that Konoe would have required substantial concessions at any summit with Roosevelt, and that Roosevelt, had he yielded any over China, would have dissolved ABCD as a whole.[60] Tojo emerges in this account as a prime

---

59 Studies of attempted links between China and America early in the 1930s are Justus D. Doenecke, *When the Wicked Rise: American Opinion Makers and the Manchurian Crisis of 1931–1933* (Lewisburg, PA, 1984); and Frederick W. Marks III, *Wind over Sand: The Diplomacy of Franklin Roosevelt* (Athens, GA, 1988).
60 Iriye, *Origins*, 161. Iriye does fault Roosevelt for not agreeing to a summit anyway in

minister dedicated to his emperor's wish to make a final try for peace, a portrait reinforced by recent studies of Hirohito himself.[61] But the facts were that both Plans A and B aimed to break up ABCD and, for that very reason, were unlikely to succeed. Iriye closes with the observation that Japan's war plans, while brilliant for a brief campaign, were completely inadequate for anticoalition warfare, much less war termination.[62]

These new studies emphasized the importance of coalitions, and the roles of China and the Soviet Union in forming them. Suitably, yet another conference of scholars gathered at Lake Yamanaka in 1991 to consider the origins and course of the war in Asia and the Pacific, with Chinese, Russians, Koreans, Germans, British, Japanese and Americans all in attendance. Perhaps at last a truly comprehensive synthesis of the war's beginnings was at hand.

Such hopes would have proven premature. The conference papers, thus far published only in Japanese, have gone some distance in providing answers, but only at the price of raising some new and not so new questions.[63] China bulks large in four chapters. Sumio Hatano traces the debate within the army over whether to continue to insist upon a bilateral solution to the China Incident or turn to Washington for help in ending that conflict. Konoe and influential officers in the Army Ministry felt that the Americans were deeply involved in Europe and would be willing to appease Japan over China. The General Staff officers were more cautious. They appeared vindicated in late June 1941. Hull's proposal hardly seemed appeasing, and the Americans apparently not only had known of the impending Nazi-Soviet war but actually welcomed it and now plotted to force Japan into a "Southward Advance," not a northern one. Clearly a Washington so inclined was not going to let Japan off the Chinese hook. For this

order to buy time and further confuse the political landscape in Japan. (Ibid., 167).

61   See Stephen S. Large, *Emperor Hirohito and Showa Japan: A Political Biography* (New York, 1992); and Masanori Nakamura, *The Japanese Monarchy: Ambassador Joseph Grew and the Making of the "Symbol Emperor System," 1931–1991* (Armonk, NY, 1992).

62   Iriye's arguments are summarized in his essay in Iriye and Cohen, eds., *Perspectives*.

63   Chihiro Hosoya, Nagayo Homma, Akira Iriye, and Sumio Hatano, eds., *Taiheiyo senso* (Tokyo, 1993).

reason, the General Staff vehemently opposed Konoe's idea of a summit with Roosevelt. Although the German alliance might be finessed, Konoe would have no choice but to accept humiliation over China, which the army could not permit. For that same reason, the army strongly opposed "Plan B" because it would do nothing to resolve the China affair, but viewed "Plan A" as a significant and major concession because it would limit Japan's presence in China. Its officers felt vindicated when the United States rejected B, dashing hopes in the Foreign Ministry that American acceptance would have permitted a return to a bilateral path with the Chinese.[64]

Warren Cohen provides a historiographical overview of China as an issue in American-Japanese relations for the entire decade before Pearl Harbor. Cohen concludes that Schroeder was right and wrong. China was not important to the United States for moral or idealistic reasons (nor for its economic value), but it was a symbol for more important concerns, such as restraining Japan directly and forging a global coalition against Germany. This latter was the key. Only after Japan's Southward Advance and alliance with Germany were American partisans for China such as Roger Greene able to persuade Washington to offer assistance. Schroeder was correct to see that Roosevelt switched tactics in the summer of 1941, but the president's objectives had not changed.[65]

Tetsuya Sakai and Waldo Heinrichs placed the Soviet Union at the center of their studies.[66] Sakai chronicles a success story for Soviet diplomacy, from obtaining recognition from Washington

---

64   Wang Xi's contribution echoes the centrality of China in Japanese diplomacy from 1940 to 1941. Katsumi Usui's chapter highlights the importance of Plan A, at least to Japan, since it offered a settlement of Chinese issues. Usui observes that Washington never showed Plan A to Chiang, but simply rejected it. An excellent study of China's coalition building is Youli Sun, *China and the Origins of the Pacific War, 1931–1941* (New York, 1993).

65   Greene was one subject Cohen examined at some length in *The Chinese Connection: Roger S. Greene, Thomas W. Lamont, George E. Sokolsky and American-East Asian Relations* (New York, 1978).

66   Regrettably, the papers by Russian scholars focused on events after Pearl Harbor. But an excellent examination of Soviet-Japanese diplomacy can be found in Jonathan Haslam, *The Soviet Union and the Threat From the East, 1933–41: Moscow, Tokyo, and the Prelude to the Pacific War* (Pittsburgh, 1992).

as a byproduct of Japan's actions in Manchuria to diverting Tokyo's attention from any northward advance in 1941.[67] Heinrichs does not count Soviet-American relations as overly friendly at any point. Washington was displeased by Moscow's neutrality pact with Tokyo, but unwilling to appease Japan in the south if the result was a northward advance. Still, he would not dissent from Sakai's high marks (at least in the Pacific) for Stalin's diplomacy.

Hitler's statecraft does not fare so well, nor Ribbentrop's. Nobuo Tajima demonstrates that Ribbentrop used the Anti-Comintern Pact and subsequent collaboration with Japan almost entirely as a way to shore up his own power base within the Third Reich. He argued strongly for a northward advance in the summer of 1941, but more for increased personal influence than out of any appreciation for the wider realities involved. Bernd Martin comments that the German-Japanese alliance was an empty instrument. German war planning seldom considered Japan. Hitler openly dismissed the idea of a northward advance, preferring that Tokyo attack the British at Singapore. Although he wavered briefly, when his own intelligence reported stiffened Soviet resistance, he openly welcomed an October confirmation of Japan's decision to strike south, confident that he could finish Stalin swiftly.

One of Martin's most interesting points concerns Germany's declaration of war upon the United States on December 11. The alliance with Japan did not require the declaration, and Japan requested one only on November 18. Germany was amenable, so long as Japan agreed to no separate peace with the Americans. Japan consented on December 11; the German declaration immediately followed. In this way the two wars merged completely.[68]

---

67   As Sakai notes, the first Soviet ambassador to the United States was an expert on Japan.
68   A detailed study of the Axis connection on Pearl Harbor is Gerhard Krebs, "Deutschland und Pearl Harbor," *Historische Zeitschrifte* 253 (October 1991): 313–69. On the Allied side, Canada beat everyone to the punch in declaring war on Japan. The role of Britain's Pacific Dominions is discussed in Hiroaki Shiozaki's chapter, "Taiheiyo Eiteikokuken no tai-Nichi senso e no michi," in *Taiheiyo senso*, 281–307. Three British scholars, Anthony Best, Ian Nish, and David Reynolds, generally concur that Britain never considered appeasing Japan, with the brief and coerced exception of the closing of the Burma Road from July through October 1940.

Although it is not proper to term *Taiheiyo senso* a synthesis, its studies do point to an emerging consensus of the origins of the war in Asia and the Pacific. That view emphasizes the construction of coalitions, one successful, one not. While it would not tolerate a return to a strictly American-Japanese focus on those origins, this new synthesis does reemphasize the central roles of Washington and Tokyo in the coalition-making process. It also serves to refocus attention on leaders. The United States was blessed with one of the best, a president who combined tactical flexibility with a firm vision of what he wanted to accomplish. Japan was riven with factions pursuing their own narrow agendas. Only two of these had any long-range goals. One, the Army's "total war" officers, lost their battle for eventual autarky in the summer of 1937. The other, Hull's "moderates," would restore Japan to the Western universe only after Allied military power had obliterated the other contestants by 1945. A new synthesis on the origins of the war in Asia and the Pacific will comprehend internal politics in Tokyo and Washington and how those politics blocked or permitted successful coalition-building and, ultimately, military victory.

Index